MERCHANT PRINCES

*An Intimate History of
Jewish Families Who Built
Great Department Stores*

Leon Harris

HARPER & ROW, PUBLISHERS
New York, Hagerstown, San Francisco, London

Grateful acknowledgment is made for permission to reprint: "Days of Lemonade and Crystal" by Armand S. Deutsch. Reprinted by permission of *Chicago* magazine. Copyright © 1977 by WFMT, Inc.

FIRST EDITION

Designer: Gloria Adelson

Library of Congress Cataloging in Publication Data

Harris, Leon
  Merchant princes.
  Bibliography: p.
  Includes index.
  1. Jews in the United States—Biography.
2. Merchants, Jewish—United States—Biography.
3. Department stores—United States.   4.   United
States—Biography.   I.   Title.
E184.J5H34   381[B]   79–1667
ISBN 0–06–011797–4

79 80 81 82 83 10 9 8 7 6 5 4 3 2 1

Merchant
Princes

This book is for
my father
his father
and for all the women and men who made
A. Harris & Company

Contents

Introduction   ix

1. The Filenes of Boston   1

2. The Strauses of New York—Five Generations   36

3. The Gimbels, Albert M. Greenfield, and Other Brotherly Lovers   69

4. The Kaufmanns of Pittsburgh   91

5. The Goldsmiths of Memphis   112

6. The Riches of Atlanta   135

7. Dallas and the Marci   156

8. The Wild Southwest   201

9. The Jewish Argonauts of San Francisco   237

10. The Meiers and Franks of Oregon   259

11. Sears, Roebuck and the Rosenwalds   280

12. Legions of Lazari, or How Fred Lazarus, Jr., Ate Up Everybody Else   336

Acknowledgments and Notes   359

Bibliography   382

Index   397

Introduction

The Jews are members of the human race—worse I can say
of no man.
                                                —Mark Twain

This is a book not about stores but about storekeepers and their
families. Even more specifically, it is about Jewish storekeeping
families and their influence in their communities, cultural and
political as well as economic—an influence so large as to be dispro-
portionate both to their number and to their wealth.

If this were only a book about stores, it could not be limited
to those owned by Jews because such stores were no different
from those owned by non-Jews. Department stores were neither
a Jewish nor an American invention. To the doubtful degree that
there was a first one, it was Aristide Boucicaut's Bon Marché in
Paris, but in fact such stores grew up over about the same period
in America, France, Great Britain, and wherever else the size and
wealth of the population made them possible.

Most of the first and biggest department stores in America were
started by non-Jews: A. T. Stewart's, John Wanamaker's, Marshall
Field's, Jordan Marsh, Macy's. Successful stores run by non-Jews
were no different from those run by Jews—the differences were
in the families.

Non-Jewish families that grew rich from storekeeping—the Jordans in Boston, the Fields in Chicago, the Daytons in Minneapolis—lived no differently from other rich non-Jewish families in their community. They built homes in the same part of town and went to the same schools, clubs, dances, dinners, and resorts. But the Jewish families that grew rich from storekeeping came from a different cultural background and often did not live in the same part of town or go to the same schools, clubs, dances, dinners, and resorts as the non-Jewish rich of their community.

The fortunes accumulated by these Jewish families from storekeeping never approached the enormous sums that were amassed from mining resources such as oil or copper, from manufacturing such as steel or automobiles, or from banking—excepting only the Rosenwald and Straus family riches. But these Jewish storekeeping families in the years from just before the Civil War to shortly after World War II played a vital role in America, a role that far exceeded the relative size of their fortunes.

This book is about a dozen or so of these families and the roles they played in business, politics, education, the arts, and charities.

For obvious reasons of space, I have omitted many more such families than I included. In New York City even a brief look at the Strauses meant omitting the Bloomingdales, Benjamin Altman, the Goodmans of Bergdorf Goodman, Franklin Simon, who led the parade to Fifth Avenue, to mention only the most obvious. Similarly, choosing a dozen areas of this country meant ignoring many more. No chapters on Brooklyn, Baltimore, Washington, D.C., Richmond, or St. Louis meant that the book contains nothing substantial about the Abrahams, Gertzes, Hutzlers, Hechts, Garfinckels, Thalhimers, or Mays. The list is long, but to have done all would have been to have done none, to have done more would have been to have done less.

That a storekeeping family left out of this book may be no less important and fascinating than those included is best illustrated by the Mays. David May, who—like J. C. Penney—went as a young man to Colorado to improve his health or to die, started in Leadville and built what has become one of America's biggest and best-known department-store chains. Jack Benny is one of the reasons that the May Company is so well known. During the many years that Benny's radio program was the most popular in America, when millions of Americans listened to it every Sunday night without fail, the most important character after Benny himself was his girfriend, Mary Livingston. She was a wise-cracking salesgirl at the May Company, and her weekly comic skit took place in the store with such familiar figures as the testy, epicene floorwalker and the outrageously unreasonable customer. Week after week, year after year, almost every program continued to include a department-store sketch. The reason for this was not difficult to deduce. The store milieu and experiences were well known to everyone. All across America, local department-store characters and the local department-store scene were more familiar and more interesting to many men and women than their church and its minister and members or any other place and group excepting their own home and family.

But more unfortunate even than omitting from this book large and famous stores may be leaving out the hundreds of tiny stores in small towns and villages where the Jewish storekeeper's family were often the only Jews in town and often made a proportionally more important economic and cultural difference than in larger communities. The man who kept the dry-goods or general store in a small town might also be its postmaster and telegraph operator, its magazine and newspaper subscriber, and its bookseller, who, when business was slow, had more time to read the copies of Shakespeare and Milton than he had opportunity to sell them. He was a man of consequence, around whose stove in winter and cracker barrel in summer the questions of the community were discussed and resolved; for good or ill, he played a major role.

This book, as is always the case with any work of selection, may be criticized on two bases—what is included and what is not. But the choices were not made from either cursory or unloving study of the field. My very first recollections are of playing in a store and in its warehouse with kind, merry, fascinating women and men. My happiest childhood memories are of traveling with my father on exciting trains and ships to mysterious and foreign places—New York, Paris, Berlin, Milan, London—where he was buying things for "the store."

It had been started in Dallas in 1886 by my grandfather, Adolph Harris, who had arrived in Galveston from Prussia at the age of seventeen in 1859. He had worked there in a ship's chandlering business only long enough to earn sufficient money to marry my grandmother, Fanny Grumbach, the daughter of the rabbi of Sarreguemines in Alsace, and to move to Houston, where he did well in the dry-goods business and also served as Alderman for the Second Ward for several years.

I knew neither of these grandparents, who died before I was born in 1926, but I knew my father well enough before he died when I was eight to think of storekeepers as the most important people in the world and to think of storekeeping as the most exciting life possible—prejudices somewhat corrected in the many years since.

It was even exciting for the storekeeper's child. The son of a banker or a cotton-gin owner may well have had a father who was in fact richer and more powerful than the local storekeeper, but his name was not on every delivery truck and he did not have the right, as the storekeeper's son was mistakenly believed by his contemporaries to have, to march into the store's toy department and take whatever he wanted.

The storekeepers' children I have known seem to have early enjoyed this misplaced admiration and also to have suffered from delusions similar to my own as to the importance, power, and infallibility of their family—delusions also known to other children. I remember in some resort in France, probably Deauville or Vichy, meeting a Straus who had the impertinence to suggest that "Our store is bigger than your store—it's the biggest store in the whole world!" I laughed at that idea and hinted that Macy's wasn't even his store, since his name wasn't on it. When my father told me that it *was* his store and it *was* bigger than ours, I could scarcely believe it.

Other inevitable disillusionments came as I slowly and reluctantly learned that my father's friends such as Lord Marks of Marks & Spencer did not own London, the Wertheims did not own Berlin, Mr. Edgar Kaufmann did not own Pittsburgh, and that my father did not own or even run Dallas.

Such illusions are permissible, perhaps even necessary, to small children; but I began writing this book after I had reached the age of fifty, and I have tried to avoid both hagiography and what the historian Jacob Marcus calls "ethnocentric schmoose." In some detail I have illustrated that these storekeepers were not invariably courageous, patriotic, noble, artistic, hardworking, shrewd immigrants who inevitably progressed from peddlers to merchant princes because of their limitless virtues. I have described how they were sometimes moved by greed as well as generosity, by lechery as well as love.

I hope, however, that I have avoided that Olympian attitude with which we are often tempted to view the errors of our predecessors if not our own.

When, at the age of twenty in 1947, I graduated from Harvard, I went to work at the store as automatically and unquestioningly as the son of a medieval stonemason would have followed his father's craft. Or perhaps more accurately, it was as some minor noble's heir assuming his father's fiefdom, for despite the disadvantages of their religion, these Jewish merchants resembled the petty German princes in their own localities. My uncle died in 1950, whereupon his son and I ran the store until we sold it in 1961 to Federated Department Stores.

There is, therefore, probably no retail practice, moral or im, legal or il, successful or un, that I have not tried myself; not an important merchant of the period whom I have not met; not a way to support (or undermine) a local institution I have not learned; not a mistake I have not made—at least once.

It has seemed to me that the recorder of a history in which he and his family took part cannot at all times be only a recorder.

It would be arch to pretend that my family and I were not responsible for acts and omissions, good and bad, that could appropriately illustrate this history. Therefore, I have on occasion found it justifiable, despite the temptations of modesty and pride, to mention some. This puts me in the position of exposing my own family's closet, which seems only fair given the other family closets I have revealed.

The number of first-generation storekeepers I have known, such as Herbert Marcus and Carrie Neiman, is very small, but of the second, third, and later generations I have known a great many. Merely because the subjects of this book played their roles very recently they are no less a part of history than much earlier merchants such as Marco Polo in the thirteenth century. Most of us are simply accustomed to perceiving even minor captains general, lesser kings' mistresses, or picayune politicians as figures of history than storekeepers and their wives. At the same time I have tried not to exaggerate their importance, and not to underestimate the role of happenstance in their success—the same kind of unpredictable accident as the war that blocked the return of Polo's father and uncle to Venice and so caused their entirely unanticipated journey to Kublai Khan's western capital at Kaifeng in 1266.

Even though the fortunes of the American storekeepers were small potatoes compared to those of a Rockefeller, a Ford, or a Guggenheim, their influence was great. As the historian Daniel J. Boorstin has explained, for example, newspapers in America received most of their income from retail advertisers and so remained relatively independent and free to report the news impartially. This was in contrast to the partisan-dominated press of France and Italy, where most newspapers were owned by party powers and served as their party's voice.

Those storekeepers were very important in determining the economic climate of their towns. Where they chose to locate their stores affected real estate values. They were among the largest bank depositors, often the largest, and so they frequently sat on the bank's board and influenced who received loans and who did not. How many employees they hired or fired was felt throughout the community.

Because some of these Jewish merchants and their families genuinely yearned for music and theater, and because they revered learning, they were often instrumental in founding the local symphony orchestra, library, college, and in the building of the first opera house, museum, and private primary and secondary schools. The fact that they were usually welcomed on the boards of trustees of the various cultural institutions was not unrelated to their frequent willingness to pay more than their proportional share of the costs of these enterprises. Support of the arts served too as a means of social climbing, but few merchants or their wives were so foolish as to be taken in by such limited acceptance. Most agreed with the New York Jewish banker Otto Kahn, who was fulsomely praised by his Christian brothers for his lavish generosity to the Metropolitan Opera, but who, when asked once the meaning of the word "kike," replied, "Any Jewish gentleman who has just left the room."

The power these storekeepers and their families exerted in politics, in the arts, and on each community's economic affairs was inevitably a mixed blessing for themselves as for the community. None of us is perfectly pleased by power in hands other than our own, and so community attitudes toward these merchants were mixed.

There is scarcely a village in any state of the Union that did not once have a "Jew storekeeper" and his family. The kaiser and the czar made more merchants than the Harvard School of Business or Pennsylvania's Wharton School—men who preferred peddling in the coldest county in New England or the hottest humid parish of Louisiana, preferred even the risk of being scalped in Arizona, to serving as a private in the Prussian army or as a victim of Cossack amusements. The variety of their experiences is as great as the size and diversity of America itself.

Like the other immigrants in the quarter century from 1840 to 1865, the German Jews gave America a new shot in the arm, a new vitality and creativity, just at the moment when the heirs

of earlier immigrants and pioneers were settling down to the con-
formity and ease their parents had won.

Then the tidal wave of millions of Eastern European Jews arrived
between 1880 and the outbreak of World War I, giving America
the stereotype of the Jew as a pale, weak, bespectacled, crouching
tailor, terrified lest he offend the sweatshop owner. Of course,
there were such. There were also the strong, strapping adventurers
whose courage and physical endurance led them to crisscross the
American continent, to settle in some crossroads village, and to
leave their imprint on it after they had made enough money at
storekeeping to take themselves and their families to an urban
center less lonely and less barren of the intellectual and artistic
pleasures they craved.

Perhaps even more striking than the physical strength of these
Jewish storekeepers is their obvious confidence and joy in their
own powers, which contrast so markedly with the mid-twentieth-
century literary image of the contemporary Jew as the ambivalent
paralyzed intellectual—insecure, indecisive, and afraid.

In much of the rest of the world, the shape and character of
big cities were determined by Indian rajahs, Persian emperors,
European kings. Frequently in America, especially in the South
and West, this determination was made, or at least much influenced, by a recently arrived Jewish former peddler.

Although this book is about such men and their influence on
America, I want early to state the obvious, that I do not believe
they did everything in this country worthy of note. There is always a danger of attributing more effectiveness than they deserve
to one's friends, one's enemies, or the subjects of one's book.
However, although fortune, good or bad, played an important
part in the success of a few merchants and in the failure of many,
no great store was built by accident.

Vastly underestimated then, and therefore difficult to assess
now, is the role of wives and other women in these families and
in their stores. A few who were the owners of their businesses—
Carrie Marcus Neiman and Beatrice Fox Auerbach—were visible
managers. And a few matriarchs, such as San Francisco's Mary

Ann Magnin and Portland's Jeannette Meier, so dominated their families and enterprises as to be visible. But almost all other women were kept, or—in the Victorian tradition—kept themselves invisible. The fact that they played an important role in the family and influenced or in many cases dominated business decisions is as certain as it is unrecorded and unremembered.

This is especially unfortunate in a business whose customers have always been chiefly women and whose largest echelon of executives, buyers, often were and are predominantly women. Even in our own day, when the department-store chains have taken over from the families and, purportedly, ability is the only criterion for leadership, women as chief executives of important department stores are still rare exceptions that prove the rule: the late Dorothy Shaver of Lord & Taylor; Mildred Custin, formerly of Bonwit Teller; the present Geraldine Stutz of Henri Bendel; and Ann Stegner of Harzfeld's. It is a disgracefully short list.

What little there is about women in this book comes most often from oral rather than written sources and the line between unquestionable fact and apocrypha is less than absolute. Throughout this book I have been much more interested in the revealing and probable anecdote than in tiresome facts of unquestionable accuracy. I willingly confess my feeling, as expressed by the Abbé Raynal about Benjamin Franklin, that he would rather recount some men's stories than other men's truths.

In these final decades of the twentieth century, many Americans are never so happy as when a Lockheed or Penn Central exposure confirms their conviction that all business is a shabby game in which the wicked invariably win and the virtuous inevitably lose. In such a climate it is difficult to believe that the businessman, with equal exaggeration, was once viewed as the quintessential American hero, especially in the three decades after the Civil War. It is perhaps even harder to believe that there were cases that justified that view.

At the turn of the century, Upton Sinclair and the other muckrakers demonstrated quite correctly that many businessmen were greedy scoundrels; but they effectively ignored many who were not. Admittedly some of America's most successful business-men labored long and hard to deserve the bad name they have today, when businessmen as a class are often disdained as being merely nimble parasites who reap without sowing, who do things but do not make things. Most of the Jewish merchants in this book were justifiably respected because they were respectable, as some but not all businessmen today are hated because they are hateful. The merchants did not pay their employees a penny more than they had to; in their private lives, they were no more saintly than men have always been. But they were grateful for their good fortune in America, and expressed that gratitude gener-ously and effectively in their communities.

One of the oldest jokes is that the Jew has only one reaction to any and all events, no matter how apparently far removed they are from him: "Is it good for the Jews?" Some say, instead, that Jewish actions are invariably motivated by the perceived an-swer to the question: "Is it good business?" For these storekeepers the answer was often yes when both questions were asked about the same thing—what was good business was also good for the Jews and, indeed, simultaneously good for the whole community.

For many years the comings and goings and gossip of great storekeepers were as fascinating to many Americans as the doings of singers, actresses, politicians, and important criminals. This is no longer the case. Even today, however, the affairs of stores and storekeepers are sometimes considered newsworthy. Like wars, earthquakes, important divorces, and other natural disasters, they occasionally make front-page news as when *The New York Times* of May 8, 1976, announced that "Brooks Bros. Will End Custom Tailoring." On November 19, 1977, the demise of Aber-crombie & Fitch inspired an editorial in the *Times*'s painfully peda-gogical prose explaining Thorstein Veblen's theory of the leisure class and declaring that Abercrombie's, "a citadel of the Leisure Class . . . is a victim of democratization." Ever since "the oddest people began to appear in Cannes" and "the ordinary working stiff" took up tennis and skiing, the "leisure explosion [has been]

. . . under way." Rather than paying Abercrombie's high prices in genteel and wasteful surroundings, all sportspersons, including the rich, now buy at discount stores and are doubtless the better for it, opined the *Times.*

Recently, after the funeral of one of my former buyers, I was approached by a mourner who had been a salesman in our store's men's furnishings department in my father's time and then left to be a traveling salesman of men's wear. He wanted to reminisce and told me at great length about a Sunday before Christmas in the 1930s—in those days it was not unusual to work on Sunday. In both newspapers that Sunday, there had been a half-page advertisement, he said, "on one of those really fabulous buys your father used to make—these were regular three-dollar silk neckties from Cheney Brothers—that was an expensive tie then—and we were offering them at a dollar apiece. To get them at that price, your father had bought two thousand dozen—that's more than one tie for every white adult male in the city—the kind of big buy that used to scare your uncle to death but excited the rest of us."

He then spent perhaps half an hour lovingly describing the patterns, colors, weaves, and feel of the various silk ties, remembered clearly from some forty years earlier.

"Your father had come down to the store early to make certain that we properly assorted and displayed the ties, but when he arrived the ties were not there! No one knew where they were and those two ads had already run. You can imagine the hell that broke loose, frantic telephone calls to New York, feverish searching all over the store, the warehouse, the depot. Finally we found them at the express office.

"And we sold them all in three days—twenty-four thousand ties in three days—every last one of those beautiful Cheney silks for just a dollar in just three days."

He had a smile on his face and tears in his eyes. "It was fun," he said. "It was such fun."

It is perhaps difficult for someone who is not a merchant to understand how much fun it is to buy and sell a lot of something, although St. Augustine in his *Confessions* recognized the *play* aspect of business. Edward A. Filene, the Boston storekeeper, said: "I think shopkeeping is like sin, first you endure and then you embrace it."

Not all the storekeepers in this book built their stores on precisely the same set of principles. The Riches in Atlanta built theirs on almost grotesquely liberal customer credit, whereas Rowland Macy and the Strauses built theirs on "strictly cash." There were more similarities than differences, of course; but the one thing they shared, despite all the talk of hard work and sacrifice, was fun. Only that explains why almost all of the most successful men continued to work when they were old, when they were rich, when they had sons, grandsons, and professional executives to do the work for them. Long after they were too old for sports or for sex, which for some had never been their favorite games anyway, they could still play and win at the store.

Whatever else this book may do, I hope it gives some sense of that fun.

1

The Filenes of Boston

Lord, I ascribe it to thy grace,
  And not to chance as others do,
That I was born of Christian race,
  And not a Heathen or a Jew.
                              —Isaac Watts, *Divine Songs for Children*

Like Huck Finn, some present-day Fundamentalists believe that God wrote the Bible in English. But many of the early New England Puritan divines, who were also its scholars and political leaders, were Hebraists. In those days, every graduate of Harvard was required to be sufficiently fluent to read the Pentateuch in Hebrew at sight, and Yale included Hebrew as well as Latin in its seal. Ezra Stiles, as president of Yale, delivered his inauguration speech in 1778 in Hebrew, a language not only "essential to a gentleman's education" but, said Stiles, even more essential in heaven.

From the very beginnings in New England, its settlers saw themselves as the children of Israel, God's Chosen People. They named their own children Isaac and Ishmael, Rachel and Rebecca, Abigail, Amos, and Aaron. Obsession with the Jews was such that it even led to speculation that the Indians of America might be descended from Israel's Lost Tribes. The practice of circumcision among the

Indians supported the hypothesis, but one Hamon L'Estrange offered an irrefutable syllogism—Jews are not permitted to marry
whores, all Indian women are whores, thus the Indians could
not be Jews!

For more than a century, the analogy between British tyranny
over the colonists in America and Egypt's over the Jews continued.
The persecution by the Church of England of the various noncon-
formist Puritan sects had caused the flight to America—comparable to the flight from Egypt. A century later, the analogy was
still a constant—the rhetoric of the Revolution compared George
III with the wicked Pharaoh. Franklin, Jefferson, and Adams
recommended for the seal of the United States a design of the
children of Israel escaping from Pharaoh's hosts whom God is
about to drown in the Red Sea while Moses stands on the far
shore. Inscribed on the Liberty Bell was the injunction from Leviti-
cus: "Proclaim liberty throughout the land unto all the inhabitants
thereof."

But the influence of the Hebrew Bible and affection for the
People of the Book "was generally operative in inverse proportion
to the presence of flesh and blood Jews." In 1649, when a Jew
named Solomon Franco proposed to settle in Boston, he was paid
to leave. In Connecticut there were no votes for Jews or such
other natural "inferiors" as Roman Catholics, blacks, Indians, or
women. Only white Anglo-Saxon males rich enough to own property and wise or devout enough to pay dues to the Congregational
Church had the right to vote.

Although Roger Williams founded Rhode Island as a refuge
from religious discrimination, the same disenfranchisement common throughout New England existed in Providence until 1843.
But the right to vote was not invariably coexistent with the ability
to make money, and a few colonial Jewish merchant families—
Rivera, Lopez, Levy, Seixas, and Hart, for example—made considerable fortunes in whale oil, spermaceti candles, rum, and slaves.
Most of the few Jewish families that became rich enough to have
portraits painted by Gilbert Stuart and to help finance the Revolu-

tion were assimilated into the local aristocracy and ceased to be Jews.

Much more typical of the few Jews in New England were the peddlers, from "David the Jew," who was arrested for peddling in Hartford in 1659, to his hundreds of nameless nineteenth- and early twentieth-century counterparts who trudged to Maine and even to Canada. Peddling was much harder in the North than in the South, not only because of the weather but because Southern planters were richer than hardscrabble Yankee farmers and there were fewer stores in the South.

In addition to country peddlers, there were city peddlers, and female as well as male peddlers. Boston's "Aunt Rachel" in the 1880s peddled in the Irish sections and so learned an English as accented by its Irish brogue as by her native Russian and Yiddish. Most New England peddlers barely eked out a living, but a few became rich. Gerson Fox (Gershon Fuchs) began peddling in Hartford about 1830, and in 1840 started a small store that is now the biggest in Connecticut.

Another was William Filene, who at eighteen came to America after the failed German Revolution of 1848. Filene knocked around New England, working as a peddler, a tailor, a glazier, until he met Clara Ballin in Hartford and fell in love. He then decided that he must save enough money to marry her, which he did within four years. By 1856, at twenty-five, he had enough to open a small store in Salem, Massachusetts.

Once the most prosperous port in North America when Boston was still insignificant, Salem was now dying—its harbor silting up, its young leaving, its businesses closing and moving away. But Filene's pattern would always be to buy what was down, especially at moments of panic when others despaired but he believed that hard work could accomplish a recovery.

Filene did so well in Salem that eight years later he could afford to send Clara, the children, and an Irish nursemaid on a trip to Germany. Near Poznan they visited William's mother and father, about to celebrate their golden wedding anniversary; then they went to Clara's parents near Frankfurt, who had been rich enough to send their daughter to New York to learn English and who had shipped her as trousseau thirteen cases of household furnishings when she married William.

While his family was in Germany, William bought a wholesale business in New York at a bargain price during one of the financial crises caused by the Civil War. Thereafter he traveled between Salem and New York, running both enterprises until the New York business grew so big and profitable that he could move his family to a luxurious house in New York at 92nd Street and Fifth Avenue between Central Park and a pasture. Years later his second son, Edward, recalled: "Coming from old contracting, close-packed Salem to New York was like moving to the country. I remember a blur of summer days, of the house being incredibly spacious and cool and rich."

But if financial panics could offer William Filene opportunities, they could also ruin him. In the panic that followed Jay Gould's infamous Black Friday in 1868, Filene was wiped out.

He was left almost penniless after the brief years of luxury in New York. Once again he started from scratch. This time it was a tiny dry-goods shop in Lynn, the dreary shoe-manufacturing town that sometimes served as the symbol of all such bleak New England mill towns. All his life Edward Filene would remember Lynn's depressing, windowless red-brick shoe factories, the acid stench from the tanneries, the silent, dazed men and women walking slowly down the center of narrow, muddy, cobblestone streets to his father's store that had to be kept open until midnight because these factory hands worked such late hours.

But the observant Edward also watched the town's factory owners, many of them ostentatious, *nouveaux riches* Civil War profiteers. During a particularly bitter strike at the shoe factories, one owner drove past his starving employees in a brand-new, extravagantly expensive carriage drawn by four matched horses and with a black footman to open the door. Edward saw blind hatred overwhelm the starving strikers, who suddenly began stoning the arrogant factory owner. As an adult, Filene repeatedly spoke of this episode, invariably snorting his ultimate expression of contempt: "Kindergarten! Waving a red flag at a bull—it's *Kindergarten* stuff."

Helping in his father's store, the boy observed the contrast between the rich women, who bought quickly and lavishly or refused to buy because the merchandise was "not fine enough," and the poor wives of the workingmen, who held a bolt of cheap goods for an intolerably long time, turning it over and over, wondering not about its quality so much as whether this pitiably tiny expenditure might later mean too little money for food or rent or medicine.

In Lynn, William Filene once again built a successful store; and from its profits he bought in the next few years four additional ones at bargain prices, a men's store in Lynn, a dry-goods store in Bath, Maine, and two stores in Boston's Winter Street, one for gloves, the other for laces. He wanted each of his four sons as well as the future husband of his daughter to have a business of his own, but only Edward and Lincoln would prove to be able businessmen.

As a child, Edward was chronically sickly. Once, after staying in bed for a whole year, he had to learn to walk all over again. The weak, crippled boy, unable to keep up with his brothers and their friends was, as he later wrote, constantly urged by his mother: " '*Go play,*' with a curious intonation on that word 'play.' It came to mean bushes that pulled at your clothes and scratched your hands and face. I got the idea that playing was something you were forced to do, like going to bed early, because adults expected you to. I never hated any part of my work so much as I hated being made to play."

A burden or a joke to his contemporaries, Edward became a friendless loner who identified himself with Hans Christian Andersen's "Ugly Duckling." In Filene's revised version, the agent of his transformation into a swan was to be Harvard College. He kept books hidden in each of his father's stores to study when he had a moment of leisure. When he was carrying cash or merchandise from one store to another on the streetcar or the ferry, he brought along Bancroft's *History* or Darwin's *Origin*.

At twenty, in 1880, the painfully self-educated scholar passed his Harvard entrance examinations. But before college opened, William Filene had a stroke and Edward, as the ablest though not the oldest son, had to take over managing the stores. Fifty-eight years later, in a private file to which no one except Edward had access while he lived, his executors would find a painful keepsake cherished secretly for more than half a century. It was Certificate Number 276, certifying that he had passed his examinations and was eligible to enter Harvard.

Early every morning, Edward now went to Boston to oversee the two shops there. When they closed, earlier than the two in Lynn, he walked to Rowe's Wharf, took the ferry and the cars to Lynn, and worked in those two stores until they closed about midnight. His older brother, Rudolph, had already proven himself irresponsible, and a younger brother, Bert, was demonstrating his incompetence to run the store in Bath. Lincoln, the youngest of all, was only sixteen. Faced with the possibility that his father might never again actively run the stores, Edward determined to run them so well that ten years later, at thirty, he would have accumulated $100,000; $50,000 of this would protect his parents, even if the stores were lost; the other $50,000 would, he hoped, put him through Harvard and launch him on whatever career he might then choose.

When Edward had to go to New York to buy for the stores, he took the midnight train from Boston, got breakfast at the station, worked all day and as late into the night as necessary, then took the next train back to Boston. In this way he avoided both the cost of a hotel room and the company of other buyers who played cards, went to the theater, and partook of the city's many amusements.

Edward was bewildered by the terrifying variety of merchandise offered for sale in New York, and even more by the inexplicable and sudden shifts of fashion that destroyed the value of merchandise in stores. He promptly determined that he would somehow devise scientific methods of merchandising so as to decrease the terrible risks these presented to the retailer. This determination would continue throughout his life and would long cause him to be an object of scorn among merchants who were smugly certain that success in merchandising depended not upon science but upon such inexplicable mysteries as superior taste and a prescient nose.

The argument between "instinctive" and "scientific" merchandising increased in the great storekeeping families as second- and third-generation sons were sent off for training at the Harvard Business School and similar institutions that had been built in part by generous contributions from first-generation, unscientific merchants. As scions returned from the Wharton School, they were quick to display their new, more formal business methods and occasionally even an ill-disguised feeling of superiority *vis-à-vis* older family members. A classic family story is repeated in virtually every city across America—always told as though it were unique to that family. The founder grandfather (or father) passing by the store on Sunday sees an inventory in progress, with very complicated methods and forms devised by very costly accountants. "What's all this expensive *mish-mash?*" demands the Patriarch.

"It's an inventory," explains the New Generation.

"What's it for? Who needs it? All these people cost money and they're not *selling* anything!"

"But it's necessary," the New Generation explains patiently. "We must do this regularly or we can't know what our profit is."

Thereupon the Patriarch takes the New Generation by the sleeve and guides him to the Patriarch's office, where he unlocks a desk drawer that the New Generation has never seen unlocked before and so has always wondered what secret it contained. From the drawer the Patriarch takes out an old, worn, dirty canvas pack, and from the pack he removes and spreads on the desk a few dozen spools of thread, papers of pins, darning needles, and sets of buttons.

"This," says the Patriarch, pointing to the pack's pitiful contents, "is the inventory." And then, with a gesture that embraces all the floors of the enormous store and all the millions of dollars of merchandise the store contains, the Patriarch intones: "Everything else—that's the profit."

Young Edward Filene in only three years had all the stores doing very well. Then suddenly the eczema that had always plagued him returned. On October 12, 1883, he awakened to find his face, armpits, and groin red and inflamed. Soon the inflammation covered him entirely. He had long looked upon his body with distrust and never with more reason. Now every morning for an hour and a quarter his whole body had to be slathered with zinc salve and every evening for a like period with tar. Also prescribed was acid potash, to be taken internally.

Completely bedridden, Edward continued these treatments for two years, during which time his hair fell out, the pain increased constantly, and great patches of skin dropped from him, leaving raw, burning flesh.

Even under these conditions, he continued to observe and speculate: "I wonder if Socrates ever had a toothache, and how he bore it if he did. I would rather know that than know the account of how fearlessly he took the poison that was to kill him. I can easily imagine a state of feeling made so exalted by innocence and the presence of weeping and sympathetic friends as to take from death all its terror. But common toothache, or some disease disgusting but not dangerous—how did he meet that?" At last the agony became so terrible that he refused further medicine; thereafter, he gradually improved.

It was during this long illness that Edward's youngest brother, Lincoln, began to play an important role in building the family business. The two men could scarcely have been more unlike. Lincoln was as modest, friendly, even-tempered, ready to compromise, and free in giving praise and credit as Edward was prideful, prickly, stubborn, and often hypercritical. Lincoln abhorred fights—Edward reveled in them. Practical and loving, Lincoln would become a happy family man, who viewed his top business associates as extensions of his family. E. A., as he was always called in the store, remained a frequently irascible bachelor who—

once he had become rich—saw the store and its employees as means of testing his torrent of ideas and theories, a few of which were brilliant to the point of genius. But had they all been put into effect, they would have bankrupted the store. This disparity would finally lead to one of the very few bitter and bloody palace revolutions in the great Jewish merchant families. However, between 1891, when E. A. and Lincoln took charge, and the end of World War I, it built one of the greatest stores in the world.

But not without competition. Boston had not waited for the Filenes to arrive. There were dozens of other stores, including Jordan Marsh, which was already well on its way to becoming the largest department store in New England.

In 1836 Eben Dyer Jordan, then fourteen, had arrived in Boston from Maine. He was descended from a once wealthy family, whose first settler in Maine in 1641 was a Church of England clergyman. But when Eben was four his father died, leaving the family so desperately poor that Eben's mother had to "farm out" the boy to neighbors to work for his keep.

The first time Eben as a child was sent into the village general store—for a dozen "soft crackers"—he witnessed a miracle no less crucial to his development than Paul's on the road to Damascus or Rousseau's on the way to Vincennes. He paid the pennies he had been given, received the crackers, and, hypnotized by this communion, he stayed and stared as again and again he witnessed money exchanged for goods. For him it was a sight that would never lose its thrill.

Eben's first retail job in Boston was as an errand boy. He opened the store before daylight, got the fires going in winter, swept out, and learned everything by doing everything. He was, even for that day, so industrious that he impressed one of the important Hanover Street dry-goods merchants, who set up the nineteen-year-old in his own little store.

Jordan was successful as his own boss. He developed $8,000 in sales the first year and almost $100,000 the fourth. But because he decided that he should also educate himself in wholesaling and importing, he did the unbelievable: at twenty-five he sold his successful store to go to work once again as an employee. He stayed two years at James M. Beebe & Company, a big importing and jobbing house, where Junius Spencer Morgan was a member of the firm.

Then, satisfied that he now knew enough, Jordan joined with his friend Benjamin L. Marsh. On January 20, 1851, with a capital of $5,000, they began what would become one of the half-dozen greatest department stores in America.

With the store's enormous success, Eben and his son, Eben, Jr., would become lavish supporters of music in Boston both at the New England Conservatory of Music and by giving the city its opera house. Eben, Jr., also would live in a rather grander style than the Back Bay Boston Brahmins considered suitable, leasing Inverary Castle in Argyllshire and subsequently Drummond Castle in Perthshire for his family's summer vacations.

When, in 1891, Edward and Lincoln Filene took over the management of their father's Boston store, it was not a department store like Jordan's. It was a specialty store. Jordan's sold everything—men's wear, women's wear, housewares, furniture—but Filene's sold only women's fashions and accessories. Like most other specialty stores, including Bergdorf Goodman and Neiman-Marcus, it would later add children's and men's wear but never become a full department store.

The Filene brothers not only concentrated on merchandising for women but also, remembering how much more difficult it was to sell to poor women than to rich ones, tried constantly to raise the quality of their stock and their service. While Edward devoted his time chiefly to merchandising, the more equable Lincoln was in charge of personnel and customer relations. If Edward was on occasion less able than Lincoln at dealing with employees individually, he was no less interested in them as a group.

In 1898, at the height of American *laissez-faire* capitalism, E. A. created the Filene Cooperative Association. The move was not made in response to any threatened strike or unrest among the store's five hundred employees; in fact, quite the opposite. E. A. had enthusiastically set up a variety of employee welfare projects—a medical service, an employees' dining room, an insurance fund—only to find that the employees, despite their obvious need, refused to take advantage of these. Never one to accept failure easily, he investigated and found that the employees distrusted these gifts. They feared that the medical service, for example, would reveal their secrets to management, with the result that anyone who was ill would be fired.

E. A. effected an immediate solution to this problem: he turned over each such enterprise to the employees to run themselves, as they chose, for their own benefit. With a candor not always evident in a boss's speeches to his employees, E. A. admitted at a meeting of the Association in 1904: "My brother and I had tried to do the work for our people under well-meant but still despotically benevolent principles. But grown wiser and more democratic by our failures, we agreed to do nothing for our people, but to try to help them to do everything for themselves."

The Association was self-governing. Its officers and executive committee were elected by secret ballot. E. A. was convinced that this kind of industrial democracy would assure not only the survival of free enterprise but also its optimum profitability. He preached his gospel to any and every business group that would listen and, like all evangelists, was easy to make fun of. But unlike many of them, he knew how to take the sting out of his critics' jibes. When someone said he was "a cross between a pack peddler and Isaiah," E. A. agreed.

But he kept preaching industrial democracy. He boasted that the Association "decides by vote all the rules of the store, hours of opening and closing, in fact everything, the question of wages and discharge." This was an exaggeration, but not a big one, for although the management had the right to veto decisions of the Association, it did not do so.

At a time when the salaries of ordinary department-store employees ranged between $5 and $12 a week, most could not, despite pious Victorian platitudes and preachments, put away anything for a rainy day, and when the inevitable rainy day arrived they could not get bank credit. This made them easy prey for the loan shark. A woman or man who needed $30 desperately would accept terms that led to paying interest of $1,080, to find the original $30 still owing.

Aware of this problem, E. A. discovered what he believed could be its solution; as with many of the ideas he supported, he found it while traveling. In 1907, he visited India, and learned about the Agricultural Cooperative Banks in Bengal. Fascinated, he then went on to Germany, where cooperative banks had been successful since the middle of the nineteenth century. A year later, with the help of a priest, Alphonse Desjardins, who had already established credit unions in Quebec, E. A. started a movement to make them legal in Massachusetts. He then founded and supported the Credit Union National Extension Bureau to propagandize for and help legalize credit unions throughout America against the resolute opposition in every state of bankers and loan sharks.

The formation of these unions was simple. In some states, as few as seven men from their pooled savings could subscribe shares of $5 or $10 par value. They and their fellow employees could then deposit further savings and borrow small sums.

This movement would grow into one of E. A.'s greatest successes. In one year in which 7,000 banks failed and 5,000 were kept from failing only by the intervention of the Reconstruction Finance Corporation (RFC), not a single credit union failed and only five borrowed from the RFC. The reasons for the contrast were edifying. Bank officers and directors borrowed lavishly from their own banks or from other banks on a mutual backscratching basis. The officers of credit unions, however, could not borrow from its funds, nor could they become endorsers for borrowers in excess of the value of their own shares. And credit union officers (who were unpaid) did not frequent the expensive restaurants or exclusive country clubs that seemed mandatory for well-paid bank officers. Therefore the operating expense of credit unions was minuscule.

In their attempts to defeat legislation legalizing these credit unions, the bankers had asked contemptuously: "Do you really believe that shopgirls and plumbers can go into banking?" The shopgirls and hundreds of thousands of others swiftly proved that they could, and the monument to Edward A. Filene on Boston Common was erected in 1959 as a tribute to his role as godfather to the credit union movement in America.

In a speech he made to the American Academy of Political and Social Science on April 7, 1907, "Conditions of Working Women," E. A. ended with a poem of his own entitled "How to Make a Poet."

> First get a good piece of land.
> Build a factory.
> Govern it wisely,
> That is, with knowledge plus sympathy.
> Make it a business success.
> Make the factory and the village beautiful.
> Make conditions just;
> And then more just;
> And then more just;
> And one of the sons of one of the workers
> Will be a poet.

If not much as poetry, it nevertheless expresses the optimistic conviction of man's perfectibility that was then thought to be no less a certainty than the opposite view is today. The believer in progress, necessarily an optimist, is now widely thought to be a fool or a fraud in America, despite the fact that his eighteenth-century fathers, here and in Europe, believed that morals, politics, emotions, indeed all of life, could be scientifically and logically understood and codified and that, in Jeremy Bentham's phrase, "knowledge is rapidly advancing toward perfection."

If Filene's meliorism had an emphasis on matters material rather than moral, it was nonetheless descended from Franklin's, Jefferson's, and Paine's. It included the same nineteenth-century boosterism that proclaimed each person who came to town was one more customer, one more client, one more patient, one more taxpayer who could help to build the Athens of the South, the Paris of the West, the New Jerusalem. Such boosterism is easy to laugh at; but it built America's cities.

In cities and villages all across the country, Jewish merchants—
Joseph Pfeifer in Little Rock, Adolph Schwartz in El Paso, David
Lubin in Sacramento—possibly even more than their Gentile fellow Americans, were buoyed by a boundless optimism. They believed that finally, here, Isaiah's vision could become reality: "Every valley shall be exalted, and every mountain and hill shall
be made low; and the crooked shall be made straight and the
rough places plain."

As the eighteenth-century *philosophes* were certain that science
would solve mankind's historic dilemmas, so Edward Filene believed that science could solve the storekeeper's. And the greatest
of these was markdowns. One of the few certainties in retailing
is that some of the merchandise bought enthusiastically in the
wholesale market, where it looks eminently saleable, will, when
it reaches the store, prove stubbornly unsaleable. But despite this
inevitability, buyers, like the rest of humanity, are reluctant to
admit and address their errors. They find endless excuses for the
slow sale of such merchandise: the weather's still too hot; the
weather's still too cold. Easter's late this year; Easter was early
this year. It hasn't been advertised; the ad was lousy; the ad
ran on the wrong day; the ad ran in the wrong newspaper.

The danger in these rationalizations is that they usually increase
markdowns. A coat that does not sell early in the fall may still
tempt customers if it is marked down early by as little as 25
percent. But as the season ends, it must be marked down far
more drastically to tempt a customer who, having done without
a new coat so long, may otherwise reasonably decide to wait
until the next season.

To combat the buyer's tendency to postpone taking markdowns,
E. A. in the early years of this century devised his automatic
markdown system that has since made Filene's Automatic Bargain
Basement the most famous store in New England—better known
and far more often visited than Faneuil Hall or the Old State
House. The system is, in E. A.'s phrase, "an auction in reverse";
it overcomes the buyer's reluctance to admit error by the simple
device of entirely removing decision making from the markdown
process.

After various evolutionary changes, the system is now absolutely automatic. The price tag of every article in the basement is marked with the date it is first put on sale. Twelve selling days later, if the article is unsold, the price is automatically reduced by 25 percent. After the next six selling days, Filene's first price (which itself was often less than half the article's original retail price) is reduced 50 percent; six selling days later, it is marked down 75 percent. And after another six—a total of thirty selling days—the article is given away to charity.

Over 90 percent of the merchandise disappears within the first twelve days and only one-tenth of 1 percent goes to charity. Because these markdown rules are as inflexible as the laws of the Medes and Persians, customers have learned that, unlike upstairs, it is useless to wait before buying an item until a favorite salesperson telephones announcing it has been marked down. Indeed, there are very few salespeople in what is essentially a self-service operation, and those few merely write the sales ticket and take the cash—there is no charging in the basement.

Although it was ten years before Filene's Automatic Bargain Basement became profitable, it eventually accounted for more than 25 percent of the store's sales and throughout the Depression its profits would more than offset the rest of the store's losses. The further profits resulting from customers who come to the basement and then make their way to the upper floors to buy more cannot be calculated.

E. A.'s automatic markdown system is at the heart of the basement operation; but of course *what* is bought is also important (although not always crucial, because when the mullets are feeding, they often snap up anything in their frenzy). Today, some sixty buyers scour the world for surplus stock, imperfect and damaged merchandise, going-out-of-business opportunities, and other "distress" bargain possibilities, in much the same spirit that inspired William Filene's search for business bargains in times of panic.

However ghoulish the role of these buyers, they are nevertheless welcomed by the victims of fire, flood, and failure, because they offer the great essential—immediate cash. At the beginning of

World War II, just before Paris fell to the Germans, Filene's buyers shipped home through Spain some four hundred dresses from such couturiers as Lucien LeLong, Elsa Schiaparelli, Coco Chanel, and Maggie Rouf. Norman Hartnell, couturier to England's royal family, also had models sold in Filene's basement.

Because a business in millions of dollars, often attracting more than 100,000 customers a day, cannot rely upon such fortunate disasters as Neiman-Marcus's fires to supply its needs, Filene's basement has also worked out regular buying arrangements with such stores as Neiman's and Saks Fifth Avenue. When the unsold merchandise of these stores has been so greatly reduced that further markdowns and offering the merchandise so long after the season would be damaging to the store's prestige, it is packed up and sent to Filene's. Customers in those communities have learned that the ads announcing: "LAST FOUR DAYS before we ship away this sale merchandise forever," mean what they say.

For generations of New England shoppers (including Joseph Kennedy's children, Harvard presidents, and Back Bay Brahmins) as well as for visiting national and international stars of movies, television, and sports, shopping in Filene's basement has also provided a blood sport. Every morning at the opening gong at 9:30, there is a crushing stampede of customers who have been waiting at the entrances. They burst into the hot, smelly, narrow aisles, snatching from gas-pipe racks and intentionally shabby wooden counters as they run. Individual fights between customers, clawing, biting, and cursing over the same article are everyday affairs, and near-riots are not uncommon.

For those who enjoy spectator sports and for voyeurs as well, there is an endless show. Most women refuse the inevitable wait for the few fitting rooms, preferring to strip in the aisles to try on their treasures. And while the customer is pulling a new dress over her head, she risks losing not only the others she has torn from the racks and must put down for an instant but also her own.

The enormous success of this basement has of course inspired numerous imitations, all over America and abroad as well, for example at Selfridge's in London. But in more than half a century it has never been successfully duplicated anywhere.

The Automatic Bargain Basement was E. A.'s most successful attempt to make merchandising "scientific" and to accomplish what he had set as the primary mission of his life—to prove that lowered distribution costs would sell more customers and make greater profits than higher and higher prices. In the last decades of his life, he would characterize it as "doing for distribution what Henry Ford did for manufacturing," although he had started his efforts years before Ford's production line.

E. A. wrote half a dozen books (one was translated into five languages), on the subject of better and cheaper distribution, as well as articles for such popular periodicals as the *Saturday Evening Post, Survey Graphic, Atlantic Monthly,* and *The New York Times.* This scientific approach extended not only to manufacturers and professional store buyers but also to customers. He pleaded for professional and demanding, "hardboiled customers," who would take the time and trouble necessary to be certain they were getting the best prices and quality obtainable. "It is economic treason to shop carelessly," he said.

While E. A. was combing the world for ideas and addressing himself more and more to problems unrelated directly to the store, Lincoln Filene was managing a constantly growing and more profitable business and bringing in talented executives from the outside to help him.

The Filene brothers had made a rule against any nepotism in the store. This was in strong contrast to the practice of most Jewish storekeepers, and may not have been entirely unrelated to the fact that E. A. had no children and Lincoln only daughters. It of course encouraged young executives, who saw that there was no impediment to promotion on their own merit.

The most extraordinary of these executives brought into the store and the one who, except for the brothers themselves, was most responsible for its success was Louis Edward Kirstein—one of the great eccentrics of American retailing.

He had begun early by running away from home on his six-

teenth birthday. A great hulking fellow, he not only played baseball well enough to earn his keep in the bush leagues as a player
but was smart enough to manage various small ball clubs. Yet
he never stayed anywhere very long, preferring to "hobo" around
and see the country.

Of his picaresque adventures, the most extraordinary took place
in St. Louis. Kirstein was convicted of peddling a bottled panacea
whose chief ingredients were sand and muddy Mississippi water.
He was sentenced to pay a $5 fine or spend five days in jail.
Kirstein did not have $5, but he convinced the judge to give
him a few hours to raise the money. First he ran to the local
Reform rabbi, who curtly refused to lend him the required sum.
He then returned to the whorehouse where he had been living
and working as a janitor, and asked for a $5 advance from the
madame, who earlier in her career had had an eye gouged out
in a fight with another whore. She lent him the money.

For the rest of his life he frequently pointed out the contrast
between the charity "of the man of God and that one-eyed whore.
I am convinced that she saved my life, that if she had let me
go to jail, I would have become a criminal. I always wanted to
repay her kindness and years later spent a lot of money on private
detectives trying to trace her. But I never found her again."

When Kirstein returned to his native Rochester, New York,
where he bought and managed the baseball team, he was still
too proud to ask for financial help from his family, who could
easily have supplied it. He often said later that he learned what
he knew about hard trading from trying to get the very highest
possible price for selling his best players in order to raise enough
money to pay the rest.

In 1894, at twenty-seven, he married an heiress, Rose Stein.
She was the daughter of Nathan Stein, the founder of Stein-Bloch,
one of the pioneer men's clothing manufacturers in America. Kirstein then went to work for Stein-Bloch, where it did not endear
him to his brothers-in-law that he was smarter than they and a
harder worker. In order to avoid family friction, he left and joined

Filene's as a junior partner in 1911. He was soon in charge of all merchandising and publicity.

A taciturn-looking giant, who spoke alternately in growls and grunts, Kirstein cultivated a reputation for imperious ferocity but was worshipped by his buyers. At Filene's he finally became a manager with enough money. He no longer had to sell off his stars. Now he could go out and hire star buyers away from other stores, or even take the often more costly alternative of training his own stars. He surrounded himself with women and men who enjoyed winning and hated losing as desperately as he did—"winning" consisted of regularly outperforming anyone else in Boston, whether at Jordan's, Stearn's, Gilchrist's, or White's. And when that became habitual, he and his team were only satisfied if they could outperform the other great specialty stores throughout the country.

Kirstein had a gift for aphorism and was widely quoted by other storekeepers:

"Advertising pays, when it is believed."

"The expense rate cannot be lowered by worrying about it."

"Retailing needs less figuring, more fingering."

"One thing wrong with business is that businessmen do not attend to it."

This last dictum was almost certainly inspired by the conduct of E. A. Filene. It was probably inevitable that so powerful and acerbic a figure as Kirstein would eventually fall out with E. A., but what insured it was E. A.'s reappearances in the store after months of traveling, whereupon he expected to reassume his role of undisputed chief.

Had this been the only problem, Lincoln Filene, whose skills as a peacemaker were legendary, could perhaps have handled the situation. But there was a more basic and irreconcilable problem. By the second decade of the century E. A. was a millionaire, who now wished to use the store as a vehicle for his social experiments, and even to give it away to all the employees. Kirstein and three other of the top executives wished to become millionaires themselves and were outraged at E. A.'s "damnfool Socialist experiments." They wanted to run a profitable business enterprise; E. A. wanted a laboratory to test his flood of ideas.

In Lincoln's house at Weston, a collection of which he was enormously proud was displayed on a wall. It was made up of gavels given to him after countless conventions, meetings, arbitrations, and conferences at which he had presided and kept the peace with skillful sweetness. In 1916, at a meeting he had arranged at the Aldine Club in New York, he proved that he could combine both E. A.'s yearning for a more scientific approach to storekeeping and Kirstein's itch to excel at the game. Lincoln had invited representatives of eighteen other successful American stores, including Detroit's J. L. Hudson Company, the Dayton Company of Minneapolis, San Francisco's Emporium, Pittsburgh's Joseph Horne Company, and Columbus's F. & R. Lazarus & Company, to the meeting.

He suggested to the assembled group that a scientific study of common merchandising problems might lead to reduced expenses and higher profits. To undertake such a study, he said, would require that they form a Retail Research Association, to which they would submit—honestly and fully—detailed figures from their own stores. This exchange of figures was, of course, a revolutionary suggestion. One of the traditional imperatives of business was secrecy. You didn't tell your wife more than you had to; you didn't even tell your oldest boy everything until the very end or close to it. If the glove buyer for Horne's had access to the figures for Filene's glove department, she could see in what respects Filene's was doing better than she, and vice versa. If she then was hired away from Horne's to work at Jordan Marsh, wouldn't that be a disaster? And wouldn't it be an even greater disaster when buyers knew their profit figures and how well they were doing in relation to other stores and therefore demanded appropriate raises? Still worse, when salaried executives higher up in the store knew *everything,* wouldn't they go into business for themselves?

Despite many doubts, the Retail Research Association was

started in 1918, but overcoming the traditional insistence on secrecy and fear of candor was only the first problem. Another was to make the sets of figures genuinely comparable, for the systems and records in each store were as individual as the original store owners.

Bernard Foreman, a Russian-born ladies' tailor who had built a fine ladies' specialty store in Rochester, was as innocent of the concept of depreciation as of English syntax. When a bookkeeper from the Retail Research Association relentlessly insisted that Foreman must charge the depreciation of his store building against profits if his figures were to be comparable, the horrified man made a special trip to Boston. He went to see Kirstein, whose wife had set Foreman up in business. Weeping uncontrollably, he sobbed: "Vunce already, Lou, I paid for the building and now your *meshuggener* bookkeeper says again a second time I gotta pay for it. For your Rosa I would do anything, but *that* never!"

Despite all the fears and birth pangs, however, the Association was so successful that two years later the stores started a second organization, the Associated Merchandising Corporation (AMC), whose chief purpose was cooperative buying for member stores (in the face of the increasing buying power of Sears, Roebuck). As it too flourished, the AMC took on additional cooperative chores, including recruiting executives, improving advertising, and exchanging personnel policies. Despite any laws to the contrary, there was of course an unwritten agreement that member stores did not steal employees whose abilities were revealed in the figure exchanges and at AMC meetings.

In 1920, Kirstein opened cooperative AMC buying offices in Europe. Other stores that used the buying offices included Bullock's of Los Angeles, Philadelphia's Strawbridge & Clothier, Baltimore's Hutzler Brothers Company, and Dallas's A. Harris & Company. From these same cooperative first steps would evolve the great American department-store chain, Federated Department Stores.

As E. A. and Lincoln had over the years given and sold 12 percent of the shares of their store to each of four top executives, the brothers had, with their remaining 52 percent, kept control—provided that they voted together. And despite differences of opinion, they had always done so. But finally E. A. had grown too removed from everyday storekeeping and too concerned with reform.

It was the era of the great reformers, both the muckrakers who believed America's promise had been corrupted but could yet be saved, and also the more revolutionary anarchists and Communists. Perhaps nowhere in America was the need for reform more evident than in Boston. Long ago the city had been a hotbed of revolution: James Otis, like Sam Adams, was a constant troublemaker, an agitator who, sometimes secretly, sometimes openly, whipped up public fury to violence over injustice and discrimination. But now radicals such as Sacco and Vanzetti could not even expect due process, and, instead of the Boston Tea Party, the 1919 suppression of the Boston police strike symbolized the city.

In point of fact, the love of liberty, free speech, and justice was not invariably the chief concern of New England's citizens. In 1692, two hundred years after Columbus's discovery of America, the anniversary had been marked in Salem by the burning of twenty witches.

E. A. was scarcely a Tom Paine or a John Brown, but his style of reform was better suited to the fat-cat mood of Boston than theirs would now have been.

E. A. was well aware that all Boston's important elements would have to join forces and act together if there was to be any hope of correcting the city's ills. To overcome the class, racial, and religious divisions that prevented such united action, he chose a means that at first glance seemed precisely the worst possible—another men's club.

Boston was perhaps the clubbiest city in America, yet the Catholics, the Jews, the Irish, the Italians—indeed everyone except the Brahmins—were rigorously excluded from the most important and powerful clubs. E. A. decided that there must be a City Club, where all the diverse Bostonians could meet and eat and come to know one another. He found and hired an able organizer who met individually with the most powerful member of each existing club to explain the purpose of the proposed new club: to discuss, to listen, to try to determine the common good for Boston, but never to go into politics.

Knowing that in addition to a convenient location, the *sine qua non* of a successful club was good, cheap food, E. A. himself undertook to find a chef. A constant traveler, wherever he ate a good meal he asked to meet the chef, and finally hired one. His City Club became one of Boston's most successful, but instead of developing into the forum for progressive ideas and the force for reform he had hoped it would, it soon became as conservative as the city's other institutions and a force for protecting the status quo.

E. A.'s lawyer and adviser, Louis D. Brandeis, declared: "Filene is forever making weapons for the enemy." Other examples of this ironic truth abound. In addition to the Boston City Club, E. A. organized Boston's Chamber of Commerce, then a national Chamber of Commerce, and finally an international Chamber of Commerce. Each of these he conceived as a force to make business more humane, progressive, and democratic; each, instead, became a powerful force for reaction and repression.

E. A., like many thoughtful Americans, had been enormously impressed by the exposures in Lincoln Steffens's *The Shame of the Cities* of the corruption and waste in big-city governments. Through the medium of the Good Government Association, which he had also organized, E. A. hired Steffens for $10,000 a year "to muckrake Boston," not only to investigate and expose but also to suggest cures for the city's ills.

In October 1903, Steffens brought an entourage that included his mother-in-law, servants, dog, cat, bird, and some seventeen trunks to a house on Beacon Hill. There he began "the biggest piece of work I ever attempted," work he hoped might lead to "the establishment by me of a profession, a new calling; that of a city manager or municipal architect." Just as the application of scientific methods to solving storekeeping problems had excited E. A., even more did this same approach to curing the problems of the city. But Steffens finally had to admit failure in his role as municipal physician. "New England," he diagnosed, "is dying of hypocrisy."

Slowly Steffens was approaching the view that attempts at reform are useless, a view best expressed by H. L. Mencken's dictum: "It will never get well if you pick it."

On his yacht at Marblehead, E. A. discussed at length with Steffens his two great ambitions: to increase the world standard of living by lowering distribution costs, and to promote industrial democracy and so save the free enterprise system. No less a political analyst than Lenin himself took note of E. A.'s efforts to correct the faults of capitalism and the possibility that they might postpone or prevent the world revolution Karl Marx had declared was inevitable. "So, Mr. Filene!" Lenin wrote, "you think that all the workers of all the world are fools!"

But even the ebullient E. A. had begun to have a few doubts about the effectiveness of democracy. In the speeches that he was delighted to give anywhere and anytime at the merest drop of an invitation, his most repeated story now was about the village priest whose poor congregation was determined to honor him. In an effort to combine their pitifully meager resources into one adequate gift, the members of the flock had decided that each of them would pour one bottle of wine into a cask and so give him one important gift. In the dead of night, each man brought a bottle to the priest's house and emptied it into the barrel that had been secretly brought to his front yard. The next morning when the priest tapped the cask, out flowed pure water—each man had expected that his failure to do his duty would be hidden by the honesty of his neighbors.

E. A. confessed to Steffens aboard the yacht that the store's employees misused the democratic tools he had given them. They were concerned with what he considered relatively minor matters—shorter hours, longer holidays—instead of with taking over the company itself and making it more profitable for themselves as owners. Would Steffens, E. A. asked, come to the store and lecture them? Steffens came.

"I told them," he later wrote in his *Autobiography*, "how . . .

the people had votes with power to govern, but did not exercise their rights; they let their bosses rule them scandalously. My hearers laughed at the people of New York, Philadelphia, Missouri, etc. . . . But when I paused and took up them and their store, there was silence. Pointing at Mr. Filene, I said that he said that they, his employees, were as weak and as ridiculous as the citizens of any city . . . that he had given them power to take over the company and that they used it only for trivialities, not always in the interest of the business. . . . I asked Filene to withdraw a moment and then asked that hunk of 'the people' to say something. Not a word."

Lincoln Filene, Lou Kirstein, and the other stockholding executives were not so silent; nor were they anxious to give the store to the employees. In fact, their desire to form a holding company with Abraham & Straus and F. & R. Lazarus was inspired by E. A.'s talk of giving the store to its employees as well as by the advantage of a geographic spread of risk. When E. A. refused to go along, and instead fought the merger, Lincoln betrayed him. After so many years of joint control, based upon their always voting together, Lincoln voted with the store's other stockholding executives against his brother.

Just as E. A. had lost control of the City Club and the other reform vehicles he had created, so now in 1928 he lost control of his own store. But perhaps a defeated opponent was never more generously treated. He kept the title of president of the store; he was paid a salary of $100,000 a year—the same as his brother and Kirstein. Outside of the store, and especially in Europe, he was still considered the great merchant prince. But he was totally and permanently stripped of authority within the institution that he had built into the greatest specialty store in the world.

For E. A. it was a mixed curse, because now he was free to concentrate entirely on his nonretailing interests, and they were extraordinarily diverse. Like his father, E. A. was a tinkerer and inventor. With Captain Gordon Finlay, E. A. had designed the first simultaneous translating system for his International Chamber of Commerce. This Filene-Finlay system was subsequently produced by IBM for the Nuremberg war-crimes trials and the United Nations.

Long a liberal Democrat, E. A. could now devote more time to politics, serving as the Massachusetts administrator for the New Deal's National Recovery Administration and campaigning for Franklin D. Roosevelt. Prominent businessmen who supported FDR were in acutely short supply, so that Democratic National Chairman James A. Farley used E. A. nationally in an effort to disprove the charge that Roosevelt was the Public Enemy Number One of American business.

At 12 Otis Place, in his Back Bay brownstone overlooking the Charles River Basin, E. A. lived quite modestly for a millionaire. His only extravagance—other than his yacht—was that he surrounded himself with a staff of secretaries, speech writers, ghost writers, and biographers. Filene had paid Charles Wood to write his biography and then suppressed it. On Steffens's recommendation he had then hired Robert Cantwell to write another, only to fire him before he was fairly started. Although politically a liberal, especially in comparison to most millionaires, E. A. was not sensitive to problems of free speech. When asked about the domination of newspapers by advertisers in a 1911 interview by Hutchins Hapgood for *Collier's,* E. A. admitted candidly, "there has been a tacit agreement that we would be displeased if the newspaper published, for instance, news of an accident in the store."

As his role in the store ceased entirely, E. A.'s need to feel effective as a reformer increased. Egotism played a significant role in his activities and the loss of power increased his vanity—he removed his date of birth from his biography in the 1928 *Who's Who.*

Perhaps no love is fiercer than that of a writer for his own words. Filene was never happier than when his clipping services revealed that one of his speeches was reported on at length or one of his aphorisms on business was widely quoted. Although not a felicitous writer, he was an excellent reporter because he was relentlessly curious and questioned almost everyone, railroad brakemen, salesgirls, barbers, waitresses, making careful notes of what they said about their jobs, their homes, their politics, their lives.

Edward Filene's defeat at the store increased his always terrible longing for kudos. But his efforts for publicity and public recognition were, he insisted, only to prove that a capitalist could be useful and socially concerned. Beginning in 1929, he briefly paid $15,000 a year for the services of the publicist Edward Bernays, who says: "The Filenes' real family name was Katz. They were Polish Jews or at least *hinter Berlin,* which amounts to the same thing. The father thought 'filene' meant 'cat' in French and was classier than Katz. That's what E. A. told us when we were working for him."

Jews, who upon their arrival in America or who later changed their surnames from Nusbaum to Norman, from Lapowski to Dillon, or from Rabinovitch to Raab or Robinson, have often been made figures of fun. Not infrequently they have even been incorrectly characterized—by Jews and non-Jews—as cowards who thereby betrayed their heritage and tradition. In fact, surnames have historically had virtually no meaning for Jews.

For centuries, as with most peoples in the West (and in the Bible), Jews had only single names, although as with other peoples (Lars, Anders's son, or Richard, Jack's son), a given name might be followed by a patronymic for better identification (Moses ben Jacob).

In the late Middle Ages, surnames for Englishmen developed from a variety of sources, including patronymics (Richardson, Wilson), trades (Cooper, Weaver), and places (Lincoln, Garfield). The same happened throughout Europe, but not to European Jews, who, segregated in small groups and often in flight, avoided taking surnames.

This practice prevailed until Joseph II in Austria in 1787 and Napoleon in France in 1808 decreed that Jews must adopt definitive family names in order to facilitate military conscription and tax collection. The same laws soon obtained everywhere and the Jews complied, but they did not take seriously these names that they had assumed under duress. Many indeed gave no more thought to choosing a surname than a man might today if required to select a social security number.

Their most common choices of names are obviously casual if not frivolous. Many took place names such as Halle or Bamberger, Thalhimer or Moskowitz. Many merely took a patronymic for their family name, such as Lazarus or Meier or Abraham or Marcus (usually derived from the Hebrew Mordecai).

In those days, when illiteracy in Europe was still the rule rather than the exception, a house had, instead of a street number, an identifying sign painted and cut in the shape of a red shield or a fox or a rose tree. Many Jews simply and somewhat whimsically took as surnames the sign on the house where they lived, Rothschild or Fuchs or Rosenstock. Straus in German means not only bouquet and knight's crest, both frequently used as house signs, but also ostrich, another popular house sign and the one that Bobby Straus of the storekeeping clan thinks was the derivation of that family's name.

My own grandfather, from the moment of his arrival in Galveston in 1859, gave Harris as his name and that of his parents, Israel and Hannah. The appearance of the name Harris in any records in Prussia is almost unimaginable. His family name, taken perhaps fifty years earlier, was probably Hirsch, the German for "hart," and so possibly derived from a house sign, or more likely, the Germanization of Naphtali, a patronymic. Cerf is the equivalent in French.

The variety is endless. Many took the names of trees, flowers, jewels, or precious metals—Rosenwald, Bloomingdale, Diamond, Goldwater. Some took nicknames as their surnames, Altman (old man) or Hutzler (wrinkled, shriveled one), while others took occupational names, Sanger (singer), Schneider (tailor), or Wechsler (money changer). Still others adopted surnames from personal characteristics, such as Klein (short), Schwartz (black), Weiss (white), or Kuhn (brave).

That name changing has frequently had at least overtones of snobbery (East European Jews wanting to appear Western or Jews wanting to be thought of as non-Jews) is undeniable. And there were often very practical aspects to such name changes. At the end of World War II, Harvard's Dr. Albert Sprague Coolidge testified before a committee of Massachusetts legislators: "We know perfectly well that names ending in 'berg' or 'stein' have to be skipped by the board of selection of students for scholarships in chemistry" because of the "gentlemen's agreement" between the university and the chemical companies donating the scholarships.

"The only profession I know that does not bar Jews," explained Rabbi Stephen S. Wise, "is the rabbinical profession."

The subject of name changes as a method of circumventing anti-Semitism is a very serious one, as is made evident by the many Jewish jokes about it.

Neither E. A. nor Lincoln was ever a practicing Jew; in fact, their father had ceased to be one before he emigrated. E. A. was quietly agnostic and had nothing to do with any organized religion. But Lincoln, at the insistence of his wife, Therese, and for the social benefit of his two daughters, Catherine and Helen, became a Congregationalist. "It was a harmless deception," one observer recalled, "and it fooled nobody. It was like the big vase of fake forsythia Aunt Therese kept on the piano in that enormous, cathedral-ceilinged living room at Weston. She explained to me that she always scattered a very few fake forsythia petals on the piano and on the floor so no one would suspect the flowers weren't real."

Catherine Filene was, everyone said, almost as ambitious and difficult as her Uncle Edward, outspoken, self-promoting, and essentially a loner. After the failure of her first marriage to Alvin Dodd, she married a right-wing congressman, Jouett Shouse, who having had a brief moment in the limelight as president of the American Liberty League conveniently died.

Thereafter Catherine enjoyed the role of one of Washington,

D.C.'s rich and lavishly hospitable widows. But it was her generosity—shown, for instance, in her support of the arts at her Wolf
Trap Farm in Virginia—rather than her family's religious conversion that brought her the social recognition in the capital for
which she yearned.

The Christian community usually perceived the Jewish department-store owner as the most prominent leader of the local Jewish
community because he was the most visible, even when (like
the Filene brothers in Boston, Dick Rich in Atlanta, or Stanley
Marcus in Dallas) in his own eyes and those of the Jews he was
not perceived as Jewish. In Boston the most important Jewish
figure for many years was Louis Kirstein. In addition to his role
as the most powerful person within the Jewish community, Kirstein was also its leading representative to Boston as a whole,
the "Jewish trustee" of the Boston Public Library and of various
other business and nonbusiness institutions. As such, Kirstein
was himself the chief fighter against the automatic, unquestioned
anti-Semitism of Back Bay Bostonians. When the future Boston
philanthropist Henry Lee Higginson was, at twenty-four, on his
first European tour, he wrote home from Vienna that he had
made "excellent warm friends" with his piano teacher, "a most
captivating man and a great artist . . . [and with] a violin-player
in the opera, a beauty, a prime fellow. These are both Jews; and
I never saw a Jew before coming here." That, of course, was
the heart of the matter. In Boston the rich, educated Brahmins
did not come into contact even with rich, educated Jews—not
in grade school, not at prep school, not in college, not at work,
not in clubs, not on holiday. No wonder, therefore, that Higginson
should express shocked surprise that the Jews "whom I have
known in Vienna are very talented, true, liberal in views of life
and religion and free handed to a marvelous extent."

This same strict separation helped to perpetuate such long-held
convictions as the one at the Harvard Medical School that "Jews
are too nervous to do surgery at the MGH [Massachusetts General
Hospital]." Such prejudice had made necessary—all across America—the building of separate Jewish hospitals to train Jewish medical students and doctors who were unacceptable elsewhere. What

drove Kirstein and other Jewish merchants like him to fury was
not only the initial injustice that led to the creation of separate
Jewish hospitals, law firms, and country clubs, but the subsequent
allegations of anti-Semites that "Jews are clannish and prefer to
be with their own kind," which excused and perpetuated the
original injustice.

In 1922 Harvard's president, A. Lawrence Lowell, announced
that Harvard was considering a quota limitation for Jews such
as obtained at other Eastern private colleges. Lowell's proposal
was rejected in 1923 by the faculty committee considering it,
but Lowell defended a 10 percent quota for Jews, and informally
the quota was enforced in both the college and the graduate
schools. The appointment of Jews to professorships was also kept
to a minimum, restricted to men like Paul Sachs of the banking
family who brought with them the gift of a priceless art collection,
or like Felix Frankfurter, an undeniable genius.

Kirstein was a pragmatist, who cared no more for Therese
Filene's snobbery than he did for what he considered E. A.'s pipe-
dreams. His concern for the college's *numerus clausus* derived from
his practical judgment—later borne out by scientific surveys—
that the average income of Harvard, Yale, and Princeton graduates
was 75 percent higher than that of college graduates in general.
In czarist Russia as in Soviet Russia, Jews constituted a much
larger percentage of the college population than of the total population until numerical limitations were imposed on top of academic
criteria.

Because the store was an important advertiser and because the
quota story was interesting news, Kirstein was able to raise hell
in the Boston papers about this situation. Kirstein worked constantly to establish and strengthen relationships between Boston's
Beth Israel Hospital and the Harvard Medical School. To him
Harvard seemed to be the key, because although the Boston Brah-
min families were nominally Congregationalists, Episcopalians,
or Unitarians, in fact their only passionate religious feelings (other
than for money) were for Harvard. If enough Jews were distinguished professors at Harvard College and at its graduate schools,
this holy imprimatur, Kirstein believed, would surely make Jews

acceptable in Boston society, and so end anti-Semitism in Boston's banks and other big businesses.

When in 1933 Harvard conferred upon Kirstein an honorary degree, it was the high point of this school dropout's life. For years thereafter, store executives who walked unexpectedly into his office would occasionally find Kirstein sitting at his desk, tears in his eyes, staring at the framed degree he had taken down from the wall and was holding firmly in both hands.

"It was a cowardly sellout," declares his older son, Lincoln Edward Kirstein. "He accepted that degree from Harvard when the university was enforcing a rigid quota system against Jews and when Father's accepting the degree therefore meant much more to Harvard than it should have to him. It absolved Lowell of his racism and only proved to the amused Brahmins how desperate for their approval Father was."

Giving absolute, outrageous, bad-tempered, and often brilliant judgments was Lincoln's specialty even as a child, when his terrified mother used to beg him, as he indulged in one of his peevish temper tantrums: "Please, Lincoln, don't be creative in front of the servants!" and when he "harbored vengeful fantasies" because his parents failed to take him to the ballet.

"We never saw Father when we were children," Lincoln goes on. "He dealt with us only through his secretary, Miss Effie Beverly. He had a file on each of his children as he did on each department in the store."

After Lincoln's graduation from Harvard, where he had associated almost exclusively with other rich Jewish students, such as Edward M. M. Warburg, he disdained any thought of entering trade. Certain that he had been called to be America's preeminent total aesthete, he experimented widely. Finally, through a meeting with George Balanchine in London in 1933, he found his life's chief interest, the ballet, to which he has made a significant contribution. Despite an apparently irresistible longing to shock and despite his ostentatious eccentricity, he has been a great force for the arts in America.

A number of the children of the great founding merchants

across America attempted to make original contributions to the country's culture and history, but no others were nearly as successful as Louis and Rose Kirstein's three talented children.

Lincoln's older sister, Mina Curtiss, taught English at Smith College and wrote important books about Bizet, Proust, and herself. While researching these she met the Duchess of Clermont-Tonnerre, the Prince and Princess Bibesco, and others of that circle. She was rich enough to be dressed by Mainbocher, but even his genius may have been challenged by her resemblance to the Duchess in *Alice in Wonderland.*

The most attractive and modest of the three is the youngest, George, who left Harvard for Hollywood, where "life, if you had money during the Depression, was rather livelier than in Boston." To please his father, he returned to Harvard, graduated in 1932, and subsequently worked at Bloomingdale's. "But luckily I am not motivated by guilt as my father and so many Jews of his generation were, even those who were, like him, agnostic. That's why their charitable giving is so much greater than normal. They wanted to appease an angry God whose vengeance they expected any minute, probably in the form of a pogrom. It's why he never owned real estate in Boston and rented the house at 506 Commonwealth Avenue for forty years—the diamonds-sewn-in-the-hem-of-your-coat-for-a-quick-flight-in-the-night mentality.

"I have concentrated instead on having fun. Whenever I so far forgot myself as to do anything 'worthy,' which was blessedly infrequent, it was not because it was worthy but because I thought it would be *fun,* like buying *The Nation* in 1955 to fight McCarthy."

Most observers believe that George's father got no less fun out of his fights, from his defeat of E. A. in the store to his support of Sacco and Vanzetti. For some years his driver was Dante Sacco, Nicola Sacco's son.

Among the burly, bearlike Lou Kirstein's great joys was food. "At lunch at the store, he always ate a lobster omelette," recalls a younger contemporary. "In those days in Filene's then excellent dining room you got an entire lobster in your omelette, but Kirstein's omelette was special. It had *two* lobsters and was so big it was served on a platter. I quickly learned that if you were lunching with him and also ordered the omelette, they brought you one like his. I can still see and smell and taste and *feel* it."

Despite Kirstein's seventy-five-year affectation of ferocity, even as he lay dying in 1942 he was characteristically kind. He invited not only his stars at the store to come to the house to say goodbye but the second stringers as well.

Lincoln Filene died at ninety-two in 1957, the last link with the era of the great founding merchants: John Wanamaker, Marshall Field, and the Gimbel brothers.

E. A. had died an exile, twenty years earlier, at the American Hospital in Paris on September 26, 1937. Until the fatal pneumonia, it had been just another typically busy trip for the dapper, always hurrying E. A., whose clipped mustache and bushy eyebrows were now white but whose bright brown eyes behind the pince-nez glasses were as alert as ever. He had climbed with friends high in the Austrian Alps shooting chamois. He had conferred with Czechoslovakian president Eduard Beneš, French Finance Minister Georges Bonnet, President Roosevelt's mother, Sara Delano Roosevelt (whose grandson James he had employed at the store), as well as with every waiter, customs officer, and chambermaid he met.

He had been driven across Europe by his personal assistant, Miss Lillian Schoedler, in her roadster—he never owned a car or learned to drive. It was she who brought back the urn containing his ashes on the luxury liner *Île de France*, helped to scatter them in the Charles River, and inherited his Otis Place home.

Until the end, at seventy-seven, E. A. was still what he modestly called "a picker up of good ideas lying loose around the world." Many of the once radical ideas he had picked up and fought for were now becoming commonplace, at least for American employees: minimum wages, paid vacations, health clinics and insurance, credit unions, all the details of what he had urged as a "buying" wage rather than merely a "living" wage. Other ideas on which he had worked and spent money, such as cooperative retail stores, never took hold.

He, like the eighteenth-century founders of America, had been an optimist. "The modern business system is at present more or less lawless," he wrote, "but I believe we are now in the morning hours of a better social order, where the average man will not be compelled to exhaust himself in merely providing food, clothing and shelter for himself, wife and children with virtually no energy left for the higher things of life."

He was not a Pollyanna. He recognized his failures and the reason why he and Lincoln had become "practically estranged. It's . . . my own fault. I was too one sided—not human enough to play more with my brother instead of working only with him."

Despite his many defeats, E. A. continued to believe that both democracy and capitalism had not failed, but rather had not been sufficiently tried and developed. And he had created the Twentieth Century Fund to continue his "work rather than play" after his death.

He had never been interested in personal charity but in the economic and social research that might end the need for personal charity; therefore the Fund was to focus on such research. Forty years after his death, the Fund had investments of over $26 million and was doing research in such disparate fields as the international oil crisis, legalized gambling, political surveillance in the United States, and the dissemination of news.

Although he worked to sell his ideas for a happier world until the moment of his death and even beyond, he may secretly not have been the optimist that meliorists are usually thought to be. E. A. suggested as an appropriate title for his biography "The Story of an Unsuccessful Millionaire."

2

The Strauses of New
York—Five Generations

Tyre, the crowning city, where merchants are princes.
—Isaiah, 23:8

The only Jewish merchant family in America that approximates the Rothschilds in Europe is the Straus family. They have been the only family—with the exception of the Rosenwalds—to amass a great fortune and to create a style of life as notable as the Rothschilds' in terms of luxury, of generosity, and of service. A few Jewish banking families in America may have been richer, but none set such an example.

Most nineteenth-century immigrants to America were, as Emma Lazarus pointed out, poor and wretched. Not many people who are rich and powerful yearn irresistibly to give up luxury and position for the hardships of beginning again in a foreign land.

At the end of the eighteenth century the Strauses were already landowners and commodity traders in the Rhenish Palatinate. Jacob Ben Lazar, the first member of the family who would adopt a surname, was a contractor of oats and clover for the horses of Napoleon's army. He was one of only seventy-one Jews in Europe at a Sanhedrin convened by the emperor in 1807 in Paris to try to define and improve their status. Bonaparte also hoped for an answer to the question he posed to the theologians at the University of Leyden: "Why are the Jews still here?"—a mystery that has obsessed non-Jews for centuries.

Jacob's oldest son, Lazarus, was active in the abortive liberal Revolution of 1848. Discouraged by its failure, Lazarus like his friend Carl Schurz emigrated to America in 1852. As Lazarus's youngest son, Oscar, pointed out in his memoir *Under Four Administrations,* these German revolutionaries who fled to America had fought "for constitutionalism and democracy . . . for American principles: they were Americans in spirit even before they arrived."

Lazarus left behind his wife (and first cousin), Sara, and their children, Isidor, Hermina, Nathan, and Oscar. He landed in Philadelphia, but instead of staying in the East as most Jews did, he went south to Georgia. There, at forty-three, and long accustomed to the comforts of riches, he had to start at the bottom. He began by peddling, but within two years had his own tiny general store in the village of Talbotton.

A peddler got his merchandise on credit from a wholesaler, whose risk was not great because the monetary value of the goods a peddler could carry on his back or in a wagon was small. But even a tiny store required the wholesaler to grant or refuse much more credit, which increased both because of the increased inventory and because the now stationary merchant had to sell on credit to match his competitors. Inevitably, the wholesaler based his decision on his assessment of the would-be storekeeper's character.

Lazarus Straus was rich in character.

In August 1854, on the maiden voyage of the steamship *St. Louis,* Sara and the four children came to America. Once settled in Georgia, each of them contributed to the family's survival and success. The children made candles, helped in the vegetable garden, and at the store, which was open until 9:30 every night. It was lighted by kerosene lamps and so was a fine place to study when there was no work to be done. Lazarus gave Sara a monthly allowance of $20, from which she was able to save something even after such luxuries as buying a piano for Hermina.

Their occasional luxuries were made possible by constant thrift. Isidor, the oldest son, who would become one of the most famous millionaires in America, recalled half a century later that only once did he own a schoolbook that was "bought new." When a relentless search for a used copy of Liddell and Scott's Greek Lexicon failed, his father bought a new one on a buying trip to Philadelphia. "What a feeling of exultation it created, and how proud I was of such an elegant prize."

Lazarus believed in religious instruction as well as general education for his children. There were only two houses of worship in the village, so he sent Isidor to the Baptist Sunday School, Hermina to the Methodist. Lazarus himself had an advantage in his biblical discussions with local and circuit-riding ministers. When they argued over the meaning of some phrase in the King James Version of the Old Testament, Lazarus could turn to his copy and translate from the original Hebrew.

Isidor hoped for an appointment to West Point. When the outbreak of the Civil War made that impossible, he settled instead upon the Georgia Military Academy at Marietta. But on his arrival to take the entrance examinations, he was the victim of a "hazing" prank. Having had a pan of water emptied on his head, Isidor decided not to put up with this sort of nonsense and left the next morning.

Instead of serving in the Confederate army, at eighteen as a Southern agent he set off for Europe—via New York, where he risked imprisonment as a spy. Soon he was traveling all over the Continent trying to sell Confederate bonds and to arrange for ships, steam or schooner, that could break the increasingly effective Yankee blockade. As the older men he dealt with in England, Holland, Germany, and France came to appreciate Isidor's shrewdness, his courage, and his integrity, he was sent on a series of secret missions to Havana, to Nassau, and even back into enemy territory, to New York and Philadelphia. In the course of these

Scarlet Pimpernel adventures, Isidor also traded for his own account. He speculated in Confederate bonds, and at first made large profits, but later suffered losses that "proved a blessing in disguise for me; they cured me of all speculative tendency."

Despite these losses he came back from Europe after the war with $10,000 in gold, all of which he spent to buy his parents a house in New York City on West 49th Street.

Lazarus, now fifty-seven years old, had concluded that economic recovery for the South would take many decades and so had moved north and bought a New York wholesale crockery business. He brought each of his three sons into the business, which soon grew to include china, glass, and bric-à-brac. Then they decided to try selling these at retail as well. On St. Patrick's Day, 1874, they leased a space about 25 by 100 feet in the basement of the store of one of their customers, a Nantucket-born Quaker whaler turned storekeeper: Rowland Hussey Macy. Thirteen years later, the Strauses had bought "Captain" Macy's entire store.

Macy had marked his merchandise clearly with one price and refused to budge from it. This was one of the two chief reasons for his great success. Until near the end of the nineteenth century, American storekeepers, like those all over the world, marked their merchandise with a secret coded price. But this merely established a minimum below which they would not sell; they and their salespeople started by asking a higher price and bargained for as much over the minimum as possible. Although beating down—"Jewing-down," as it was unfortunately often called—a price was fun, many customers were less than perfectly secure and always wondered whether they had in fact got a bargain or might with more time and hard trading have done better. "By adopting one price and never deviating," Rowland Macy advertised, "a child can trade with us as cheap as the shrewdest buyer in the country."

This was neither a new nor an American idea. Two centuries earlier, in 1653, the founder of English Quakerism, George Fox, had urged his followers to set a fair price, the same for everyone, and refuse to haggle. In Paris as early as 1852 the great Bon Marché department store had a single price policy, and ten years later A. T. Stewart's store in New York did the same. Stewart's already had 2,000 employees, virtually all of them underpaid, and it would have been impractical as well as dangerous to trust each of them to set prices.

The other chief reason for Captain Macy's success was that he sold only for cash. Because he did not have to wait for his customers to pay, he had cash in hand with which to buy bargains and to obtain the lowest prices from wholesalers, and could sell merchandise cheaper than his credit-granting competitors.

The three Straus brothers continued these policies and inaugurated new ones. For customers who did not want to carry cash for their purchases, the store offered "Depositor's Accounts" into which the customer could deposit cash and thereafter charge purchases against the account, but only until the balance was used up. These "D.A." accounts were also a method for the store to borrow substantial sums of money at no interest from its customers, just as American Express does from the purchasers of its travelers' checks.

Its reputation for consistently selling merchandise for less than its competitors was the most important of the many factors that built Macy's into the largest store in the world. Year after year after year the store advertised the same story in different words: "We sell goods cheaper than any house in the world," or "Save 6% at Macy's," or, as America grew richer and anything other than conspicuous consumption might appear to lack chic, "It's Smart to Be Thrifty." But Macy's did more than merely advertise that its prices were lower. It also kept an army of professional shoppers employed to make certain that the claims were true by constantly comparing Macy's prices with those of New York's other stores and lowering its prices as necessary—sometimes several times in a single day.

Its price wars with competitors such as Hearn's were exciting. Japanese silk that started at 41 cents a yard would be lowered a cent or two per yard by each store trying to undersell the other, until at the end of the day the price was a penny a yard and the crowds were close to riot trying to get in on the bargain. Replenishing its stocks overnight, Macy's the next morning offered the same silk at "two yards for 1 cent." The war continued again all day, as the newspapers reported, "until at 6 o'clock at Macy's when the bell rang, the quotation was '11 yards for 1 cent,' amid scenes of the wildest excitement ever witnessed in a retail store." Although it lost money on each such sale, the store made up the losses many times over in reputation as each "war" was reported and exaggerated in the newspapers and by word of mouth.

Macy's reputation for selling for less became so fixed in the minds of New Yorkers that its chief competitor's slogan (invented by a former Macy's advertising woman) protested for years that "Nobody but nobody undersells Gimbel's!"

From the moment the Strauses became the sole owners of Macy's in 1887, the rise in their wealth and reputation was meteoric. In 1893 they bought a half interest in a Brooklyn department store, known thereafter as Abraham & Straus, for $1.5 million. In 1902, four years after Lazarus died, the Straus brothers completed their enormous new Macy's store at Herald Square between 34th and 35th streets, opposite the site of New York's two most famous brothels, the Pekin and the Tivoli. This move had required a loan of an additional $4.5 million.

The Straus brothers had no difficulty in borrowing such sums without putting up security and (to the fury of their investment banker friends) often without the professional help of money brokers. One reason for this was that after the Civil War, most Southern merchants had ignored their debts owed to Northern wholesalers when the war broke out. But Lazarus Straus had sought out and paid every creditor—a phenomenon still remembered in credit circles half a century later.

These large borrowings were quickly repaid from Macy's huge profits, and with their increasing wealth the younger Straus brothers could afford to expand their activities outside the store.

Isidor's chief role was always as storekeeper. On his stately

walking tours of the great "retail palace," his costume never varied: high hat, frock coat, fresh buttonhole flower, stiff wing collar.
The hat was never removed until he returned to his office. Away
from the store he was marginally less formal. In 1884 he had
moved from 26 East 55th Street to the "Straus farm," that ran
from Broadway (then called Grand Boulevard) to West End Avenue on 105th Street. It had once belonged to Matthew Brennan,
the sheriff who had finally arrested Boss Tweed as Jay Gould
stood by to guarantee Tweed's $100,000 bond.

Isidor's brothers and sister—and later, his children and grandchildren—maintained far grander homes. But the farm provided
what, even then, was lacking to most New York families: space.
It had an apple orchard, a barn, and for rainy days an ample
attic that even had a cupola.

With isolation came adventure. After the Great Blizzard of '88,
the family was snowbound and short of food until the coachman,
Pat MacDermott, tore apart a barrel and from its staves made
snowshoes for himself and the two oldest Straus sons, Jesse and
Percy, who could then go to Amsterdam Avenue for supplies.

There were six children: Jesse, Percy, Sara, Minnie, Herbert,
and Vivian. Every summer they were removed from New York
to "Sunnyside," the house Isidor and his wife, Ida, had built on
the New Jersey seashore. Rich Jewish merchants and bankers at
the turn of the century were quite as certain as their non-Jewish
counterparts of the conventional Victorian wisdom that declared
sea air and salt water to be sovereign cures for city ills accumulated
during the winter. These were also sure means by which to "build
up your strength" and so resist the ills of the winter to come.
They had therefore built a "Jewish Newport" at Deal, Elberon,
Long Branch, and Sea Bright, where some of the imitations of
Italian palazzi and a copy of Versailles' Petit Trianon compared
not unfavorably for pretentiousness with Newport's "cottages."

In these enclaves (or, for Midwestern families, the one at Charlevoix, Michigan) the children could meet only other children
of "the right sort." This meant other rich German Jews, who
would later make suitable boarding-school and college friends

and, eventually, suitable spouses. Later generations of children were sent for the same purposes to spartan but expensive summer camps in Maine—the boys to Androscoggin and Kennebec, the girls to Tripp Lake and Accamac—where there was little danger of meeting "the wrong sort," that is, the children of rich Russian or Polish Jews.

Snobbery derives as much from economic as from other factors. No less than in other aristocracies at other times and places, the rich American Jewish families wanted money to marry money, power to marry power. And to a considerable degree they succeeded. More extraordinarily, to a much more limited degree they are still succeeding.

Because each generation grew up together, went to school together, danced together, worked and played together on the same civic boards and country-club golf courses, rich Jews often married one another as did rich non-Jews—Cabots and Lodges, Medills and McCormicks.

In just one such Jewish storekeeping family, the Strauses, the evidence is endless and continuing. Roger Williams Straus married Gladys (American Smelting) Guggenheim. Nathan Straus, Jr., married Helen (Goldman, Sachs) Sachs; his son Ronald Peter Straus married Ellen (New York *Times*) Sulzberger; and his sister Sissie Straus married Irving (Lehman Brothers) Lehman. Herbert Nathan Straus married Therese (Kuhn, Loeb) Kuhn; Percy Straus married Edith (Abraham & Straus) Abraham.

Country club and other intimacies also led (with the increasing acceptability of divorce) to intramural multiple marriages, as when Minnie Straus Weil's daughter, Evelyn, took as her second husband one George Backer, whose previous service had been as one of the husbands of Dorothy (Kuhn, Loeb/New York *Post*) Schiff.

In the Straus family there were, of course, at least as many exceptions to prove the rule as there were adherents to it. For example, a son of Vivian Straus (from her first marriage) married an actress (Geraldine Fitzgerald), and her daughter (from her second marriage) Vivian so far forgot herself as to marry Rodman

Wanamaker after divorcing his cousin Dennie Boardman.

Like beauty, whether one has married above or below one's self is in the eye of each observer. When Carola Warburg married Walter Rothschild of Abraham & Straus, some said she had married beneath herself, while others observed that at least in Warburg eyes, whenever a Warburg marries anyone except another Warburg, it is a step down.

When Alva Bernheimer married Bernard Gimbel, those whose chief occupation was analyzing and categorizing such matters diagnosed the match as unfortunate because she was marrying a "shopkeeper." One of the givens in the laws that governed this society, at least as the laws were interpreted by bankers' wives, was that lending money at interest was a higher calling than storekeeping. Not too surprisingly, the Strauses and other storekeepers laughed at this. Bankers could sometimes bring more power to bear than merchants and they often built greater fortunes than merchants did, but across the country from New York to Arizona the banker's influence on his community was frequently less significant than the merchant's.

Perhaps even more than the rest of the Strauses, it was Nathan, Isidor's middle brother, who established the family's reputation for philanthropy. For years his chief concern was public health. In the terrible winters of 1892 and 1893, he distributed millions of tickets to the poor of New York City that cost them a nickel and entitled each to a bucket of coal, a basket of food, or a night's lodging and breakfast.

Such stopgap efforts brought him much praise; but more significant was his work as one of the first pioneers in preventive medicine. Nathan led in the bitter fight for the compulsory pasteurization of milk, against the combined ignorance and indifference of doctors and the greed for profits of milk producers and distributors.

In 1891, 241 out of every 1,000 babies born in New York City died in their first year, but in control groups who received only Nathan's pasteurized milk the death rate was reduced to a fraction of that.

Nathan opened pasteurized milk depots at his own expense and was attacked for this by an alliance of dairymen, milk distributors, physicians, and corrupt politicians, who managed to have him arrested on charges of watering his milk. But by 1920 he had almost three hundred milk stations in thirty-six American cities and abroad.

In 1914 Nathan had resigned from Macy's to devote himself full time to charity. Between his resignation and his death in 1931, he would give away almost two-thirds of his fortune.

A variety of causes appealed to him. In 1916 he sold his yacht, *Sisilana,* and gave the proceeds to war orphans. He was generous in small private matters as well as large public ones. Among the messenger boys at the Postal Telegraph office there was fierce competition to deliver messages to the millionaire who, refusing to hide behind a secretary, always shook each boy's hand and gave him an unheard-of tip—a $1 bill.

But the bulk of the fortune that he gave away went to Palestine. At the entrance to Nathan's health clinic in Jerusalem, an inscription in Hebrew, Arabic, and English declared it was to serve all citizens. He was, in President Taft's phrase, "a great Jew and the greatest Christian of us all."

The youngest of Lazarus Straus's sons was Oscar—not to be confused with Oskar, the Viennese composer of *The Chocolate Soldier,* who was, in fact, a cousin. Other members of the various European branches of the Straus family were also much involved in the arts. Another cousin, Emil Straus in Paris, was rumored to be the illegitimate half brother of the Barons Rothschild—Alphonse, Edmond, and Gustave. Unfortunately he was only their lawyer. His chief role, however, was as the Swann-like, adoring husband of Geneviève Halévy Bizet.

Geneviève was the daughter of Fromental Halévy—who wrote the opera *La Juive*—and the widow of Georges Bizet. She was mistress of one of Paris's two most important salons below the level of the nobility and was the friend of Degas and Proust. At the Straus's Trouville villa, "Clos de Muriers," as well as at their Paris salon, Geneviève and Emil were important Dreyfusards. Deserted by many of their non-Jewish friends over the Dreyfus affair, like other of the most brilliant, rich, and well-assimilated Jews who considered themselves French, they learned that in the eyes of many Frenchmen they were only damn Jews.

The Dreyfus affair, perhaps more than anything else before Hitler's atrocities, stood out as a warning that assimilation was no guarantee against anti-Semitism even in the land of the Enlightenment where the Revolution had promised *"Liberté, Egalité, Fraternité."* It would have been difficult to discover a more assimilated Jew than Alfred Dreyfus, who at thirty-three had risen to be captain and the only Jew on the French army general staff. But when he was charged with treason and the attempts to prove that he had been falsely accused first began, demonstrations of virulent anti-Semitism burst forth not only from the army, the aristocrats, and the politicians but also from a large part of the ordinary citizenry.

In every country the Jews who had arrived earliest and become the richest and most assimilated came to think of the Passover prayer "Next year in Jerusalem" as merely rhetorical. Most scorned Zionism when it came and were genuinely convinced that the longer they had been where they were, the more likely was their safety. But early arrival often proved to be of as dubious value as assimilation. Jewish merchants had followed on the heels of the Roman legions and were pioneers in the towns the Romans founded along the Rhine—a historical fact of limited interest to the murderers of their descendants from the Dark Ages through our own.

In America the questions of how much assimilation and in what forms were as difficult as anywhere else. Within the Straus family, the answers ranged from explicit pride in their Jewish heritage to conversion to Episcopalianism and change of surname. Isidor's youngest brother, Oscar, the first Jew to serve in the Cabinet, was publicly proud of his Judaism and actively concerned with Jewish problems all over the world.

After receiving his law degree from Columbia in 1873, he had joined the family crockery business. But he also interested himself in New York and national politics, that is, he made substantial political contributions to candidates in both parties with whose policies he agreed.

As a result of his "mugwump" support of Grover Cleveland in 1884, Oscar at thirty-seven was offered the post of minister to Turkey, an offer that stirred up considerable opposition because, as his opponents pointed out, the minister's chief role at the Sublime Porte was the protection of Christian missionaries and Christian colleges. Carl Schurz and *The New York Times* expressed support for Oscar, but his most effective supporter was the enormously popular Brooklyn preacher Henry Ward Beecher, who wrote to President Cleveland: "The bitter prejudice against Jews, which obtains in many parts of Europe, ought not to receive any countenance in America. It is because he is a Jew that I would urge his appointment as a fit recognition of this remarkable people, who are becoming large contributors to American prosperity, and whose intelligence, morality, and large liberality in all public measures for the welfare of society, deserve and should receive from the hands of our government some such recognition."

A man of obvious probity and irresistible charm—two characteristics not invariably found in the same person—Oscar became a favorite of the Sultan, who offered him 1 million francs (some $200,000) to arbitrate between the Ottoman Empire and Baron Maurice de Hirsch, whose disputed claims against Turkey for building the Oriental Railway linking Constantinople to Europe totaled 132 million francs. Oscar refused to take any fee but mediated a settlement that instead of making for him an enemy of each disputant—the reward for many mediators—made him the lifelong friend of both.

In the summer of 1905, Oscar Straus and other prominent American Jews met with Count Sergius de Witte in Portsmouth, New Hampshire, where Witte, under the auspices of President Theodore Roosevelt, was working out Russia's treaty of peace with Japan. But the czar's Envoy Plenipotentiary, like his Communist successors, ignored Straus's complaint against the Russian dogma that "the question of the condition of the Jews in Russia is a purely domestic one with which the people and governments of other countries have no concern."

In December 1906, Roosevelt appointed Oscar to the post of Secretary of Commerce and Labor. It was the first time in American history that a Jew served in the Cabinet, but not the last time that there was some confusion as to whether the appointee was the best possible person to serve in the post or had been chosen because religion, race, or sex served a symbolic or political purpose.

In a long, rambling speech at New York's Hotel Astor on January 18, 1911, "the Colonel," as Oscar always called Roosevelt, said that he had personally selected Straus for no other reason than that he was the right man for the job. Old Jacob Schiff, the toast-master of the evening, then proved that he had become so deaf he was unaware of what TR had said. He rose and explained that when Roosevelt had earlier called him to the White House and said he wanted a Jew in his Cabinet, he had suggested Straus to the President.

Schiff was distressed when he learned of his gaffe, but Oscar laughed with the rest of the audience. Unlike some of his nephews and their progeny, he never sought to play down his Jewishness nor to play up his Americanism but rather thought of them as perfectly complementary. He wrote about the historical basis of the American commonwealth in the earlier Hebrew common-wealth and its laws. In 1892 he founded the American Jewish Historical Society chiefly to study and celebrate the history of Jews in America.

But Oscar's most interesting book was a memoir written in 1921, five years before he died. Ten years earlier, Isidor had pri-vately published his own reminiscences and had introduced them with the typical Victorian disclaimer, apologizing for the apparent immodesty, the inescapable use of the pronoun "I," and protesting that he had written only after importunings by friends and chil-dren, and only for the purpose of edifying his grandchildren. By contrast Oscar, without false modesty—indeed, with the can-dor and good humor that characterized his happy life—admitted to the same motive as Benjamin Franklin's: "I may as well confess it, since my denial of it will be believed by nobody, perhaps I shall a good deal gratify my own vanity."

But if Nathan and Oscar were setting such exemplary and happy patterns of philanthropy and public service, this was in large measure made possible by Isidor, who was minding the store. And it was the relatively retiring and private Isidor whose name ultimately became the most famous of any of his clan.

On April 15, 1912, Isidor and Ida were on the maiden voyage of the *Titanic* as the great new White Star liner pushed full steam toward New York. The passenger list was full of the most distinguished American names—Astor, Widener, Ryerson, Guggenheim—along with an equivalent of English swells, including Sir Cosmo and Lady Duff Gordon as well as the Chairman of the White Star Line, J. Bruce Ismay.

In the period between 11:40 that night, when the *Titanic* collided with an iceberg, and 2:20, when she foundered, a full range of human behavior was displayed as it became increasingly evident that there were too few lifeboats and that no rescuing steamers would arrive in the nick of time.

In the tradition of "women and children first," Ida Straus was repeatedly urged to enter a lifeboat. Having spent over forty years with her husband, she said, she did not propose to leave him now, and they died together.

In memory of Isidor and Ida, their children built Straus Hall in the Harvard Yard and the many other gifts of various Strauses to Harvard reach from the Fogg Museum across the river to the Business School.

A few years before the *Titanic* tragedy, Isidor had written letters of advice to be followed by his family when he died. To his much-loved Ida, who was four years younger than he but who shared his birthday, February 6, he urged: "You have an ample income, enjoy it; deprive yourself of nothing which can contribute to your comfort and happiness. I know you are fond of doing good, indulge yourself in this enjoyment without stint and if you use up your entire interest it is the best use you can make of it."

He wrote the same day to his three sons, Jesse, Percy, and
Herbert: "Look to his [Nathan's] reproves or his approvals as
you would to mine. . . . Cultivate between yourselves frankness
and cordiality. . . . Never let any differences, should they arise,
rancour in your breasts; he loves me best and honors my memory
most sincerely who will be readiest to forgive and forget any
misunderstanding, and who will be first and most anxious to re-
store the good feeling which constitutes the basis of brotherly
love and filial piety. . . . I should consider my life's work a failure
if ever there would arise any serious differences between you."

The similarity between this and Polonius's speech to his son
lies not only in what today may seem a comically pretentious
style but in the fact that the advice is good. A frequent reason
for the success of certain Jewish storekeeping families as opposed
to the failure of others was their stern refusal to succumb to
the joys of family feuds, to the inevitable and enormous temptations of envy, contempt, greed, and competitive ambition; and—
perhaps most tempting of all—to justifiable but unacceptable criticism.

But making enough money so that some of the brightest and
strongest heirs could—if there were too many of them—go into
other fields, helped, too.

At Isidor's death he and Nathan had owned everything half
and half, Oscar having long since devoted himself entirely to
public service. Despite Isidor's letter, his sons frequently found
themselves at odds with their Uncle Nathan, who was well aware
that his own sons, much younger and less experienced than his
nephews, were in far less important positions than they and unlikely to catch up.

Jesse, Percy, and Herbert therefore offered either to sell their
half interest in the store to Nathan for $7 million or to buy his
for the same figure. Nathan chose to sell, taking in partial payment
his nephews' interests in Abraham & Straus and the family crockery business.

The upbringing of this third generation of Macy's owners had
been strict and unbending. Isidor had been by his own admission

"subject to many nervous anxieties" and unable "not to forbode troubles which in many cases I admit proved imaginary." Therefore, he was forever offering his oldest son the advice he could not follow himself: "For Heaven's sake, Jesse, relax!"

No less strict was Jesse's training at New York's Sachs School. There, along with Herbert Lehman, Henry Morgenthau, Mortimer Schiff, and Walter Lippmann, he was under the unrelenting eye of Dr. Julius Sachs, who was strong on German, Greek, and Latin, history and literature, but relegated the study of music and art to "the elementary grades only."

The proper education of young gentlemen also included such nonscholastic graces as riding properly. One June 26, as a joint birthday gift—Jesse's birthday was on the 25th and Percy's on the 27th—the brothers received a pony. Neither, however, was allowed to use a saddle until he could keep a silver dollar between each knee and the horse's ribs.

Ballroom dancing was also essential, and if it was said of Jesse that "he was the best dancer among Isidor's children," it was quickly added, "But that is not quite the highest praise for a dancer."

Jesse longed to get into "the store" and begged his father to allow him to go to work rather than to Harvard. But Isidor refused.

In Cambridge, away from strict paternal supervision, Jesse followed the advice for gentlemen: "Never get higher than a C, and never get your name in *The Crimson*." His suite at Weld had the extraordinary luxury of a bathtub, in which his less fortunate friends could "tub on Jesse." His lavish allowance, $100 a month, also helped his popularity, but in a notebook always carried in the upper left-hand pocket of his waistcoat he kept strict account of every penny. It was scrutinized at intervals by Isidor.

Over six feet tall, slim, brown-eyed, darkly handsome, Jesse was meticulous about being elegantly dressed—exaggeratedly high, stiff collar, double-breasted waistcoat, wide Ascot ties that he selected carefully in London. Once when he was ill and a high fever had seemingly rendered him speechless, he suddenly admonished the nurse who was changing his pajamas: "The tassels belong in the front, Miss Smith, not in the rear."

Even after Jesse's graduation, Isidor refused for three years to
take his son into the store. During this period Jesse trained first
by clerking at the Hanover Bank, where his duties included filling
inkwells, a task about which he complained to his mother but
not of course to his father. At least by comparison, his next post
as salesman at Abraham & Straus was splendid.

Despite or perhaps because of this strictness, Jesse worshipped
his father. After Isidor's death, Jesse always insisted that any
printed reference to himself be in full, "Jesse Isidor," and not
merely "Jesse." It was, a Harvard classmate said, Jesse's "Isidorsyncrasy." Until his own death in 1936, Jesse referred to Isidor
as "Poppa" and his ultimate argument in store and family discussions was: "Poppa would want to have it thus."

When Jesse finally got to the store, life became as exciting as
he had always been certain it would be. And it was the same
for his younger brothers. With the booming growth of the city
and the astute business leadership that the brothers either provided personally or hired, Macy's became the greatest store not
only in America but in the world. In a competitive male society,
to be the captains of the perennially championship team is not
the least satisfying of life's pleasures.

After their father's death the brothers, with exactly equal shares
in the store though not in talent and energy, ruled as a triumvirate.
If in terms of directing the store Jesse was closer to Caesar, and
Percy and Herbert to Pompey and Crassus, the public saw no
evidence of this. When the brothers disagreed, they retired and
conferred privately until they had reached a point that one of
them could announce: "My brothers and I have decided . . ."

By 1919 the store was doing an annual business of $35 million
(Rowland Macy's first day's sales had totaled $11.06), and in the
next ten years the brothers bought stores in Toledo, Atlanta, and
Newark. The Thanksgiving Day Parade, begun in 1924, added
to the public perception of Macy's as the biggest and therefore
by American definition the best. "Macy's basement" became the
metaphor for any jam-packed crowd; "Macy's window" was the

cliché for the most public place to do anything.

Just as America's historic love of a feud was profitably exploited by radio figures—Ben Bernie and Walter Winchell, Fred Allen and Jack Benny, Charlie McCarthy and W. C. Fields—so both Macy's and Gimbel's pretended to a feud whose personal animus exceeded mere business competition.

The owners of so public an enterprise were, therefore, public figures whose private lives aroused as much curiosity as those of theater people, politicians, and important criminals. Public service, by now a family tradition, only increased their celebrity.

In 1931, Jesse was appointed by New York Governor Franklin D. Roosevelt to head the state's Temporary Emergency Relief Administration. To help him disburse $20 million to the unemployed, Jesse selected young Harry Hopkins. Although politically quite conservative, Jesse was a Democrat. He had supported Alfred E. Smith's presidential campaign, while his brother Herbert supported Herbert Hoover no less enthusiastically.

When across America in local and national elections different members of the same storekeeping family publicly supported opposing candidates, it frequently gave rise to cynical comments. To the much-asked question, why the Dallas merchant Edward Marcus supported Adlai Stevenson when his brother Stanley was so vehemently in favor of General Eisenhower, the standard reply was: "Because Eddie lost the toss."

Jesse, like Boston storeowner Edward Filene, was one of the few prominent businessmen to support Roosevelt for the presidency in 1932. His reward, it was said, would be the same Cabinet post as his Uncle Oscar had held. But FDR already had three New Yorkers in a Cabinet of only ten, as well as greater debts to pay to others. The President toyed with the idea of sending this Jew as ambassador to Hitler's Germany but instead offered to appoint Jesse ambassador to France, despite the long tradition against appointing a generous supporter to any country whose language he actually spoke. With that happy facility for soothing ruffled feelings that was no small factor in Roosevelt's success, the President overcame Jesse's hurt at not being offered the expected Commerce Department post. Neither man was afraid to say no to the other. (When, as governor, FDR had asked Jesse for money for a Boy Scout fund, Jesse replied: "As my brothers have already contributed and as I am otherwise rather heavily committed, I must ask you to excuse me.")

To his son Robert, Jesse contrasted the Frenchman, "surly and resentful," to the Englishman, "cheerful, clean-minded, clean-bodied." But Jesse accepted the post and a cartoon in *The New Yorker* pictured him announcing on his arrival in France: "Galeries Lafayette, we are here!"

He and Irma obviously relished their ambassadorial social duties: attending a championship match at the Polo Club; being guests of President Lebrun at Auteuil's Grand Steeplechase and at Longchamps' Grand Prix de Paris; entertaining and being entertained by Mr. and Mrs. John D. Rockefeller, Jr., General Pershing, Mrs. William K. Vanderbilt, Miss Anne Morgan, and the mysterious munitions magnate Basil Zaharof, whose Avenue Hoche house had "flowers always at its windows, even when the owner was absent from home—'So the poor can see them'—[and] where guests ate from gold plates."

At the invitation of Ambassador and Mrs. Robert W. Bingham, Jesse went to London and donned black silk knee pants and black silk stockings so that Irma could be presented at Court. But when virtually every American in Paris came to the American Embassy, Straus left town and so "avoided the Fourth of July reception with the motley crowd."

Whether or not such snobbery played an important role, what some people found shocking in Jesse's conduct as ambassador was his resolute refusal to comment publicly on the increasingly terrible problem of Hitler's Jewish policy or even to make a private effort to influence President Roosevelt. His silence was thundering.

In retrospect it seems inexcusable. But given his milieu, it is understandable. He was perhaps America's quintessential German-Jewish assimilationist. When the prominent Wall Street lawyer Samuel Untermeyer began to organize an anti-Hitler movement in America, Jesse objected to Percy: "Untermeyer keeps on stirring up trouble in things that are none of his business." When Felix Warburg and Rabbis Stephen S. Wise suggested that the American government might protest the Nazi Jew-baiting, Jesse complained privately: "Wise, Warburg & Co. are doing American Jewry harm by their activities. They certainly give color to the accusation that Jews are a race apart, with a group solidarity that prevents them from becoming a sincere and patriotic part of the country in which they live."

In today's climate of ethnicity, it is difficult to feel or perhaps even to imagine the fervor once experienced by new Americans for ethnicity's opposite—the melting pot, Americanization, assimilation, the promise and prayer on every coin and banknote, *E pluribus unum.* Just as a century from now the present ideal of ethnicity may be viewed as having been the most serious threat to (or as having destroyed) the polis, so the nineteenth- and early twentieth-century ideal of Americanization seems in retrospect to many a cowardly sellout.

Then, however, it was almost a substitute religion. For many German Jews who arrived in the United States, their nominal religion was virtually meaningless. Its ritual seemed barbaric, its magic merely superstition; its dietary laws like its holiest prayers had been destroyed not by centuries of oppression (which actually preserved and strengthened them) but by a few decades of Enlightenment and increasing toleration. For many, these were outworn forms appropriately replaced by a fervid patriotism for this new Canaan. Later, Rabbi Wise would declare in his funeral tribute to Oscar Straus: "America became his religion, patriotism or love of country the sovereign motive of his days. His Americanism was his religion." Across the land, Rosenwalds in Chicago, Riches in Atlanta, my own parents in Dallas—all stressed to their children their obligation to America, but what they said and did often contained obvious contradictions.

Children were told frequently that we were first and last *Americans,* no better and no worse than our Christian neighbors and schoolmates. For a group that had for so many centuries and in so many places been "inferiors," equality was no small step up. Logic told us that if we could be "better" we could also be "worse" than non-Jews and that therefore equal was safest. Besides, "better than" would excite envy and punishment.

This of course conflicted rather obviously with what we were taught in Sunday school about "God's chosen people" and the purportedly incomparable, heroic history of the Jews.

At home as well, children heard contradictions to the we-are-all-equal parental pronouncements. In fact, there were numberless invidious comparisons. "Our stores" were better (more honest, more profitable, more compassionate) than "their stores." The greatest movers and shapers in history were "ours"—Christ, Marx, Freud. (The fact that a Marx or Disraeli or Freud had specifically renounced or repudiated Judaism did not prevent his appropriation as one of "ours.") The number of Nobel Prize winners who were "ours" was disproportionately large, and with each new one there was a glow of pride and an at least implied sense of superiority.

It was constantly stressed to us that we were no different from any other Americans and yet Max Baer and Benny Leonard were claimed as "Jewish" boxing champions, Sidney Franklin (Frumkin) was a "Jewish" bullfighter, Charles Goren was a "Jewish" bridge player, Al Capp was a "Jewish" cartoonist. En famille, they were all "ours," despite the fact that if our Christian friends characterized Paul Muni as a "Jewish actor" or Felix Frankfurter as a "Jewish judge," we had been taught to protest immediately: *"No, they're Americans!"*

I grew up in the era when J. Edgar Hoover was building his then hero's image by regularly selecting America's "10 Most Wanted Criminals" and promptly capturing them. Children in school were taught that if John Dillinger or Al Capone had turned his energy and talent to honest pursuits, he might have become chairman of General Motors. When I suggested to the teacher that if the actual chairman, Alfred P. Sloan, had turned his talents to crime, he might have become the greatest criminal in history, I was sent home from school to be whipped by my father, who instead laughed with delight.

But when once I suggested to my father that if his favorites such as Sarah Bernhardt and Camille Pissarro proved something about the Jews, so must such criminals as Arnold "The Brain" Rothstein, Louis "Lepke" Buchhalter, and Benjamin "Bugsy" Siegal, he answered—with an almost suppressed smile—that a smartass does not prosper in either the business or the criminal world.

There was in many of the great department-store families a pervasive self-contempt or self-hatred or at least regret because they were Jewish. The same Rabbi Wise who had praised Oscar Straus wrote about Jesse: "I am very much afraid that he might have felt what Heine once said—'Judaism is a misfortune.' . . . His attitude toward Zionism and the Jewish Question was dictated by a spirit which to me is not only foreign but incomprehensible. It is the spirit of complete assimilation."

There was relatively little anti-Semitism in the United States for the first century of the country's existence. This was especially true among its richest citizens. Jew and Gentile, they founded and supported the same clubs and went to the same resorts, just as they invested in each other's businesses and served on each other's boards of directors. In 1877, when Jewish New York banker Joseph Seligman and his family were excluded from the Grand Union Hotel in Saratoga, it was reported and discussed nationally because it was so surprising. It quickly became, however, a practice widely copied.

The chief reason was that the number of rich men—very small before the Civil War—had now become so large that new noneconomic criteria of exclusivity had to be created and this method was convenient and easily applied.

Some form of it may be basic to human nature. Perhaps the chief pleasure of the tree house for children has always been, once they were safely in themselves, to pull up the ladder and keep the others out. But the Strauses and many other rich German Jews in America laid much of the blame for the increased social anti-Semitism elsewhere. From 1881 to 1914 the major problem of America's Jewish aristocracy was assimilating some 2 million Jewish refugees from Russian barbarism. After the murder of Czar Alexander II in 1881, official policy in Russia was to get rid of all Jews in any of three ways: force them to convert; force them to emigrate; or kill them—either by starvation or by massacres that ranged from small Cossack amusements to the Christmas night bloodbath of 1881, the worst such butchery in the 300 years since the St. Bartholomew's Day massacre of the Huguenots.

This flood of Russian Jews was swelled by thousands of other Eastern European Jews, and their arrival in America changed the perception of Jews by America's non-Jews. Before this influx, Jews had comprised only a small fraction of 1 percent of the population. In many communities there was not one Jew, and in others so few that they were exotics.

But after the flood, which the Strauses thought no less a disaster than the biblical one, even though the Jews never reached as much as 4 percent of the country's population they were perceived as a much larger percentage—and in many cities they were so.

First-generation German Jews who had not lost their own foreign accents, along with their children who had none, were appalled at the accents of these parvenu Jews. Like most rich Americans, these earlier arrivals aped British affectations, including understatement and surface unflappability. By contrast the new arrivals were publicly emotional, vocal, and, therefore, embarrassing.

This influx of Eastern Jews undeniably played a role in diminishing the social acceptance—real and imaginary—of the Strauses and their kind. The resultant anger of the earlier group was therefore understandable, although the forms it took were often distressing. To express the contempt the German Jews felt for the ragged, new arrivals whose names often ended in k-sounds—Potofski, Zhitlovsky, Kautsky—they coined the insulting name "kikes." With a rarely seen poetic justice, the new deprecation was soon applied by American non-Jews to all American Jews.

Despite their anger at these poor newcomers, however, the Strauses and their kind not only continued to help thousands to come over but also to feed, house, find employment for, educate, and try to Americanize them, although this last effort often met with contempt instead of gratitude.

Sadly, these generous and often wise efforts were frequently marred or even negated by both real and imagined condescension, a recurrent tone of *noblesse oblige* on the part of the rich "uptown" Jews that infuriated the "downtown" Jews who lived in lower East Side slums worse than those of Bombay.

The German Jews, for example, spent large sums on the unfortunately named Removal Office. Its purpose was to channel the new Jewish immigrants through Galveston, Texas, and New Orleans rather than New York, and to send butchers to such stockyard centers as Fort Worth and Kansas City, carpenters to such furniture towns as Grand Rapids. As Secretary of Commerce, Oscar Straus supported the so-called Galveston Plan and other programs to keep Jews from the already overcrowded ghettos of New York, Boston, Philadelphia, and Baltimore. But most Jews resolutely refused to be settled in the hinterlands of Colorado and Nebraska—fewer than 80,000 of nearly 1.5 million who arrived between 1901 and 1917 were settled by the Removal Office.

In the Isidor-Nathan-Oscar generation, the Straus reactions to anti-Semitism had been swift, unembarrassed, and public, ranging from personal appeals, to American presidents, to direct economic retaliation for social snubs. When Nathan Straus was excluded from a resort hotel at Lakewood, New Jersey, he immediately built one next door twice as big and "for Jews only."

In the next generation, however, the response to social anti-Semitism was often to pretend that it did not exist. Jesse, like all Jews, regardless of their refinement and wealth, was barred from the best Park Avenue apartment houses. He responded by building his own. In 1927 he bought the northwest corner of 70th Street and Park Avenue, the site of the old Presbyterian Hospital, and there built 720 Park Avenue, at least the equal of those tall, luxury buildings from which he was excluded. He subsequently built 730 Park as well.

All this investment, however, was carefully characterized as being merely a method of keeping his friends and especially his family about him, just as his earlier purchase of a "farm" at Mt. Kisco had been made with the view that his children when they had families of their own would build country places on the same property.

Although prominent Jews were debarred from some apartment buildings, clubs, and resorts, they were scarcely social pariahs. When Oscar Straus's son Roger married the copper heiress Gladys Guggenheim, the wedding guests included Mrs. Theodore Roosevelt, Mrs. Nicholas Longworth, and Mrs. Andrew Carnegie.

To the children of the Jesse-Percy-Herbert generation, however, their parents' pretense that obvious anti-Semitism did not exist, and indeed the careful avoidance of references to their Jewishness, led to confusion and tragedy.

Percy had three sons, Ralph Isidor, Percy Selden, and Donald Blun. Ralph was sent to Groton despite Paul Warburg's warning against it. Founded in 1844, Endicott Peabody's new school shamelessly imitated the British public schools but was more successful in reproducing their architecture, brutality, and strange practices than their scholarship. The eighty-four-pound, fourteen-year-old Ralph was regularly taken to the basement where, because he was a "dirty little Jew who doesn't belong here," he was beaten almost senseless by the older boys. Unlike his grandfather, who had left the Georgia Military Academy after his first experience of hazing, Ralph was long too ashamed and afraid to tell his father. When he finally did, Percy ordered him to "Stick it out."

After two years of hell, Ralph broke down and wept to his mother. She was the beautiful daughter of Abraham Abraham, the founder of Abraham & Straus. She was slowly dying of multiple sclerosis and only because Percy could refuse her nothing, Ralph was permitted to finish at Hotchkiss. Years later when a close relative had a breakdown, his Uncle Percy's entire sympathy was expressed in the brief suggestion: "Get back on your horse."

Percy's own tolerance for discomfort may perhaps best be gauged by the fact that he changed his name from Percy Solomon Straus to Percy Selden Straus for reasons resolutely unknown because the subject was never allowed to come up. His second son completed the operation, dropped the name Straus, and so became Percy Selden, moved to Houston, and withdrew from the family. When he died in the crash of a balloon along with his daughter Marjorie, who was its pilot, his aunt, Mrs. Herbert Straus, wondered: "Why couldn't Junior have died in his bed and surprised us by doing something normal for once in his life?"

Opinions as to why he became the family eccentric vary. According to his older brother, Ralph: "It was because he was spoiled. Mother kept him in long curls and dresses for years and always took his side in fights."

"Quite the opposite," says cousin Bobby. "His own mother couldn't stand him and made no bones about it. His was a cruel childhood."

"My parents both felt guilty about their treatment of Percy," recalls Percy's younger brother, Donny. "That's why he got their entire art collection instead of its being divided among all three of us. Father hoped that if it all went to the Houston Museum as a collection, it would give Percy some position there, a sense of belonging that he never had at home. But it didn't."

Donald Blun Straus's recollections of growing up are vivid and often poignant. "Jewishness was like sex. It was absolutely taboo as a subject for discussion with either of my parents. By example rather than by word, they raised the three of us to be anti-Semitic. One did not go to a Jewish school or country club or summer resort. As a matter of duty and tradition only, one might serve as a director of a Jewish charity, but the goal was to get on the boards of directors of non-Jewish charities, museums, and businesses. It was just as clearly preferable to meet and take out Christian girls and of course we all married Christians.

"Our loyalty and our duty were not to the Jews but to the family and its traditions. Our father and uncles revered their father and we were expected to do the same and to be as close to our cousins as the brothers were supposed to have been to one another.

"We didn't get much fun from the tennis courts and stables and grooms and servants because fun, like wealth, was denigrated. Power and money only brought responsibility for achievement, for making a place in life. But it was all a Catch-22 because if you made it, it was because you were a Straus, and if you didn't, it was because you were no damn good.

"With that kind of a no-win situation, I got out early and made my career away from the family and away from the store. Poor Ralph, as the oldest son, had no choice. He had to go into the store and he never recovered from not delivering what was expected of him. Even Percy and I had to be tops. If you didn't make a career at the store that was like deserting from the army, but you might be somewhat redeemed by a great enough success elsewhere. If you should become a distinguished professor of history at Harvard, that would be failure, but to become president of Harvard, that might be acceptable—for a younger son. . .

"Work hard. Aim high. Be uneasy if you're enjoying yourself. You should never sleep with a girl until you married, not only because it was a dangerous game that led to disease and blackmail, but because it was fun. Even art was not something to be enjoyed, but a duty. We went to Italy every year and Father built up rather a fine collection. But for him it was not a passion, not a thrill, not even an investment—it was what you did. And for us the gallery in the apartment at 875 Park was not a place to look at the Bellini or the Michelangelo bronze and enjoy them, it was just a place where you had to walk, not run.

"Even for those days, life was terribly elaborate. At Sunday lunch everything was in aspic. I promised myself that when I grew up I would never have to eat anything in aspic again.

"We were punished often, by not being allowed to ride, in a very horsy family, or by not being allowed to go out. Many children think themselves unjustly punished, but I never did. I always thought I was unworthy and deserved punishment. But I was never spanked, just as I was never taken in either parent's arms and kissed and hugged.

"There was no comfort in religion either. All religions were merely a cause of wars, cruelty, and prejudice. The only religious training I ever had was occasionally going to the Presbyterian church on Madison Avenue if my Canadian nurse wanted to go on Sunday."

If Donny, long the president and guiding force of the American Arbitration Association, failed to enjoy the luxury that surrounded him, other family members did not. His Uncle Herbert spent $3 million during the Depression to build an enormous house on 71st Street between Fifth and Madison avenues. The rooms, all eighteenth-century, were brought over from France.

The blame for this unseemly extravagance and public ostentation—as it was judged by some critics in the family—lay with Herbert's wife, the former Therese Kuhn of Cincinnati, known as "Aunt Teddie" to her face and "The Duchess" behind her back. She was the unquestioned art connoisseur of the clan, but Herbert himself was no slouch. When Lord Duveen was once attempting to sell Herbert an especially expensive rug, Herbert felt certain the rug had been doctored. "Joe, where's the other half?" he demanded.

"In the Victoria and Albert," Duveen admitted sheepishly.

It was The Duchess, however, whose insistence upon absolute excellence was relentless. Once, discussing a staircase she was having brought over from France, she was assured by her architect: "I can duplicate it over here, save you $50,000, and no one will know the difference."

"But I will know the difference," The Duchess explained.

Before they could complete and enjoy this palace, whose greatest treasures are now in the Metropolitan Museum, Herbert had a heart attack and died. "That damned house killed Herbert," declared his brother Jesse. The ambassador's youngest son, Robert Kenneth, publisher, wit, family historian, Bobby to everyone and everyone's favorite Straus, maintains that his own parents enjoyed the same kind if not the same level of extravagance at Mt. Kisco. " 'Northview' was Mother's own WPA project, and we used to tease her that she spent more millions rebuilding it than Father spent as Governor Roosevelt's unemployment administrator."

Such lavish public expenditures, especially during the Depression, ran contrary to the single most repeated rule of all these rich storekeeping families, "Don't make yourself conspicuous"—but some things are more essential than others. And despite the dicta against public displays of wealth, some of these were deemed to be unavoidable. On October 17, 1935, headlines in dozens of newspapers from coast to coast announced: STRAUS BROTHERS GIVE AWAY $5,619,740 OF STOCK! The wire service stories under the headlines explained that these were gifts not to charity but to members of the family, made to avoid the new tax schedule that would go into effect on January 1, 1936. Other sizable gifts to their children, the article explained, had been made by Samuel J. Bloomingdale, J. J. Newberry, John D. Rockefeller, Jr., and George F. Baker.

Despite the regrettable publicity, the timing could scarcely have been better for Jesse, who died a year later. A recent codicil to his will, pointing out the increased taxes on estates, revoked public bequests of $878,512. Luxury is addictive and it is easier to countenance others doing without their needs than one's self.

In the long years after the ambassador's death, it seemed to his older son, Jack, that Mrs. Jesse's style of living might now without any hardship be somewhat reduced. He was not suggesting anything as drastic as buying clothes anywhere except Paris. But perhaps, he intimated, she might without too much discomfort cut down on the apartment at 720 Park Avenue whose maintenance cost was $1,000 a week.

When Robert Dunkelmann, a servant she had brought back from Hamburg in 1916, grew progressively less able to work, Jack thought he might retire to Florida on a suitable pension. "Robert has been with me longer than your father was," Irma Nathan Straus explained patiently to her son, "and if all he can do is stay and watch television, then *that's* what he'll do."

Nor did she propose to be rushed. Like her father, she lived ninety-six years, and when she died had ten servants.

At home Jesse dressed for dinner every night, even in the country. In Europe, at least for his children, life was sometimes a bit less formal, but never so unbuttoned as it was occasionally for the Warburgs. Young Jack Straus might go out in Paris on an all-night spree with Paul Warburg, but when they returned by dawn's early light, Jack did not so far forget himself as Paul did—wandering into the wrong room at the Ritz and throwing his evening cane at something in the bed. It turned out to be his mother who said quietly: "Your father will speak to you about this in the morning."

By Jack's generation, the fourth in America, the early emphasis on thrift and making money had been replaced by an inordinate stress upon being "socially attractive." Jack was nothing if not that. His parents had not only agreed to but encouraged the expensive lessons and long hours of practice that had made him an excellent amateur jazz pianist. But neither that nor his undeniable charm was sufficient to overcome the tradition at Harvard that Jews were simply unacceptable in the exclusive "final clubs."

As with all such rules, of course, there were exceptions. James Warburg was, much to his surprise, elected to a final club. When he said that he would be delighted to join if the club had abandoned religious discrimination, but not as an exception to a continuing anti-Semitic policy, he was told he was an exception. "Regretfully, I said I would have to decline the invitation. Having done so, I could not help wondering whether it might not have been more constructive to join and break down the prejudice, thus opening the way for other members of excluded minorities. But whether I was right or wrong, this is the course I have pursued throughout my life. I have refused either to be made an exception to a prejudice or to retreat in the face of it into the sort of defensive ghetto symbolized by Jewish country clubs and a general aping of the Christian community."

Jack as well as other Strauses of his and subsequent generations joined New York's socially eminent St. James's Episcopal Church. "Not in terms of numbers but in terms of financial support, the formerly Jewish ladies who are communicants of St. James's are very significant," says Donny Straus.

Only the crass or the envious can believe that social acceptance was invariably either the exclusive or the strongest incentive in the conversion of many German Jews. There were many forces at work, including the same spirit of humanism and of skepticism that was reducing the acceptance of ritual and tradition in many Christian churches.

It affected even the most religious. Felix Adler, the son of the rabbi of New York's Temple Emanu-El, was sent to Germany at the Temple's expense to receive rabbinic training. The hope was that he would succeed to his father's pulpit. Upon his return in 1873, he decided that he could not accept even such loose guides as obtained at this nothing-if-not-Reform synagogue, and so in 1876 he founded his own religion for contemporary needs, the Ethical Culture Society. It was Felix Adler who had married Irma Nathan and Jesse Straus in an Ethical Culture wedding.

If even a religion so historically based in a sense of special mission as Judaism was to become little more than a loosely organized force for social justice, why cling to it, many of these rich Jews wondered. When virtually identical Protestant churches were available in an overwhelmingly Protestant country, did not the refusal to convert smack of masochism, stubbornness, sloth, arrogance, cowardice, or some combination of these?

One of the arguments most often heard against the conversion of the Jews is similar to Thorstein Veblen's argument against Zionism in his 1918 essay, "The Intellectual Pre-Eminence of Jews in Modern Europe." If, as Veblen suggests, "the Jewish people have contributed much more than an even share to the intellectual life," it is because the pressures of life in an alien and unfriendly society have given the Jew "a skeptical animus . . . [but] the skepticism that goes to make him an effective factor in the increase and diffusion of knowledge among men involves a loss of that peace of mind that is the birthright of the safe and sane quietist." Veblen argues that given a country of his own, the Jew would lack the cruel but effective pressures that made him "a disturber of the intellectual peace" and kept him "among the vanguard, the pioneers, the uneasy guild of pathfinders and iconoclasts."

Presumably, if American Jews converted and were perfectly assimilated, they would under reduced pressures produce no more than other Americans—as great a gain for the Jews as it would be a loss for the world, according to assimilationists.

Not only Jews but also other rich, upper-class Americans not born into the Episcopal Church blended themselves into what Clarence Day described as "a sect with a minimum of nonsense about it; no total immersion, no exhorters, no holy confession." It was so relaxed a religion as could absorb a skeptical, intellectual, bon vivant such as Thomas Jefferson no less easily than dour Scotch Presbyterians and more-or-less ascetic folk, New England Puritans, Pennsylvania Dutch Reformed, and Lutherans. There is something appealing, however, about the Americans who even if not at all devout in their religious observance, resist the centripetal force toward Episcopalianism's easy uniformity—Boston Unitarians who did not follow Phillips Brooks, Philadelphians who remained Quakers even if they rarely visited the Meeting House, New Orleans's aristocratic Creoles who continue to be Catholic, Jews who stay Jews.

Even among some of the least-practicing Jews, there is a vague and sad feeling that with conversion comes an undefinable loss that will be costly to America or to the world. Of course no single example can prove a general premise, but the career of C. Douglas Dillon seems at least to point the other way. His grandfather and great uncle, Sam and Jake Lapowski, were Polish-Jewish storekeepers in West Texas and friends of my grandfather.

When Sam's son, Clarence Lapowski, went away to Worcester Academy and Harvard, he became Clarence Dillon. When he had made enough of a success in business to be listed in *Who's Who*, in his biography his father, too, was named Dillon. His son "Doug" went to Groton, where he left the Presbyterian church of his mother to embrace the school's Episcopalianism and where, he says, he neither suffered nor witnessed such barbarities as were visited on Ralph Straus six years earlier.

Ambassador to France in 1953, Secretary of the Treasury in 1961, president of the Metropolitan Museum, and having served in many other posts with distinction, it is almost impossible to imagine that he could have contributed more as a Jew. It is completely impossible to imagine that as a Jew he could have achieved

such a list of clubs as New York's Racquet and Tennis, Knicker-
bocker, Links, River, Recess, Pilgrims, and Washington's Metropolitan. After years on the waiting list of Washington's Chevy
Chase Club, Dillon was finally admitted, according to Arthur
Krock in *The New York Times,* "only on the solemn assurance to
disturbed traditionalists that his percentage of origin in this group
[Jews] was a maximum of 25."

In the fourth and fifth and sixth American generations, the
Strauses proliferated to more than 200, and some achieved distinction in fields far removed from the store. Allegedly to help keep
track of them and to distinguish them from prominent world
citizens, living and dead, who spelled their names Strauss (including Levi Strauss, the pants man; Lévi-Strauss, the man man; Anna
Lord Strauss, no man's woman; and atomic Admiral Lewis L.
Strauss, who inexplicably pronounced it "straws"), *The New Yorker*
magazine commissioned the late social analyst Geoffrey Hellman
to write "Straightening Out the Straus(s)es," which cannot be
done.

One may, of course, make lists of Lazarus's progeny, including
Roger Williams (Farrar, Straus & Giroux) Straus, Jr.; his mother,
Gladys Guggenheim *(Gourmet)* Straus; Ronald Peter (WMCA, Voice
of America) Straus; and descendants of female descendants who
enormously complicate matters because they have no Straus in
their name, such as the writer Barbara Levy. But that way lies
madness.

It would be difficult to suggest an American family whose
breadth of interest and force for good have been greater. More
difficult yet would be any predictions as to the future of its members, except to remember that when Alice asked, "Would you
tell me please, which way to go from here?" the Cat replied,
"That depends a good deal on where you want to get to."

3

The Gimbels, Albert M. Greenfield, and Other Brotherly Lovers

In Boston they ask, How much does he know? In New York, How much is he worth? In Philadelphia, Who were his parents?

—Mark Twain, *What Paul Bourget Thinks of Us*

In recent years Philadelphia is, at best, praised with faint damns. Although W. C. Fields, who was born there, suggested as his own epitaph, "On the whole, I'd rather be in Philadelphia," it was once the greatest city in America. The national capital both during the Revolution and from 1790 to 1800, it was also a political, economic, moral, and cultural capital, occupying the keystone position between the Northern states and the Southern. All of which may help to explain why in our own century its attitudes have increasingly been those of a once great beauty who has lost her looks, an impoverished former millionaire, a revolutionary artist whose work is now passé and forgotten.

In colonial Philadelphia there were a few Jewish merchant families that had prospered—Levy, Franks, Gratz. When the Revolution came, it divided families much as the Civil War would later. David Franks was loyal to the Crown and was exiled from Pennsylvania to England. His kinsman, David Salisbury Franks, an aide to Benedict Arnold, was exonerated of any complicity in Arnold's treason and became a courier and confidant of Jay, Franklin, Jefferson, Livingston, and John Adams. Aaron Levy lent money to the Continental Congress, as did Haym Salomon, who also served the revolutionaries as a secret agent.

After the triumph of the Revolution, rich Jewish merchants were as welcome in the social as in the economic life of Philadelphia, just as they had been in colonial times. When the city's fifty-nine most prominent families formed the Dancing Assembly in 1748 (still today Philadelphia's most exclusive clique), the families of David Franks and Samson Levy were among them.

Here as elsewhere, however, most of these earliest prominent Jewish families were, by conversion or marriage, gradually absorbed into the Christian community. An exception was the Gratz family, whose Rebecca Gratz was said to be the model for Rebecca in Sir Walter Scott's *Ivanhoe.* Various Gratzes were members of Philadelphia's other most exclusive institution, the Philadelphia Club, founded in 1832. But again as elsewhere, in Philadelphia after the Civil War the automatic exclusion of Jews became virtually absolute not only in its clubs but in its most important business and cultural institutions as well.

As Philadelphia grew less important, it became proportionally more snobbish. Pennsylvania still had underground lakes of oil and mountains of coal, but these were owned and controlled by New York families and New York banks. The resulting bitterness over its has-been status was understandable: snobbery is far more essential to a failed society than to an expanding one.

This same pattern was repeated among America's Jews. As financial, intellectual, and artistic power slipped increasingly from the German Jews to the parvenu Eastern European Jews, the last resort of the earlier arrivals was an even angrier and less effective exclusiveness.

The Gimbel family did not begin as storekeepers in Philadelphia but in 1842, in Vincennes, Indiana—the fur-trading outpost fortified about a century earlier by the youngest sieur de Vincennes. In 1835 Adam Gimbel arrived in New Orleans from the tiny Bavarian village of Rhein-Pfaltz. He was eighteen. With a rifle and an oilcloth pack on his back, he peddled up and down the Mississippi before starting his store in what was still little more than a village on the banks of the Wabash. He called it "The Palace of Trade," and if "Palace" was considerably grander than the actual facts, "Trade" was not. In the beginning, most of his business was done by trading as neither he nor his customers usually had cash.

Adam's business was based on fair dealing—even with Indians. He had nothing else to base it on. He posted a sign prominently in the store: "If anything said or done in this store looks wrong or is wrong . . . we shall set it right as soon as it comes to our knowledge," and he promised: "Fairness and Equality of All Patrons, whether they be Residents of the City, Plainsmen, Traders or Indians."

More important, of course, than the declaration of such self-serving advertisements was the increasing word-of-mouth reputation throughout the territory that Adam actually lived up to them.

The most often repeated story was that when Bishop James M. Maurice de Long rode into town, he once dropped a bag of gold coins on Gimbel's counter and announced: "I have not counted it. You count it and credit me with what you find it to be. When we both count it you sometimes find more than I find. Besides, why should I bother to count money given to Adam Gimbel?"

Probity is not inescapably profitable, however, unless it is accompanied by at least a portion of good luck, of which Adam was to have a generous share. On his first trip to Philadelphia he met Fridolyn Kahnweiler, the daughter of a dry-goods merchant, and their marriage produced seven sons: Jacob, Isaac, Charles, Daniel, Ellis, Louis, and Benedict. Not a man to rely entirely even on excellent luck, Adam adopted yet another son, an orphan named Nathan Hamburger.

With such a swarm of sons, Adam inevitably sought to expand his success in Vincennes. After a venture in Danville, Illinois, the cohort of Gimbels in 1887 invaded Milwaukee. They were not the first—Edward Schuster had started his store in 1884—and not the last—in 1897 Julius Simon opened the Boston Store. But no one else had the advantage of "a surplus of capital and a surplus of Gimbels."

In an era when a woman sometimes gave more thought to her hat than to her virtue, the Gimbels shocked and delighted Milwaukee with the latest hats from Paris, Berlin, and London, displayed in an enormous millinery department "encircled by huge mirrors . . . palms, plants, flowers, ribbons . . . roses attached to invisible wires extended from the ground floor of the store to the ceiling, with a hundred white doves flying around."

This kind of chic and showmanship impressed Milwaukee's population, which in 1890 numbered some 204,000. Even more impressive to a smaller group, the doyennes of the city's Jewish society, was the prospect of so many obviously eligible young Gimbels. Rich, unmarried young men with prospects of becoming richer, if not younger, presented a challenge that distracted the mothers of daughters from Milwaukee's everyday domestic trials, including "servants [who] think much of themselves—almost necessarily the mistress waits on them. Wages are very high. The cook gets two dollars a week."

The young Gimbels, however, found the blandishments of *le tout Milwaukee* resistible, and were soon employing their Milwaukee experience and profits to the conquest of Philadelphia, where in 1894 they bought out Granville B. Haines & Company for $1 million.

Here again they were not the first. The Snellenburg family had been building their store since before the Civil War and, like the Lit family, also storekeepers, the Snellenburgs were leaders in Philadelphia's Jewish community. The two most important stores, however, were not owned by Jews. One was Strawbridge & Clothier, founded in 1862; the other had already dominated the city for some years: Wanamaker's.

Only half a dozen other men, if indeed that many, were as important to storekeeping in America as John Wanamaker. Born in 1838 of German, Scottish, and French Huguenot ancestry, he never completed grade school. He went to work at thirteen as a publisher's errand boy and in 1857 became the first paid secretary of the Young Men's Christian Association in the country, at $1,000 a year. By 1860 he could afford to marry and a year later to open his own men's clothing store.

In 1876, the year of the Philadelphia Centennial Exposition at which Alexander Graham Bell's telephone created a sensation, Wanamaker with the showmanship that was the greatest cause of his success took over the enormous old freight depot of the Pennsylvania Railroad at 13th and Chestnut streets. To his usual men's clothing he now added a selection of dry goods, and his "Grand Depot" was as impressive to the city's centennial visitors as anything at the fair.

When the fair ended, Wanamaker was determined to create a "new kind of store," with a much wider selection of different kinds of merchandise under one roof than had ever been seen before. He invited the city's best specialized merchants to lease spaces in his oversized building, which he was determined to make into the greatest bazaar in the world. When they refused, he opened dozens of specialty shops himself. He had created one of the earliest department stores and was soon one of the richest merchants in America.

Wanamaker instituted various practices that would lead to the success of department stores all across the country, such as the one-price system and the refund for unsatisfactory merchandise. But the single factor most likely to immortalize Wanamaker was the simple motto he invented, which becomes more moving as it is less and less observed in America: "The customer is always right."

Wanamaker's ran the first full-page newspaper advertisement in the country in 1879 and was soon running them regularly. But no newspaper advertisement, no policy, no merchandise, could be as important as what American department stores offered their customers free of charge—theater, diversion, relaxation, education, celebration, a never-ending indoor fair full of hoopla, novelty, variety, performance, drama, sensationalism, and *fun*. And no one provided these better than John Wanamaker.

On the day after Christmas in 1878, he introduced the gala new miracle of electric lighting. From the St. Louis Exposition of 1904, he brought back to his first floor a leviathan pipe organ and a huge, 2,500-pound, 10,000-piece bronze American eagle. Its perch three-quarters of a century later is still the main meeting place for Philadelphians.

In April 1912, as another publicity stunt, Wanamaker's installed a wireless station on the roof of its New York City store. Its operator, young David Sarnoff, the future millionaire tycoon of RCA, caught first in America the wireless message: "S.S. *Titanic* ran into iceberg. Sinking fast."

This New York store—the old A. T. Stewart store at Broadway and 10th Street, which John Wanamaker had bought in 1896—would prove to be Wanamaker's only major blunder. No matter how great a merchant's success elsewhere, to try to duplicate it in New York City was a dangerous game. For Wanamaker it proved to be an impossible one when he refused to move uptown with the rest of the city's stores.

The world of Philadelphia's Wanamakers, Drexels, and Cadwaladers was not open to the Gimbels; but for some time that made no difference. The Gimbels were too busy minding their new store. The same year that they began in Philadelphia, 1894, Adam died, and Isaac—not the oldest, but the smartest—became president. His older brother Jacob was of course made chairman of the board and was referred to by his brothers as the "Judge," both as a mark of respect and because of his height and erect carriage. Jacob and Daniel returned their brothers' kindness by remaining bachelors and notoriously frugal ones: "When Uncle Daniel opened his purse, which was not often, moths flew out." Therefore, when they died, their considerable fortunes and their shares in the stores were concentrated in the family rather than becoming even more widely distributed.

That Ellis's role too was often ceremonial is not to say that it was useless. He was the public relations Gimbel. In 1921, in Philadelphia, three years ahead of Macy's, in New York, he originated the Thanksgiving Day Parade, just as in 1915 he had begun the tradition of every year buying circus tickets for the city's orphans regardless of race or religion. He had been called to other duties as well. Barred from the city's best country clubs, Ellis was one of the founders in 1906 of a new club for his fellow German Jews, the Philmont Country Club. Until his death at eighty-four in his Rittenhouse Square apartment, this last surviving Gimbel brother struggled, not always successfully, to keep the Philmont free of Jews from Eastern Europe.

The only scandal in the second generation of Gimbels might have resulted from Louis's special sexual tastes. The scandal was suppressed, however, locally at least, by "collusion between the prostituted press and the wicked capitalists," as the perpetually outraged muckraker Upton Sinclair explained more excitedly than accurately in his exposé of the press in America, *The Brass Check:* "One of the Gimbel brothers was arrested in Philadelphia, charged with sodomy, and cut his throat. Not a single newspaper in Philadelphia gave this news! This was in the days before Gimbel Brothers had a store in New York, therefore it occurred to the 'New York Evening Journal' that here was an opportunity to build up circulation in a new field. Large quantities of the paper were shipped to Philadelphia, and the police of Philadelphia stopped the newsboys on the streets and took away the papers and the Philadelphia papers said nothing about it."

One of Louis's sons, Lee Adam Gimbel, killed himself by jumping from a window of the Yale Club.

By 1909 the Philadelphia store had been brought to such success that it would take several generations of aggressive incompetence to wound it seriously. Isaac decided that the next challenge must be the most dangerous one: to build a large new department store in New York City. To take charge of this undertaking he chose his older son, Bernard, whom he made a vice-president at twenty-four.

"Bernie," as he was to almost everyone, contradicted the frequent pattern of diminished energy and talent in the third generation. Educated at Philadelphia's Episcopalian, exclusive Penn Charter School and at the University of Pennsylvania's Wharton School, his attention was always more firmly fixed on sports than on his studies. He played football and water polo, and in 1904 and 1905 was the university's heavyweight boxing champion. Long after he graduated, he continued to spar with such famous boxers as Bob Fitzsimmons, Stanley Ketchel, Jack Johnson, and especially Gene Tunney, who was one of his best friends. After Tunney won his second world's championship fight with Jack Dempsey in 1927 in Chicago with the until-then-unheard-of gate receipts of $2.28 million, Gimbel was so excited that he walked fully dressed into a steaming shower with the naked Tunney.

On April 4, 1912, at New York's Plaza Hotel, Bernie married the petite, elegant, and no-less-assured-than-he Alva B. C. Bernheimer, who briefly tried to direct at least some of his interest toward the arts. "One night she took me to the Metropolitan Opera," Gimbel loved to recall. "There I was, snoozing quietly in my seat, minding my own business, while Caruso was singing, when from the balcony above me fell a pair of binoculars that missed my head by inches and smashed to pieces on the floor. Two inches the other way and they would have killed me! Since then, I've never been back to the opera—it's too dangerous! I go to the [Madison Square] Garden or the Polo Grounds where it's safe."

If Alva failed to turn the sportsman into an art lover, he more successfully encouraged her to become an athlete, a first-class horsewoman. For many years the handsomest sight at the Madison Square Garden Horse Show was the jumping team of Alva and her daughters, Caral and Hope, superbly tailored, black-silk-hatted, perfectly coordinated, as they sailed over the obstacles on a trio of matched hunters from their stables at "Chieftains," their 200-acre estate in Greenwich, Connecticut.

In pleasant contrast to the cultural and intellectual pretensions of some New York Jewish storekeepers, Bernie affected a good-natured yahooism. "When I got married, my wife tried to make an intellectual out of me. She made me sit on those hard chairs down at the New School with all those brainy guys. The only fun I ever got out of it was when someone asked me, 'Bernie, do you know Walter Lippmann?' and I answered, 'Sure. He used to sit next to me at the New School and look over my shoulder and copy my answers.' When Lippmann heard about it, he didn't like it."

Such tales often had as much truth in them as his claim that he had taken his large suite at New York's expensive Pierre Hotel because it was "handy to the subway."

As foreign to him as intellectual pretensions were the various social pretensions and snobberies typical of his one-time brother-in-law, M. Robert Guggenheim, whose first wife was Alva's sister, Grace. When Bob converted to Catholicism to marry his second wife, Bernie's only comment was: "Who's he kidding?" Bob's own father, Daniel, was rather more caustic on the subject. "I'm delighted," he told reporters. "My son has always been a very bad Jew. I hope they'll make a good Catholic out of him." In fact, they did not, for Bob soon divorced his second wife to marry a third and fourth, both Protestants.

Bernie was 6–1, 190 pounds, as rumpled in his expensive tailor-made Saks Fifth Avenue suits as though he had bought one off the rack at Gimbel's. Indeed, everything about him, from his smile to his hands, was outsized. He ate too much corned beef, drank too much Jack Daniels bourbon, worked too hard, played too much gin rummy, had too many friends. He and Alva even had two sets of twins (Hope and Caral, David and Peter), in addition to their first-born son, Bruce. None of his children was his equal in *joie de vivre* or in success.

"Bruce was defeated before he began," explains an old family friend, "because you can't be a jock if you're born with a withered arm. Caral's unsuccessful second marriage to baseball star Hank Greenberg was to please her father, and I agree with Albert Lasker's analysis of Caral's earlier marriage to his son, Edward: 'Never heard of getting a good omelet out of two spoiled eggs.' The only one who comes close is Peter, now that he's stopped landing his plane in the vegetable garden at Chieftains and had some success as a deep-sea filmmaker."

If none of his children was a match for Bernie, the tiny, tenacious Alva was at least his equal and had been since she first saw him at sixteen and decided to marry him despite the objections of her family and friends.

He called her "Baby." She called him "Beany." And for more than half a century their marriage was the despair of the envious, the delight of their friends.

Alva's thirty-first-floor aerie in the Pierre obviously reflects her taste, not his, a completely catholic mixture of Rouault, pre-Colombian pottery, period English furniture, a Baskin sculpture, a Bouché portrait of her, Chinese Export lamps, and an inscribed photograph of the black dancer Arthur Mitchell, whose Harlem Ballet she supports. Floor-to-ceiling windows give a spectacular view of the city on which her husband had a significant influence.

Likewise the winter place in Palm Beach, "Chieftains South" (where the whole crew of servants is transported for January, February, and March), and the baronial keep in Connecticut, are *hers*, African sculpture, malachite candelabra (from the Hearst sale), faux malachite breakfast room looking on Long Island Sound.

Bernie was born in Vincennes in 1885 and had lived as a boy in both Milwaukee and Philadelphia. Therefore it was not surprising that like so many other out-of-towners he should finally become a quintessential New Yorker, boosting it as enthusiastically as any small-town Western merchant would his local community. He became, in fact, "Mr. New York," but first he had had to prove himself in the big city.

To attempt to build a big new store in New York City in 1909 was considerably more unsafe than attending the opera, but that may, in fact, have been its chief appeal to Bernie. For his site he picked the block on Broadway between 32nd and 33rd streets, the terminal of the Pennsylvania and Long Island railroads, thus assuring a flood of commuter traffic. It was also only one block from Macy's, giving him the opportunity to go toe-to-toe with the champion.

On the advice of Sears, Roebuck's Julius Rosenwald, Bernie had the store built by Louis J. Horowitz of the Thompson-Starret Company, who became one of Bernie's intimate friends and invariably referred to him as "Big Casino." The whole undertaking was a big gamble—the "most costly lease in the real estate annals of the city," declared *The New York Times*; the rentals would total $60 million if all renewal options were exercised. Bernie increased even that risk by convincing his reluctant father and uncles not to lease but to buy the Greeley Square land and store outright: more than 27 acres of floor area and 2 acres of window glass, it was a formidably greater investment than they had in either Philadelphia or Milwaukee.

Also an enormous risk, quite as difficult to sell to his family and finally no less profitable, was Bernie's 1923 purchase of Saks & Company. This included both the store that covered the block between Gimbel's and Macy's and the new $4.25 million Saks store being built way uptown between 49th and 50th streets on the east side of Fifth Avenue. Typically, Bernie worked out the whole deal with Horace Saks sitting on top of a coffin in the baggage car of a train taking them back to the city after a weekend in Elberon. It offered a more informal and private place than the smoking car full of Wall Street bankers.

By 1922, Bernie, a closet smart beneath his dumb-jock pose, had already understood the advantage of buying what he wanted with other people's money, and so had taken Gimbel's "public." He put both common and preferred shares of Gimbel's on the New York Stock Exchange in the pre-1929 boom market, while keeping control firmly in the hands of his family. Rather than parting with always precious cash in order to expand, he was therefore able to pay, with printed- paper stock certificates, some $8 million of which brought him the Saks stores.

When Horace Saks died in 1926, Bernie put in charge of the Fifth Avenue store the other star of the Gimbel third generation, Charles's son Adam Long Gimbel. Not the least of Bernie's talents was the ability, once he had a proven executive, to let him run his own show. For years Adam L. Gimbel and his in-store *couturière* wife, Sophie, made Saks Fifth Avenue the most profitable fashion specialty store in America. Adam lacked Stanley Marcus's genius for personal and institutional publicity, but unlike Neiman-Marcus, Saks Fifth Avenue was a prodigious moneymaker.

For Bernie Gimbel, as for John Wanamaker and every American storekeeper, showmanship was an essential element that must be fostered: the ability month after month and year after year to get for his stores the kind of publicity that Americans equate with success and that therefore makes success. Supplying the stewards' and library's equipment for the great transatlantic liner *Leviathan*; being the first to offer from Paris "colored wigs more brilliant than the rainbow, if not more beautiful"; sponsoring an indoor golf tournament on the store's fourth floor and a $5,000-prize airplane race between the New York and the Philadelphia stores; these and other feats kept Gimbel's in the newspapers and so in the public eye. Then there was always the carefully cultivated, endlessly exploited war with Gimbel's far better known competitor, Macy's, valuable beyond measure in just the same way that years later the debates with the far more famous Richard Nixon would be to the relatively unknown John F. Kennedy.

If Bernie was indifferent to high society for himself, he was delighted when its members could be used to get publicity for the store, as when Miss Ruth Morgan, Mrs. J. Howland Auchincloss, and Mrs. Nicholas Biddle sold in the store for the benefit of Bellevue Hospital. He was even self-assured enough to know, like P. T. Barnum, that "bad publicity" can be good as, for example, when Mrs. O. H. P. Belmont, Mrs. Emmeline Pankhurst, and Mrs. Inez Milholland Boissevain made headlines because the police stopped them—ever so courteously—from distributing a demand for shorter hours for Gimbel's female employees.

But the store's biggest publicity coup (Macy's tried for it and lost) was the sale of millions of dollars worth of William Randolph Hearst's art collection. When the banks and *Los Angeles Times* publisher Harry Chandler (who held the mortgage on Hearst's San

Simeon) finally insisted upon repayment from Hearst, his only liquid asset, unless his publishing empire was to go on the block, was some $50 million of art that he had recklessly accumulated for half a century.

Even his three homes in California, his Mexican ranch, his castle in Wales, and his various New York hotel suites (at the Ritz, the Warwick, the Lombardy, and the Devon), couldn't house the collection. Tons of it filled New York and Los Angeles warehouses—much never unpacked since it was purchased—including an entire twelfth-century Cistercian monastery from Segovia, each separate piece carefully numbered and crated.

The deal was brought to Bernie's playboy younger brother, Frederic ("a soft touch for women, especially Cuban or Mexican girls") by his friend Dr. Armand Hammer, who demanded and got 10 percent off the top.

The New York police had difficulty controlling the crowds. Half a million dollars' worth had sold the first night, and more than $11 million by the end of the sale, including the monastery. Gimbel's customers got many of the greatest bargains ever bought at the store: a Teniers the Younger sold for $998 that would bring ten times as much today; and a Raffaelino del Garbo sold for $12,998 that would now fetch over half a million.

The value of the publicity to Gimbel's was incalculable. Newspaper and magazine stories appeared around the world, including one about a housewife who as the result of a newspaper photograph showing Bernie and John D. Rockefeller, Jr., examining a bowl, wrote a postcard: "Dear Sirs, Please send me a Benvenuto Cellini bowl as advertised. Kindly choose a good color to go with a blue dining room." The store answered that there was only one bowl—its price, $25,000

While Bernie and his cousin Adam were conquering New York, the rest of the Gimbels had stayed in Philadelphia, where their roles, in the store and in the city, were not invariably happy ones. When in the Depression, Bernie put Arthur C. Kaufmann of the Pittsburgh retail family in charge of Gimbel's Philadelphia store, Richard Gimbel, Ellis's son, raised such hell that finally

Bernie fired Richard and barred him from entering the store again.

From the time he was a child, Richard's cousin Rose recalls, he loved to give the impression that he was crazy. As an undergraduate at Yale his love of excitement and danger took the form of running a highly profitable tutoring school that guaranteed its student customers would pass their courses.

After graduation Richard saw no reason not to continue to indulge his whims as he could so well afford to, for example, listing in the telephone directory the name Edgar Allan Poe whose former house he owned. By Richard's generation, many of the Gimbels had become more interested in their collections (Richard collected rare books); in their summer homes (Richard had bought and made even more elaborate the Lits' "camp" at Rangely Lake, Maine); and in trying to make, for themselves and for their children, proper marriages to proper people—Snellenburgs, Lits, Guggenheims, Rosenwalds. Such family alliances were thought to be doubly strong when two sisters married two brothers, as when Minnie and Julie Mastbaum married Ellis and Louis Gimbel.

With the increasing acceptability of divorce, however, even the most seemingly appropriate alliances between rich German-Jewish families could prove to be only temporary. Occasionally practice made perfect. After Alva's sister Grace had divorced Bob Guggenheim, she married Morton E. Snellenburg, "the last smart Snellenburg." It proved to be, according to their friends, a perfect marriage because they were the two stingiest people in Philadelphia and thus made for each other. They lived at the Ritz-Carlton, but rather than be charged 10 cents for each phone call, Morton went downstairs and used the nickel pay telephone. He kept nickel cigars in his front pocket to offer to friends and fine Havanas for himself in an inside pocket. At their cocktail parties, Grace did not allow hors d'oeuvres to be served until all the guests had arrived because she prepared only one per guest.

"It was a tradition in Philadelphia," recalls Richard's widow, "that all Snellenburg men were dull as dishwater and all their wives were witty and smart and delicious."

When Joseph N. Snellenburg married Irene Horner of Chicago,

she immediately took to decorating her house with elaborate, antique, Catholic, ecclesiastical robes and linens, because they were invariably beautifully embroidered with her new initials, IHS.

Quite unknown to these proper Philadelphia German Jews, there was growing up in the ghetto of their city a little Russian Jew who would become the most powerful man in Philadelphia. Born in 1887 in a miserable straw-thatched log hut in the village of Lozovata near Kiev in the Ukraine, Avrum Moishe Grunfeld had come to the slums of South Philadelphia as a small boy. He grew up to become "the exact opposite of Bernie," says a man who knew them both well, "short, ugly, brilliant, devious, and vengeful. If anyone could give anti-Semitism a good name, it would be Albert M. Greenfield."

Greenfield was of course not the only Russian Jew to achieve wealth and power in the City of Brotherly Love, nor to inspire such contempt. There was Moe Annenberg, whose racing journals, wire services, and intimate association with criminals earned him a considerable fortune on which he failed to pay $1 million of income tax. Understandably, his children studiously ignore the years he spent in prison for cheating the government, preferring to characterize him somewhat vaguely, when they mention him at all, as one of the group of benevolent pioneer Jewish press lords that includes Baron Paul Julius von Reuter, Joseph Pulitzer, Adolph Ochs, and Samuel I. Newhouse. But even with the help of hoodlums, Annenberg never approached Greenfield's peak of power, as a brutal contest between them in the late 1930s would prove.

After a few years at Horace Binney Public School and a brief moment at Central High School, Avrum Moishe Grunfeld, relabeled Albert Monroe Greenfield, went to work at fifteen to make money. This was a career, indeed for him a calling, at which he grew more and more expert but for which his passion—unlike most passions—never diminished. Instead, it grew marvelously more concupiscent until he died at seventy-nine.

For a few months young Albert earned a salary transcribing

realty conveyances in his swift, sure longhand. But in 1904 at sixteen, he borrowed $500 to form his own real estate company. At first he dealt only in properties so shabby, cheap, and unpromising that none of the many established real estate people would bother with them. But the word soon got around that there was no property so bad that this bright, brash, pushy kid couldn't somehow sell it to somebody. His first year he made $12,000.

He never stopped climbing. The image of the ladder was his favorite. At the end as at the beginning, he told anyone who would listen: "I would rather fall off the top rung than never climb the ladder." All his life he was undeterred by those impediments to climbing that sometimes hinder the ascent of the scrupulous: a sense of fairness, avoiding a conflict of interest, a concern for honesty, truthfulness, loyalty, or love.

Marriage, if not love, helped his ascent three times. He first married Edna Kraus, daughter of the city's leading Jewish real estate man, who taught his son-in-law the building and loan business—Albert's first step toward banking. But even easy access to mortgage money was not the most important factor in making money in real estate. That was political power.

On the most primitive level, political power meant getting the brokerage on much of the city's real estate business, as well as having the power to influence real estate taxes, zoning, street improvements, public transportation for one's own properties, and not less importantly for the properties of one's competitors and clients, present and potential. On a broader scale, political power meant the ability to influence others to do one's will—whether businessmen, important property owners, or bankers. The lack of sufficient power over such men could mean disaster.

By the high-rolling 1920s Greenfield had parlayed his own explosive energy and the boost his father-in-law gave him into a multimillion-dollar mélange that in 1928 he christened the "Bankers Securities Corporation." Into and out of it he churned banks, hotels, building and loan associations, department stores, office buildings, and anything else he thought could turn a profit. Bankers Securities did not build anything or transport anything or create anything. Its purpose was to make money—not for its shareholders, not for the depositors of its banks, but for Albert Monroe Greenfield.

Only a few months after Greenfield had created it, he had Bankers Securities buy control of the Lit Brothers department store from the Lits for $10.5 million. Bankers Securities then immediately sold Lit's to another Greenfield company, City Stores, for $12.8 million. This purported profit more than doubled the market price of Bankers Securities shares, whereupon Greenfield sold the public another $19 million of them.

In fact, of course, nothing had really happened. City Stores had not paid for Lit's but had only given its note. "The deal had all the soundness of a chain letter," a witty analyst of Greenfield's flimflams has observed, adding: "To say that Philadelphia's Protestant Establishment looked upon Greenfield and his activities with alarm and apprehension is to say that it gets very cold sometimes at the South Pole."

That this upstart Jew had so profitably invaded the previously Protestant preserve of banking and that he had, in no time at all, absorbed dozens of banks and savings institutions, was simply insupportable to the Philadelphia gentlemen who for generations had monopolized these businesses. Whether, as Greenfield always claimed, he was led on and then betrayed by Joseph Wayne, Jr., William Purves Gest, E. T. Stotesbury, Edward Hopkinson, Jr., and C. Stevenson Newhall, or whether, as they asserted, it was the inevitable outcome of his insatiable greed, Greenfield was destroyed by them.

In July 1930, with their assurances of credit, he bought the troubled Bank of Philadelphia & Trust Company and all its branches and merged these into his Bankers Trust Company. Five months later, four nights before Christmas at a meeting at the Main Line home of Gest to which Greenfield had not been invited, these gentlemen decided to cut off his credit. Bankers Trust never again opened its doors and its 135,000 depositors got for Christmas their first bitter taste of the Depression. The death threats of some of them convinced Greenfield to keep an armed policeman at his children's Christmas party.

Greenfield was ruined. But he impudently refused to stay ruined. He stubbornly refused to allow his moribund Bankers Securities and City Stores to die. As others crashed in the Depression years, he picked up the pieces and with *chutzpah* in place of cash, built an empire many times greater than the one he had lost.

Even his few admirers euphemistically described him as nothing if not supple. His enemies, a much greater number, and various government bodies accused him of extortion, misapplication, bribery, and double-dealing; but none of these charges was ever quite proven against him.

Never again did Greenfield put himself in the power of others. Instead, he relentlessly increased his own power. He had for many years been a contributor to and ally of William S. Vare and the corrupt Republican machine. He had made a nominating speech for Hoover at the 1928 Republican National Convention. But he was not a man to overvalue loyalty or undervalue opportunity. In 1934 he foresightedly switched to the Democratic fold, was soon the most powerful Democrat in Pennsylvania, and for the next several decades one of the most powerful in the country.

He became the ally of Dennis Cardinal Daugherty and was blessed with the exclusive control of all the real estate business of the Archdiocese of Philadelphia—schools, investment properties, everything. Greenfield in return was blessedly generous to Catholic charities and schools, and with exemplary Christian charity showered political favors on the cardinal's favorites. When the prince of the Church visited Greenfield's home, the five Greenfield children barely suppressed their mirth as the Catholic servants knelt and kissed the cardinal's ring. Albert did not kiss the ring but neither did His Grace kiss Greenfield's.

Aware that political power needs a voice, Greenfield helped to finance Julius David Stern's purchase of the Philadelphia *Record* from the Wanamaker estate. A few years later, this led to war with Republican Moe Annenberg, who as Hearst's circulation boss in Chicago had emerged victorious from the bloody newsstand wars that left corpses on Chicago's streets. Annenberg imported hoodlums from Chicago. Greenfield, not notorious as a peacemaker, exacerbated matters by public pronouncements, including one that compared Annenberg to "a dog who had returned to its vomit."

Greenfield, whose favorite method of impressing visitors was to put through a direct phone call to President Roosevelt or Postmaster General Farley, always refused either to confirm or to deny that he had played any role in the government's tax suit that sent Moe Annenberg to prison and so ended the circulation war. His cryptic reply to inquiries on the subject was: "He who digs a grave for his neighbor is apt to fall into it himself."

The unbelievable had happened. The stubby, potbellied, whey-faced Jew with the grotesquely oversized head whom the aristocratic bankers thought they had destroyed had become the *éminence grise* of Philadelphia. Nothing of any significance happened in that city without his approval—and very little without some profit to him. Philadelphians who had never before seen a smile on his face now observed that Greenfield seemed finally to be enjoying life a bit. He had apparently discovered that if all power is delightful, absolute power is absolutely delightful.

By department-store owners all across America, however, Albert M. Greenfield was characterized as a hyena, a snake, a vulture, the Bag and Bones Man, the Angel of Death. These store owners might have argued among themselves as to who was the greatest American retail hero, but Greenfield was everyone's favorite villain. It was a judgment based more often upon hatred and fear than upon any firsthand knowledge. Under Greenfield, City Stores grew from an insignificant group of three Southern stores (Maison Blanche in New Orleans, Lowenstein's in Memphis, Loveman's in Birmingham) into a chain that owned many well-known stores, including Philadelphia's Bonwit Teller and New York's W. & J. Sloane. What frightened and angered American store owners was that City Stores frequently served as the graveyard for many once great stores—Hearn's, Franklin Simon, and Oppenheim Collins in New York; Washington's Landsburgh's; Boston's R. H. White; Philadelphia's Snellenburg's.

The individual store owner often tended to regard his store as a holy temple, an inevitably and deservedly immortal monument. Greenfield harbored no such illusions. He had ruthlessly converted Philadelphia's near-sacred but unprofitable Ritz-Carlton Hotel into a profitable office building. A store, like a hotel, candy factory, taxicab fleet, bank, or brothel, was something that was supposed to make money. If it did not, it must be disposed of.

One reason that so many of Greenfield's stores closed was that he often bought very sick stores. Fred Lazarus, Jr., who was building the Federated Stores chain at the same time, bought only the best store in a town, or at least one that with infusions of talent and money he believed could be made into the best store in town. But Greenfield wanted only bargains. He wanted the joy of beating down the price of any store offered for sale. Rather than investing more money in people or plant, once he had bought a store, his usual pattern was to cut expenses and if possible to use the store as a tenant in one of his office buildings or shopping centers, whether or not that was in the long-range interest of the store itself.

More revealing than the many apocryphal tales about Greenfield is an experience that Stockholm-born Walter Hoving had with him. No less quick to recognize a financial opportunity than Greenfield, the three-times well married, handsome Hoving was American retailing's professional WASP. Trained under Percy Straus at Macy's, Hoving progressed to the presidency of Lord & Taylor, then of New York's Bonwit Teller, and finally to the ownership of Tiffany & Co.

Greenfield was well aware that he himself lacked style and that the tall, thin, blue-eyed, well-mannered Hoving had style to spare. He had, therefore, put together a store deal in which he promised that Hoving would run the enterprise. However, when he and Hoving arrived for the formal closing of the deal,

Greenfield could not resist the temptation to try to improve the deal a bit and started bargaining. The other side, outraged, walked out. Afterward, at lunch, Greenfield suggested to Hoving, "Well, I guess I tried to trade that deal just once too often."

"Yes, you did," said Hoving.

"But don't you understand, Walter. I would rather bargain on a deal than have an orgasm."

When Greenfield died at his Chestnut Hill estate, "Sugar Loaf," in January 1967, more than 1,400 people attended his funeral service despite the cold gray rain—"To make certain the son-of-a-bitch is dead," said one.

The usual tributes from President Lyndon Johnson, Vice President Hubert H. Humphrey, and other highly placed figures were printed in the papers. A former Philadelphia mayor asserted: "Of those who are truly involved in a love affair with Philadelphia, Albert M. Greenfield was one of the greatest," which caused one observer to suggest that "Mayor Dilworth was like Al—he saw no difference between a love affair and rape."

Whenever so large a group of people is eager to revile, envy is often an important element among its motivations. But there are a few, pitifully few, individuals who have a kind anecdote about Greenfield to offer. One such is Mildred Custin, one of the tiny company of four or five women who became president of an important store. "Albert made me president of Bonwit Teller in Philadelphia and that led to my becoming president of Bonwit's in New York, although he had no connections with the New York store. I know it's chic or at least popular to badmouth him and I know he usually loved to get the best of every bargain. But he taught me a lot and I always thought I owed him a lot. Then when he lay dying of cancer—his weight had fallen from 175 or so to 90 pounds—he called me down from New York to his home in Chestnut Hill. He handed me an envelope and said: 'I want to give you this $25,000. You did a great deal for Bonwit's and for me.'"

Since Greenfield died, both his City Stores and Bankers Securities have fallen on desperately difficult times, emphasizing how very much they had depended on this imaginative, relentless, terrible little man for their success.

William Penn's City of Brotherly Love, too, in recent decades, has more often been thought of in terms of its enormous problems than in terms of the creativity and growth that characterized its first two centuries. So also with its stores. Wanamaker's, long the model and measure of originality and greatness, the paradigm of the American department store, has ceased to seek its own solutions to its many problems and sold out to the Carter Hawley Hale chain. Gimbel's, and with it Saks Fifth Avenue, has sold out to the British-American Tobacco Company and is only a small part of a part of an international conglomerate. *Plus ça change, plus ça change.*

4

The Kaufmanns of Pittsburgh

A department store . . . diversifies the temptations to buy
and at the same time it concentrates the opportunity. . . .
If the vitality of an institution may be gauged by its architecture, the department store was one of the most vital institutions of the era 1880–1914.

—Lewis Mumford

Almost until the Civil War, Pittsburgh was the Wild West. When
in 1753 the twenty-one-year-old George Washington described
in his *Journal* that point where the Allegheny and Monongahela
rivers joined to form what the French appropriately called the
Belle Rivière, its peaceful beauty had been only intermittently disturbed by humans—as when a year earlier some 250 painted Ot-
tawa and Ojibway warriors attacked and defeated a group of
Miami there and boiled and ate the stout Miami chief who rejoiced
in the name *La Demoiselle.*

Jewish merchants who were attracted to Pennsylvania during
the eighteenth century by William Penn's religious freedom guarantee of 1680 were among those who sent trappers, traders, and
surveyors to western Pennsylvania and beyond. Joseph Simon,

a merchant and land speculator, traded with the Indians and supplied the unfortunate Edward Braddock's army during the French and Indian Wars. Then, during the Revolution, Simon supplied General Washington's troops.

After the Revolution, another Jewish merchant, David Franks, sent so many pack trains from Philadelphia to Pittsburgh that the route was called "Frankstown Road" and an early map shows an area east of the village marked "Jewstown."

Even further west, Daniel Boone surveyed land in what would become Kentucky for the Richmond firm of Cohen & Isaac, whose records contain a copy of a receipt for £6 specie for 10,000 acres of land, marked on the back in American-Yiddish script: *"Resit fun Kornel Bon far 10,000 agir lant."*

But not until the railroads came to Pittsburgh in the early 1850s did any significant Jewish settlement begin; and only in 1854 was a synagogue formed, in a room over the Vigilant Fire Department. Then, after the Civil War, an increasing number of German Jews arrived.

Jacob Kaufmann settled in Pittsburgh in 1868 from the Rhenish village of Viernheim, where his father was a horse and cattle trader. As a backpack peddler of notions in the hamlets surrounding Pittsburgh, Jacob made and saved enough money to bring over his brother Isaac. Then, in 1871, he opened a 17- by 28-foot store that prospered sufficiently for him to bring over two more brothers, Morris and Henry.

Traditionally, the last in the family to arrive slept at the store and so served as its burglar alarm. Morris Kaufmann always recalled that he was often kept up most of the night emptying buckets strategically placed under leaks in the roof. He slept on the second floor, with a piece of string dangling from his toe out the window down the front of the store. A sharp tug woke him if he overslept.

The four brothers were not Pittsburgh's first storekeepers, nor was Joseph Horne, who, more than two decades earlier, opened his store only four years after the disastrous fire of 1845. When the Kaufmann brothers were just starting, Horne's was already on its way to becoming the carriage-trade and fashion store of Pittsburgh. It billed its customers only twice a year, in January and June, and was nothing if not discreet in its front-page newspaper advertisements—only gentlemen's "drawers" were mentioned, never ladies'. Well into the twentieth century, Horne's refused to advertise in the Sunday papers and closed the curtains of its display windows in order not to profane the Sabbath, this Christian piety presumably made easier by its strict policy of not hiring Jews.

Despite a lack of comparable prestige, Kaufmann's soon became a popular and profitable store. The brothers began as merchant tailors with a store for men only, but expanded their stocks and moved frequently, each time into dangerously larger and more expensive quarters. By 1885 they had arrived at Fifth Avenue and Smithfield Street, where without excessive modesty they called their establishment first "The Grand Depot" and then "The Big Store," and advertised that they sold "Everything Under the Sun." They prospered because they treated every transaction, even if it was only the sale of a paper of pins, as though it were crucial; they were almost obsessively concerned about quality and price, trying to satisfy every customer however unreasonable, and so, bit by bit, they established a reputation for being reliable.

But in addition to the Kaufmann brothers' hard work and meticulousness, what made their businesses thrive was the explosive economic growth that prevailed all across America from the 1870s into the 1920s—and especially in Pittsburgh. The seemingly inexhaustible deposits of bituminous coal nearby, the easy transport by water of rich iron ore from the shores of Lake Superior, the comparably rich flood of cheap labor from Europe, presented opportunities to other young men building fortunes. And these opportunities were seized upon by Andrew Carnegie in steel, Henry Clay Frick in coal and coke, William Thaw in freight transportation, and above all, the Mellons, who had a considerable head start.

Thomas Mellon, who had arrived in Pittsburgh from Ireland as a barefoot boy in 1823, learned and practiced the law, and invested shrewdly in businesses that desperately needed his money. Most shrewdly of all, he had forbidden his sons Andrew and Richard to indulge in the "folly of soldiering." While thousands of young Americans were being killed or mutilated at Gettysburg and Bull Run, at Antietam and Shiloh, singing their determination "to make men free" or "to live and die in Dixie," the Mellons were lending money in Pittsburgh and becoming the richest family in America. They and their heirs became major stockholders in United States Steel, Westinghouse, Koppers, Gulf Oil, Texas Gulf Sulphur, Pittsburgh Plate Glass, and the Pennsylvania Railroad; in the next generation, *Fortune* magazine would estimate that the wealth of Richard King Mellon and his sister, Mrs. Alan M. Scaife, and of Paul Mellon and his sister, Mrs. Ailsa Mellon Bruce, totaled some $3 billion, not to speak of their control of the Mellon National Bank's $2 billion in assets or Gulf Oil's $3 billion.

Compared to such fortunes, those that the Kaufmann brothers were amassing were modest, for they were not manufacturing products nor buying up raw materials needed all over the country or the world, but merely selling a variety of merchandise to the local population. Because they were not manufacturers, they were not part of making Pittsburgh what Lincoln Steffens described as physically "Hell with the Lid Off."

In many of these merchant families the men and women of the first generation were the most interesting, while those of the second and third generations became increasingly less so. But in a few cases—such as Stanley Marcus, Beatrice Auerbach, and Barry Goldwater—the greater figures were in the second or even the third generation. Edgar Kaufmann was one of these.

Born in 1885, the older son of Morris and Betty Kaufmann, he attended Pittsburgh's exclusive Shadyside Academy and Yale. In 1906 he went to Europe, ostensibly to learn storekeeping at the Karstadt store in Hamburg and at Galeries Lafayette in Paris. Whatever else he may have learned in his *wanderjahr,* he acquired and indulged there what would become a lifelong taste for women in great variety and quantity.

His handsome features were set off by a saber scar he had picked up on a visit to Heidelberg. Dashing, dark-skinned, athletic, with black hair and what were then inevitably described as "dark, passionate eyes," Edgar looked like a more virile version of Rudolph Valentino, and, like the movie idol, he had all his life the problem of dissuading many of the women who believed they had been called or chosen to come to his bed.

"The first time I met him and saw that irresistible crooked smile, I was fifteen and he was sixty-two," said one Pittsburgh doyenne, "and when he took my hand and looked in my eyes, I thought I would faint. That look made you feel that you were the only woman in the world and that you were so extravagantly desirable that not to be generous with such a great treasure would be mean and cruel. And in bed with him I felt we were like gods on Olympus."

In 1909 Edgar married Lillian Sarah Kaufmann. As they were first cousins, the ceremony took place in New York City because they could not get a license in Pennsylvania. She was as blonde and beautiful as he was dark and dramatically handsome, and she was equally brilliant, ambitious, and tireless. Wildly in love with him, she would remain so throughout their stormy marriage even when his numberless infidelities drove her to leave him temporarily, to threaten divorce, and occasionally to take lovers of her own, or so the gossips said. The same gossips suggested that whether Edgar had married her for love was less certain than that the stock she would inherit as the only child of Isaac would give Edgar effective control of the store.

In the Roaring Twenties, Edgar and Lillian lived in a style typical of a rich young couple. On a 7½-acre tract on Pasadena Drive in fashionable Fox Chapel, they built an eighteen-room Norman château, spending a quarter-of-a-million 1925 dollars on such luxuries as a fireplace in every room and on bringing over the then famous Swedish ironworker Samuel Yellin to make all the hardware in a forge set up in the living room before the floor was installed. The house had a cobblestone courtyard, wide-beam wood-pegged floors, a large greenhouse for orchids, and, of course, a name, "La Tourelle"—just as George Westinghouse's mansion was named "Solitude," Henry Clay Frick's "Clayton," and Lawrence C. Phipps's "Grandview."

But the Kaufmanns' efforts at grandeur were modest when compared to those that made "Pittsburgh millionaires" a joke, a synonym for relentlessly ostentatious and vulgar spending by the parvenu moguls whose very first shampoo, so a local barber declared, invariably brought out at least two ounces of fine Mesabi ore, slag, and cinders. According to Stefan Lorant, "They bought paintings by the yard and sculptures by the ton," and when Alexander Peacock, the former sales manager of Carnegie, heard that one of his former colleagues had bought two gold-plated pianos, not to be outdone, he installed four, although no one in his family could play the instrument.

Edgar and Lillian, whose name was in this same period transmogrified to the presumably more elegant "Liliane," were also fashionably horsy, taking their French-bred steeplechase "fencers" to race meets to compete against those of John Hay Whitney, Colonel Robert R. McCormick, and Stephen Sanford. At first Liliane especially found it exciting to mix with rich non-Jews, but for both of them it soon became tiresome to follow fashion once they realized that instead they could set fashion and that others far richer than they would then imitate them.

Liliane would have been more than enough of a mate for an ordinary man. Tall, sinuous, intelligent, curious, and stylish, she kept her provocative figure, with the help of a series of masseuses, until she was well into middle age, and she was as enthusiastic as Edgar about shocking their relatives and friends, whether by collecting modern art or nude bathing. She made a considerable reputation locally as a hostess and nationally as a breeder of long-haired dachshunds, a breed that had been virtually unknown in America until she introduced it.

When Edgar in the mid-1930s overexpanded the store—it now covered an entire block and the upper floors went begging—it was Liliane who suggested opening a branch of Elizabeth Arden's. This proved a great success, and she herself opened a shop of exquisite gifts, art, and antiques. She called it *Vendôme,* and did all of the buying for it and much of the selling as well. The *Vendôme,* like the red-doored Arden salon, was not only profitable but also helped to lessen the prestige gap between Horne's, which had always been the carriage-trade store, and Kaufmann's, which had become the biggest store in Pittsburgh by selling low-priced merchandise. Edgar was now eager to capture as much of the higher-priced trade as possible.

Despite her understandable moments of rage and despair, Liliane was no ordinary woman. She was at least as courageous and generous as her husband, and her style was as apparent in her life as at the store. When she learned that Edgar had had a daughter by another woman, she invited the by then teen-age daughter up to their weekend house and she insisted that Edgar set up a trust fund for the mother and child although the liaison had ended long before.

Edgar was not an ordinary man. Regardless of what he had, in business, in reputation, in women, he wanted more. He kept a series of mistresses, but he was no more faithful to them than to Liliane; he wanted women, as he wanted everything else, wholesale.

Edgar was a friend and a lavish customer of both Florenz Ziegfeld and George White. One evening he invited every girl in the "Follies" to sail with him the next day for Europe on the *Bremen.* They accepted. When Ziegfeld patiently pointed out the comparable effect it would have on Kaufmann's store if Ziegfeld without any notice hired away every one of its female employees, Edgar good-naturedly compromised. He took the girls to the Ritz in Atlantic City for the weekend.

Oliver M. Kaufmann, who sometimes accompanied his older brother on buying trips to Europe, maintained that they were the most exciting part of an almost always exciting and changing business. The ocean voyages over and back were especially pleasant when they corresponded with the trips of the Seventh Avenue ready-to-wear manufacturers. In those days when what was new in fashion was determined in Paris and only Paris, the best American manufacturers made at least two trips a year to buy from the spring and fall collections of the great couturiers.

These manufacturers often brought with them a favorite model whose charms they were on occasion not unwilling to share with their good customers and friends, the store owners. The manufacturers also joined with the store owners after dinner in forming the syndicates that gambled large sums in the "ship's pool," the winners determined by the exact distance traveled by the ship in each twenty-four hours. In the bidding for the most likely distances, the competition between syndicates was often fierce and the sums paid for them frequently enormous, so that there were occasional whispers about a ship's officers being bribed by a share of the winning syndicate's take.

Quite as enthusiastic about drinking as about women, Edgar would disappear with increasing regularity, and "Happy" Solomon, the chief of the store's detectives, would be sent to find him. It was not an easy job. Instead of being at the apartment he kept in the Hotel William Penn, or at one of his favorite speakeasies, Edgar was just as likely to be found in the modest apartment of some young woman who had just caught his eye for the first time (although she may have had hers on him for a long time) and who was just as delighted to have the handsome and generous gentleman come home with her as he was. But as often as not he was discovered at the lavish brothel of Billie Scheible, on the corner of Halket Street at 3400 Fifth Avenue.

It is difficult in today's climate of permissive sex and egalitarianism to understand fully the comfortable and comforting role played before World War II by the expensive and high-class whorehouse. At least one prospered in every town in America and was thought of as a local showplace no less than the best hotel, the finest store, or the opera house.

Sex was not the most important blessing available there, although it existed in far greater variety than was probably dreamed of by the patrons' wives, "nice" women, most of whom had been taught that sex was at best a duty, at worst a cross to bear, and were therefore often afraid to express any natural feelings to the contrary.

These brothels were in fact clubs where the rich, Gentile and Jew together, and those not rich but powerful—the governor, the mayor, the chief of police—met in a climate of easy conviviality and a relaxing absence of the pretensions that were mandatory in upper-class Victorian society.

It would have been unthinkable for Edgar Kaufmann to visit, let alone to belong to Rolling Rock, the country club where only the closest intimates of the Mellons were allowed to belong and to build country houses marginally less luxurious than their mansions in town. But at Billie's, Rolling Rock members met with Edgar as equals, in a relaxed and joyful atmosphere not even possible at the downtown men's clubs such as the exclusive Duquesne Club or the handsome Concordia Club built by rich German Jews because they were excluded from the Duquesne. Jews were of course not the only undesirables excluded from clubs in America, but their exclusion was often so taken for granted that it was not even specified in the by-laws. The first rule of the Chicago Club read that no admission should be granted to "dogs, women, Democrats or reporters."

At Billie Scheible's the furniture and furnishings, the liquor and the service, were at least as luxurious as those provided in the Pittsburgh downtown clubs. And on any afternoon or evening a number of the men who ran Pittsburgh would drop in, if only for a drink and some easy conversation.

In the society of "nice" women in those days, when even chickens had "white meat" and "second joints" instead of vulgar "breasts" and "thighs," there was an endless list of subjects and words not suitable for polite conversation. Polite society was, therefore, frequently a tedious trial when compared to brothels like Billie's, where the delightful company of women put no boundaries on the conversation and the madams as well as occasionally the girls could enter into conversations about business, or the real pleasures and tragedies of life far more interestingly than most "nice" women—even those who had gone to the best private schools and then to "finishing" school or college.

These whorehouses were carefully protected from annoying incursions by the lower ranks of police officers and were, along with the best hotels and the best department stores, considered evidence of the city's culture, places where the most important "visiting firemen" were taken with pride by local leaders in the certainty that their needs would be provided for, from check cashing to specialized sex services.

There was usually no crowd and no rush at a place like Billie's except on very rare occasions, as when a police convention came to Pittsburgh and Billie held open house for anyone who could show a badge—apologizing to local clients who showed up during the unwonted lack of calm that she was doing her best to build the reputation of her city.

Billie had as her employee and lover a young man named Joseph Ryan. For protection against an "outlaw" police raid and perhaps also as insurance against some future rainy day when Miss Scheible might lose her taste for his services, Ryan had taken to his mother's home many of Billie's business records containing the names of prominent Pittsburgh and out-of-town clients.

Charlotte Ryan finally concluded that despite her earnest urging, her son would not leave his "unhealthful" employment. Therefore, after consulting with her priest, she turned over these records not only to the local constabulary, in whose hands they would doubtless have been carefully lost, but also to federal agents of the then-called Internal Revenue Bureau, who were delighted to have the opportunity to determine whether or not Miss Scheible was properly declaring all her income.

When it was revealed in the Pittsburgh press that in one year Miss Scheible had paid only $6 of income tax, although her books disclosed an income of $92,000, a number of the most prominent sources of that income, with a mixture of joy and sadness, generously and swiftly financed her immediate move to New York City and set her up in an equally luxurious business on the fashionable upper East Side in a many-roomed apartment on East 74th Street.

Fear of publicity doubtless motivated many of her supporters, but not Edgar Kaufmann, who either ignored or enjoyed the scandals that constantly surrounded his name from almost the moment he passed puberty. Not the least talked about of these resulted from his refusal to pay the Joseph Horne Company for six platinum and diamond bracelets and sixteen hats charged to his account there and delivered at his instruction to the Tudor Hall apartment of one Josephine Bennett Waxman.

Apparently, upon reflection, Edgar was less grateful to Miss Waxman than he had been initially. But when he tried to return his purchases, Horne's had refused to accept them for credit because they were returned after the seven-day limit and Horne's was not in the business, they said, of selling used merchandise, including used diamond bracelets.

Horne's 1933 lawsuit reminded delighted Pittsburgh citizens of other hard feelings between other competitors, as when Thomas A. Edison, furious at George Westinghouse's alternating current system that threatened Edison's profits built on direct current, declared publicly that AC was a "horrible menace, a vehicle of instant and painless death" and that Westinghouse was "a man gone crazy."

Newspaper reports of gossip and scandals were just as essential to Pittsburghers as to everyone else and were rarely in short supply, from Thomas Quart's June 5, 1834, advertisement in the Pittsburgh *Gazette* that his wife Sarah Anne had left his bed and board and he would not be responsible for her debts to the 1906 murder of architect Stanford White by the thirty-four-year-old Pittsburgh transportation heir Harry Kendall Thaw, described by one historian as "A sadistic pervert who became insanely jealous over the fact that someone else had been intimate with a girl . . . with whom he enjoyed an almost incredibly unnatural relationship."

In excoriating the undoubtedly loathsome Thaw, however, historians and other reporters frequently forgot that if the heroine of the drama, the stunningly beautiful chorus girl Evelyn Nesbit, had left such attractive lovers as "Stanny" White and the young John Barrymore for the unspeakable Thaw, the love of money may have played a part in her decision. Nor is it perhaps too skeptical to suggest that when Thaw stopped flogging her with a dog whip long enough to go out and murder White, in full view of the audience at Madison Square Garden, Evelyn's testimony at the subsequent trials, that Thaw was really not a bad fellow, perhaps had some causal relationship to promises of more money from Thaw's mother.

Those who endlessly declare that a different justice is meted out to the rich than to the poor and that the rich are thereby deprived of the remedial effects of the prison system would do well to note that Thaw's few days of trial, jail, and in the madhouse had an edifying and salutary effect upon him. When, for example, several years later he was arrested for kidnapping a new playmate, instead of a girl it was a nineteen-year-old boy, Thaw did not this time waste the taxpayers' money with a trial but settled out of court. However, in saving them money he was also depriving them of something they wanted much more than economy, the details of a juicy scandal.

When Thaw returned to Pittsburgh after one of his trials, he was cheered in the streets by his fellow citizens, who, like most red-blooded Americans of both sexes, expect "law and order," if at all, only from the lower orders and not from the rich and famous.

The lawsuit brought by Horne's against Edgar was the result of mutual miscalculations. Edgar was too generous-hearted himself to believe that the Hornes and the Sheas and Burchfields, who had inherited that store, were pettish enough actually to bring a court action. They, on the other hand, believed that just as they carefully kept their adulteries and other unacceptable amusements hidden behind closed doors, Edgar would also prefer to do so. In fact, Edgar laughed at the publicity that titillated his fellow citizens until the lawsuit was settled by the efforts of Arthur C. Kaufmann, a distant cousin of Edgar's who was then running another Pittsburgh store, McCreery's.

Horne's had a summer camp for employees just outside the city. The women's tents were of course segregated from the men's, and guards patrolled at all hours to see that there was no dancing, drinking, or card-playing, and especially no "hanky-panky in the woods," even between husband and wife. At meals the blessing was said by A. H. Burchfield, Sr., who, like Edgar, occasionally took a female companion with him to New York on the train, but never on Sunday and always with a circumspection Edgar thought laughably hypocritical.

Kaufmann's, too, for many years had a similar camp for its employees in the lovely foothills of the Allegheny Mountains in Fayette County, where rhododendron and mountain laurel and the waterfalls of Bear Run gave relief from the smoke and soot and sounds of the city. Here Edgar had Frank Lloyd Wright build a weekend house called "Fallingwater" that is one of the great works of art of the twentieth century, but when it was built in 1936, it shocked proper Pittsburgh even more than Edgar's sex life.

Most of the rich of Pittsburgh had kept themselves at a safe distance from art and the corruptive influence of beauty. Artists born there from Stephen Foster to George Kaufman (no relative) fled the city as soon as they could. This was also true of the remarkable number of women among them, including Mary Cassatt, Gertrude Stein, and Martha Graham.

Only a very few storekeepers, such as Benjamin Altman and some of the Strauses, had the wealth and the conservative taste to compete even occasionally with the Mellons and Morgans in collecting works of art by old masters. More storekeepers and their wives were timidly *avant-garde.* On their buying trips to New York and Europe they were essentially in a race to find merchandise for their stores that was new—but not *too* new—that could be bought, sent home, and offered to customers ahead of the competitors. This constant search for "what's new" of course had an effect in other areas of their lives as well. In New York and Europe they were exposed to the new shape in hats, the new Poiret silhouette; but they were also exposed to what was new at the theater, the opera, the ballet, in restaurants, and in the homes of friends on the walls, at the dinner table, in the garden, the bathroom, and even the bedroom.

It was pleasant when they got home to be the first in their community to talk about a new painter or composer, to suggest to the local symphony conductor a new fiddler, to have seen an actor or ballerina as yet unknown to their friends. Anti-Semitism also often moved them toward the not too *avant-garde.* In those older cities where, because they were Jews, they were excluded from the boards of directors of existing arts institutions despite their known willingness to give more than their share of financial support, they were the more inspired to help initiate new institutions that would discover and support contemporary dance, sculpture, painting, and to a lesser extent theater and music.

The observations of visitors to Pittsburgh were uniformly unflattering in regard to its culture—or rather, the lack of it. Henry Mencken described it as "a scene so dreadfully hideous, so intolerably bleak and forlorn that it reduced the whole aspiration of man to a macabre and depressing joke. Here was wealth beyond computation, almost beyond imagination—and here were human habitations so abominable that they would have disgraced a race of alley cats. I am not speaking of mere filth. One expects steel towns to be dirty. What I allude to is the unbroken and agonizing ugliness, the sheer revolting monstrousness of every house in sight."

Edgar, who loved Pittsburgh, saw this same ugliness, but he was determined to change his city from what Trollope had called "the blackest place I ever saw." He was aware that Herbert Spencer, the inventor of Social Darwinism, had said that a month in Pittsburgh would justify anyone in committing suicide; but instead of accepting as immutable the terrible conditions that most other Pittsburghers either took for granted or in which they took a kind of perverse pride, he was resolved to correct them. His role in helping to change Pittsburgh from one of the ugliest and least humane to one of the most beautiful cities in America was as disproportional as everything else about him, and he set an example for men and women much richer and more powerful than himself.

He was, of course, neither the only one nor the first to notice and to care. Andrew Carnegie had written to Prime Minister William Gladstone: "Pittsburgh . . . has never been anything but a center of materialism; it has never had a fine hall for music, nor a museum, nor an art gallery, nor public library." Carnegie, whom Morgan had congratulated "on being the richest man in the world," proceeded to give Pittsburgh a library, an art gallery, a music hall, a natural history museum, and Carnegie Institute.

Edgar Kaufmann was never in the same financial league as Carnegie or the Mellons and yet his impact on Pittsburgh was not less significant. He was determined to make his store a leader and to set an example in the movement to link industry and contemporary art. So in 1930, when the store's first floor was redesigned, its chief decoration was a series of murals by Boardman Robinson, commissioned by Edgar to illustrate the role of commerce through the ages.

Carnegie had hoped that the annual exhibition of paintings chosen by an international jury would result in the Pittsburgh museum acquiring a collection of modern masterpieces; Monet, Matisse, Rouault, and Picasso all submitted works. The museum instead bought only relatively unimportant conventional work.

Into this climate in 1936 Edgar brought Frank Lloyd Wright, who exercised a talent for personal publicity far more inflammatory than Edgar's and who gazed upon Pittsburgh and later declared contemptuously, "It would be cheaper to abandon it than to rebuild it."

Kaufmann gave Wright *carte blanche* in planning the weekend house, and Wright built what art historians would soon proclaim one of the milestones of civilization. Its modern materials were dramatically cantilevered over a waterfall, yet the glass and concrete and stone blended with the surrounding woods and water as perfectly as the top of the untouched boulder on which the house is perched formed the hearth of the living-room fireplace. Equally complementary and shocking were the pieces of contemporary sculpture by Jacques Lipschitz and Henry Moore that Edgar placed around Wright's work.

Diego Rivera's judgment that the house was "three hundred years ahead of its time" seems to be holding up. Forty years after it was built, "Fallingwater" was judged by the American

Institute of Architects to be one of the half-dozen most significant buildings in America's 200-year history. Another of the six was the Chicago department store Louis E. Sullivan designed for Schlesinger & Mayer, that now houses Carson, Pirie, Scott, & Co.

Edgar also had Wright design for him a new office on the store's tenth floor; but typical of Edgar's catholicity was his insistence upon also keeping and using the splendid office he had brought back from an early buying trip to Europe, which had once belonged to a merchant prince of the Hanseatic League and had also served as the taproom of a monastery.

But for Edgar, as for everyone else who loved Pittsburgh, the greatest problem and one that most people considered insoluble was not in the arts. It was how to halt and then reverse the obscenely brutal effects of a century of unrestrained commerce and industry. Already in 1842, Charles Dickens on visiting the city had complained of the "great quantity of smoke hanging over it." A century later the industries that had made Pittsburgh rich had made it almost uninhabitable, had turned the *Belle Rivière* (celebrated in American song as "The Beautiful Ohio") into a giant sewer, and had turned day into night. Frequently the smog was so dense that the downtown streetlights had to be kept burning even at midday.

The need for reforms and controls was obvious, but the indifference or opposition of many industrialists had stopped repeated efforts. The St. Patrick's Day flood of 1936 was only one of a series of such catastrophes, none of which had resulted in any serious efforts toward flood control. As late as 1939, the Bureau of Smoke Regulation was actually abolished by the city council.

Just as no one would accept the blame when the city was an inferno, so everyone was willing to claim a generous share of the credit when Pittsburgh changed from an international joke to an international example, and of course many different men and women played a significant role, but none more extraordinary than Edgar Kaufmann's.

Two of Edgar's most felicitous gifts were his charm, as irresistible to men as to women, and his ability not only to get along

himself with prickly people but to bring them into effective coop-
eration with others like themselves. When the Dallas storekeeper
Stanley Marcus engaged Frank Lloyd Wright to design a new
residence for him, their equally monumental egos made it impossible for them to function together and before anything was built
they fell out with each other with considerable acrimony. Edgar
not only worked successfully with Wright on "Fallingwater" and
a new office and a parking garage for the store, but also later
hired the less-than-genial genius to create a design for The Point
(the original site of Fort Duquesne) with a stadium, two new
bridges, and a park. The project was never executed, but—along
with others, such as Robert Moses's 1939 proposal for a new
Point Park—it helped to inspire the remarkable renaissance that
transformed Pittsburgh after World War II.

Kaufmann was one of the six incorporators of the Allegheny
Conference on Community Development. Through it he worked
together with such different men as David L. Lawrence, the Democratic former mayor of Pittsburgh and then governor of Pennsylvania, and the arch-Republican Richard King Mellon, who refused
to join the Conference but whose long arm served it well. In
1947, representatives of the Pennsylvania Railroad in the State
Senate at Harrisburg opposed smoke-regulation legislation. According to Lawrence, when word of this opposition was telephoned to Mellon in Pittsburgh, Mellon "called the president
of the Pennsylvania and let him know that there were other railroads besides the Pennsylvania that would be only too happy
to ship the products of the Mellon enterprises, and the railroad
called off its lobby."

The Mellons of earlier generations had been as conservative
in their tastes as they were generous with their money. In 1935
they donated $4 million toward the building of a neo-Gothic
cathedral, the East Liberty Presbyterian Church, that irreverent
Pittsburghers called "the Mellons' fire escape." The Mellons were
also openhanded with the University of Pittsburgh, whose hideous
skyscraper, pretentiously christened "The Cathedral of Learning,"
led wags to dub the neoclassic Mellon National Bank and Trust

Company "The Cathedral of Earning." But by the time of Richard King Mellon and Paul Mellon, they were insisting that not only Mellon Square Park but also the new office buildings being built in Pittsburgh by companies they controlled (United States Steel, Alcoa, Gulf Oil) should use the very best modern architects in precisely the pattern set by Edgar Kaufmann.

When the slums that had been the ghetto of immigrant Eastern European Jews in the 1890s were torn down to build the new Lower Hill, the dominating structure was the Civic Arena with its retractable roof. It cost some $22 million, of which Kaufmann had given the first $1 million; but even more important than his seed money were his fresh ideas and example.

Whether he was commissioning historian Stefan Lorant to write and edit "a de luxe book" to illustrate and glorify the reborn Pittsburgh or architect Richard Neutra to design a winter house for him in Palm Springs, Kaufmann, like Oscar Wilde, was easily satisfied; all he wanted was the best.

Philanthropy and lechery took so much of Edgar's time that, according to his brother Oliver, "He usually appeared at the store no oftener than two or three days a week. But he could accomplish more in those two or three days than an ordinary man could in seven." Furthermore, Irwin Damasius Wolf, Edgar's brother-in-law from Paragould, Arkansas, was a great merchant who ran the store efficiently when Edgar was absent. Stores that were not well run, even successful department stores such as Rosenbaum's and Frank & Seder's, disappeared. But Kaufmann's, Horne's, and Gimbel's remained.

Like his father and his uncles, indeed like most such first- and second-generation German-Jewish storekeepers, Edgar more than anything else wanted his store to be "the best." Because most were not accountable to their stockholders or to Wall Street securities analysts if they failed to produce absolutely optimal profits, these successful storekeepers often ignored their own controller's advice on expenses and turnover in a kingly fashion that would later seem grotesque to the post-World War II, Harvard Business School, professional executives who were chosen to run these stores when they were eventually sold to the chains whose shares trade on the New York Stock Exchange. These hired managers, however, were not *building* great stores from tiny shops into community institutions as the owners had. Rather, they were merely expanding already dominant businesses, mainly by adding suburban branch stores.

Edgar was so obsessed by his desire that his store should first become and then remain the biggest in Pittsburgh, that he focused his energy only on the downtown store; in this, he badly underestimated the importance of such branches. Similarly, he wanted his store to maintain the reputation: "We have whatever you want," so that when former President William Howard Taft needed an outsized pair of white flannel trousers, Kaufmann's received national publicity because they were able to fit him out of stock. Edgar was delighted, although he, like other store owners and his own controller, knew that it meant Kaufmann's turnover must be too slow if they carried such a stock.

Once, when upon his return from a European buying trip Kaufmann was warned by his distressed controller that the store was "overbought" some half a million dollars, he answered cheerily, "Oh, don't worry about that—there's a million and a half more on the water that I haven't told you about."

And when he hired the Hungarian-born architect and stage designer Lazlo Gabor, instructing him that his only concern was to create the most beautiful windows and interior displays possible, the expenses rose abruptly. But after that, few if any stores in New York and none in Pittsburgh could equal Kaufmann's.

Despite all this pride, in 1946 Edgar sold his store to the May Company, a chain well known to be unconcerned about prestige and very much concerned about net profits. His reasons were many, but his son's unwillingness to work at the store was one.

In the third and fourth generations of these merchant families, the sons (to the mixed anger and pride of their fathers) frequently refused to come into the store or otherwise soil their hands in the marts of trade. They preferred often to join professions that poverty and prejudice had closed to their fathers and grandfathers, and when they became attorneys or physicians or professors, their performance could not readily be compared to that of a father or grandfather.

Even after Edgar's death on April 15, 1955, in Palm Springs, he provided Pittsburgh's citizens with the scandal they expected from him and so enjoyed. Liliane had died on September 7, 1952; and on September 4, 1954, the sixty-eight-year-old merchant married his stenographer, nurse, and constant companion, one Grace A. Stoops. The newspapers reported breathlessly that she chose as her wedding outfit a beige-colored Italian wool costume suit by Hattie Carnegie, and as her flowers, cymbidium orchids. At thirty-four, she was precisely half her husband's age.

When Edgar died seven months and eleven days later, the relatively new Mrs. Kaufmann declared, perhaps not entirely unreasonably, "I think charity begins at home!" She brought a lawsuit in Orphan's Court seeking one-half of his $10 million estate, the bulk of which he had left to charity.

She was accustomed, her attorneys and accountants stressed, to such gifts as a $22,850 emerald-cut 6.32-carat diamond ring and an $11,000 Russian sable jacket, and to a style of living appropriate to the wife of Mr. Kaufmann, whose living expenses in 1953 and 1954 totaled $268,059 and $210,023, respectively, and whose gross income for those two years was $446,307 and $441,200. She could not, they pointed out with irrefutable arithmetic, live in this style on the gross income of $40,000 for life (a mere $23,000 after taxes) left to her from a $700,000 trust of 20,000 shares of May Company stock established under the will. And in fact she could not on such a paltry sum maintain the $140,000 Palm Springs mansion she had inherited outright and whose cost of operation for the two prior years was $68,434 and $30,700.

In turn, the ungallant attorneys for the estate, her stepson Edgar, Jr., and the Edgar J. Kaufmann Charitable Foundation pointed out that this "young, attractive, ambitious woman" in the years from 1942 to 1953 had earned a total of only $18,240—and never more than $2,383 in one year. They also presented to the court a premarriage agreement surrendering her widow's rights signed by Grace the day before her wedding. When her attorneys suggested that she might not have signed the agreement if she had known what Edgar, Jr., was receiving and that taxes would eat away half the money, an unchivalrous State Supreme Court Justice commented: "Maybe Mr. Kaufmann wouldn't have married her if she hadn't signed it."

The gossip stopped abruptly, however, when in 1961, after losing her last appeal, Grace Kaufmann, now a victim of multiple sclerosis with almost no use of her hands or legs, died one morning in her apartment in a small fire caused by her heating pad, only about fifteen minutes before her maid arrived.

If even after his death this horse trader's grandson continued to provide his city with scandal, he also continued his efforts to make Pittsburgh the best city in the world through the charitable trust that received more than half of his estate. A horse trader is quite the other end of the stick from a philanthropist, but as a skeptic might observe, that men only one and two generations removed from the Rhineland horse trader could be such lavish philanthropists as Edgar and his uncles was possible only because they were also such successful horse traders.

A skeptic studying the philanthropies of Kaufmann, Rosenwald, Altman, and the majority of Jewish storekeepers across America might suggest that these gifts were in fact only a milder form of the ransom (rançon) that their ancestors paid in Europe—in the duchy of Burgundy, for example, from the ninth through the end of the thirteenth century, for the right to live there. These blackmail payments did not, however, deter the duchy in the late fourteenth century from expelling all Jews.

To a less skeptical observer, the history of these Jewish storekeepers and of America seems a bargain—for both.

5

The Goldsmiths of Memphis

I really cannot seriously consider converting to Christianity until I have seen it practiced.

—Anonymous

Even since the advent of the railroad and the plane, very few cities that were not ports have grown to importance. In the last thousand years, for a city to become great, it did not have to be a seaport; indeed it could, like Paris or London, be well inland, but almost invariably it had to have water access to the sea.

Memphis is such a river port, at the junction of the Wolf River and the Mississippi. The city's growth has been up from the banks of the Wolf along Front Street that parallels the river, as well as eastward along the streets such as Gayoso and Pontotoc that run at right angles up from the docks. The most famous of these, Beale Avenue, is never called anything but Beale Street.

At first by flatboat and barge, then beginning in the 1830s by steamboat, river commerce made Memphis one of the great ports of America. And in the 1830s and 1840s, enterprising Jewish peddlers followed the traffic to Memphis, upriver from New Orleans and Vicksburg, downriver from Cincinnati, Louisville, and St.

Louis, joining those Scots and Germans who were the other early settlers of Tennessee.

A century earlier, when there was not yet a single white settler in what would someday become the state of Tennessee, an extraordinary and eccentric Scottish baronet, Sir Alexander Cuming, had promoted in England a scheme he declared would be enormously profitable—to found in the wilderness west of Carolina a colony of some 300,000 European Jewish families. The relentless industriousness for which these Hebrews were well known would purportedly pay off handsomely not only the investors but also the national debt of England. And as a kind of spiritual special dividend, the colonists, as well as the Cherokee Indians in whose tribal mountains Cuming proposed to build the colony, would eventually convert to the Church of England.

Cuming, like John Law and the other great eighteenth-century confidence men, was a genius at bluffing, able to inspire simultaneously greed and prodigious confidence; his own self-assurance was unshakably based upon a perfect ignorance and an equally solid egotism. But George II's government finally turned down the plan, so that the few Jews who came to Tennessee in the three decades before the Civil War came in ones and twos and in a manner that was anything but grand or organized.

In Memphis as elsewhere, most of them began as foot peddlers. The wives of the great plantation owners, much less those of small farmers and tradesmen, rarely left home even on those few occasions when their husbands traveled to a larger town to sell produce or to buy supplies. So these women were delighted when a peddler arrived with new fashions, with necessities, and with the equally essential gossip of the outside world that had also for the medieval minstrel been no less important than his stock-in-trade of songs. For the peddlers as for the minstrels—who were also of necessity strong young men—any limit to their methods of pleasing these customers were usually set by the customer.

If she felt enough confidence in him, a customer would place orders with a peddler for things he didn't have with him but could bring on his next visit. This assured them both that there would be another visit and these repeat sales seemed no less important to the peddler than to a storekeeper.

One such peddler was Benedict Lowenstein. When at nineteen he reached New Orleans from his native Darmstadt, his remaining capital was 35 cents, but he impressed a coreligionist wholesaler sufficiently to be extended credit to the extent of one 90-pound pack full of linens, shawls, silks, and laces. Very quickly Benedict developed for himself a summer route in western Tennessee and Kentucky and a winter route in southern Arkansas and Mississippi.

When a peddler started a shop in a village that remained a village instead of developing into an Atlanta or a Little Rock or a Dallas, it was often not a misjudgment of locality but rather, as the peddler would later explain repeatedly to his sons and grandsons—"It was where the horse died."

Years later, the social pecking order among rich Jews in communities all across America was frequently determined by who had first ceased peddling and opened a shop, no matter how modest, even if the time difference was a matter of months rather than years.

One Memphis woman was so satisfied and impressed by young Lowenstein that she lent him $500 to buy a horse and wagon, the traditional middle step between pack peddling and opening a small store. These enabled the peddler to carry a larger and more profitable stock of goods as well as more and larger special orders, and also to service a wider territory, thereby increasing his chances of finding a place where business possibilities seemed sufficiently promising to open a small store, once he had saved enough money and built up enough credit.

Benedict Lowenstein, with the small capital he had saved from peddling, brought over his younger brothers, Elias, Abraham, and Bernard. They opened tiny stores on the corner of Front and Poplar in Memphis in 1855 and briefly in the village of Paris. When Lowenstein's Memphis shop had developed into one of the two largest department stores in town as well as an important wholesale dry-goods company, he was visited by a small-town merchant whose store had burned down and who was unable to get a stock of goods on credit to start another. As soon as Benedict heard the storekeeper's name, even before the man had been able to explain his dilemma, Benedict assured him that he could have whatever stock he wanted on whatever credit terms he thought appropriate.

Delighted but astounded by Benedict's generosity, the merchant asked why he was willing to take such a risk. "One night on my travels as a peddler," replied Lowenstein, "a severe storm broke suddenly and I knocked at your back door. You were just a small boy then and probably don't remember, but your parents gave me food and shelter for the night. I tried to pay them for their kindness, but they wouldn't let me. Since then I've always regretted that I was unable to do anything for your family, and now this gives me the opportunity."

In the years before the Civil War, Memphis developed into the largest inland cotton market in America and one of the largest markets in the South for lumber and slaves. The Jews were in banking, barbering, and auctioneering (including slaves); they even operated a racetrack. A good number of them were in several businesses simultaneously. If a customer absolutely insisted on paying the merchant in bales of cotton rather than in cash (as in the West a customer might pay in buffalo hides and in the Northwest in fur pelts), the merchant was not inclined to refuse the business and send the customer to a competitor. Nothing if not adaptable, he took the barter merchandise, as he had occasionally done even as a peddler, and sold it as profitably as he could. If it happened often enough, this led to his becoming a cotton broker or fur trader in addition to a retailer.

There were a few Memphis Jews in the professions (including the self-styled doctors Spiegel and Reinach, who advertised themselves as "Resident Physicians and the most successful cancer operations [sic] in the world") but most were small storekeepers, who dealt in clothing and dry goods, in groceries, and in hardware—the only businesses in Memphis, except for cotton, that totaled over $1 million a year.

Until the Civil War, there was little anti-Semitism, perhaps because there were so few Jews; in Memphis, as in Nashville, the members of the synagogue numbered fewer than 100. But the war brought to Memphis one of the few clearly anti-Semitic acts by the United States. General Ulysses S. Grant issued General Order No. 11 of December 17, 1862, expelling all Jews from the department of Tennessee within twenty-four hours after the is- suance of the order, because "the Jews as a class [were] violating every regulation of trade established by the Treasury Depart- ment."

Grant's order was unjustly discriminatory in implying that the Jews were different. Like the majority of the city's other white citizens, most of its Jews were intensely loyal to the Confederate cause and did not become less so after the city was captured by Grant late in June of 1862. Wars help business communities that are not ravaged, and Memphis suffered almost no war damage. Once the city was captured, not only such necessities as medicine and salt but also such luxuries as cigars and coffee flowed freely downriver from Pittsburgh and Cincinnati. The Memphis mer- chants, Jewish and Gentile alike, found it as gloriously profitable as it was patriotic to smuggle these goods into the increasingly beleaguered Confederacy.

Dead mules were hauled south from the city, their bellies packed full of quinine, because very few people object to anyone hauling a dead mule *away*. And the increased number of funeral processions that found it necessary to pass out into the country in order to reach "family graveyards" beyond the Union lines was quite extraordinary. The brilliant and furious General Sher- man declared that Memphis was far more valuable to the South after its capture than before.

But with the South's blockaded cotton so severely needed in the North, and the salt essential to curing bacon bringing $100 a barrel just south of Memphis, Union officers, ex-slaves, and, of course, all the city's merchants joined in the booming and illegal trade that flowed both ways.

The injustice of Grant's order was that it was directed only at a small minority of the smugglers; indeed, it delighted the city's Gentile merchants, whose business it temporarily increased.

In 1863, when Jews complained about the order to President Lincoln, he promptly had it canceled because, as General H. W. Halleck wired Grant, "it . . . proscribed an entire religious class, some of whom are fighting in our ranks."

In both the Union and Confederate forces, there were considerable numbers of Jewish volunteers; and, as in many Christian families, there were those Jewish families whose loyalties were painfully divided. In Knoxville, Bertha Ochs, the mother of the future publisher of *The New York Times*, was a strong supporter of the Confederacy—her brother was in its army—but her husband enlisted in the 52nd Ohio Infantry and came out of the war a Union captain.

Like Grant's, many men's prejudice against Jews as a race has often not precluded their friendship with individual Jews. Typically, Grant, after he was elected President, offered to appoint as Secretary of the Treasury his old friend Joseph Seligman, who in little more than twenty years had worked his way up from just another Jewish immigrant foot peddler to one of the most powerful bankers in America.

Not the least remarkable thing about these Jews, who wisely would not have dared to fight the many injustices they had fled, was how quickly they learned to fight in America. Their traditional sense of humor, which had helped such men in Europe, also helped them to adapt to their great, wild, free new country. The police and the courts in America were sufficiently less terrifying than in Europe that a few of the men even felt secure enough to enjoy disturbing the peace, by "indulging in a little fisticuff on the street" or "by throwing eggs upon a house kept by Rebecca Shell for infamous purposes."

After the war, more young French and German Jews, courageous and lucky enough to escape from their limited lives at home, found their way to Memphis, including nineteen-year-old Isaac Goldsmith and his brother Jacob, who was two years younger.

Their uncle, Louis Ottenheimer, had come to America before

the war. He had lived in the back of a tiny log cabin in the front of which he had kept a "last-chance" provisions store at the frontier crossroads of Taylor's Creek, Arkansas. Here, pioneers in covered wagons bound for the "Western lands" could buy overlooked clothespins or calf weaners or a washboard. After a few years of this lonely life, he had made enough money to open a small store in Memphis. It prospered sufficiently that in 1867 he could visit his family at Hainstadt in Baden, and bring his two nephews back with him to Memphis, to work in his store and live in his home.

The nephews proved to be appropriately industrious and intelligent clerks. They worked from before the store opened for business at seven o'clock in the morning until however late was necessary after it closed at ten or eleven at night. Very soon the brothers were obviously more than earning their board and their $10 a month salaries. But Jacob was so ungrateful and saucy as to fall in love with his employer's daughter, Dora, and she was so foolish as to return the clerk's love. Because this contradicted her father's plans for her, he sent her 1,000 miles north to school in Philadelphia.

Jacob was no longer welcome to live in Ottenheimer's home or to work in his store, and family loyalty required that Isaac follow his younger brother. With the almost $500 they had saved in the three years since their arrival, they opened their own tiny store at 81 Beale Street and lived there as well. The "store" was scarcely more than a long, dimly lighted room, some 15 by 60 feet in all.

For the Jewish peddler or shopkeeper, the first customer every day is of symbolic, indeed superstitious, importance. If the customer buys, it will be a good day; if the first sale is lost, it bodes ill. With the very first customer in a brand-new enterprise, the importance grows geometrically.

As Jacob loved to tell the story in his later years, on the morning the store first opened—its stock looking pitifully meager even in so limited a space—he stood at the open door, grateful that at least it had not rained and alternately hoping for and dreading the arrival of the first customer. He saw a little girl turn off Main Street. She headed down Beale. She did not pass by I. Goldsmith & Bro., but instead entered their tiny store and bought the two spools of cotton thread that her mother had sent her out for. As Loretta Pool grew up and even after she married, she received every Christmas a finer gift than the year before from Jacob Goldsmith for fifty-one years until she died in 1921.

The store's business prospered. Five years later, it was clear even to Louis Ottenheimer that the twenty-five-year-old Jacob's prospects were good and since his now twenty-year-old Dora was still in love, he allowed them to marry.

Memphis in 1878 was little better than any city of the Middle Ages 500 years earlier. It did not provide sewers, garbage removal, or even pure water, and in the unpaved streets (except for a very few in the business district paved with wood blocks), filth, both human and animal, stagnated and stank in the summer sun. Not until the turn of the century would it be understood that yellow fever, also known as Negro Vomito or Black Vomit, could only be transmitted by the bite of the *Aedes aegypti* mosquito that multiplied in the stagnant pools.

When in the summer of 1878 it became evident that the outbreak of yellow fever was far worse than those of 1855, 1867, and 1873, much of the city was sprinkled with lime, the streets were washed with carbolic acid, and cannons were fired "to clear the air of miasma." But the epidemic raged on, and some 30,000 citizens fled (by boat, train, horse, and on foot) as far as St. Louis or to makeshift camps in the country to which many refugees were soon turned back at gunpoint by terrified people living along the escape routes. Of the fewer than 20,000 who remained in the city, only some 6,000 were white; two-thirds of these died. Of the nearly 14,000 blacks, almost 1,000 died.

Dr. William J. Armstrong reported: "The number of sick exceeds anything you can imagine. . . . We poor doctors stand by abashed at the perfect uselessness of our remedies. . . . I tell you it breaks the stoutest hearts." And the Hebrew Hospital Association account described "whole families down sick at one time and in one room with no relative or friend to even pass them a glass of water to quench the thirst caused by the burning fever."

All businesses and even the churches closed. Funerals were forbidden. In six weeks, Jack Walsh, the undertaker for paupers, buried 2,500 bodies. But finally, with a severe frost on October 20, the epidemic ended. At least 17,600 of the 19,000 who had remained in the city had caught the fever, and some 5,150 had died.

Among the few heroes who had voluntarily stayed to tend the stricken and who themselves died of the fever were Nathan D. Menken, whose store until then was the most important in the city, and an even more successful entrepreneur, Anna Cook, whose Mansion House on Gayoso Street was the finest brothel in Memphis. Sending her girls out of the city, she herself had stayed, opened her elegant rooms to the fever victims, and nursed them until she died in September.

Both Goldsmith brothers had fled with their families to St. Louis, where a number of the wholesalers offered to help them open a new store. But in the fall, they returned to Memphis and reopened their store.

Beale Street was then the best retail street in town—and the liveliest. The best customers were the planters from Arkansas and the Delta country of Mississippi, who several times a year drove their wagons to Memphis to buy the essential supplies that no peddlers could bring them: sheeting and other fabrics, plow handles, shovels, and all kinds of hardware; canned and dry groceries and white flour, as well as delicacies and luxuries. If on the trip before winter a man forgot to buy double-breasted, double-backed, all-wool undershirts, he would be cold all winter. If he forgot to buy enough coffee, the plantation would run out and there would be no more until spring. There was no corner drugstore and no local supermarket, and in many areas the roads in winter were impassable even to the hardiest and hungriest peddler.

It usually took all day for a planter to reach Memphis, where he arrived in the late afternoon or evening. He left his rig in

Fred Schwanz's or some other wagon yard behind the Beale Street stores, then unhitched his horse and tied it to the back of his wagon, into which he had poured some feed (unless he was a freeloader who put out no feed for his own horse but tied it so loosely that it could pull free and eat from various other wagons). He then took his harness and tack (so that they would not be stolen) to a storekeeper to keep and also left the list of his planned purchases with him.

Next, he proceeded to a bar or saloon—in those days there were fourteen bartenders on duty at Gallina's bar—and then either to a hotel or a brothel.

The following morning, or several mornings later, he would reappear at the store, sometimes with his partner from the brothel if she had proven especially pleasing, in which case he might buy her a lavish assortment of gifts. He checked over the merchandise that the storekeeper had assembled from the list: Saturday-night bathtubs, stove wicks, long-handled underwear (different for each sex), cowbells, pig-snout rings, skeleton keys, patent medicines, 100-pound bags of sugar, bolts of flannel, gingham, linen, and silk, barrels of whiskey, tea, and books, along with whatever else would be needed or wanted until the next trip many months later. These were then carefully packed in the wagon, the merchant was paid, and the planter headed for home.

In American cities and towns from about 1860 to 1900, there were many small stores, sometimes dozens of them. By the end of World War I, two or three or at most four of these in each town had grown into the important department stores, while the other little stores had disappeared. One essential of a successful retail enterprise was endless hard work. Not all of these storekeepers, Jewish or Gentile, could continue to work for twelve to fifteen hours a day, day after day, year after year. Some preferred to play cards, to drink, to chase women, or, once they had assembled a small fortune, to invest in real estate or in some other business that was not such an irreducible aggregate of small details. Some were unlucky. They had no children to help carry the burden, or illness struck them down.

But among those who both worked hard and who also had good luck, the difference between those who built big department stores and those who did not was boldness.

Occasionally this boldness manifested itself in merchandising, as when Al Neiman and Herbert Marcus determined to stock their store with more expensive merchandise than other Dallas merchants dared, years before the East Texas oil fields had been discovered.

Fred Lazarus, Jr., of Columbus, Ohio, put together a chain of great department stores that spread from Filene's and Bloomingdale's in the East to Magnin's and Bullock's in the West. He often explained that between his grandfather's men's clothing shop and the railroad depot in Columbus, there were more than 100 other little stores, and that the most important of the many reasons why the F. & R. Lazarus store finally became the only large department store in town was his grandfather's decision, in an era when men who wore suits had them tailor-made, that the moment of the ready-made suit had arrived. The clothing factories in the North had learned to pour out uniforms for the Union army. When the war ended, Lazarus ordered a dangerously large inventory of their unproven ready-made civilian suits. But as he had anticipated, when the discharged soldiers came home and found that they didn't have to wait to get rid of their hated uniforms if they went to Lazarus's, that they could have a new suit in the few minutes it took to hem trouser legs and shorten sleeves, that's where they all went. It gave Lazarus's not only a sudden small fortune but also a very important lead in reputation as the place to go.

More usually the crucial boldness manifested itself less in merchandising than in real estate terms, such as moving from an old, established retail area to a new one that promised to be the best in the future, or renting or building a much bigger store than those of the competitors. Some storekeepers went broke doing this. But for others, it gave them a head start and a favorable reputation with the city's customers that the less bold storekeepers never caught up with.

In 1881, the Goldsmith brothers moved their store to Main

Street. Four years later, after Isaac had died and Jacob had bought his interest, the store was moved to an even larger building on Main and Gayoso. Then, in 1892, Jacob moved across Main into a new five-story building so much too large for his current needs that he could scarcely fill the first two floors, even after larding out the merchandise on the shelves with empty boxes. This new store was built for Jacob by Napoleon Hill, one of the more colorful entrepreneurs of Memphis, and the manner of their making a deal is revealing of both men. The old building on Hill's property across from Goldsmith's store caught fire and Hill and Goldsmith stood together watching it burn. Goldsmith's lease would soon be up for renewal. Hill would now have to build a new building. So while the old one burned to the ground, the two men struck a bargain.

Abraham Schwab came to Memphis from Alsace-Lorraine. He married Dora Ottenheimer's sister Sarah and opened a store at 163 Beale Street in 1876. But he could never bring himself to move from Beale Street. Indeed, his little store is still there, as is his grandson, selling cotton picker's knee pads, magic dragon's blood, and policy books on how to beat the numbers to its now virtually all-black clientele.

For the bold there was always a risk in moving boldly; but there was also a risk in not moving. It was just less obvious.

To make a small store grow so that its sales increased and it both needed and could afford more space, the owner must attend to literally tens of thousands of details. He had to see that he kept in stock all the sizes and colors of whatever merchandise he regularly carried so that his customers could expect to find it whenever they came to the store. He had personally to satisfy himself of the quality of the merchandise as it arrived and before it was put on sale because—strange as it must seem in the present era of disposable everything—quality was absolutely essential to success. Any customer who was displeased with the quality of her purchase was not only certain to return it but also likely thereafter to go to another shop where she would not have the bother of returning her purchases.

As a peddler, the store owner had first learned how essential quality was. He had discovered the hard way that it was far better for him to pay his supplier a bit more in order to get the best yarn, thimbles, darning needles, and combs than to be turned angrily away (after trudging many miles and often in bad weather) from the door of a former customer whose new button hook had snapped the first time she used it and whose anger had grown month after month as she repeatedly broke her nails buttoning her shoes.

Such work as checking inventory, inspecting for quality, book-keeping, and paying bills was done before the store opened or after it closed. While it was open, the store owner could not be in an office or a stockroom but had to be "on the floor." There he supervised his salespeople to make certain that they gave the proper service, and he made many sales himself, often to custom-ers who would believe no one else or who would have considered themselves insulted had they not been waited on by "the boss."

On the floor he also watched carefully for stealing, whether by customers or by employees. An employee who was caught stealing or, in those days before unions, even suspected of it, was usually fired on the spot. But a customer was treated with considerably more care. "In the early days," Jacob loved to explain, "many of our customers paid by barter—with butter or eggs or whatever they had—and one day I noticed a customer making off with a three-dollar ball of butter I had taken in earlier in the day. He put the butter on top of his head, jammed on his hat, and headed for the door. Instead of accusing him of stealing, I called him over and began chatting with him, but as we talked, I edged him little by little back to the big potbellied stove in the middle of the room.

"It got hotter and hotter by that stove, but I kept talking and the butter kept melting. It trickled down from under his hat, down his neck and over his ears. When he nodded his head in agreement with what I said, it poured down over his eyes and dripped off the end of his nose. I lost the butter, but I had much more than three dollars' worth of fun."

It was frequently a cause of wonder that well into the 1920s and 1930s, long after their little shops had developed into enormous establishments, these first-generation merchants spent so many hours every day standing on the first floor greeting customers—not only any of the several thousand they knew by name but also the many more thousands they did not. They understood that the store owner himself was the most important asset he had.

Jacob did not know every soul in Memphis who had enough money to buy a shirtwaist or a collar button or at least to look, but virtually all of them knew him by sight. And saying "Good morning, Mr. J." gave a citizen the same sense of importance, the same momentary glow of status, as seeing Admiral George Dewey or John L. Sullivan or Adelina Patti pass in a parade. The glow could be rekindled by telling everybody you met for weeks, "I spoke with Mr. Goldsmith the other day."

If you had a bit of courage and perhaps a moment to wait, you could easily get him to help select a necktie for your husband or just the right handbag to go with your fall outfit or your child's first doll. And *that* you could talk about all your life, to your children and even your grandchildren.

Mayors usually came and went and were soon forgotten, and not infrequently some aura of dishonesty or at least shady practice attached to their names. The president of the bank, however powerful and rich, was usually unknown to most citizens. But "Mr. Goldsmith" in Memphis or "Mr. Thalhimer" in Richmond, "Mr. Halle" in Cleveland or "Mr. Weinstock" in Sacramento was known to virtually every citizen in his community—and he was an enduring public figure.

To most people he seemed an American hero. He was a success. He had made money. He was upright. He had built a great store that employed hundreds of people. And from that store had come the citizen's Flexible Flyer or first long pants or long dress or the first baby's layette.

For the store owner himself, this daily duty on the first floor was fun. It was fun to be the center of attention and admiration, a sage and even a wit. It was fun to escape from the big eighth-floor office and its decisions. And it was a habit, dating from those days of the original 15-foot-front shop, when he was "on the floor" all day, every day.

One winter afternoon when I walked onto the ready-to-wear floor at A. Harris & Company, I saw a customer who was an old friend of my mother's. She was surrounded by dozens of coats, on racks, on chairs, and she was obviously undecided.

"Help me, Leon," she called to me. "Which of these coats is best for me?"

I surveyed the battlefield, then picked up a red wool chinchilla coat from one of the chairs and declared with the absolute authority of a twenty-three-year-old, "If you take any coat but this one, you're wrong. It was made for you."

"It's the one I wore into the store!" she squealed delightedly, and left.

Although the saleswoman whom I had cost a commission was justifiably furious, even my fatuous advice was probably in the long run good for the store. The woman told the story to everyone in Dallas for years because it was so funny, but she also told them that she never again bought a coat without asking my advice because she knew I'd tell her the truth.

When a store owner grew old, he often spent all the time he could on the sales floor because that was how he met the people and found out what was going on. The store had become so large that he could no longer see with his own sharp eyes most of the merchandise and most of the sales. Therefore, he now had reluctantly to rely on others. He was isolated by executives and relatives who were often inclined only to agree with and flatter him. Now being on the floor kept him on his toes.

One day as Jacob Goldsmith was watching a hearteningly large crowd that had come to a big basement sale, he was approached by an old black man he had known for years, "Uncle Robert."

"Mr. J.," complained Uncle Robert, "I seen these same identical dollar shirts as you got on sale here for seventy-nine cents over to Lowenstein's and they're selling them two for a dollar. Won't you sell me these two for a dollar?"

"Why didn't you buy them at Lowenstein's, Uncle Robert?"

"Because they didn't have my size," answered the black man.

"Well, when we don't have your size," laughed Goldsmith, "we sell them *three* for a dollar."

In their dealings with blacks in the South, the Jewish peddlers and storekeepers rarely risked endangering their own safety, but their way of treating blacks frequently differed considerably from that of the typical Southern white. In the days before "one price," these Jews bargained with the blacks, whereas Gentiles dealt with blacks, if at all, only on a take-it-or-leave-it basis. And Jewish merchants usually called their black customers "Mr. Flynn" or "Mrs. Watson," instead of using only their family name as was the more common practice.

The South was segregated, so the stores were segregated; the Jewish merchant, like all employers, paid his black employees as little as possible, just as he did his white employees. But because the Jews' own days as slaves in Egypt and their own mistreatment as a minority for centuries was never far from their thoughts, they frequently dealt less harshly than many other white Southerners with the blacks.

These Southern storekeepers often had a bad conscience about refusing to serve blacks except in segregated areas of the store. This bad conscience is revealed by a story that was told by many storekeepers in many versions. When an obviously well-to-do black woman came into the Better Millinery Salon at Neiman-Marcus and took a seat, the manager, rather than risking a scene by refusing to serve her, showed her only one hat, told her that it was the only one he had in her size, and that it cost $250.

The black woman carefully tried the hat on and then suggested, "The price is fine, but don't you think it makes me look Jewish?"

After the War and Reconstruction, the exploitation and consequent hatred of the "niggers" on the part of many Southern whites diverted much of the hostility that might otherwise have been directed at Jews. But because the population of the South was so homogeneous compared to the mixed immigrant makeup of the East or the ever-changing population of Western frontier towns, these resolutely indigestible Jews stood out more there. The Fundamentalist Protestantism of the South could not lightly dismiss God's Holy Word in the Old Testament that described His Chosen People as heroes; but the same fundamentalism bred hatred of the Christ-killers who so peevishly refused to be born again and accept their Savior, thereby wickedly calling into question the validity of the New Testament.

Fear of anti-Semitism was the main reason that even after their stores had become among the largest business enterprises in a city, many of these Jewish merchants often tried to avoid taking a public stand on controversial political issues. But, of course, they did not avoid politicians. Politicians fixed real estate and *ad valorem* taxes as well as public transportation and traffic patterns. Politicians controlled the police who determined where trucks were or were not allowed to park and could also usually be counted on to break up unionization or strike efforts and forcibly convince union organizers and leaders to leave town.

Not surprisingly, therefore, Jacob Goldsmith called himself a good friend of Edward Hull Crump, "Boss" Crump, "the Red Snapper." Goldsmith supported Mayor Crump financially and Crump supported Goldsmith's interests accordingly. Quite often their interests in a particular matter were the same. Crump, a frequent gambler, was against horse racing in Memphis because he thought it was bad for the citizens. Goldsmith was against horse racing because it hurt sales and the collection of charge accounts. During Crump's reign, there was no horse racing in Memphis.

Crump insisted on low streetcar fares because they brought him votes. Goldsmith knew that they brought customers to his store. Crump had an insurance agency that sold fire insurance to the city's big real estate owners and insisted that the city maintain a first-rate fire department, which each month thoroughly inspected his insured properties. Goldsmith had valuable property to protect.

Goldsmith's success was due in the main to his own efforts.

But unexpectedly a change in the circumstances of his major competitor made a significant difference.

The last of the Lowenstein brothers, Elias, died in 1919 in his Jefferson Street mansion, whose gargoyles on the roof, Italian stained glass, and splendid mantels and fireplaces had made it one of the city's showplaces. With the brothers gone, the store was sold to the Newman family of New Orleans who owned the Maison Blanche store there, and it suffered thereafter from different absentee owners—to the benefit of Goldsmith's.

Common to many of these first-generation storekeepers who built great businesses were long life, long and happy marriages, and many sons and daughters to help in minding the store. Jacob and Dora were married for fifty-eight years and had three sons and four daughters. Not only all the sons and grandsons in such families but also any sons-in-law or grandsons-in-law who wanted in were welcomed into the business. But female heirs inherited real estate or assets other than stock in the store; that was reserved to male heirs.

As matters of authority and rights, women were only marginally, if at all, less discriminated against in the Jewish tradition than in any other. Even today among Orthodox Jews the prayer is heard, "Blessed art thou, O Lord Our God, who hast not made me a woman." But as a practical matter, the power exerted by many Jewish women was frequently no less important because it was exerted informally and privately. There has always been a tradition of the strong-willed Jewish wife and mother who will not be gainsaid, and every family has its favorite tales of such women.

Jacob Goldsmith's favorite daughter-in-law, the former Aimee Landman, was married to his oldest son, Fred. Shortly after she returned from her honeymoon, Aimee, the beautiful, independent, and spoiled daughter of a whiskey millionaire, walked into the store where Jacob greeted her and remarked, "That's an exquisite lace jabot. Did you buy it here in the store?"

"No, I bought it at Marshall Field," answered Aimee.

"Now that you're married to a Goldsmith," the patriarch explained, "I think you had best buy what you wear from Goldsmith's."

"My husband works for his money," replied Aimee, "and earns every penny of it, and where I spend it is nobody's damn business!"

Jacob loved the story, repeated it endlessly, and was honored when he was invited to his daughter-in-law's house where she unquestionably ruled the roost.

Dora Goldsmith and her daughters and daughters-in-law all stayed out of the management of the store. But Jacob's sons, "Mr. Fred," "Mr. Elias" (pronounced "alias"), and "Mr. Leo" were all in the business, and the grandsons were sent off one by one to Culver Military Academy. Then to train to be storekeepers they went either to the Wharton School at the University of Pennsylvania or for on-the-job training at another great department store such as Kaufmann's in Pittsburgh.

These Jewish merchant families were the major newspaper advertisers in their cities. Not only were they rich but also somehow permanently foreign and mysterious, regardless of how long they had lived in the community, so that they were the subject of even more curiosity than the Gentile rich. As a result, the merchants, their wives, their children, and even their servants, were frequently featured in newspaper stories.

Although they were not members of Memphis society nor of its exclusive clubs, they were often to be found in the society section of the papers on occasions no more newsworthy, for example, than young Fred Goldsmith, Jr.'s, return home for Christmas from Culver Military Academy. Of more widespread interest were the frequent visits of fashion celebrities, such as "Hair Style Dictator" Antoine, the famous and shrewdly eccentric Paris hairdresser who relentlessly revealed such secrets as that he slept in a glass coffin whose lining he had recently changed from blond antelope to white wool. These well-known fashion figures were often pictured in the papers with the store owner or his current wife.

Even more than weddings, divorces were news, especially if a divorcing wife intimated what "indignities" and "cruelties" she had allegedly suffered or, if like Wanda E. Goldsmith, the wife of Elias, Jr., she was awarded a $531,000 alimony trust.

The store owners tried to avoid unfavorable publicity; but if they felt sufficiently that they were being taken advantage of, they were willing to fight. According to the custom of the day, the gallant husband invariably allowed his wife to sue for the divorce regardless of fault. Yet the handsome and ordinarily equable Jack L. Goldsmith sued his first wife, Jen, and sought custody of their two-year-old daughter, Joan. Divorced in September 1937, Jack and Jen remarried three months later and divorced again a year after—confirming Dr. Johnson's dictum that a second marriage represents the triumph of hope over experience. Nothing if not hopeful, Jack would go on to take two more wives of his own, the last eminently satisfactory—to date.

When a sixty-seven-year-old maid in Fred Goldsmith, Jr.'s, home killed the yardman with a well-placed 410-gauge shotgun blast through a den window or when Elias J. Goldsmith's chauffeur crashed into a police car in a 90-mile-an-hour chase through eleven red lights and six stop signs, such incidents made interesting newspaper reading, sometimes for several days.

But the reputations of both the family and the store were far more lastingly affected by such actions as Fred Goldsmith's support of the failing American Savings Bank. When in 1926 the president of the bank killed himself at the bank, his brother-in-law, Abe Plough, called Fred Goldsmith to tell him. Plough, who had begun by peddling drugs and medicines door to door in Memphis, was already well on his way to becoming the dominant figure in Schering-Plough Corporation and supposedly the richest man in the South. Fred Goldsmith suggested and Plough agreed that it would be a disaster if the bank's small depositors lost their Christmas savings accounts. The two of them underwrote some $232,000 of checks to pay the depositors who would otherwise have had no Christmas. Even half a century later, this kind of gesture is not forgotten in Memphis.

These Jewish merchants practiced, or at least professed, a religion in which tradition was enormously important. In America's South, Midwest, and West, where their stores were frequently as old as the community itself, the men and their institutions were often parts of the community's own tradition; at the very least, they had helped to create it. Soon after he moved from Beale to Main Street, for example, Jacob had originated the "Spirit of Christmas" parade. In the days before radio and television, street festivals had great importance to adults as well as children, and this parade became the most important such event in Memphis, remaining so even into the 1960s.

Jacob Goldsmith died at eighty-three on November 24, 1933, "just before the peak Christmas business," he would have said. Dora died one year later, on November 23.

Long before Jack L. Goldsmith became president of the store his grandfather had started, he had learned that he had better not make any significant changes in it before preparing the city's citizens, who considered it "our" store. He faced the same kind of problem when he bought the badly rundown Gayoso Hotel, into which he planned to expand the store.

Fifteen presidents of the United States had been guests at the Gayoso, as had even locally more important men, such as Henry Clay and John C. Calhoun; but what made every brick of the hotel sacred to Memphis citizens was an incident one early August morning in 1863, when Confederate General Nathan Bedford Forrest's cavalrymen rode their horses into the hotel lobby. It was a daring sortie designed to capture the city's Union commandant, who was quartered in the hotel but unfortunately for them had bedded elsewhere the night before.

In the tradition of his grandfather's sidewalk deal with Napoleon Hill, when Jack heard at 7:30 one Saturday morning in 1948 that the hotel was about to be leased to a hotel chain for twenty years, he bought it immediately for $1.2 million ("Luckily it was raining or I'd have been off fishing"). That same morning he offered it to the family for the same price.

If, however, they thought he had been too precipitate, he said he would keep it himself until they were certain they needed it to expand the store. But in that case, he said, it would cost them $2 million. They took it on the same day.

"We closed it down gradually, only twenty rooms at a time," said Jack, "so there was no shock. But what I worried most about was how the hell to get rid of two big murals depicting Hernando DeSoto's discovery of the Mississippi in 1541 and his burial in the river. I'd have been delighted to burn the damn things, but I didn't dare. Then I got a bright idea and gave them to the DeSoto County Courthouse at Hernando, Mississippi. My God, what a relief!"

But tradition or no, in 1969 Jack sold the family store to Fred Lazarus, Jr.'s, Federated Department Stores for $13.5 million. "The need for more and more fixed capital to build branch stores would soon make it impossible for the members of the family to pay inheritance taxes," Jack explained. "I held the Lazari off for eleven years, but the day of the family store was over."

In Memphis, as virtually everywhere else when a national chain took over a family store, support for the local arts and educational and charitable institutions was reduced from the generous levels that had been acceptable to family stockholders but ostensibly not to the out-of-town stockholders who had bought the store because of its local reputation but who now apparently cared only how much profit generated in Memphis could be siphoned out of the city and into their pockets.

In recent increasingly skeptical, indeed cynical, decades, some have suggested that the scrupulous honesty and often lavish generosity of the early Jewish merchants had no moral basis, but was instead a matter of policy that assured the financial credit they needed and was, in addition, a very effective form of advertising.

Whatever his private feelings about such a view, Jacob Goldsmith would have been far too proud to contradict it. In fact, he might have told about the poor black woman he once saw repeatedly poking a stick through the iron grating in the sidewalk in front of the store. "I watched a good while and then I asked her what she was doing. She said she was trying to get back a quarter she'd dropped, so I naturally reached in my pocket and gave her a quarter. She thanked me and left. I then went down to the basement to see if she had really dropped a quarter and under the grating there it was. And next to it was a silver dollar."

6

The Riches of Atlanta

The gentleman will please remember that when his half civilized ancestors were hunting the wild boar in Silesia, mine were princes of the earth.
                    —Judah Benjamin, replying to the slur of a
                        Senator of German descent

Perhaps more than any other storekeeping family anywhere in America, the Riches created in their community the conviction that their store was not merely a store but an institution—like a church, a school, a family—and one whose honesty, compassion, and credit the individual members of that community could count on absolutely. More than any bank or public utility or branch of local or state government, Rich's was perceived by virtually everyone within a radius of several hundred miles of Atlanta as reliable, responsive, and humane. And virtue was more than just its own reward. With its great reputation came great business, until finally no other store in the South even approached Rich's success.

The Riches themselves were latecomers, but there had been Jews in Georgia since the beginning. In 1733, the same year that James Oglethorpe had arrived to found a refuge for imprisoned British debtors, another ship with some forty Jews also arrived in Savannah. Among them was Dr. Samuel Ribeiro Nuñes, who upon landing saved the colony from a raging epidemic and so earned Oglethorpe's recommendation to the colony's directors in London that the Jews be allowed to stay.

It was, of course, their usefulness that made these Sephardic Jews as well as the other early refugees—Welsh, Scottish, Piedmontese, Swiss, and a group from Salzburg—welcome in Georgia. It had always been thus. In 803, in the first record of Jews in Salzburg, Archbishop Arno had requested the settlement of a Jewish physician in his archbishopric. Need for their skills as merchants and bankers in the centuries that followed had brought other Jews to the diocese. But need can lead to resentment as well as to gratitude, and at the beginning of the fifteenth century all those Jews in Salzburg who were not burned at the stake were driven out and fled to other towns in Austria and Hungary.

Most of America's great Jewish store builders came from Germany; but a few—especially in the South and West, including Birmingham's Louis Pizitz from Russia and Arizona's "Big Mike" Goldwater from Poland—were from Eastern Europe. Even lower on the social scale, if that was possible, than Russian and Polish Jews, in the eyes of German Jews, were Jews from Hungary. It was there that Morris Rich had started life in the town of Kaschau, now Košice, in Czechoslovakia. With his older brother, William, Morris came to America in 1859 at the age of twelve.

For six years Morris peddled Yankee notions in Ohio at the same time that John D. Rockefeller's father was peddling patent medicines there. This Hungarian Horatio Alger did well enough that he and William could bring over their two other brothers, Emanuel and Daniel. Then, after the Civil War ended, at a time when many Southern Jews were moving north from the defeated South—the Strauses from Georgia, the Lehmans from Alabama, the Baruchs from South Carolina—the Riches moved to Georgia. On May 28, 1867, three years before Georgia was readmitted to the Union, the twenty-year-old Morris opened a store in Atlanta with $500 borrowed from William.

Just as the terrible fire in Chicago in 1871 made possible that great city by destroying it, so with the burning of Atlanta by Sherman's troops on November 15, 1864, its growth began in earnest. It had been nothing before the war, not even incorporated or named Atlanta until more than a century after Georgia's founding. But after the war it boomed, not as part of the antebellum cotton-plantation economy but as a new distribution and manufacturing center. And in the main, this new Atlanta was made by newcomers such as Morris Rich.

There were already dozens of stores there, owned by both Jews and non-Jews. For decades Chamberlin's remained the carriage-trade store until it failed in 1932. Keely's, Ryan's, and Dougherty's were for many years at least the equal of Rich's. Other stores could be more innovative; for example, in 1873 Regenstein's was the first to employ a woman as a salesperson. The woman, Mrs. Martha Owens, was the widow of a Union soldier. Advised by Julius Regenstein that in the South a lady simply did not go out to work, she told him that she was destitute and could not afford to be a lady. Furthermore, she insisted, she could sell his merchandise at least as well as any of his salesmen—and for twenty years she did.

But what made Rich's outlast most other stores and surpass all of them was its treatment of customers, its insistence that "People are more important than things." For decades in the South after the war, the second most hated creatures were the "carpet-baggers," outsiders who descended on the defeated South to cheat and blackguard their way to wealth. Even more hated than these were the "scalawags," those Southerners who cooperated with the parasitic carpetbaggers in fleecing the locals.

The Riches were the opposite of these. In each generation there were dozens of tales—the true stories often more remarkable than the apocryphal ones—of how Rich's resolutely, unremittingly, satisfied its customers no matter how unreasonable, outrageous, or provocative. The store refunded the full price of an unused pair of high-buttoned shoes thirty years old, of an unworn man's shirt ten years old, of a dead canary. It accepted for credit or exchange merchandise that customers had bought not at Rich's but from its competitors, because when a customer alleged that she had bought it at Rich's, the Riches did not propose to call her a liar.

A customer complained that a wedding cake, joyfully and completely devoured by the wedding guests, had been yellow inside instead of white inside as she had ordered. The store sent another cake, with an undeniably white inside, proving that she could eat her cake and have it, too.

Rich's insisted that it had no complaint department, that any employee, whether a salesperson or a bookkeeper, must accept goods for return without question—what came to be known as "You make your own adjustment at Rich's."

At Rich's as at other stores across America—most of which tried some version of this same policy—such a liberal program was very difficult to enforce because a store's employees usually felt that they were giving away *their* money, *their* profits, that *they* were being taken advantage of.

This employee reluctance to be taken for a sap led to what became the best-known dictum in American retailing. One day when the white-gloved, stiff-backed Marshall Field was walking through his great Chicago store, he came across one Lindsay T. Woodcock, an assistant manager, who was in the midst of a heated conversation with a female customer.

"What are you doing, sir?" demanded the furious Field.

"I am settling a complaint," offered the unfortunate Woodcock.

"No, you are not, sir," snapped Field. *"Give the lady what she wants!"*

Better than any other storekeepers, the Riches trained their employees to do precisely that. The store's liberal return policy (even today Rich's returns are 50 percent more than at most stores) was only one aspect of the family's insistence that the store must be run to suit the needs of its customers. Rich's credit policy was tolerant to a fault. If a farmer could pay his family's bill only once a year, when he was paid for his crop, that suited Rich's; if he couldn't manage even that in bad years, that too suited Rich's. To a quite startling degree the customers made not only their own merchandise adjustments but their own credit and payment program as well.

In the 1914 depression and again in the 1920s, when the price of cotton fell to unheard-of lows, Rich's advertised that it would buy and store bales at well above the market price and urged others to do the same. The farmers did not forget.

After the disastrous Atlanta fire of 1917, the store's open-handed credit policy was an important factor in the city's rehabilitation. The citizens did not forget.

In 1918 the store announced that it would accept at par Liberty bonds presented in payment of merchandise by patriotic Atlantans who were short of ready money. The beneficiaries did not forget.

And in 1930, when the virtually bankrupted city had no money to meet the schoolteachers' payroll, the store's president, Walter Rich (Emanuel and Bertha's son), called the mayor to suggest that the city issue scrip to pay the teachers, which the store would not only accept in payment but also cash at full value with no obligation that a penny be spent at the store. Rich's paid out $645,000 for this scrip and held it until the city could redeem it. The schoolteachers did not forget, nor their children, nor their grandchildren.

The determination that the store be an accepted and essential part of the community prompted hundreds of different actions every year, year after year, including such seemingly insignificant things as supplying uniforms, musical instruments, floats, bunting, flags, Japanese lanterns, sports equipment or megaphones for the baseball team, the marching band, the Masonic picnic, the firemen's ball, the pig, sheep, cattle, horse, or flower show. Every church, grade school, high school, ladies' book club, poetry reading society, barbershop quartet, debating league, sewing circle, and china-painting club had at least one annual printed program that required an advertisement, in addition to the gift of door prizes and the purchase of raffle tickets or baked goods or handmade felt pen wipers.

Some activities that Rich's sponsored—especially in the store itself—were obviously beneficial to it as well as to the citizenry—

classes in knitting, embroidery, crocheting, sewing, dressmaking, cooking, canning, gardening, contract bridge, and mah-jongg. In 1917 Miss Lulie T. Hall, a registered nurse, began advising expectant mothers on infant care and, if asked, helped to select a layette. Mrs. Daisy Browne not only gave free needlework classes to adults but urged mothers to send in their children to learn tatting and how to make flowers.

In the Bible Belt careful attention had to be paid to such matters as contract bridge lessons in the store, because many people considered card-playing sinful, even if not done on the Sabbath. When as early as 1914 Rich's used live corset models in the store to demonstrate correct fitting, it was a daring, indeed a risky thing to do. But it was successful—it caused talk but not scandal.

In addition to building sales by bringing women into the store where many of them then bought merchandise, these teaching activities were often an important part of the building of America's "consumer society." America's department stores constituted an absolutely essential link in the technological chain between the inventor/manufacturer and the consumer. The far-off creator was at the least unknown, perhaps even a flimflam artist, and certainly not to be trusted; the local merchant, on the other hand, was well known and would stand behind what he sold. Especially if it was some "new-fangled" thing that might not function as well or last as long as what one was accustomed to. Only the imprimatur of the local storekeeper made the risk worth taking.

"Why trouble and make up underwear for yourself or children when you can go to M. Rich & Bro. and get them ready-made at much less than you can make them up for?" And if they shrink or discolor or itch excessively or if in any other particular, real or imaginary, they "just don't do right," the store will take them back. The family store was the *sine qua non* for ready-made underwear and similar giant technological steps along America's road of progress and perfectability.

Of course, the activities of the Riches did not alone account for their enormous success. If they had started and stayed in Savannah or Macon, they could not have flourished to such an extent. Atlanta was a boom town: $3 million in trade in 1860, $8 million in 1873, $40 million in 1878. And it was not a one-crop or one-industry town; it manufactured railroad spikes and candy, bags and barrels, and what it did not manufacture, it distributed to its neighbor states. But this did not account for why Rich's survived when other stores expired, nor why it steadily put so great a distance between itself and the few surviving competitors. What the Riches did better than anyone else was to identify their store with their area; not only to advertise it as "a Southern Institution," but to make it just that.

Even more successfully than their native-born competitors, these recent Hungarian immigrants wrapped themselves in the flags of Georgia and the Confederacy. All Atlanta merchants contributed to local institutions such as Georgia Tech; but if Tech had a championship football team, if Georgian Ty Cobb had an especially glorious season in the big leagues with the Detroit Tigers, if Atlanta golfer Bobby Jones outdid himself, frequently the store's advertising somehow made it appear at least partially another triumph of the brothers Rich.

I was in Atlanta in 1939 when the premiere of the film of Margaret Mitchell's *Gone with the Wind* attracted almost as much attention as Sherman's burning of the city seventy-five years earlier. My Aunt Irma, an intimate of the Riches, teased their general manager, Frank Neely: "I enjoyed the film, but I was surprised that you didn't cast Dick [Rich] as Rhett Butler instead of Clark Gable and that there were no Rich's labels in Scarlett O'Hara's clothes."

Especially after 1925, when Macy's bought the Davison-Paxon store in Atlanta and then when Sears, Roebuck came to town, the Riches stressed mercilessly that theirs was the home-town store, "Atlanta Born, Atlanta Owned, Atlanta Managed." They were helped enormously when Macy's Jack Straus ingenuously informed an Atlanta dinner audience that his wife, the former Margaret Hollister, was a descendant of William Tecumseh Sherman.

Robert W. Woodruff was the president of Coca-Cola, the only

Atlanta institution (except perhaps for the federal penitentiary there) better known than Rich's. Woodruff, who was a director of Rich's, was also on the board of Gimbel's. When Bernie Gimbel came to Atlanta as Woodruff's guest, the Coca-Cola tycoon gave him a dinner party to which he invited his friends from Rich's. The rumor ran through the city that, like Macy's and Sears, Gimbel's would invade Atlanta and the announcement would be made at the end of dinner. When Bernie rose to speak, however, he declared: "We have no intention of seeking out for ourselves a competitor as unbeatable as Rich's."

The one individual who was "Mr. Atlanta" during the second quarter of the twentieth century, who more than anyone else in the city determined what did and what did not happen there economically, politically, and educationally, was the chief executive officer of Rich's. But he was not a Rich. A mistaken belief usually found in these storekeeping dynasties—frequently quite contrary to all evidence—was that business ability is invariably transmissible in the genes. When once-great stores that were doing badly sold out to one of the chains, the new owners brought in expert, professional management. But vanity and false pride often made this impossible in a family-owned store. Not so with Rich's.

In 1924 it seemed to Walter Rich, a quiet, shy man with a cast in one eye, that the store might have overexpanded—and in a doubtful area downtown. It had also grown fat and careless with success. To straighten matters out, he hired Frank H. Neely, a forty-year-old mechanical engineer with not one day's experience in retailing.

A small-town boy from Rome, Georgia, Neely was raised from the age of four by relatives after his preacher father had died, leaving nine children and no money. An indifferent scholar until suddenly he was excited by an exhibition of farm machinery, Neely then applied himself, graduated with honors from Georgia Tech in 1904, and made a career for himself, first with Westinghouse Electric and then with Fulton Bag and Cotton Mills. When Walter Rich tried to hire him, Neely said, "You can't afford me."

"Name your own salary," replied Rich, and when Neely specified a figure they both knew was much higher than his salary at Fulton, Rich merely asked, "How soon can you come to work?"

In Atlanta there was no office Neely wanted that he did not get, from chairman of the board of the Sixth Federal Reserve Bank to the leadership of informal and often unnamed groups that determined where streets, schools, public transportation, or storm sewers would go. The city's important bankers, real estate men, politicians, and newspaper publishers all recognized Neely's power. It was said that newspaper proofs of his competitors' advertisements were delivered to him along with his own several days before they were due to run so that he was never surprised. Everyone, women no less than men, wanted to be his friend— and Neely loved friends.

To please Rae Schlesinger, whom he married in 1908, Neely converted to Judaism; but the non-Jews carefully took no notice and Neely enjoyed the best of both worlds. He was a member of and a generous contributor to Atlanta's German-Jewish synagogue that was named simply The Temple, just as the country club in Brookline, Massachusetts, is named The Country Club, as though it were the only one in the world. Neely was also a member of the Piedmont Driving Club, the most exclusive club in Atlanta, from which Jews were excluded. At the same time he was a member of the Standard Club that admitted only Jews. "Frank is an engineer," said a waggish member of Rich's board of directors, "and when he was circumcised in order to please Rae he saved the foreskin and designed a zipper for it. Now when he plays cards at the Driving Club he zips it on, and at the Standard, he zips it off."

Despite Oglethorpe's tolerance, there was a tradition of anti-Semitism in Georgia politics. When Raphael J. Moses, who had been a major in the Confederate army, ran for Congress in 1878, his opponent taunted him with being a Jew. Moses answered in a widely reprinted and praised Open Letter: "I feel it an honor to be one of a race whom persecution cannot crush . . . whom prejudice has in vain endeavored to subdue. . . . Would you honor me? Call me Jew. Would you place in unenviable prominence

your unchristian prejudices and narrow bigotry? Call me Jew."
But Moses lost the election.

Sex has historically played a significant role in race hatred in
America as elsewhere. Catholic priests and Mormon patriarchs
were said to commit unspeakable licentious atrocities. Depending
on the preferred sado-masochistic fantasies of the hater, Masons
were accused of disembowling, lashing, and raping recalcitrant
women. Not very surprisingly, some Southern men who during
and after slavery had abused black women were certain that black
men were ceaselessly planning to rape white women and many
white men secretly feared that their own particular white woman
would find sex with blacks more satisfactory.

The beautiful, dark, mysterious, virginally erotic, sexually desirable and desiring Jewess (usually with a rich wicked father) is a
constant of the literatures of the West—Marlowe's Abigail, Shakespeare's Jessica, Lope de Vega's Raquel, Racine's Bérénice. Her
ancestors fill the Bible on which rednecked Georgians were
raised—Dinah, the first rapee; Bathsheba, Judith, Salome, the
temptresses; and Mary Magdalene, the whore. Of the many American writers of fiction, none more fervidly than Thomas Wolfe
described this inevitable sexuality of Jewesses who "were as old
as nature, and as round as the earth: they had a curve in them.
. . . Female, fertile, yolky, fruitful as the earth, and ready for
the plow, they offered to the famished wanderer . . . escape and
surcease of the handsome barren [Christian] women [who] had
no curves or fruitfulness in them. The Jewish women waited with
rich yolky cries for him . . . there was still good earth for the
plow to cleave and furrow, deep cellars for the grain, a sheath
for the shining sword, rich pockets of spiced fertility for all the
maddened lunges of desire."

Even more exciting to many Klansmen and other Southern big-
ots than their fantasized yearnings of the Jewess was the purported
concupiscence of male Jews, projections of the hater's most favorite fantasies. Not only in Klan propaganda but in best-selling,
lip-smacking cheap novels, the evil Jew storekeeper seduced,

raped, bought for money, or otherwise violated his poor, young, innocent Christian female employees.

In April 1913 in Atlanta the most horrific projection of such a mind appeared to have come true when Leo Max Frank, a twenty-nine-year-old Cornell-trained Jew, was accused of murdering a fourteen-year-old girl who was an employee in his uncle's factory. More than any other American court case involving a Jew, more even than the Leopold-Loeb murder trial (in which Richard Loeb, the son of a Sears, Roebuck executive, and Nathan Leopold were convicted of a cold-blooded homosexual murder), the Leo Frank case became a *cause célèbre*, the American Dreyfus case. Unlike Leopold and Loeb, Frank—in the judgment of many— was not guilty of the murder; but as Sacco, Vanzetti, and Mooney were at least guilty of having the wrong ancestry and the wrong politics at the wrong time, so Frank was guilty of multiple sins— being the rich boss's nephew, being an intellectual, being a damn Yankee and a damn Jew; that is, being the perfect victim for angry, poor, confused Southerners not yet recovered from the war and now further disturbed and displaced by industrialization and urbanization.

Macy's Nathan Straus and Sears, Roebuck's Julius Rosenwald were among those who contributed to the Frank defense, but they were much less effective than racists such as Tom Watson, who ceaselessly howled for the death of "the filthy, perverted Jew of New York." When Georgia's governor, John Slaton, courageously committing political suicide, commuted Frank's death sentence, an armed midnight mob dragged Frank from prison, drove him 170 miles to the girl's birthplace, and hanged him from a tree near her grave. No one was ever punished for the lynching.

Despite many strong and some sincere protestations to the contrary, it is not reasonable to believe that most Jewish storekeepers between 1850 and 1950 were substantially less or more inclined than non-Jewish employers to try to take sexual advantage of their female employees, although there was of course the Victorian pretense that this was unheard of.

It could scarcely have been otherwise. In the last half of the nineteenth century and for more than the first quarter of the twentieth, the only other employment open to most women was schoolteaching, domestic work, and unskilled labor in factories. Only in a department store could a smart, hard-working woman rise quickly, becoming a buyer. That meant trips to New York and even to Europe, fine restaurants, fancy hotels, the great world that otherwise was only open to rich women and even to many of them only as frequently and in such areas as suited their husbands. Rich and educated women were excluded by prejudice, by cultural restraints, and by their husband's ego from most interesting work. But department-store buyers were independent. In New York or Munich or Florence they did and saw and tried and repeated whatever they pleased. Their salaries, although they were the highest that most women could then earn outside the theater, did not permit them unlimited luxuries, but there was almost always a manufacturer who wanted their business enough to take them to the expensive nightclub or wherever else they wanted to go.

At home, the smaller the town the more difficult it was for women who wanted to have sexual adventures as men did. But on buying trips, it was easy and relatively safe. For many of them a trip to New York meant several days and nights on the train. It was a luxurious and exciting kind of travel—smooth, spotless, white linens; extraordinarily good food (prepared in unbelievably difficult conditions); the beauty of the whole country visible from the windows, day and night.

The greatest pleasure of Pullman travel, however, was found— as on transatlantic crossings—in meeting people. Buyers who traveled regularly on the same route got to know the train conductors, dining-car headwaiters, club-car attendants, and the invariably polite, welcoming, anxious-to-please Pullman porters—whatever the terrible reality of the porters' lives. Meeting other passengers was easy, often romantic, and sometimes thrillingly dangerous. If on the train a buyer, most of whom were women, met a drummer or a professional man or an executive from another store, whom she found attractive enough to want to bed with, getting him in and out of her upper or lower berth without being seen or heard by the twenty or so other passengers in the same car was an adventure. If she found the experience worth repeating in New York, that was easy.

Like ships, every Pullman car had a name painted on it. For years afterward, a buyer might remember with tenderness a particular trip from Kansas City to New York on the "Beaver Falls" or the "Lafayette Mountain" or the "Oneida Lake."

Small wonder that so many of the brightest, bravest, smartest, and most attractive women in America went to work for the nearest department store. What first moved Frank Winfield Woolworth toward building a multibillion-dollar chain of five-and-ten-cent stores was his hatred of farming. Despite the myth of a blissful life on the farm that persists only among city dwellers, Woolworth's hatred was epidemic in America and afflicted women no less than men, although their chances for escape were fewer. That an Iowa farm girl gave up backbreaking chores to go to work at Younkers' in Keokuk and later Des Moines, that a Nebraska farm girl fled the brutal weather and brutalizing attitudes to work at Brandeis's in Omaha, that a Georgia farm girl left the endless boredom to work at Rich's was easy to understand.

That these courageous and self-confident women only succeeded if they succumbed to the boss's lust is of course nonsense. That those who acquiesced invariably found it unpleasant, degrading, or impermanent is equally untrue. A good many of the greatest merchants in America—including Stanley Marcus and Grover Magnin—married their own employees.

Of course if a member of a store owner's family was too blatant in his attempts to force his attentions upon many women employees, and they objected, he could be eased out. After something somewhat similar happened at Rich's to a member of the family whom I shall call Leon Levi, it was said in Atlanta: "Rich's will take anything back—except Leon Levi."

Rich's, like the other most successful stores in America, had made itself into the greatest show in town. An important part of this ability was having both the courage and the profits to seize upon whatever the new technology was making possible. A city's store, like its railroad depot and its hotel, had to be a source of pride, a symbol of the city's faith in its own growth and future. Rich's boasted the first plate-glass show windows in town. Like other stores across the country, it early on introduced its customers to electric lights and the telephone, as well as letters and statements written not by hand but by machine.

Even, or perhaps especially, during hard times, the public wanted evidence of progress. It was during the Depression years of the 1930s that Rich's was air-conditioned.

For centuries whatever was new and beautiful had been available only to royalty, nobility, or at least the rich. The ordinary citizen would not have presumed to enter the small exclusive shops where his betters were shown the finest laces and silver, the newest firearms or Jacquard silk. It was Émile Zola, the defender of Dreyfus, who pointed out that the new department store was "democratized luxury."

Whereas formerly the greatest architects and inventors had worked for temporal and ecclesiastical princes, now their greatest splendors and newest ideas were often seen first in what Daniel Boorstin has called "consumers' palaces," where not only "quality folks" but also quite ordinary citizens could enter, *free of charge,* and see the goods on display (that had formerly been taken out of drawers one at a time for rich clients) as well as actually touch and examine them. One didn't even have to be a serious customer—"just shopping" gave a new meaning to what "shopping" had formerly meant.

Perhaps the most important single technological leap in American architecture was the increasingly inventive use of cast iron by such pioneers as Daniel Badger and James Bogardus. A. T. Stewart's luxurious "Marble Dry-Goods Palace" of 1846 was abandoned only sixteen years after it was built—superseded by his new "Cast Iron Palace," for the moment the largest store in the world.

Cast iron made possible not only taller buildings but also airier, more open ones, whose weight was supported by the outer walls that replaced the once-mandatory enormous and frequent interior columns with slim iron columns that did not obstruct the exciting vistas of tempting merchandise. This same cast iron was easily and quickly and cheaply cast into facades that looked like the most elaborately carved Venetian *palazzi,* that had taken decades to carve. Most of these splendid structures, such as E. V. Haughwout's 1857 department store at Broadway and Broome Street in New York, have long since been replaced by buildings whose sterile "skin" offers no aesthetic substitute; but Chicago's Carson, Pirie, Scott & Co. remains to remind America of its elegant destroyed palaces.

As stores became unbelievably big, lighting presented problems unknown in the earlier small shops—problems now solved by electricity but formerly by improved technology in glassmaking. This progressed from blown glass through small laboriously hand-ground and polished sheets, through the eighteenth- and especially nineteenth-century French and English improvements in casting glass and using rollers to make "plate glass" of almost any length.

These "show windows," as they were quite properly christened, became a most important part of the show-business aspect of storekeeping. They created a brand-new, consummately democratic pastime, "window-shopping," which French slang called *"lécher les vitrines,"* literally, "licking the windows." Like the scantily clad women exhibited briefly by the barkers in front of the "girlie shows" at the fairs, these show windows were primarily designed to tempt passers-by to come inside. However, they also served an educational function. When Rich's used its windows to display such merchandise as "genuine oriental curtains imported by us from Damascus, in Syria," it was teaching not only geography but also what it called decoration "a la oriental," these more than compensating presumably for the dubious French.

Elisha Graves Otis sold the public on his "safety" elevator when at New York's Crystal Palace Exposition in 1854 he was pulled high up in his elevator cage and then he melodramatically cut the supporting rope, proving that his elevator's teeth and ratchet safety device worked. Three years later, in the Haughwout Department Store, Otis made the first permanent installation of his safety elevator and the public was able to enjoy the sensational thrill it offered *free of charge.*

Ordinary Americans had always shopped on foot—only the rich had horses and carriages—and so their stores had been within walking distance, that is, 2 miles or so. With the advent of cheap public transportation, first horsecars and mule cars, then electrified trolleys, citizens could easily live 6 to 10 miles out and come into town to shop and work.

Ironically, what was probably the greatest single technological boost to America's storekeepers came from one of its worst anti-Semites, Henry Ford.

The rising cost of labor in America made many technological improvements economically practicable. Running water inside was increasingly common when it became costly to hire people to carry buckets full of clean water in and dirty water out. Similarly, once department-store clerks had had to wrap each purchase in paper and tie it with a string, but making these parcels took time. After 1870, machines to make paper bags solved this problem more quickly and so more cheaply and soon these paper bags became a method of advertising the store as well.

Not every technological step, great or small, was an improvement and some were blessedly short-lived. For example, most American department stores including Rich's sold (until they were replaced by radios) many of the player pianos that caused John Philip Sousa in his "The Menace of Mechanical Music" to quote an astonished child's shout: "O mamma, come into the drawing-room; there is a man in there playing the piano with his hands!"

Being first with the new technology was part of the show business of retailing. Another was for the storekeeper's family and his store to be identified in whatever way was possible with what the average customer perceived as "high society" and visiting celebrities. This meant not only paying an at least appropriate share of the $20,000 cost of Atlanta's "Great Southern Musical

Festival" in 1909 but also taking not one but two of the fifty-six boxes on opening night so that the newspapers could describe the elegant clothes of Mr. and Mrs. Morris Rich, Mrs. Emanuel Rich, Mrs. W. H. Rich, Mr. Walter Rich, and their various relations, connections, and guests.

The Riches appeared to participate in Atlanta's socially important horse show, in which they did not ride, and in the debutante ball, from which they were excluded. They accomplished this by large newspaper advertisements explaining with a combination of grave authority and excitement what should be worn to these events.

Nationally prominent society personages could also be made to contribute to Rich's social status. On July 1, 1923, in the *Journal,* Rich's fashion director managed to tie the names of various Whitneys, Morgans, and Rockefellers to the store, however peripherally, by means of an on-the-spot report of the Harvard-Yale Boat Races flashed back to Atlanta with the breathless fashion news that "Mrs. J. P. Morgan wears a white flannel suit with a black straw hat. Isabel Rockefeller—watching her cousin row—wears a white crepe sports dress trimmed with yellow and a yellow, felt cloche." The implied connection between these Olympian figures of American society and the Atlanta store of which they were almost certainly completely unaware was no more false and a great deal less expensive than paid television endorsements of cosmetics and coffee makers by Hollywood and sports stars.

The constant concern with the public perception of the store that had resulted even at the height of Georgia's Negro-lynching, Jew-baiting fervor in Rich's being considered "a Southern Institution" to be cherished, rather than a "Jew store" to be boycotted, was not forgotten in the family's third generation. Morris and "Honey" Rich's favorite grandchild and only grandson, Richard, was the son of Rosalind, their favorite daughter, whom they had unsuccessfully tried to stop from marrying a "shoe man" considerably below her social station, one Herman Rosenheim. The "well-uncled," as they said in Atlanta, Richard Rosenheim, born on Christmas Eve of 1901, was raised as much by his grandparents as by his parents. He was the dynasty's only male heir and no one was surprised when he changed his name to Richard H. Rich.

Dick, as he was more often called, trained for his role, first at the University of Pennsylvania's Wharton School and then at L. Bamberger & Co., the Newark department store. The significance of the merchant-prince-as-public-benefactor was nowhere in America more importantly illustrated than at Bamberger's. Its lifelong bachelor founder, Louis Bamberger, along with his sister, Carrie Bamberger Fuld, in 1930 gave $5 million to found the Institute for Advanced Study at Princeton, New Jersey. Fascinated by their educational institution—new for the United States—dedicated to advanced research, the two of them gave the Institute (that brought Albert Einstein to America) some $18 million.

Dick's role from the moment he was transmogrified from a Rosenheim to a Rich was to be the outward and visible sign of the store's concern with Atlanta and Georgia. He joined and eventually led dozens, possibly hundreds, of charitable, educational, cultural, and civic groups, until gradually he approached and finally equaled Frank Neely's position as "Mr. Atlanta." Dick represented the store as a president or board member of Atlanta's Chamber of Commerce, Rotary Club, Community Chest, Symphony Guild, the Southern Bell Telephone Company, the Trust Company of Georgia, *et alia.* He did not concentrate either his efforts or the store's gifts of money to create a single superb monument, as Louis Bamberger and his sister had done. Rather, because everybody shopped at Rich's, he continued the store's policy of "spreading it all around," and everybody got a bit— Baptists and Catholics, blacks and whites. Not that on occasion he did not use the store's gift or his own prestige to build a sizable sum with gifts from others. In 1962 when 122 Atlanta art enthusiasts died in an air crash at Paris's Orly Airport, Dick led the fund raising for an Atlanta Memorial Arts Center that originally had a goal of $1 million but eventually raised $13 million.

Within the store he continued the traditions such as unlimited returns and liberal credit, explaining: "The old saw that 'Credit is like lending someone an umbrella and taking it away from them when it rains,' does not exist at Rich's."

Often the store's various roles—good civic citizen and show business, for example—complemented one another. The "Lighting of the Great Tree" at Rich's grew over the years until finally 120,000 people or more attended what had become for Atlanta the traditional beginning of the Christmas season. It was difficult for most people to think of its sponsors as Christ-killers.

Invited to join the exclusive Piedmont Driving Club, Dick asked whether he was an exception to their practice of excluding Jews or the first example of a new policy. Told he was an exception, he refused to join. His son, Michael Peter Rich, would later convert to Presbyterianism and seek to join the Piedmont, only to be blackballed. With considerable good humor, however, Mike told a recent visitor: "I am considering converting to the Episcopal Church and then perhaps I'll get into the Driving Club, when they're able to say, 'No, he used to be a Presbyterian.'"

Dick was not without vanity and, therefore, behind his back, sometimes a figure of fun. Until his death at seventy-three in 1975, he dressed always in the manner described as "shoe" in the Ivy League of his youth. In the store's publicity releases he was invariably portrayed as having "done postgraduate work at Harvard University" whereas in fact he had merely visited for a very few weeks, auditing nondegree summer lectures. His prematurely white hair was always carefully cut short; his mustache was always meticulously clipped. His clothes were painstakingly and expensively tailored, not at Rich's but by Rosenberg, one of the fewer than half-dozen Jewish "New Haven tailors" (including J. Press, Fenn-Feinstein, and Chipp's irrepressible Sid Winston) who for half a century set the resolutely understated and unchangeable fashion for America's male Establishment.

Dick and his wife, the former Virginia Lazarus who died in 1957, built in northwest Atlanta's Buckhead area, on West Andrews Drive, an adequately ducal estate with tennis court and swimming pool. A participant in his regular all-male, early morning, fiercely contested tennis game remembers that immediately

after the game was over, Dick stripped naked and dived into
the swimming pool, as oblivious of the black maids setting out
breakfast as had been the French royalty who dressed, bathed,
and made love in front of servants who were considered to be
no more than part of the furniture.

If considerably less than wildly liberal about blacks, Dick was
much less traditionally intransigent than Frank Neely about such
once absolute articles of Southern faith as lily-white lunch counters. Dick's chief concern was that violence, such as would so
badly impair the economic growth of Little Rock and Birmingham,
not be permitted in Atlanta.

Slowly, Georgia seems to be changing, or perhaps it is reverting
to its pre–Klan, pre–Civil War traditions as when, in 1801, David
Emmanuel became the first Jewish governor of any state in the
Union.

Atlanta is also changing. In 1969 the city elected Sam Massell,
Jr., its youngest and first Jewish mayor. Of course, not everything
changes. The Piedmont Driving Club that had traditionally by
means of Rule 18 of its by-laws granted club privileges to the
mayor of Atlanta rescinded the rule and happily so, since in 1973
it would have faced an even worse problem when Atlanta elected
a black mayor, Maynard Jackson.

Sadly but necessarily, Rich's changes, too. In 1976 its directors,
against the wishes of Mike Rich, agreed to merge it into the almost
$4 billion Federated Department Stores. At the news, individuals
all over the South worried about "What will happen to *our store?*"
The anecdotes of over a century were retold, including the one
about the three-year-old boy who, having heard from his parents
that Rich's would exchange anything, tried to swap his baby sister
for a helmet. The store sent him the helmet as a gift, along with
its strong assurance that a baby was too valuable to trade for
anything else.

There were some who remembered what the store had done
for the schoolteachers in 1930, others who remembered when
in 1945 at nearby Fort McPherson troops were ready to be discharged on the Sunday before Labor Day. The base's vault had

mistakenly been time-locked for the long weekend and the men could not be paid. Rich's opened its safe and sent over the payroll money so that the men would not have to wait to go home.

As the news about the sale of Rich's spread, to be at first laughed at, then finally believed, its customers asked: "Will it stay the same?"

Sadly but inevitably, the answer is no.

7

Dallas and the Marci

Thus sayeth the Lord of hosts, the God of Israel, unto all that are carried away captives, whom I have caused to be carried away from Jerusalem unto Babylon;

Build ye houses, and dwell in them; and plant gardens, and eat the fruit of them;

Take ye wives, and beget sons and daughters; that ye may be increased there, and not diminished.

And seek the peace of the city whither I have caused you to be carried away captives, and pray unto the Lord for it: for in the peace thereof shall ye have peace.

—Jeremiah, 29: 4–7

When Al Neiman and Herbert Marcus opened their store in Dallas on September 10, 1907, they were already late.

The town's very tentative beginning had been some sixty-six years earlier, when John Neely Bryan with his Cherokee friend Ned, his pony Neshoba Tenva (Walking Wolf), and his dog Tubby arrived in November 1841 at an uninhabited ford in the Trinity River. Bryan too was late. He had come to open an Indian trading post, but the Indians were gone.

There was no good reason for a town to grow here. There was no confluence of important rivers; in fact, the Trinity was at best only intermittently navigable and on occasion went dry. There was no mountain pass through which travelers would have to go; on the contrary, this was flat country and Bryan could quite as well have begun 50 miles away. From its very beginning, therefore, Dallas was a place made not by nature but by men. Promotion was what built Dallas, early and late, and Bryan was only the first in a long line of expert promoters, reluctant to use hyperbole if an outright lie might prove more effective. An early victim of Dallas flackery arrived from Missouri in 1844 and complained in his journal: "We soon reached the place we had heard of so often; but the *town*, where was it? Two small log cabins—this was the town of Dallas, and two families of ten or twelve souls was its population."

For any village that was neither a seaport nor a river port, the one essential for growth was good railroad service. In 1872 the Houston & Texas Central Railroad completed its line from Houston to Dallas. The Texas & Pacific Railroad was already planning a transcontinental road that would bypass Dallas, but Dallas businessmen by a happy combination of political tricks in the state legislature and a $100,000 purchase of T & P bonds secured an east-west connection to complement the HT & C's north-south line. This was the decisive coup upon which others would follow; without it, Dallas would have remained a village or disappeared entirely.

Once Dallas had railroad connections, its chances for growth were at least sufficient to tempt the braver—or more footloose—Jewish "terminal merchants," such as the brothers Sanger who followed the building of the Houston & Texas Central from Houston through Millican, Bryan, Hearne, Calvert, Bremond, Kosse, Groesbeck, Corsicana, and finally to Dallas.

The Sangers were from the Bavarian village of Obernbreit, where Elias Sanger had ten children to help with his various efforts to earn a living, from weaving and winemaking to selling whatever might yield a profit at nearby markets and fairs. "These fairs were always on Sunday," Lehman Sanger later recalled, "and Mother always accompanied Father as his main clerk, riding on top of one of the cases on the wagon carrying the goods to the fair."

Traditionally, women and even children were put in charge of the stall at a fair, while the man moved about buying or peddling or both. And in fact as well as in Jewish fiction, there were women peddlers both in Europe and America.

How essential Jews were to the fairs of Europe was proven almost as often as the prejudice against Jews. At the beginning of the ninth century, Archbishop Agobard complained because the weekly market at Lyons had been changed from Saturday because otherwise Jewish traders would not attend. In Poland, Lithuania, and many areas of Europe, it was forbidden by law to fix the dates of fairs and markets on either the Jewish Sabbath or on Jewish holidays.

When in 1741 France's controller-general polled the provincial governors, all agreed that Jews must not be excluded from markets, indeed must be encouraged to attend them, because they forced down the prices, at least during the market, of the monopolistic guilds and Christian merchants.

In order to protect themselves from physical violence and excessive discriminatory Jew-taxes, the Jews frequently formed themselves into a cooperative group and boycotted fairs where they were too abused. And in many areas and in many different commodities—including furs, feathers, textiles, tobacco—they were so essential to the trade that persecutions against the Jews were suppressed by nobles and monarchs who considered the pleasure too costly. Even in places where they were forbidden to live, in Switzerland or Saxony or Brandenburg, Jews were often encouraged to come to market lest the prices on local livestock or other crops suffer from their absence.

The first Sanger to come to America was Isaac, who arrived in 1851. He clerked with cousins in New Haven and New York until he had saved enough money by 1858 to indulge his "Texas fever," opening a store in McKinney, a village so far north from Houston that goods sent up by ox wagon were four weeks in transit.

In 1854 Isaac helped to bring over his brother Lehman, who "went to New Haven where I stayed with my uncle Mandelbaum for a while . . . and in order to brighten up in the language went to peddling with a basket of notions about the city." Such relatives and connections were of incalculable value to a greenhorn when he arrived. They paid him at first pitifully little (if anything in cash), but they provided him with room and board and the opportunity to "brighten up" sufficiently to run his own business, in which they often helped to set him up.

After four years of such brightening up in Chicago and Georgia, Lehman joined Isaac in McKinney, where he took charge of the store while Isaac opened a branch at Weatherford, Texas.

In 1856 Isaac and Lehman brought over their sixteen-year-old brother, Philip, who went to work in Georgia peddling for their cousins the Hellers. Many of these German Jews who came to the South before the war remembered in later life that they had enlisted in the army of the Confederacy from a sense of patriotism. They were, of course, grateful to their new fatherland; but, in fact, among the reasons most of them had left Germany was to escape military conscription, and not the least important reason for their enlistment in America after the Civil War broke out was the increasing effectiveness of the Yankee blockade, which soon made it virtually impossible to get goods for their stores.

Isaac, Lehman, and Philip all enlisted in the Confederate army and Philip was slightly wounded. All of them were proud of their service for the rest of their lives and felt a camaraderie and an obligation to help their fellow veterans. Their nostalgia for their years of service is almost unimaginable to some American veterans 100 years later.

At the war's end, Lehman was too poor to buy a horse so he "tramped it afoot" back to Weatherford, where a friend with whom he had left $300 in gold miraculously still had it and turned it over. Lehman then set off by stagecoach for Waco and Houston. He passed through the village of Millican, the northern terminus of the Houston & Texas Central, and decided it was a good place to set up as a storekeeper with Isaac. So, after a brief buying trip, Lehman returned to Millican where, for $5 a month, he rented half of a tiny store from a cobbler who occupied the other half.

His entire inventory of dry goods and groceries could be "contained in one small Saratoga trunk. I paid cash. Could have bought goods on credit, but things looked rather 'squally' and it was against my policy to involve myself until things looked more settled."

How conservative Lehman was and how good his estimate of Millican were demonstrated when "it took us only about twenty-four hours to close out most of our stock and go back to Houston to replenish."

Shortly thereafter, while the conservative Lehman was away on a trip, twenty-four-year-old Philip Sanger showed up in Millican and was of course welcomed and put to work in the store by Isaac. When Lehman returned he did not recognize the much-aged war veteran whom he had not seen for six years, and he was furious at Isaac's apparent extravagance in hiring without any discussion a clerk they could not afford.

"Oh, he's not just a clerk," protested Isaac with a straight face, "I've made him a partner!" Then, before Lehman could explode, he drew him over to the young man and said, "Allow me to introduce your brother Philip."

Millican was a "tough" town made up of hated Yankee soldiers from the federal garrison and a scruffy floating population of freed slaves and bitter whites. "The goods for which there was the greatest demand were shot-guns, revolvers, and musical instruments—the most popular instruments being what the negroes termed 'Cordials,' that is, accordions, of which we could not get enough to supply the demand."

Lehman required payment in gold, for which "we realized, for a time, from $1.30 to $1.40 on the dollar in exchange for greenbacks. This money 'picnic' however did not last very long—competition soon became very sharp."

To help meet the sharpening competition, Isaac and Lehman took on as a partner Morris Lasker, the younger brother of the German Liberal politician Edouard Lasker. Morris later moved to Galveston, where he became a prominent merchant and banker. His son, Albert Lasker, was first a pioneer and then a giant in national advertising—the new form of merchandising that would determine how most Americans spent their money.

In perhaps no other American business except motion pictures, certainly not in department stores, have Jews had so great an influence as in advertising. Lasker of Lord & Thomas, Lawrence Valenstein of Grey Advertising, as well as Milton Biow, William Bernbach, Norman Norman, Julian Koenig, and Frederic Papert are only the most famous names in a business replete with Jews at every level.

Although Morris Lasker and the Sangers would in a few years become rich, "In those days we all slept in the store by making pallets on the floor. Beds were a luxury, the limited space of the room did not permit beds and we preferred to sleep in the store as a matter of precaution."

As the competition at Millican became sharper and as the railroad continued to push north, the Sangers opened a new store in each promising town along the route and closed any store, old or new, that was not profitable. The operation of several stores at a time of course required more family, especially after Isaac moved first to New Orleans and then to New York in order to be "in the market" and so able to snap up goods at bargain prices for the family stores.

The Sangers therefore brought over the rest of the family— their parents, four brothers, and three sisters, who settled first in Cincinnati and constituted a reserve force to be called on as business increased.

"Late in the summer of 1867," Lehman recalled, "the railroad was extended to Bryan, 20 miles north, and it became necessary for us to follow it in order to retain our trade." Brothers Dave and Jake were sent to Bryan. A scourge of yellow fever swept through Texas that year and killed them both.

But if brothers were lost, brothers-in-law were gained as the Sanger sisters married. The Sanger women, both sisters and wives, were often at least as strong as the Sanger men. Sister Sophie from Calvert came to Bryan in 1873 to visit Lehman's family. After she arrived, word came that yellow fever had broken out in Calvert. Lehman later recalled that "the Bryan Board of Health attempted to compel us to leave town. My wife was determined to hold the fort, and when they threatened to make us move, she told them she would shoot the first man that crossed her threshold, and they concluded to leave her alone."

As the railroad pushed north to such now almost forgotten villages as Calvert, Kosse, and then Groesbeck, the Sangers had to push forward too, because their customers were very widely distributed, often from several hundred miles away, and if the terminus of the railroad moved 30 miles closer to them and the Sangers didn't open a store there, another "terminal merchant" would take over the trade. In 1870 the Sangers opened a branch at Bremond and later that year another at Corsicana; and finally in 1872 on the courthouse square of the newest terminus, Dallas.

As Dallas boomed, so did Sanger Brothers, until by the turn of the century it was the greatest dry-goods company west of the Mississippi. Not only did it have large retail department stores in Dallas and Waco but also a wholesale business second in importance only to that of Marshall Field's in Chicago.

With their escalating wealth, the brothers enjoyed an ever grander style of living and at least as grand a manner. There was, of course, a rationale to justify why the exemplary thrift of many years was now replaced by lavish luxury. If the storekeeper, so the reasoning went, was authoritatively to set the style for what people should wear, the storekeeper's family had to set the style as to how families should live—how they should build, furnish, and decorate their houses, train and costume their servants, and how they should entertain.

The first posh residential area, away from downtown Dallas by only a dozen blocks, was called "The Cedars"—and the two most important houses in it were those of Philip and Alex Sanger. Philip's was an outright copy of a summer mansion he had seen at Long Branch, on the Jersey coast. Built in 1885 at the corner of Ervay and St. Louis streets, Philip's home was grand enough that even half a century later as critical an observer as Edna Ferber would declare: "It's worth a trip to Texas just to see it!"

Philip's enormous house, its wide, railed verandah and the double stairway leading up to it, the attic turrets (where the white servants slept) and lacy trellises were all of wood painted a deep beige. Inside, too, wood declared the wealth of the family: Honduran mahogany, cherry, rosewood, and oak, 4-foot-high wainscoting, dark-stained paneling, and mantels intricately carved by Italian workmen Sanger brought down from New York.

Some of the workmen stayed on in Dallas and applied their talents to other homes in the booming city. In Philip's home their elaborately carved shelves, nooks, brackets, cabinets, and columns displayed a bust of Sarah Bernhardt as L'Aiglon, the mandatory Italian marble sculpture of Cupid and Psyche, and countless bisque, porcelain, terracotta, and glass bibelots, bric-à-brac, gewgaws, knickknacks. In those days in America there was an endless supply of maids to dust them. The same endless supply often guaranteed the immediate replacement of any maid who was so wickedly careless as to break one of these Victorian treasures, or so stubborn and foolish as to resist the sexual opportunings of the master of the house or the first fumbling efforts of his sons.

But more than the rich fabrics that covered its walls and French furniture, more than the oriental rugs or the mullioned or leaded windows whose stained glass glowed at night and so edified outsiders on the meaning of culture and luxury, even more than the greenhouses or carriage houses or "quarters" (where the black servants lived), what significantly differentiated the homes of the rich Jewish merchants from those of most of the non-Jewish rich was the inclusion of artists as guests—visiting actors (from Anna Held to Otis Skinner), singers (from Melba to Pinza), instrumentalists (from Paderewski to Heifetz), and writers (from Wilde through Sinclair Lewis).

Not all members of the Sanger family displayed equally good judgment as to how to entertain such artists. When the very young Horowitz arrived in Dallas to play his first concert, he was turned over to Philip Sanger's grandson, Joe Linz, to look after until the evening performance. The equally young and fun-loving Linz decided to augment the virtuoso *wunderkind*'s limited education by teaching him to roller skate, until Linz's uncle, Eli Sanger, looked out the window and ordered the lesson stopped at once before a fall resulted in a sprained wrist and a cancelled concert.

Not until well into the twentieth century would Dallas's non-Jewish rich (and even then far from all of them) enjoy the excitement or see the social utility of entertaining visiting artists. Before that, whether it was an insecure snobbery or the fear that their ignorance of the arts would prove an embarrassment, most Christian Dallas doyens and doyennes limited such entertainment of important visitors to politicians and businessmen, whereas the signatures in the guest books of the Sangers, Harrises, and Marci ranged from Paderewski and Pavlova to such even more controversial figures as Margaret Sanger (no relation) and Alexander Meiklejohn.

In the decades when such men as Jay Gould were easing themselves onto and up New York's social ladder by building—and, even worse, attending—the Metropolitan Opera, in Dallas most public spectacles were less esoteric. At a cock-fighting tournament in 1886, more than a 100 breeders from across the country entered some 500 birds, thus helping to maintain Dallas's and Texas's "supremacy in the cocking world." The following year a local hall "was packed from pit to dome by the sporting elite" for a dog fight between Spot and Rowdy who had, according to the Dallas *News*, "physiognomies that would do credit to a New York alderman."

However, prize fighting, "the protest against effeminacy or dudeism," did not prosper in Dallas, especially after 1890, when a local carpenter was killed at the Dallas Opera House in a challenge match against one of Jake Kilrain's touring "troupe of fistic entertainers."

On occasion there were, of course, more cultural entertainments at the Opera House than prize fights, sometimes even opera, but there was not a whole season of it to support and attend. The Opera House sold out a week in advance despite a $15 price for tickets when Edwin Booth played *Hamlet* on February 24, 1887, and the storekeepers were not displeased that in addition to its critic, the Dallas *News* sent its society editor to describe the dresses in the audience.

Alex Sanger's three-story cream-brick mansion was designed to be, if possible, even more elegant than Philip's, with chandeliers from Louis Comfort Tiffany, an ivory board in the library on which children and neighbors were expected to list the books they borrowed, and—an almost scandalous luxury—a "powder room" with inside plumbing just for guests. The butler's pantry had a sink used only for washing fine crystal, and there were two extra dining rooms, one for white servants and poor relations, another for blacks.

In her late eighties, even Mrs. Herbert Marcus, who had long since progressed from her modest Russian-Jewish beginnings to a grandness she obviously relished as the matriarch of the Marcus family, remembered the Sangers with a touch of envy and wonder: "They were the very epitome of royalty."

Their usual style of living followed wherever Alex Sanger and his family went with children, grandchildren, guests, and servants to escape the torrid Texas summers: on a European grand tour, or to Marienbad or Mackinac. Often it was to Rangeley, Maine, where other retail royalty—the Hutzlers of Baltimore, the Gimbels of Philadelphia—also had "cabins" that approached the common concept of a cabin about as nearly as the "cottages" of Newport approximated the usual cottage. "All the way to Maine, for three days and three nights, we were fanned by Annie, our black nurse," Alex's beautiful granddaughter Frances Mossiker remembers. "She had wet-nursed my father and my Uncle Eli, but what impressed me much more was that her daughter had run away to Chicago and 'passed.' I admire anyone who has that much courage."

Although family rivalries, envy, and greed for personal advancement were not allowed to injure "the store," competition in social matters—especially among female members of the family—was intense and unrestrained, and it extended to every level of the household. Adolph, Philip Sanger's German gardener, was not satisfied merely to supply every room of the house year round with flowers and plants from the cutting gardens and greenhouse. These had to be better, rarer, more surprising than those supplied by Alex's gardeners. If at Cornelia Sanger's first tea party after the New Year the center of the table boasted an enormous epergne full of forced violets and lilies-of-the-valley long before any such had graced the Alex Sanger house, it was a triumph for Adolph as much as for his mistress.

Cornelia's black lady's maid, Australia Center, felt a personal responsibility to try to keep Cornelia better coiffed and dressed than Evelyn Sanger, Alex's daughter-in-law, who was the mistress of his widower's house until he died in 1925. Australia Center's goal was not an easy one, because Evelyn was a "tearing beauty," who floated through Dallas society in her famous pastel chiffon gowns inspiring the admiration—some said inflaming the passions—of generations of Dallas men, of whom the millionaire Dallas mayor Henry Lindsley was only the most prominent.

Philip's black butler, Leaptor Louis, held up his end of the competition by his strict supervision of every detail in the Ervay Street mansion. Pity the coachman who did not see to it that the coach horses "Dewey" and "Syntax" were perfectly groomed, and that even the pony and pony cart of Philip's children, "Miss Jessica," "Miss Lois," and "Mr. Eli," were perfectly turned out. And when Louis "strutted his stuff" among his own people on his one-night-a-week-off, it was often in a carefully brushed frock-tail coat secretly borrowed from "Mr. Philip" to maintain the family name.

But no other event offered so great an opportunity for competitive elegance and extravagance as a family wedding. When Philip's beautiful daughter Lois married the handsome and notorious Clarence Linz—an heir to the finest jewelry store in town, Linz Brothers—Dallas's always overwrought society journal, *Beau Monde,* was sorely taxed to describe adequately "one of the most fortunate marriages of all times."

Clarence Linz would prove to be one of the most compulsively adulterous husbands in Dallas history and perhaps its most extraordinarily inept businessman as well, repeatedly snatching failure from the very jaws of success. A partner in the city's first dial telephone company and in what is still one of its greatest insurance companies, he would lose both these potential fortunes and make himself instrumental in the family's loss of Sanger Brothers to outsiders. Yet the marriage would last for over fifty years.

Clarence and Lois spent the night after their wedding at Dallas's Southland Hotel. The next morning when the waiter wheeled in their elaborate breakfast and saw the startlingly lovely Lois propped up in bed in an elegant lace peignoir, he stammered: "Lawdy, Mr. Clarence. She's surely the prettiest one you *ever* brung here!"

"I knew at that moment," Lois always recalled when she recounted the incident over the next half century, "that I had to leave him right then or laugh at such things, and I decided to laugh."

Not to be outdone by Philip, Alex's only child, Elihu Sanger, had laid on a wedding feast for his Cousin Lois that, according to *Beau Monde,* was "so preeminently smart it was right up to the minute according to the swellest New York edicts."

Even in that day of extravagant and fatuous society reporting, perhaps no one in America surpassed the *Beau Monde*'s editor, Iowa-born Mrs. Hugh Nugent Fitzgerald, in her ability to combine malapropism with hyperbole and cliché with tautology. Every rich Dallas family, Jewish or Gentile, had its favorite Fitzgeraldism. In my own family it was her reportage of the honeymoon plans of my father's older brother and his fiancée, including the breathless revelation that "The bride will air her lingerie at Atlantic City." Admittedly, this is not quite up to her description of Helen Adams, whom Mrs. Fitzgerald reported she saw on the golf links "gracefully swinging her caddy."

The Sanger family had already for many years provided the model and measure of elegance when young Herbert Marcus began his Dallas retailing career as a shoe clerk at Sanger Brothers. Born in Louisville in 1878 of recently arrived immigrant parents, he had at fifteen followed his older brother Theo to the Texas village of Hillsboro, some 55 miles southwest of Dallas, in the hope of earning enough to help support his parents and three sisters.

Marcus never finished grade school, let alone high school or college, and this was a source of acute embarrassment to him all his life. But it was probably also a significant factor in his great success. My uncle, Arthur Kramer, was put through both the University of Texas and its law school by the sacrifices of his large family, but he early left the bar to marry my grandfather's ugly daughter Camille and so enter A. Harris & Company. At any dinner, cocktail party, or meeting, Kramer invariably seized the first opportunity to tell his Herbert Marcus Story. "For years Herbert was so humiliated by his lack of education," Kramer would confide with obvious relish, "that he finally decided to educate himself by reading the entire *Encyclopaedia Britannica* from cover to cover. And so, when you heard him at a dance, apropos of nothing at all, begin to expound on Dickens and Dostoevski, you knew he was in Volume D. But he became successful so fast that he gave it up in the middle of Volume M and, therefore, if you ask him about Thackery and Tolstoi, he thinks it's a cloak and suit manufacturer on Seventh Avenue."

Kramer, of course, meant the anecdote to diminish Marcus, but on most people who knew both men it had the opposite effect. It illustrated the peevish envy Kramer felt for Marcus's obviously far greater abilities, an envy that led Kramer to imitate Marcus in business. And it illustrated Marcus's irresistible determination to achieve by hard work in every area of his life those things that were important to him.

Marcus's enormous ambition and, even for that day, phenomenal hard work were not lost on Philip Sanger, who soon made Herbert the buyer of boys' clothing. Herbert had married Minnie Lichtenstein when he was so poor that they had to live with her parents, who were Russian-Polish immigrants. The Marcuses said that they were German Jews, and Theo refused to attend

Herbert's wedding because Herbert was "marrying beneath himself." "I resented it then and I still resent it," Minnie remembered at ninety. "We hadn't a penny, and Papa said, 'You have to save five hundred dollars the first year of marriage,' so every day Herbert went to work carrying his lunch in a brown bag. I remember how odd it looked; he was always so elegantly dressed, even then, and that brown bag just didn't fit."

When Minnie became pregnant, Herbert asked for a raise. All his life he was fond of saying that if Alex Sanger had then offered him just a bit more than a $1.25 a week increase, he would probably always have remained at Sanger Brothers. The offer was not only insufficient for his growing need but, perhaps more important, it so wounded the growing ego of the poverty-proud Marcus that he quit.

I cannot point out Alex Sanger's lack of prescience without candidly confessing that my own grandfather's was equally deplorable, for he allowed to escape from his employment Herbert's slim, dark, doe-eyed, pre-Raphaelite younger sister Carrie, who had become one of the best saleswomen at A. Harris & Company. There she revealed a sure sense of fashion not only extraordinary for an uneducated and untraveled woman not yet twenty, but one never equaled either by her brother or her nephew Stanley and not surpassed by any other American retailer.

Carrie had married the colorful Abraham Lincoln Neiman, always called "Al," who was an occasional employee of my grandfather. Al's business was "putting on sales." This consisted of helping merchants to sell their markdowns (and even augmenting this sale merchandise by skillfully buying for them closeouts from manufacturers and jobbers) by whatever flamboyant means could be assembled: a local brass band or drum-and-bugle corps, a fire department parade, hyperbolic banners promising unbelievable bargains hung across the town's main street. In those days long before movies, radio, or television, street theater, usually in some form of parade, was the people's chief (and free) entertainment; it brought out most of a town's citizens and farm families from miles around. The imaginative and often outrageous Neiman was a wonder at whipping up excitement and helping less imaginative merchants to move their mistakes.

It would be difficult to overstress the circus and theater role of the department store from 1870 to 1920. There were, of course, other entertainments. The Dallas *News,* like all newspapers across America, provided an endless supply of vicarious violence in its simultaneously prurient and pious reportage: AND YET ANOTHER HORROR TO SHOCK THE VIRTUOUS PEOPLE OF DALLAS; A WOMAN KILLER HANGED; or LYNCHERS AFTER JOHN DOE. Evangelists such as Dwight Moody and his songmaster, Ira Sankey, painted powerfully exciting pictures of the sinful pleasures of the flesh and the terrifying torments of Hell these led to—alternating with blessedly brief but restful descriptions of the comparatively tiresome life in the Kingdom of Heaven. And there were the free shows of leather-lunged politicians and temperance orators. But day-in, day-out, the best show in town, and often the only one, was the ever-changing spectacle at the department store.

After he quit Sanger Brothers in 1905, Herbert moved to Atlanta with Minnie and their six-week-old firstborn, Stanley. Herbert convinced Al and Carrie to join him there, and for two years they operated the American Salvage Company, a delightfully profitable but depressingly un-chic enterprise that put on sales for merchants all over Georgia.

But Minnie missed Dallas, and all of them increasingly dreamed of opening their own store there and becoming as rich and important as their former employers. So they saved scrupulously. By 1907 they were able to return to Dallas, where with the financial help of Theo, now a successful cotton broker, they opened their own store.

The Marcus family's publicity has often tended to minimize the importance of Al Neiman's role in the store's first two decades before he left in an atmosphere of scandal and acrimony. But the new store was not called "Neiman-Marcus" rather than "Marcus-Neiman" because Al was less important than Herbert.

Herbert was twenty-nine, Carrie twenty-four, and Al only

twenty-seven, and to Dallas's already successful merchants what these young new store owners were doing seemed risky to the point of foolhardiness. They proposed to open a frankly expensive store (years before the oil boom) in a town as yet far from rich. Even riskier was their insistence that this store's high-priced clothing would not be custom-made but ready-to-wear.

Fashionable rich women of Dallas in 1907 still had their clothes made to order in New York and by the best local dressmakers, including Miss Ward of Sanger Brothers, Madame Bartel of A. Harris & Company, and Titche-Goettinger's Madame Snow. Neiman-Marcus promised that its revolutionary ready-made clothes would be even finer than made-to-order fashions. To ensure the proper fit for these off-the-rack outfits, Neiman-Marcus hired Madame Bartel away from A. Harris & Company, but made plain that she would only fit and alter ready-made fashions—thus offering the best of both worlds.

The "piece-goods" department of most fashion stores of that era was usually the most important contributor to the store's reputation, turnover, and profits. The department supplied both the store's dressmaker and the many private dressmakers then in every community, as well as the great majority of women who made their own and their family's clothes. Neiman-Marcus had no piece-goods department.

For American business, 1907 was a very bad year; thirteen New York banks and several railroads failed. But Neiman-Marcus flourished from its inception. Al Neiman provided both the promotional flair and the bargains that protected the store from a reputation of being exclusively for the very rich. Throughout its existence, Neiman-Marcus has been extraordinary in its ability to maintain its reputation and supremacy as a rich women's store, while at the same time attracting and keeping a large trade of middle-class and working women without whom it could not have survived and grown. The store had to preserve an exclusive and expensive atmosphere for its rich clients, make them feel protected from hoi polloi, and keep them from feeling like suckers for buying high-priced fashions rather than the cheaper equivalents available in the same store and advertised in the newspapers. It had at the same time to guard against frightening away the less than rich.

Just five days after its posh "Grand Opening," the store addressed this problem in the Sunday newspapers of September 15, 1907. The owners announced that they felt it essential to contradict the impression "that because of the elegance and general high character of the Neiman-Marcus establishment, prices would be proportionately high."

While Al concentrated especially on the promotions and bargains, Herbert and Carrie put much of their emphasis on buying only what was most fashionable and of the best quality. If what the markets provided did not suit them, they specified the improvements they required and paid extra for them, as of course did their customers.

Herbert Marcus always remained fanatical about quality. Until after World War II, every piece of expensive ready-to-wear received by the store was put on a form and thoroughly inspected. If any detail of fit, any handmade buttonhole, the pressing and shaping of a suit lapel, or the hang of a skirt was less than the best, the garment was returned to the manufacturer.

But the chief cause of the store's success was that Al, Herbert, and Carrie all spent endless hours on the selling floor and in the fitting rooms with customers, carefully, ingratiatingly, patiently explaining those elements of quality that made their things more expensive as well as the new fashion elements that they promised would differentiate the customer from less demanding and knowledgeable peers, precisely as they differentiated Neiman-Marcus from lesser stores. It was the "highfalutinest" kind of selling Dallas had ever seen, but it was selling at its best—and it worked.

Many years later, when Neiman-Marcus had become famous, a granddaughter of one of the brothers Sanger took a visiting New York friend through the store and was embarrassed by Herbert's relentless selling. "He followed us everywhere, with a cashmere throw over one arm and a mink coat over the other. And as he described the virtues of each, he stroked it as one would a lover. It was mortifying—he was like an Arab in front of his souk. I never saw my grandfather do anything like *that!"*

In fact, Alex Sanger had long since given up selling customers and become quite grand. Perhaps not entirely coincidentally, Sanger Brothers by 1926 was broke. Never the merchandising genius his brother Philip had been, Alex's role had been that of the exemplary public citizen. He was the first Jew to be appointed a regent of the University of Texas, and was a director and generous supporter of every civic enterprise of any significance in Dallas. But after Philip died in 1902, Alex could not control the store's inventories and expenses nor the credit that its wholesale department extended to smaller Texas merchants. He failed to bring in nonfamily management when it became evident that the second generation of Sangers was not really interested in storekeeping and had not been given the necessary training and experience to correct matters.

In the decades following Philip's death, Alex Sanger's concentration on social and civic activities seemed to increase in proportion to the store's diminishing competitive position and huge losses. And charity began at home. The store's payroll was bloated with both incompetents and old employees, but Alex was no more able to bring himself to fire them or to reduce their salaries than he was to cut off the credit of longtime customers who would or could not pay their accounts, even after his New York bankers, Goldman, Sachs, had cut off his own credit. In the face of increasingly serious problems, instead of retrenching, Alex expanded the Dallas store and opened a new store in Fort Worth. This was precisely the opposite of the careful policy in Millican sixty years earlier that had limited the inventory to what would fill a small Saratoga trunk and could be bought for cash, until things looked less "squally" and credit might be risked.

So enormous was Alex Sanger's prestige because of his inordinate public service that his local and St. Louis bankers would not foreclose him; but with his death in 1925 their tolerance ceased, and the store was shortly sold out to a Kansas City promoter.

Many of these storekeepers overextended their credit; but unlike the Sangers, not all of them who did so lost their store as a result. In 1915, when my grandfather's store was unable to pay its debts, its suppliers accepted a settlement of twenty-five cents on the dollar and wrote off the balance instead of forcing it into bankruptcy. In the boom years during and after World War I, A. Harris & Company flourished under my father's merchandising.

The store had no legal obligation to repay any of the 75 percent its creditors had lost in 1915, but my father felt (and convinced his brother-in-law, Arthur Kramer) that it was a debt of honor. In thirds, in 1919, 1920, and 1921, A. Harris & Company paid off its defaulted debt, and in cases where the suppliers had gone out of business, the store donated the money to charities in each supplier's community. The checks for the final third were sent out on February 14, the anniversary of my grandfather's death in 1912.

Most of the creditors had forgotten the debts and a flood of letters came to the store expressing shocked surprise and admiration. One large St. Louis jobber returned his check to my father suggesting "I should like you to donate this in your name to some commendable charity in your city," and a Jersey City glove manufacturer wrote, "I intend to have your letter framed and hung up in our New York office as an example of the highest grade of integrity."

Of course not all of the Jewish department-store keepers were so conscientious—there were trimmers and even scoundrels, but not many.

Stanley Marcus, who has never suffered from excessive modesty nor attributed too much of Neiman-Marcus's success to outsiders, admits that the sellout of Sanger's in 1926 was a turning point for his father's store. The new management discontinued buying Sanger's expensive lines of merchandise and summarily fired many of its oldest and best employees, who were then hired by Neiman's, bringing with them the bulk of their established clientele. "One salesperson, alone, sold over $200,000 her first year at the store," Stanley remembers. "Loyal customers of Sanger's were incensed by the ruthless treatment of employees who had given years of faithful service, and they switched to Neiman-Marcus in appreciation."

If Alex Sanger had become too grand to sell to customers, Herbert and Carrie had not, nor would Herbert's sons. All their lives they loved selling to customers and hated losing a sale—selling became their ruling passion.

It was while listening to a top traveling salesman for the jeweler Harry Winston describe his sale of an especially expensive emerald and diamond rivière to the wife of a banker in a small Texas town that I first became aware of how very similar the sale of a high-priced luxury item is to seduction—not rape, but mutually satisfactory seduction.

Slowly, pridefully, relishing the recollection of every detail, he described his flirtation, her flicker of initial interest, his gradually increasing ardor, her gradually diminishing *pro forma* refusals, and how finally she joyfully, excitedly, "opened up, gave up, gave in, and I *had* her!"

As I listened, I was struck both by the reciprocal and the ritualistic aspects of the prolonged seduction: "She really made me work for it. It took me two hours to get her to say 'Yes!' " It was as formally choreographed as a ballet or Kabuki performance, and performance was an essential of the total experience.

"It sounds when you describe it as though you had seduced her," I told Winston's salesman, "as though you both had an equally glorious time, furious foreplay leading to climax and mutual satisfaction."

"And the satisfaction is not just momentary, it's permanent," said Winston's man. But in this last judgment he soon made it evident that he was mistaken, for as I listened to him describing other important sales he had made, it quickly became obvious that in selling he was a psychiatric textbook example of Don Juan—endlessly unsatisfied, permanently priapic. It was precisely this priapism that made him such a great salesman.

During World War II at a dinner party at my mother's house, Stanley Marcus pulled out of his pocket a small, square suede box that contained a splendid yellow diamond ring he proceeded to try to sell to the guest of honor. When all the guests had left, my mother gave way to the anger she had until then successfully hidden. "How vulgar! By the second generation the Marci really should have learned you don't do that sort of thing as a guest in a private home."

Born Lucile Herzfeld in New York in what Stephen Birmingham called "Our Crowd," educated in Europe, my mother was a woman of great elegance—a quality rarely in excess supply anywhere and certainly not in Texas then. She was aware that elegance not only is a product of grace and refinement but also requires discipline and on occasion sacrifice, neither of which Stanley had displayed. But in one particular, she was mistaken. Many seductions begin at private dinner parties and for the sedulous seducer, the proper place to begin is wherever you are.

Stanley is always selling. In 1946 in France, Stanley was introduced to Dwight Eisenhower, then commanding general of SHAEF. It was a time when Truman still hoped the general might someday run for the presidency as a Democrat and some Republicans hoped to convince the carefully uncommitted soldier to run as a Republican. Stanley's concern, however, was not with party. Although the old soldier had until then never heard of the store, Stanley urged him: "If you do decide to go for the nomination, and get it, and if you are elected, I hope that as an ex-Texan, you will buy Mrs. Eisenhower's inaugural gown from us." Six years later Eisenhower did just that.

Even more important than any sale, however large or noteworthy, made by Stanley or his father or Carrie, was the example set and the techniques demonstrated for the salespeople. If a woman was trying on Adrian and Hattie Carnegie suits in one of the large, flatteringly pink-lit fitting rooms on the expensive second floor, as if by magic handbags, shoes, scarves, blouses to complement the suits she selected appeared for her inspection. If lunchtime arrived or a cup of tea seemed called for to renew the customer's strength, the necessary refreshments also appeared—of course at no charge. But the keystone was the "clientele book," in which each salesperson was required to keep as complete a record of her customers as could be assembled by careful listening and discreet questioning. The customer's birthday (or her husband's or child's) offered an extra opportunity for a phone call and the proffer of assistance a few weeks before the date to demonstrate "personal interest." And a call announcing the arrival of "a perfect blouse that will make the herringbone suit you bought last fall seem brand new," demonstrated not only such personal interest but a generous effort to save the rich customer money when so many were trying to get money away from her.

For the rich, middle-aged woman who was Neiman's best customer, whose husband ignored her for his work, his mistress, or both, whose children were hostile or had left home, Neiman-Marcus offered a blessed balm that combined cosseting, concern, flattery, attention to her desires and complaints—valuable, like her psychoanalysis, because it cost so much money, but ever so much more enjoyable.

At Neiman-Marcus as in other stores, customers loved being waited on by "the family," and there was always an abundance of family available. For many years Herbert's father, Jacob, sat by the front door of the increasingly elegant store, nodding to customers and offering each child a piece of candy. And there was no shortage of Minnie's relatives, relations, and connections. "Sometimes the relations made a contribution, sometimes not," Stanley recalls, "but no member of the family was ever fired."

But if family can be a blessing to the growth of a business it can also be a curse. Al Neiman loved life, good food and drink, gambling and joking, and most especially women. Born in Chicago, he had been raised in a Cleveland orphanage, and throughout his adult life, in good fortune and bad, he enthusiastically tried to make up for his miserable childhood by having as much fun as possible. In Victorian Dallas, sexual adventures by married men who could afford them were not only acceptable but practically *de rigueur*—provided they were suitably discreet. But Al's indiscretions were too indiscreet. And a number of them were with women in the store—a pastime not unknown to other of the store's owners, but like everything else about him, Al's affairs were joyously flamboyant. And to make matters still worse, unlike the ideal Victorian wife who remained blissfully ignorant at home, Al's wife worked in the store.

Al's adulteries were particularly painful to Carrie, a shy and rigidly correct person who in the many long years after her divorce was called, in the Southern style, "Miss Carrie" and was widely believed to be an old maid.

As the 1929 stock market crash and the subsequent Depression approached, Herbert borrowed $250,000 and bought out Al's interest in the store. For Herbert, the bad feeling between his sister and Al had been terribly trying. No less troublesome had been the increasing ill-will between Al and Herbert's oldest son, Stanley—a man difficult to like and impossible not to admire.

In his memoir, written when he was over seventy, Stanley recalls that at public grammar school, "many a day I was run home by a gang of schoolmates shouting, 'Ikey, Ikey, little Jew-boy.' My mother would pay a prompt visit to the school principal in protest; he would lecture my tormentors, and they would lay off me for a while."

Stanley's, of course, was not an uncommon experience. Edna Ferber as a small child in Ottumwa, Iowa, regularly ran a gauntlet not only of children but of adults as well who shouted at her: "Oy-yoy, sheeny! Run, sheeny, run!" Part of the time she was able to console herself that these persecutors were barbarians and her inferiors, but much of the time she felt the inferiority was hers, "and out of that inferiority doubtless was born inside me a fierce resolution, absurd and childish, such as 'You wait! I'll show you! I'll be rich and famous and you'll wish you could speak to me.' Well, I did become rich and famous, and have lived to see entire nations behaving precisely like the idle frustrated bums perched on the drugstore railing."

Stanley's looks were never a blessing. "In my senior [high-school] year, I received the dubious honor of being voted by my classmates 'The Ugliest Boy' in the class. When my mother heard of this . . . she immediately paid a visit to the principal, Mr. Parker, and protested so vigorously that he persuaded the class to change the title of the award to 'The Most Natural Boy.' "

At a Jewish summer camp in Maine, where his mother was not there to protect him, the young Stanley also had problems getting along with his peers. "I was a poor athlete, a poor crafts-man, a poor camper, and I vowed I'd never go back," he later recalled. But at another camp, two years later, "I made up my mind in advance I was going to enjoy it by being a good camper. I resolved to go out for every sporting event, whether I was any good or not, to play the game as hard as possible, to be a good loser. . . . My athletic prowess hadn't improved, but my efforts were noticeable, and by early August I was awarded the camp's top camper award . . . my first overwhelming success."

The camp recollections of two other Texas merchants' sons, Morton Sanger and Eddie Kahn, differ markedly from Stanley's on the cause of his sudden popularity—not any heroic if futile athletic efforts but the fact that he had brought a gross of lollipops to camp and was lavish in distributing them. It was Stanley's first triumph in public relations, an area in which no other store-keeper would even approach his genius. When he was still in grade school, Stanley had done much better in elocution than in mathematics and had thought it more important. Throughout his life, public relations rather than any form of sport or any hobby would remain his chief passion.

As a boy, except for the two summers at camp, Stanley spent his free months working at the store where he was somebody and not subject to attacks by peers who did not understand this boy so strange and different from themselves. "Playing with other children never really interested me. I couldn't keep up with my peers, much less surpass them." The contrast provided by his life at the store could not have been lost on Stanley. And it seems unlikely that so brilliant a boy, who had been so unsuccessful with his peers, would not, like Edna Ferber, have harbored strong feelings about the necessity to "show them."

These feelings were almost certainly sharpened two days after
Stanley's arrival as a freshman at Amherst College, "when all
the new students had been pledged, I found myself a member
of a group of six 'barbarians' including two other Jews, one Chinese, and two blacks." All social life at Amherst in the twenties
revolved around the fraternities, and as a result, Stanley wrote:
"The year at Amherst proved to be a most unhappy year for
me, and at the same time, it was probably one of the most valuable
experiences of my life."

Stanley transferred to Harvard, where he was intellectually
stimulated for the first time. He made no close or lasting friendships there, but he had his first important experience of objects
as a substitute for friends in a course called "The History of
the Printed Book." It so excited him that while still an undergraduate he became both a collector and a mail-order seller of rare
books.

After graduation from Harvard College, he studied briefly at
Harvard Business School, but in 1926 left to work at and build
the store that for half a century would be his favorite wife, mistress, and child.

Herbert and Carrie were obsessed with the merchandise itself—
the finest weave, the softest leather, the best quality of sewing,
the most perfect shade of color, the ideal drape of fabric, the
most delicate bridal veil, the newest heel shape. What Stanley
focused on especially was not substance but image—the windows
and interior displays, the packaging, the language and manners
of the salespeople, the advertising and (most particularly and brilliantly of all) publicity as distinct from advertising. To say that
Stanley's concern was with image rather than substance does not
denigrate his contribution, for in matters of snobbery and fashion,
image is often more important than substance—in a sense, indeed,
image is substance—greatness is what is perceived to be great.

America's most successful and most colorful public relations
man was Ben Sonnenberg. He was paid enormous fees by corporations and by individuals because his advice was unorthodox and
effective. To Texaco he gave only two then shocking suggestions—

that it insist upon cleanliness in its rest rooms and that it introduce grand opera to America by means of radio.

His most amusing myths and disguises he made for himself, but as one acute observer remarked, there were only two essential things to understand about Sonnenberg: "The first is that only the most improbable things about him are true; the second, that early in life he discovered that candor is the greatest wile in the world."

Stanley Marcus as a young man met Sonnenberg, and as an old man Stanley declared: "I have learned more from him than any person except my father."

In the second quarter of the twentieth century in America, from I. Magnin's in California to Saks Fifth Avenue in New York, two dozen or so luxury fashion stores grew to considerable size and prominence. Some of the best were known only locally: Harzfeld's in Kansas City, Young-Quinlan in Minneapolis, Garfinckel's in Washington, D.C. The ones in New York became more widely known both because most rich Americans visited New York and because the New York stores advertised in the national fashion magazines. The circulation of New York newspapers reached thousands of readers who could not afford to buy at Bergdorf's, Bendel's, and Best's, whereas the readers of *Vogue* and *Harper's Bazaar* were precisely the customers these and other Fifth Avenue stores wanted.

Theirs was not just a small business. Saks Fifth Avenue became so big and so profitable that during the Depression its profits supported the whole Gimbel's chain. Gimbel's customers had to cut down their spending whereas Saks's rich customers did not. But no New York fashion store, and none anywhere else in America, even approached in reputation or mystique what was achieved by Dallas's Neiman-Marcus, and the reason for this was Stanley Marcus.

Reputation, of course, begins at home. The first principle upon which Stanley built was exclusivity. Whatever Neiman-Marcus was to buy and promote by name must, if possible, not be available at any other Dallas store. Stanley was able to convince not only small expensive dressmakers but even large cosmetics manufacturers such as Elizabeth Arden, who sold to dozens of department and drug stores in New York, to sell to no one but Neiman-Marcus in Dallas. On the most basic level, this meant that every time a Dallas woman wanted an Arden lipstick or a bottle of nail polish, she had to go to Neiman's, where she usually saw something else that tempted her. But even more important was the conditioning of Dallas women, until many (whether consciously or subconsciously) believed that what was best was at Neiman's and nowhere else, and that what was elsewhere was not the best.

The cost to Neiman's was great. By refusing to carry Revlon's products because they were in other stores, Neiman's lost a lot of trade. For years Neiman's refused to do any business with the most popular makers of sterling silver flatware, such as Towle, Gorham, Reed & Barton, Wallace, and International, because they insisted on continuing to sell to other stores. Instead, Neiman's tried, unsuccessfully, to convince its customers that no silver was worth owning except Georg Jensen's, which they had exclusively. In so doing they lost hundreds of thousands of dollars' worth of wedding-gift business until they finally gave up in this particular area and stocked the nonexclusive lines. But on balance the gain from this policy was far greater than the loss.

Many rich women all over Texas went to New York for their major fashion purchases. Stanley had to convince them that Neiman's was the equal of the Fifth Avenue stores and offered a selection as good as or better than theirs. Therefore, in the depths of the Depression in 1934, he began advertising in *Vogue* and *Harper's Bazaar,* whereupon these magazines began to mention the Dallas store on the editorial pages as a place where the illustrated new fashions were available. At the same time, he began to demonstrate again and again in regular weekly style shows that the best of what was in those magazines was available at Neiman's. In Dallas there was time for the customer to have proper fittings; in Dallas whatever was unsatisfactory for any reason could, at the customer's convenience, be returned to the store.

With all the charm, intelligence, ingenuity, flattery, and persistence at his disposal—by means of thousands of letters, phone calls, dinners, gifts, and favors—Stanley instituted the most successful campaign of public relations imaginable. No reporter or editor from a New Mexico weekly was too unimportant to talk to; no celebrity of films or radio or the arts who visited Dallas was too minor to merit some personal attention. And of course important people—bankers, publishers, aristocrats, politicians, and their mistresses or wives—were worth larger efforts and expense. In his obsession with work, Stanley not infrequently forgot he was a husband and a father; but whether on shipboard, in Europe, at work, or at play, he never forgot to promote his store, never failed to see an opportunity for publicity or else to create one.

Success, like failure, tends to snowball. The reputation of Texas was changing from Wild West to wild millionaires. And Neiman's reputation as their purveyor of wild extravagances made good reading in the Depression. *Fortune* in a 1937 article on "Dallas in Wonderland" saw what extraordinary authority Neiman's had achieved in only three decades. Its customers, *Fortune* declared, now said: " 'You know better than I do what I need.' The store is like a doctor or lawyer that people swear by. And dressing well in Dallas has become more than a personal matter, it has become a civic one. Perfect clothes are as much the cultural expression of Dallas as art is of Toledo."

But Neiman's did not just let it happen. When Louis Kronenburger arrived to research the *Fortune* piece, Herbert was ready with quotations from Plato and Flaubert, and Stanley had arranged his time to make the reporter's job easy and pleasant—as Sonnenberg had taught him to do.

Like storekeepers, magazine and wire-service editors copy one another. So each story led to more.

Little that the store did was original. Its foreign "Fortnights," of which the first provided Stanley with "the most exciting experience of my life," were copied from the Nordiska department store in Stockholm. But Stanley did much more than copy—he perfected. These "Fortnights" were not merely displays and offerings for sale of merchandise from the particular country, say France; the store also brought over French artists and designers and writers. Through his long cultivated connections with local institutions, Stanley saw to it that simultaneously the symphony played French music, the museum exhibited French art, the theater and ballet performed French works, the public libraries displayed French books. And in their own interest local restaurants, antique stores, movie theaters—all hoping to profit from Stanley's lavish publicity—offered French wares too.

Before long the countries Neiman-Marcus chose to honor with a "Fortnight" were making contributions to the store in six-figure sums. No other American store could successfully demand this kind of tribute, because no other American store could deliver comparable publicity, which was usually followed by orders for the country's merchandise from merchants who followed Stanley's lead.

It was standard practice for a traveling salesman seeking to impress department-store buyers with the desirability of his wares to say, "Neiman-Marcus bought twenty dozen of these," and if perchance the statement were true, the salesman then displayed a copy of the prestigious Neiman's order. It was, therefore, not uncommon to find on the wall of a buyer's office at Carson, Pirie, Scott in Chicago, or Bullock's in Los Angeles, or D. H. Holmes in New Orleans a sign reading: "I don't give a *damn* how many Neiman's bought!"

Many stores, like other businesses all over America, already gave prizes and citations when in 1938 Stanley inaugurated "The Neiman-Marcus Award for Distinguished Service in the Field of Fashion." But by his brilliant selection of awardees and his unequaled genius for publicity, in a short time Stanley had made his the most coveted and most widely written about prize in the fashion world—its Pulitzer, if not its Nobel Prize. Awardees included not only such designers and manufacturers as Nettie Rosenstein, Elizabeth Arden, and Christian Dior but also celebrities who purportedly "influenced" fashion, such as Mrs. Howard

"Slim" Hawkes and Grace Kelly, whose selection guaranteed the store publicity in additional places—gossip and society columns, movie and news magazines, as well as the fashion journals. Only those manufacturers whose merchandise was exclusively at Neiman's became awardees, which not only rewarded their exclusivity and reinforced it but also tempted other great designers who had not confined their wares to consider doing so.

In his memoirs Stanley admits to copying other ideas from firms as disparate as Bergdorf Goodman and Levi Strauss, although he is somewhat self-consciously partial to the euphemism "borrowed," as though the ideas could be returned.

The store's most sensational publicity came from stories, real and apocryphal, of oil millionaires who demanded original and extravagant gifts for a wife or mistress: a pousse-café of cashmere sweaters topped by a 10-carat ruby ring, or an entire Christmas window of gifts duplicated secretly in a customer's home on Christmas Eve. As the demand by the various news media for stories about such extravagant gifts exceeded the supply, Stanley began to build into his annual Christmas catalogue such newsworthy gifts as matched His and Her mummy cases, or His and Her private airplanes at $176,000 the pair.

But the facts were even more remarkable than the flackery. He ran the best store in the world and no aspect of it was beyond his improving touch—his escalators, for example. In every other store these are, at best, sterile utilitarian necessities. But by the simple expedient of separating them and decorating the generous "wasted" space between them with lavish hanging plants, Easter flowers, or Christmas decorations, Stanley made even his escalators enchanting.

As with most successful businessmen, Stanley usually got the credit for ideas and their brilliant execution when, in fact, they were often those of the women and men he employed. Perhaps even more than with successful executives in most other businesses whose needs and functions may be less widely diverse than those of a great store, a very large part of Stanley's success resulted from his ability to find and hire and keep excellent subordinate executives. Even in the area in which he was unequaled, publicity, he hired and gave a large measure of freedom to talented subordinates. To help him with reporters, to write his speeches and articles, to create and dispense a constant flow of publicity, he hired not just ordinary former newspaper reporters or the usual tub-thumping hacks, but writers with flair and wit—Marihelen McDuff and Warren Leslie—in whom he developed the same combination of *chien* and *chutzpah* as he possessed himself.

The charge often leveled against Stanley by some who disliked or envied him—that he was no more than an especially astute discoverer and exploiter of the talents of others—was in fact the opposite of the truth. This was repeatedly proven when many of his people were hired away (to be president of Cartier or Bonwit Teller or to scores of other posts) but failed to achieve great success elsewhere. Clearly, it was something of Stanley's and his store's magic that made them so hugely successful in Dallas.

With his executives he was fair and often patient, and with those who retired after long service he was—with one notable exception—generous. After Al Neiman left Neiman-Marcus at forty-eight he never again repeated his success. In his last years he was ill and as penniless as he had been as an orphan child. When old friends appealed to Stanley to join them in offering help, he refused to give any to this man who, he declared, was "egotistical, opinionated, emotional, critical, and unfortunately sarcastic"—a not too inaccurate, if very incomplete, description of Stanley himself. But Stanley changed this most uncharacteristic position, and helped to support Neiman in the Masonic old-folks home where he died.

If as an employer Stanley was usually supportive, reasonably patient, and generous, these qualities were far less evident in his private life, in which he was unfortunately like Franklin Roosevelt, Winston Churchill, and many less well-known men whose primary commitment was to their own success. The *sine qua non* of great success is the power to *do*, and according to Joseph Ross, one of Neiman's ablest vice-presidents: "Stanley castrated all his brothers, after which he was invariably generous to them. He gave them large salaries, important-sounding titles, lavish travel and expense accounts, charitable and civic roles to play, in fact, anything in the world they wanted—except power."

That all the power should go to Stanley was his father's wish. "Stanley was always Father's favorite," his brother Edward remembered only a few weeks before Edward died in 1977. "When he went to Philadelphia to meet my fiancée's parents, he spoke so incessantly about Stanley that Mrs. Blum, my future mother-in-law, finally reminded him laughingly, 'Mr. Marcus, my daughter Betty is not marrying Stanley. She's marrying Edward.' To this Father replied, a bit impatiently, 'Yes, yes, Edward is a fine boy. But let me tell you about *Stanley*.' "

Edward believed that the acute psychiatric problems that sent his younger brother Herbert, Jr., to Menninger's and even the problems that led finally to the financial bankruptcy of his youngest brother, Lawrence, were largely attributable to their father's undisguised preference for Stanley. As was traditional in these Jewish department-store families, Herbert left each son equal stock in the store; but there was never any doubt after Herbert died in 1950 that there was only one boss and his name was "Mr. Stanley."

Stanley's careful confession of fraternal frictions is limited to such generalities as "unhappy tensions did develop, as egos expanded, marriages occurred, and pillow talk exerted itself."

The matriarch, Minnie, at ninety-five in 1977 was still playing an important role as peacemaker and comforter. No family feud or acrimonious divorce or scandal or stupidity, by blood relation or in-law, present or former, removed anyone from equal access to her consideration and kindness. But even for her, and even though she knew his defects, Stanley came first.

In 1932 Stanley married an employee, Mary Cantrell, whom everyone called "Billie." Full disclosure being presently in fashion, I point out that then, at the age of six, and since then as well, I tried without success to convince Billie how much happier she would be with me than with Stanley. The reader may judge to whatever degree, if any, this has colored my appraisal of Stanley.

For her family and for the public, Billie offered an example of unpretentious simplicity that often contrasted favorably with Stanley's style. He described men who were "vitiated" by their life's struggles or who "imbibe" excessively; she said they were "defeated" or "drink" too much. She was a great and loving lady.

An important and often overlooked element in the public service of these Jewish merchants was their competitiveness with one another. Herbert Marcus was for many years the chief local money raiser for the visits of the Chicago Opera Company that brought to Dallas such stars as Tetrazzini, Chaliapin, and Mary Garden. Arthur Kramer, the president of A. Harris & Company, on every trip to New York spent time, effort, and stockholders' money trying to convince the managers and board of directors of the even more prestigious Metropolitan Opera to include a visit to Dallas on the company's annual spring tour. When after years of financial contributions and flattery he finally succeeded in 1939, he considered it the high point of his life, and having "whipped" Herbert Marcus was no small part of the victory.

Kramer had a variety of collections in the immense, pretentious Tudor mansion he had hired the English architect Alfred Bossom to design. One of these, a collection of nineteenth-century Clichy, Saint-Louis, and Baccarat paperweights, was of national distinction. But none of his other collections meant as much to him as the one he kept in an old cigar box in a locked bottom drawer of his office desk and showed to visitors with obvious joy. It consisted of some two dozen marbles, all fine agates. "I won every one of these from those rich Sanger boys," he boasted, "and all I had to start with was two chipped glass marbles and a steelie."

Kramer's reputation for clear calculating coolness in Dallas was unsurpassed. According to Morton Sanger, "He peed ice water." But under that widely admired cold exterior burned a terrible, even pathetic, yearning for recognition and approval. Alexis de Tocqueville observed that in America, business satisfied not only economic lust but other yearnings as well, for it offered more power than politics and more competitive sport than the hunting indulged in by European aristocrats. "In democracies nothing is greater or more brilliant than commerce," whose leaders participate "not only for the sake of the profit it holds out to them, but for the love of the constant excitement occasioned by that pursuit."

Kramer had come up from selling newspapers on the street to the presidency of his wife's family's store, and he also made his way to the presidency of the Dallas Museum of Fine Arts and the Dallas Symphony. According to John Rosenfield, the arts critic of the Dallas *Morning News,* "I never remember Arthur using his seats at a symphony concert. He usually came to the concerts when he was in town, but he stood at the back of the house working out problems in calculus." If Kramer did not listen to the orchestra, it was perhaps not an overwhelming love of music that led him to accept the burdens involved in the orchestra's presidency. But such an assumption need not be entirely denigrating. It may, indeed, be interpreted as a greater sacrifice than such service would have been for one who loved and knew music. Similarly, when Temple Emanu-El needed a new rabbi, Kramer and Herbert Marcus (who would, like Kramer, also serve as president of Dallas's Reform synagogue) were the entire search-and-selection committee. Both men admitted privately that they were agnostics.

The reasons that men who care nothing about music and have no religious faith seek the leadership of symphonies and synagogues are doubtless many and complicated. In Kramer's case: "His wife's constant craving for social status and his own insatiable ambition for public recognition and power were of course very important," Rosenfield remembered, "but they weren't the whole story by far. Unlike those pious platitudes in his annual Christmas Day advertisement that were pure hypocrisy, Arthur's sense of duty to the Dallas community was genuine. Modesty was not one of his failings—he gave himself at least full credit for his rise in the world—but to the limited degree that he could feel gratitude, he was grateful to the city."

This sense of debt to the public, the conviction that they owed the citizens of their community not only value for their money but also contributions of money and time to matters of public welfare was exactly the opposite of J. P. Morgan's insolent statement: "I owe the public nothing," or William H. Vanderbilt's earlier contemptuous: "The public be damned."

The greatest robber barons in America from coast to coast all had, whether or not they expressed it publicly, this same damn-the-public, dog-eat-dog attitude. San Francisco's "scrupulously dishonest" Collis Huntington boasted: "Everything that is not nailed down is mine and anything I can pry loose is not nailed down." But the Jewish department-store keepers did not practice business this way, which may explain partially why none of them became as rich as the robber barons. Or it may be argued that they lacked the courage, but, if so, it must also be acknowledged that they did not contribute, as the robber barons did, to the destruction of the great prestige that for so long businessmen enjoyed in America. Or it may be that they were as burdened with rectitude as they were with their religion.

Whether the motives that moved these Jewish merchants were a genuine love of art or a yearning for public recognition or some combination of these with other incentives is in large measure unascertainable and finally unimportant. What is important is that because of Kramer and others like him, a museum was built in Dallas, and that with supporters such as Herbert Marcus a fine private girls' school survived and grew there.

From the moment of Stanley's introduction to rare books at Harvard, he was a compulsive collector. His collections eventually came also to include primitive arts, masks, twentieth-century painting, and sculpture. In the 1920s and 1930s, and again after World War II, he traveled regularly to Europe as well as to New York, and he had the money to buy when the greatest modern art was cheap. Yet, curiously enough, in those three or four decades when he and other department-store owners across America had endless opportunities to build what could have been a great modern art collection, they assembled instead only what could be called at best interesting ones. That these men, so successful in one kind of selection, were such mediocre contemporary art collectors, seems strange. There are perhaps two primary reasons.

Bargaining about price, trying to beat the seller's price down as far as possible, has always been one of the essentials of trade. But in the art world the object sold is unique, not just so many bushels of oats or yards of flannel of which virtually identical oats and flannel can be bought from others.

According to the rare-book expert David A. Randall: "Collectors like Stanley Marcus are as absolutely essential to the trade as the really great collectors like [Josiah Kirby] Lilly. Great collectors will pay *anything* for what they really want—but they are difficult because they will only accept the very rarest, finest, perfect examples and they refuse anything else. That's what makes men like Marcus who are looking for bargains so valuable.

"On a trip to Dallas I would show him something that, if perfect, would be worth perhaps five thousand dollars, but that had a few pages missing. I would ask four thousand for it and then slowly allow him to beat me down to two thousand or even one. He was then delighted, thinking he'd gotten a five-thousand-dollar book for a fifth of its worth. I was even more delighted to be rid of it at *any* price."

An even more important reason than Stanley's burning desire repeatedly to prove himself a virile bargainer was the very genius that made him one of the shrewdest fashion merchants in America. The rich customers of Neiman-Marcus—like their counterparts at Bergdorf's, Dayton's, or Magnin's—wanted expensive new fashions in suits, dresses, bags, and shoes at a very precise moment. It could not be too early, or the customer would seem to her peers to be merely odd, wearing something new and strange that no one else wore and wearing it before it had received the imprimatur of *Vogue, Town & Country,* fashion-store advertisements and windows, or the fashion and gossip columnists. On the other hand, it was even worse if she was late, if what she wore was also being worn in cheaper copies by "every little secretary," and the rich customer's peers were therefore in a position to purr: "Oh, you're still wearing *that,* are you? I gave mine away simply weeks ago."

Great art is essentially the opposite of fashion—it doesn't go out of style. But the only time when it can be bought cheap is before it has been recognized and accepted, when it is not yet fashionable because it is still so *avant-garde* that to most viewers it appears to be distorted, even ugly.

The very timing instinct that made Stanley so superb a fashion merchant may have been the chief force that stopped him from buying the really great French and American artists early and led him instead to buy the work of such momentarily "fashionable" artists such as Vertès and Clavé. Stanley did not have Gertrude Stein's eye, but it would be difficult to imagine a worse buyer for Neiman-Marcus than Gertrude Stein.

In his sixties and seventies Stanley finally gave some stature to his own collections by buying, at the high prices by then prevailing, a few pieces by artists recognized by everyone to be the most important of this century—artists whose works he had ignored in the decades when he could have bought them cheap.

But that he collected at all, well or badly, and so finally helped to set a pattern of collection was what really counted. In as tenaciously philistine a climate as existed in Dallas until after World War II, any public identification with the arts required some courage.

When President Nixon's warning to Bob Haldeman, "The arts, you know, they're Jews, they're left wing—in other words, stay away," became public in 1974, it caused a good deal of both genuine and pretended shock, despite the fact that for most of the twentieth century, in most of America away from the Eastern seaboard, it has in great part been true. And nowhere has it more obviously been true than in Dallas when (with a few such rare exceptions as the sophisticated and generous oil man Jake Hamon, long a closet intellectual and philanthropist) the richest men in the community were resolutely illiterate oil millionaires, including Clint Murchison and H. L. Hunt. They spent vast sums, but only on their wives and children, their mistresses and gambling, their kept senators and congressmen, and most of all on making more money. They refused to spend money on art objects or on the support of art institutions, although a few gave to the schools that would accept their children, to hospitals when they had health problems, and to their churches for other services rendered or hoped for.

The grotesquely disproportional representation of Jews on the boards of Dallas's arts institutions confirmed Nixon's warning. Only in recent years have some of the second and third generations of "new" Dallas money learned the joys of buying public acclaim with tax-deductible dollars.

Dallas's only first-generation oil man to revel publicly in this game was Algur Meadows, who may have spent more millions of dollars buying fake French masterpieces than the city's entire oil community spent on all the arts in the first half of the century.

From 1936 to 1966, much of what did or did not happen in Dallas was determined by the executive committee of a small group of the city's most powerful rich men, the Dallas Citizens Council, an oligarchy not unlike those that ruled the Italian city-states of the Renaissance. When asked what it was like to be the token Jew, token intellectual, token liberal, in that arch-conservative committee, Stanley smiles. "I was of course often tempted to take my bat and ball and go home. But that would not have been useful and, besides, it was more amusing occasionally to hear an idea I had suggested ten years earlier to sniggers and rejection suddenly proposed again (and as his own) by some ignorant redneck and this time to see it accepted."

Stanley was repeatedly courageous in his public statements. He had no desire to be a martyr or a Samson. The courageous positions he took and the time when he took them would seem far from heroic in other places. But the savage spirit that had demanded that all the slaves in Dallas County be whipped in 1860 had been kept alive by the Dallas *Morning News* and similar barbaric forces, so that in 1960 Lyndon Johnson and his wife, and in 1963 Adlai Stevenson, were physically attacked on the streets of Dallas in ways that would have been unthinkable elsewhere.

Just after World War II at a public protest meeting called to demand the end of wartime price controls, Stanley, who would have profited immediately from their end, was the only man who spoke in favor of keeping controls. It was a steamy, hot summer night and as he spoke, slowly, reasonably, calmly, from the back of a truck, he was greeted with obscenities, curses, and threats by the increasingly angry and dangerous mob. It was a courageous, a heroic performance.

The worldwide expressions of horror after the murder of President Kennedy in Dallas terrified the city's business leaders because the "wrong image" might halt the city's growth. Their proposed solution was to spend a lot of money with a local advertising man to project the "right image." However, on New Year's Day, 1964, Stanley ran a large signed newspaper advertisement suggesting: "Dallas should forget about its 'civic image' as such. The best public relations comes from doing good things and by not doing bad things. Let's have more 'fair play' for legitimate differences of opinion, less coverup for our obvious deficiencies, less boasting about our attainments, more moral indignation by *all* of us when we see human rights imposed on. *Then* we won't have to worry about the 'Dallas Image'—it will take care of itself."

He was much criticized for this advertisement in Dallas, and even more when in 1968 he copied San Francisco's Levi Strauss Company by writing his suppliers that Neiman-Marcus would favor affirmative equal-opportunity employers. Because so much of Stanley's life had been an obsessive and successful pursuit of publicity, he later felt it necessary to protest that the feelings expressed in this letter were genuine, and that it "was not a grandstand play for applause, even though we received it, but an act of conviction."

Houston has now clearly and apparently permanently outdistanced Dallas in growth and quality of cultural life—to a degree that would have been unimaginable in the first half of this century when both economic and cultural evidence seemed to point toward Dallas's eventual supremacy in the state. An important reason is the fact that Houston made itself into a seaport with a ship canal. But in the view of many astute observers, the chief reason has been Dallas's repeatedly reinforced reputation for relentlessly reactionary attitudes and for violence. The NASA Center and many of the companies that in recent decades moved to Houston could quite as easily have come instead to Dallas. They did not because national government and business leaders quite correctly perceived Dallas in the image of H. L. Hunt rather than of Stanley Marcus.

One of the things that has annoyed other Dallas business leaders and nearly everyone else (except customers and possible sources of publicity) who dealt regularly with Stanley has always been his often arrogant, know-it-all manner. But that was not quite as annoying as how very often he *was* right and *did* know what he was talking about.

Many if not most of Dallas's prominent citizens were richer than he, but not one even approached his extraordinary reputation nationally and internationally. If the Murchisons wanted to be on the board of directors of a major insurance company, they had to buy it; but Stanley in 1962 was asked to come on the board of New York Life because its members such as Frank Stanton and Paul Hoffman wanted him with them.

Stanley was kept from membership in Dallas's Brook Hollow Golf Club and the Petroleum Club, just as his wife, Billie, could be kept out of the Shakespeare Club and the Junior League; but when the richest and most powerful members of those clubs went to San Francisco or London and were introduced as being from Dallas, the first thing they were asked was almost invariably: "Do you know Stanley Marcus?"

Whatever their virtues, American storekeepers, Jewish and Gentile, were not immune to breaking the law in the higher name of profit. In Dallas, meetings of the Department Store Association every month or so were attended by a top executive of each of the then-five largest stores excepting Sears, who sent no one to the meetings but cooperated with whatever programs were decided on there. The most important purpose of these meetings was to discuss three illegal things: the fixing of prices; the coordinating of prohibited personnel policies and anti-union activities;

and determining the secret cash support to be given to appropriately compliant politicians, both local and national.

Prices were not fixed by item but by category and wholesale cost, for example, in ready-to-wear, anything that cost at wholesale $5.75 had to be sold for $9.95. These retail prices were, of course, floors, not ceilings. If Neiman's had a $5.75 cost blouse exclusively for the whole state of Texas and so charged $10.95 or $12.95 for it, no other storekeeper objected—he only admired and envied.

These price-fixing, political, and anti-union activities were not unique to Dallas. They were common practices all across America throughout the first half of this century. In fact, the continuation of such price-fixing practices even into our own days, and despite the purported moral- and consumer-protecting climate of the 1970s, was made obvious in 1977 by the multimillion-dollar penalties against Bergdorf Goodman, Bonwit Teller, and Saks Fifth Avenue.

In the early 1950s I unexpectedly received an official notification that the Teamsters' Union demanded an election among A. Harris & Company's delivery and warehouse employees to determine if they wanted union representation. I was still in my twenties and almost totally ignorant in such matters, so I immediately called the other Dallas storekeepers and asked their advice, as well as that of Walter Halle (of Halle Brothers in Cleveland), Fred Lazarus, Jr. (head of Federated Department Stores, which included Sanger Brothers in Dallas and Foley's in Houston), and others. Everyone with whom I consulted agreed with Lazarus, who had cheerfully explained: "Oh, don't worry if it's the Teamsters. If it was the Clerks, you'd be in trouble—they're honest. But there's no problem with the Teamsters—just call my friend Nate Shefferman in Chicago."

Shefferman ran an organization called Labor Relations Associates. Supposedly, it only "advised on labor relations," and in fact one of its representatives came to any client store that had labor problems, interviewed employees and managers, and offered suggestions on personnel policies and labor-negotiation tactics, for which services the client was billed and payment was made by check. But, in addition, Shefferman required a large secret payment in cash—in our case, $10,000. On learning about this, I asked: "And in return do you guarantee in writing that we will win the election?"

For this I received a look such as one might bestow on an especially stupid child and an explanation delivered very slowly in a loud voice, as though I were deaf as well as retarded. "You get nothing in writing, and we don't guarantee whether or not there'll be an election or whether or not you'll win it. What we guarantee is that regardless of any election or National Labor Relations Board order or anything else, you will not be asked to sign a contract with the Teamsters."

At the trial of teamster chief Dave Beck in Chicago, Shefferman turned state's evidence and revealed that he was in effect Beck's bagman. He sold out local workers for cash, most of which he then delivered to Beck, who was sentenced to jail for failing to pay proper income taxes on these bribes. It was revealed at the trial that Shefferman's clients included Sears, Roebuck, Associated Dry Goods, J. C. Penney, Montgomery Ward, Federated Department Stores, and many of the finest individually owned stores in America.

The payment of the $10,000 cash bribe in Dallas was divided between the Dallas stores on the basis of their volume; that is, Neiman's contributed more to it than did A. Harris & Company because their volume was greater than ours. At the time I had no qualms about the payment. Wiser and far more experienced men than I assured me it was the way the game was played— which in no way excuses what was both an immoral and an illegal act.

By 1977 all the executives of other Dallas stores who had participated in this bribe were dead except Stanley. If I were to reveal in this book without his approval what we had done, it would have been a betrayal of confidence. So I asked Stanley if he objected. "Say what you want in your book," he replied, "but it seems to me an unimportant and boring confession."

With his increasing stature locally, nationally, and internationally, Stanley gradually put aside many of the pretentious and
pontifical affectations that had perhaps compensated for his being
"The Ugliest Boy" and been an appropriate adjunct to his mandatory infallibility when advising oil men's wives what furs they
must buy, but had long made even his admirers laugh. For many
years he styled himself "H. Stanley Marcus," but with his increasing self-assurance he quietly dropped the H.

He never gave up his delight in grandiloquence, and in areas
where he knew his reputation was mainly undeserved, such as
art collecting, he remains still painfully prickly and pompous.
When in his seventies he learned that some of his recently bought
Central American pre-Colombian pieces were fakes, he was excessively outraged and embarrassed. But he was unquestionably the
first citizen of Dallas, which would be a far better place if more
of its leading citizens followed his example of courage and civic
generosity rather than taking the easier path of mocking his vanities.

The oil wealth and boom times in Dallas were not infrequently
cited by disparagers of Stanley as the real causes of his success;
the facts disprove the allegation. The same factors have made
Houston a big and rich city, but neither of its stores, Foley's
and Sakowitz's, even approaches Neiman's in reputation. Nor do
San Antonio's stores, Joske's and Frost Brothers. Nor indeed does
any Texas business concern of any kind, even those that are many
times larger and more profitable than Neiman's.

In the fashion business, nothing is more certain than that anything worthwhile will be "knocked off." A new dress or a new
way of promoting or selling it will very quickly and widely be
copied.

When in 1928 Herbert Marcus finally built the big store he
had always dreamed of, it was a frank copy of the Young-Quinlan
store in Minneapolis. All Stanley's life, all over the world—in
department stores, drugstores, grocery stores, fine hotels, famous
restaurants, theaters, opera houses, museums, private homes, public palaces—when he came across a thing or an idea worth copying,

he copied it. But whereas most copies are less than the original, Stanley's were often more.

To the charge I have heard repeated all my life by other merchants: "The Marci never invented anything—they only copied others," the proper answer is: "Yes, and they did it better than anyone else in the world!"

The building of the great American department stores was not, as is sometimes the winning of great battles, the result of a single brilliant or courageous stroke; it was a success that accumulated only from endless concern with countless tiny and often tiresome details. And no one knew this better than Stanley, the builder of what was in many respects the greatest American store. In some aspects of his life he was arrogant, even insolent, but when it came to the store he was a slave. No detail was so small, so insignificant, so menial, that it was beneath him. "Specialty-store retailing in particular," Stanley wrote, "consisted of a mass of minutiae, you made and kept your customers by your ability to remember small details."

The last time I interviewed Stanley, in 1977, he had been moved out of the store he had built by the New York Stock Exchange corporation to whom he had sold it, Carter Hawley Hale. The new owners were building large new versions of Neiman-Marcus all over the country, in California, Missouri, Florida, Chicago, and Washington, D.C. But in Dallas, Neiman's had lost much of the fine-fashion business it once monopolized to small specialty shops that provided those same small services Neiman's could no longer give because it was too big and its new owners were too far away.

The loss of this prestige business that he had spent more than half a century building did not go unobserved by eyes as sharp as Stanley's. During the interview Stanley accepted a call from a customer who complained that she had been unable to purchase a certain candy she had been buying at Neiman's for years. Ignoring the interviewer, Stanley immediately called the store's candy buyer and discovered that the candy had not been discontinued but was only temporarily out of stock. "You must call immediately," Stanley insisted, giving the buyer the customer's name and address and telephone number, "and tell her when you believe it's coming in—don't promise it earlier than you can deliver it. Assure her that you'll personally see to it that she gets the one pound she wants and see if she wants to order any more as gifts or for herself for later."

The buyer, who was responsible for nine candy departments from coast to coast, had obviously been reluctant to waste time on a 1-pound sale, for when Stanley asked that he read back the customer's name and address and phone number, he could not. Slowly, carefully, Stanley repeated it all again.

8

The Wild Southwest

The Jews were men who actually lived by commerce, and apart from a few Venetians they were almost the only people who did so . . . thanks to the contacts which they maintained among themselves, they constituted the only economic link which survived between Islam and Christendom. . . . [They] "speak Persian, Roman, Arab, and the Frankish, Spanish, and Slav languages. They bring from the Occident eunuchs, women slaves, boys, silk, furs, and swords . . . to Sind, India, and China. On returning they are laden with musk, aloes, camphor, cinnamon."

—Henri Pirenne, *Mohammed and Charlemagne*

Our mental picture of the Wild West was formed by the movies. The hero was handsome, clean-shaven, straightforward, and asexual; the bad guy had at least a dark mustache if not a two-day stubble, a black hat, and an endlessly burning desire to inflict on the inevitably virginal heroine a fate worse than death. With very few exceptions, Indians were ignorant, cruel, and treacherous. Equally falsely stereotyped was the "Jew peddler." He was a figure of fun, potbellied, derby-hatted, perspiring because of his inappropriate wool trousers and vest and his comic inability to control his stubborn mule, to whom he complained constantly in a music-hall Dutch-German accent.

In fact, the Jewish peddler-turned-storekeeper was one of the earliest civilizers of the West, but never the first. The first requisite for a settlement was a saloon, and the next was a whorehouse. Only then, after the settlement had begun to grow, came the second phase signaled by the arrival of "decent" women.

Decent women soon required a church and a school and, no less important, a store where some printed fabric and a bit of ribbon or lace might briefly give the illusion that frontier life was less lonely and brutal than in fact it was.

These fashion frills were only a tiny part of the early Western store's inventory that, as Senator Barry M. Goldwater explains, was supposed to supply the pioneers' needs "from the cradle to the grave, from a baby blanket to hardware for coffins, from drill bits to black powder to demijohns of whiskey—in other words, the essentials and a few luxuries for every room, the front parlor, bedroom, kitchen, and, of course, the outhouse."

Much has been made of the undeniable fact that most of the Jewish immigrants to America were fleeing from greater or lesser degrees of oppression and were seeking better economic and social conditions. But too little has been made of another enormously important stimulus to these young men: the yearning for adventure.

The first of Christopher Columbus's adventurers to set foot on the New World was their interpreter, Luis de Torres, a former Jew who had been baptized only the day before sailing. Other Marranos—Jews who converted to avoid death at the hands of the Holy Inquisition—came with Hernán Cortés to Mexico in the early sixteenth century, with DeSoto to Florida a few decades later, and with other adventurers.

For centuries Jews had been interpreters as well as traders. At the end of the eighth century, one Isaac was sent by Charlemagne with the delegation to the caliph Harun al-Rashid. For a people who, with little or no notice, might have to flee for their lives from England to France, from Venice to Turkey, from Spain to Holland, it was mandatory to know several languages and to have the ability to learn still more languages very quickly. The Jewish

peddlers who came to the American Southwest and Far West
rapidly acquired the Spanish and English that were essential to
their survival, as well as the Indian dialects that increased their
possibilities for trade and that many native-born Americans disdained to learn.

What little civilization and safety there were then in the Southwest came and left with the army, and young adventurous Jews
were sometimes soldiers, sometimes sutlers (who followed the
troops selling tobacco and other provisions), sometimes post traders; often, too, they switched from one of these roles to another.
The traders and sutlers had a monopoly of all business on an
army post. Sutlers sold the army its necessities—corn, hay, whiskey—and were under the control of the post commander. Post
traders did the same business, but were appointed by the Secretary
of War.

In Europe, Jews had long been important contractors and sub-
contractors for armies, from those of Marlborough and Louis XIV
down to those of the petty German princes and for the worst
anti-Semites across the continent, from Isabella in the west to
the czars in the east.

In the American Southwest, these army posts were in a sense
the public works projects of their day. They alone provided in
quantity what was even rarer in the New Mexico Territory than
manufactured merchandise—cash money. For a few weeks or
months after an army paymaster arrived on a post, there was
real money, as opposed to scrip or IOUs, for the saloonkeeper,
the brothelmaster, and the merchant.

It is difficult to overestimate the importance of these forts and
the local representatives of the Superintendent of Indian Affairs
to the storekeeper-sutler. When they gave him a contract for a
large amount of local produce, such as meat or corn, they not
only paid him in cash or equivalent federal drafts on Eastern
banks, but also enabled him to collect from the local producers
of meat and corn who had usually been buying from the merchant
on credit and now paid him in produce.

In the seventeenth and eighteenth centuries when the Spanish controlled New Mexico—except when they were driven out by the oppressed Indians—they did their best to keep out all American traders, Jew or Gentile. After Mexican independence from Spain in 1821, matters were only marginally better for the *extranjero*. He had to obtain a *pasaporte* for himself and a *guía* for his cargo, that had then to be further described in detail in a *manifesto*. But this was only the beginning. There followed endless red tape requirements and excessively frequent bribery requirements, first to get into business, and subsequently to get out of troubles manufactured for no other reason than to extort bribes—and the undeniable fun of harassing the foreigner.

The Catholic Church had for centuries maintained that the lending of money at interest was so vile as to be unfit for any Christian and appropriate only for Jews. Various other profit-making enterprises were also considered unworthy of educated Christian gentlemen. Therefore one of the inconveniences to Spain and her colonies that derived from the Holy Inquisition was that after so many Jews had been burned alive or driven out, there was a shortage of folk versed in providing goods, credit, and cash in an orderly fashion.

A few enterprising Jewish traders tried to function even under the Mexican administration. Eugene Leitensdorfer and Albert Speyer were already in Santa Fe by the early 1840s. Speyer was probably related to the Frankfurt bankers who were essential to Germany's well-being in the view of the kaiser. If His Majesty had any affection for Jews it was kept rigorously under control, with the exception that when he learned that male members of the Speyer line were running out, he ennobled a Speyer brother-in-law with the title "von Speyer," because, the kaiser insisted: "There must *always* be a Speyer in Frankfurt!"

From the Middle Ages on, such Jewish merchant bankers had made themselves indispensable to rulers, from local counts and dukes to Isabella of Spain and Henry VIII of England. Indeed so indispensable did some become—that is, so enormously in debt was the ruler—that frequently the only way to discharge the debt was to kill or exile the banker.

Excluded from owning land or practicing a profession, most European Jews were limited to money-lending, peddling, and shopkeeping, and so became expert at commerce. As the commercial and industrial revolutions progressed, commercial skills were more and more needed and were especially in short supply on the frontiers. When in 1654 twenty-three Portuguese Jews fleeing from Brazil landed in New Amsterdam, Governor Peter Stuyvesant did not want them to stay and put them under painful disabilities. But their lot improved rapidly when the Jews of Amsterdam interceded with the Dutch government on their behalf, stressing how useful these immigrants would be in fighting the terrible commercial competition of the English.

When the English took over America, it was not their Christian interest in the people of the Old Testament that led them to tolerate God's Chosen People, but the much needed mercantile talents of the Jews. And after the American Revolution, as the country expanded westward, the need for these talents did, too.

Not until New Mexico became a province of the United States in 1846 did more and more commerce begin to flow along the Santa Fe Trail. A monthly stagecoach line began operation in 1850; by 1860, 3,033 wagons, 9,084 men, 6,147 mules, and 27,920 oxen were employed on the Trail. By 1868, the stage was running three times a week over the 800 miles from Independence, Missouri, to Santa Fe. The fare was $250 and baggage was free up to 40 pounds, 50 cents per pound above that.

More and more people flooded down the Trail until visitors reported that in the Plaza in Santa Fe one heard a babel of French, English, German, Yiddish, Spanish, and an assortment of Indian tongues. But by 1880 the Atchison, Topeka, and Santa Fe Railroad had killed the Trail traffic.

Prussian-born Solomon Jacob Spiegelberg served in the winter of 1847 in Chihuahua in the war against Mexico. Under Colonel William Alexander Doniphan, he was a sutler or soldier or both. In 1848 he started a store in Santa Fe, and as soon as his profits permitted, he brought over five of his brothers, Levi, Elias, Emanuel, Lehman, and Willi. By 1854 he was rich enough to return to Europe when his doctors warned that he had at most two years to live. He remained in Europe another forty-four years, married, and had five children.

Spiegelberg Brothers grew into an important retail establishment on the Plaza, the Palace Store, as well as a large and profitable wholesale establishment, selling to the army and the Bureau of Indian Affairs everything from an ambulance to tons of corn, coffee, salt, light brown sugar, and blankets for both the Navajos and Apaches. In addition to retail and wholesale dry goods, there was no limit to the variety of business that such pioneer families as the Spiegelbergs went into, including banking, freighting, mail routes, mining, insurance, real estate, and hotel- and saloon-keeping.

The saloonkeeper had been the original banker in the West, keeping in his safe the money or gold dust of miners, cowboys, and farmers. After the storekeeper arrived, his place of business and consequently his safe were at least somewhat less subject to violence than the saloon.

These storekeepers provided not only the banking function of a depository but also the often more essential one of extending credit. They grubstaked miners, giving them free beans, bacon, black powder, pick and shovel in return for a place on the discovery claim entitling them to one-fifth of whatever the mine produced. They provided farmers on credit with the necessities of life until the crop came in—and often longer if the crop failed.

The reputation for honesty and even generosity of many of these merchants was sometimes so extraordinary and so marked in contrast to the slipperiness and greed of some bankers, once these arrived, that despite restrictive legislation passed in 1902 and a special gubernatorial message in 1909, many New Mexico citizens continued to insist on banking with the merchants.

When I was a boy still small enough to ride on my father's shoulders, I asked him once why he had passed Mr. Fred Florence, a Dallas banker, and not said good morning. "Merely because prostitutes and bankers each serve a useful function," he explained. "It does not follow that they should be acknowledged in public." I remember the incident because I later asked my mother what a prostitute was and for the first time had my mouth washed out with soap.

My father was fond of telling the story of a young farmer who had never before borrowed money but suddenly had to and sought advice from a more experienced man on how to deal with the local banker. "Just go in, sit down, tell him how much you want, and he'll give it to you this time because it's so little and so much less than the value of your place. But do be careful not to stare at his glass eye. He is very sensitive about it."

"But how will I know which is his glass eye?" wondered the young farmer.

"It's the one," his friend explained, "with a little kindness in it."

Much more important to the success or failure of the Southwestern merchant than his ability to select or sell merchandise was his wisdom in matters of credit. If he proved himself worthy of credit in the eyes of local bankers and of Jewish bankers in New York, he often could and did survive his own merchandising errors, depressions, fires, and such natural catastrophes as flood and drought. If he did not prove himself worthy of such credit, his business did not survive regardless of his merchandising skill and hard work.

And nothing was more likely to ruin a merchant than extending credit unwisely to others. It was money and credit that connected the Wild West not only to New York but even to London and Paris, though the connection was sometimes reinforced by marriage, as when Emanuel Spiegelberg became the son-in-law of President Grant's friend and banker, Joseph Seligman.

The Jews, even before they were murdered and raped all over Europe by the holy crusaders in the Middle Ages, had learned the essentiality of trying to come to terms with the Church. And there had been no scarcity of similarly candid and edifying reminders in the New World from the very beginning.

Hernando Alonso was the first Jew to arrive in Mexico. A ship's carpenter, he came with Cortés in 1521 and supervised the building of the thirteen bridges necessary to attack the last Aztec emperor, Cuauhtémoc, in his palace in the middle of Lake Tenochtitlán. Like the other *conquistadores,* Alonso was rewarded with the grant of an *encomienda,* and seven years later he had the additional honor of being the first Jew burned at the stake in North America. It was similarly unequivocal anti-Semitism in South America that drove the small band of Portuguese Jews from Brazil to New Amsterdam in 1654.

An interesting contrast to the usual brutality toward Indians and Jews was displayed by Archbishop Jean Baptiste Lamy. For a number of American writers including Willa Cather (*Death Comes for the Archbishop)* and Paul Horgan (*Lamy of Santa Fe*), Lamy was a fascinating figure in the history of New Mexico. He arrived in 1850, and by his kindness and example tried to make the Indians forget, or at least forgive, the obscene cruelties committed by earlier representatives of the Catholic Church—cruelties that drove the Indians in 1581 to murder the missionary friars and that a hundred years later caused the Apache and Pueblo revolts that temporarily drove the Spanish from New Mexico.

Lamy's treatment of the Spiegelbergs was blessedly untraditional. One day on the road, Lamy saw a train of twenty-five wagons halted while some Mexican teamsters carried a man into an abandoned sod hut beside the road. On inquiry, Lamy learned that it was Levi Spiegelberg, about to be left to die because his teamsters feared he had cholera.

"We willingly make room for you in our covered wagon," the French churchman told the German Jew, "and we will nurse you until you regain your strength, for we could not think of leaving you here in this lonely prairie cabin. We do not believe you have cholera and even if you have we are not afraid of contagion."

Levi was transferred to Lamy's train and a week later was well again.

Lamy became the friend of all the Spiegelbergs and one day Willi's wife, Flora, glancing out of a front window of her Palace Avenue mansion, saw the archbishop with two willow saplings. He planted them with his own hands on either side of her entrance, and then blessed the young trees.

The most venerable object in Santa Fe was a small statue of

La Conquistadora, Our Lady of the Conquest, brought there by Juan de Oñate in 1598 and kept in her shrine in the Rosario Chapel except when, once a year to celebrate Corpus Christi, she was paraded through the streets. One year the celebrants had set down the Madonna's litter in front of Willi Spiegelberg's house and were resting. The four- or five-year-old Spiegelberg daughter, seeing this unbelievably beautiful doll, quietly took it from the litter into her house, unseen by the bearers who did not notice the loss until they had returned to the cathedral. Then terror and fury grew at the inexplicable loss.

The mystery continued until that evening when Flora Spiegelberg went to kiss her daughter good night and found the splendid statue in the child's bed.

Flora rushed to the archbishop's house where Lamy received the news with "roars of laughter."

Many months later there arrived from France a beautifully dressed wax doll and with it an apology from the archbishop to the little girl explaining that it was to replace the little Madonna he had taken from her.

Not very surprisingly, the Spiegelbergs were on the list of generous first contributors to the building fund for Lamy's Cathedral of San Francisco. And they even appointed the archbishop's nephew, John B. Lamy, Jr., to a directorship of their Second National Bank of New Mexico, despite the fact that Lamy, Jr., had murdered François Mallet—a French architect the archbishop had brought over who had become too intimate a friend of Lamy's nephew's wife. The presence of a murderer on the board may also have served as a deterrent to embezzlers from within or bank robbers from without, but its main purpose was to express gratitude to the archbishop.

Just as the pioneer Spiegelberg brother, Solomon, had remained in the Territory only ten years before returning to Europe to live, so eventually his four surviving brothers (Elias had died at twenty-three in 1855) all moved their families and their now considerable fortunes from Santa Fe back to safer and more civilized New York City. But their influence remained in the Southwest because many of the most successful pioneer families of New Mexico and Arizona were relatives, friends, connections, and employees of the Spiegelbergs.

One such family was the Bibo brothers, Nathan, Simon, Solomon, and Emil. Nathan worked for both the Spiegelbergs and the Zeckendorfs before going on his own. Encouraged by Lehman Spiegelberg to bid for his own account, Nathan won a contract to provide 100,000 pounds of corn to Fort Apache. He had a difficult time delivering at the end of October when the ground was miry, but he met the contract even though he had to build a bridge to do so. He was also a big-stakes gambler, sometimes winning or losing as much as $5,000 a night at poker. He was a successful storekeeper at Bernalillo where, as the town's leading citizen, he entertained such prominent visitors as the ubiquitous General W. T. Sherman and Lew Wallace, now remembered less often as the governor of New Mexico than as the author of *Ben-Hur*.

Nathan Bibo taught himself Apache, Navajo, and Zuñi, all of which helped both in trading with the Indians and in his work on their behalf to improve their health and living conditions—a field then far from overcrowded.

Nathan's brother Solomon married a member of the Acoma tribe and became governor of the Acoma Pueblo. There were almost no young Jewish women on the frontier, and although some of the pioneers went back to Europe or to America's East Coast to find a Jewish bride, many could not afford to spend either the money or the time for this, and so married a local girl. These marriages, mixed in religious or ethnic terms or both, frequently led to the assimilation of the husband and almost always of the children.

Quite a few Jewish peddlers married Indian women and a number of them became Indian chiefs, both through their own abilities and by the traditional expedient of marrying the chief's daughter. Julius Meyer, an Indian trader in the Nebraska Territory in 1866, taught himself at least six tribal dialects and was adopted by the Pawnees and named "curly-headed-white-chief-with-one-tongue." Another peddler, Louis Friedlander, married a princess of the Colville Indians in Washington.

Decades earlier when parts of North Carolina still constituted the frontier, peddlers who traded with the Cherokees were often referred to by them as the "egg-eaters," because they lived all week long on hardboiled eggs, the only kosher food they could obtain, until they returned home for Friday evening services and some appropriately slaughtered meat. But in the endless reaches of the West, no such weekend return to a home base was possible.

As important as the Spiegelbergs in the history of New Mexico and Arizona was the Freudenthal-Lesinsky-Solomon clan. The first member to emigrate to America was Julius Freudenthal, who, like Isidor Straus and Carl Schurz, fled Germany after the unsuccessful revolution of 1848–49, and who was followed by his brothers Louis (Lewin) and Joseph.

Henry Lesinsky, whose mother was Fanny Freudenthal, a sister of Julius, was the most adventurous member of the whole tribe. At fourteen he had left his village in Eastern Europe and gone to England, where he stayed only long enough to simplify somewhat the spelling of Leszyczynski and to learn to carve in wood and stone. He then headed for the gold fields of southwestern Australia. In 1858 he came to California, where a decade earlier he might have found gold; finding none now, he joined his Uncle Julius Freudenthal in Las Cruces, New Mexico, storekeeping, supplying flour and grain to the army, and running passenger coaches and mail through 600 miles of the most dangerous Indian country in the West.

During the Civil War, many of the United States troops that had offered some protection in the West were called back for war duty. This not only gave outlaws and Indians a fairer field but also occasionally offered opportunities to marauding Confederate troops from Texas.

When Lesinsky's Uncle Julius moved back to serve as resident buyer in less dangerous and less culturally barren New York City, Henry took complete charge, brought out his brothers Charles and Morris, and opened a store in Silver City. But his riskiest decision was whether or not to invest his money in the Longfellow copper mine at Clifton, Arizona, six days' horseback ride from Las Cruces and 3,000 feet above the San Francisco River. Knowing no more about copper than that it was then selling for 25 cents a pound, Henry decided to try to mine the rich copper ore.

The mine was 1,200 miles from the nearest railroad and there was no furnace to extract the copper from the ore. Henry hired Mexicans who built furnaces, but after two years the results were so disastrous that Henry's partners were delighted to sell him their interests for $20,000.

Now at the nadir of his career, Henry by accident discovered that he could build a furnace out of copper plates. By 1880 the Longfellow mine could produce 100,000 pounds of copper a month, but by then the price of copper had fallen to 15 cents per pound and Henry had lost some $150,000. Then the price rose again and soon Henry had not only recovered his losses but was making a profit of $100,000 a year. When in 1882 he was offered $1.2 million for the mine that had almost bankrupted him, he took it and moved to New York.

These Southwestern storekeepers had to be adaptable and inventive in all of their different enterprises. In the beginning, Henry could only move his copper ore from the mine to the furnace or ship the copper itself back east by ox team up the Santa Fe Trail—an expensive five-month haul. One means of reducing this transportation cost was by having the teams bring a return load of dry goods for his own stores or those of others.

In the growing West, the demand for merchandise was so great that selling it at a very healthy markup was usually no problem. The problem was getting it. And that problem was so difficult that many merchants also became freighters, at first to satisfy their own needs and then to make a profit on the similar needs of others. Ox teams carried the ordinary freight; for fast freight there were mule teams.

These slow-moving wagon trains were often easy victims for well-mounted marauding Indians. This problem increased after Geronimo led his Chiricahua Apaches out of the San Carlos Reservation in 1882. He and his braves terrorized the whites of Arizona, whom he viewed with considerable reason as oppressors. Even on the short haul between Henry's mine and his smelter, Apache braves constantly raided ore wagons and killed the teamsters—so frequently, in fact, that it drove Henry to build the first railroad in Arizona. It was a narrow-gauge railroad, completed in 1879.

If a man's business meant that there were jobs for his relatives, the converse was equally important—a rich supply of relatives meant that every department of the store or every peripheral business could have a family member to run it or supply it rather than some outsider.

A successful storekeeper-sutler who had helped to send relatives out into smaller villages in the territory to start businesses of their own had thereby created a two-way branch system. They bought merchandise from his wholesale department. When he got a larger contract from the army for hay or corn than he could fill locally, they helped him to fill it from their localities.

Isidor Elkan Solomon married Anna Freudenthal, daughter of Louis, niece of Julius, and a cousin of the Lesinskys. When the couple moved to Las Cruces, New Mexico, the opportunities offered to Isidor by his in-laws did not please him. He therefore moved on alone to Clifton, Arizona, to work in the Longfellow mine, where he was even less delighted with the job given him by his wife's relatives—digging ore. But it may have been the yearning to escape during two weeks of that backbreaking work that inspired him to think of fueling the smelter with mesquite charcoal.

Henry Lesinsky liked Isidor's idea and offered to pay him the market price of $30 a ton at the cave pit. And so the clan was in another new business.

Isidor brought his wife and children to Pueblo Viejo, a tiny village some 40 miles southwest of Clifton. Here he not only made charcoal but soon also bought out the only store for $75 and was in addition provisioning nearby Fort Thomas.

By the end of the 1870s, Pueblo Viejo had grown enough to warrant a post office. Its citizens suggested that because Isidor had been chiefly responsible for that growth, he be appointed postmaster and the town be renamed Solomonville. Both suggestions were followed.

Entering yet another field in order to make a career for his son Charles, Isidor Solomon in 1899 launched the Gila Valley Bank in Solomonville. The bank started in a 16- by 16-foot corner of his building with one cashier's cage, where gold dust was handled quite as rapidly as coin is today. Although all employees were armed, there was no vault and no night watchman, the books never quite balanced, and Solomon himself remained convinced that to ask a man to *sign* a promise to repay what he borrowed was degrading to both the borrower and lender. Nevertheless, it would eventually grow into Arizona's principal bank, the Valley National.

Over in Silver City, the Lesinskys had a bank in which young Samuel J. Freudenthal was employed. He later described how casually a $1,000 bank shortage was treated: "One morning just after the bank opened, a gambler known as Jack Brown came in and presented a check for $1,000. My assistant, Harry Booth, asked me to get him a supply of currency from the inner vault, and I handed him $2,000. Without looking at the roll he handed it to the gambler. After the bank closed, in checking up cash we found that we were short $1,000. Harry remembered the roll given to Brown in the morning, and like a flash he suddenly realized he had neglected to count it out. So he rushed out to look for Brown, and fortunately for the bank found him in the gambling house. The gentleman was as careless as Harry. He had not even glanced at his roll of bills as yet and cheerfully surrendered them to Harry. . . . Harry subtracted $1,000 from the roll; and our cash account was once more balanced."

Samuel J. Freudenthal, Joseph's son, was the second generation of his clan to follow Horace Greeley's dictum (borrowed from John Babsone Lane Soule) to "Go west, young man, and grow up with the country." Sam was born in 1863 at Sag Harbor near the eastern end of Long Island, and his most exciting childhood adventures there consisted of trapping muskrats and selling their skins to the local hatter for 15 cents apiece.

But in 1878 he set out for Las Cruces to work in his Uncle Henry Lesinsky's store, and discovered that little if any of the excitement of that trip had disappeared since his uncles took it a generation earlier. There were no surprises on the thirty-six-hour journey from Trinidad, Colorado, to Santa Fe, or on the stops made about every 25 miles to change mules and allow the passengers to eat and refresh themselves. He found Santa Fe "quite an imposing city. Its whitewashed adobes . . . trees and flowers were refreshing to the eye after traveling through a desert country."

But after a day's rest in Santa Fe, on the 400-mile trip to Las Cruces, Sam was robbed of one of his suitcases during a stop at Paraje. A merchant there discovered the thief some months later, appropriated his horse, and sent it on to Sam. "Being a good saddle horse, it was disposed of to good advantage, so my loss eventually became a profitable one to me."

The tenderfoot set about learning Spanish and the customs of the country: that whiskey or the local wine made better "refreshment" than the beer, which was "expensive and owing to the lack of ice, not very palatable"; that whiskey with quinine was the specific for malaria and cured him of it; that for coming young men like himself, there was a constant "epidemic of marriage," from which as it turned out he would be spared until he was forty-two and against which the best preventive medicine was regularly to "dance with the señoritas."

The workers in the Longfellow mine were paid in *boletos,* company scrip that saved the extremely rare real currency for more essential and profitable purposes. The workers could spend these *boletos* at the company store where Sam clerked and absorbed "that fine old business maxim: 'Charge all the traffic will bear.' No wrapping paper or bags were furnished, the purchaser utilizing a hat or dirty handkerchief to carry the goods in."

The workers, not only the Mexicans but even the several hundred Chinese, were also graciously permitted to spend their *boletos* at another family enterprise that, like the store, was the only one allowed in town, the saloon. When Sam noticed that David Abraham, who ran the saloon, had a man whose job seemed to consist in bringing up water from the river, he asked why. "I elicited from Dave a frank admission that he was watering his whiskey on a 50–50 basis. As he himself put it, if he sold the Mexicans the pure whiskey, the company would have no men at work."

This wonderfully coordinate concern for the workers' well-being and the family's profits extended even to the practice of medicine during the many years when Clifton had no doctor. Anyone in need of medical attention was sent to Sam's cousin, Louis Smadbeck, who had no medical training whatsoever but was the owner of "a big book which gave the symptoms of, and the cure for, all diseases which flesh is heir to. With such success did he practice that he could make the enviable and unusual claim of having never lost a patient."

Very conveniently justice was also provided by an interested amateur, a company bookkeeper, one Colonel Bennet, who "had seen better days, but fondness for drink and lack of stability had been his undoing. . . . When a man was brought in for an offense against the peace and dignity of the Territory, he was usually fined a pretty stiff amount, all fines being payable in *boletos*. The money from the fines was kept in a cigar box, and when the total got up to around the $100 mark, the Colonel would have a grand jamboree with all his friends, which would last until the box was empty. Once when the Colonel had to go away for a couple of weeks, he asked me to fill his position as justice and I did so. . . . A Mexican was brought up before me and received the usual fine. The money was deposited in the cigar box, and I was an honored guest at the next jamboree. The county seat and capital of the Territory were several weeks' travel distant, and nobody was worried about such trifles as the enforcement of law and order in a faraway mining camp. Clifton was an independent republic in those days, and we were not worried by any official red tape."

For the miner or merchant, the banker or bandit, who made

his living and met his death in the Southwest, any political differences between New Mexico and Arizona were usually imperceptible. In fact, Arizona was part of the New Mexico Territory until 1863; for almost half a century after that it remained the Arizona Territory, until in 1912 it became the forty-eighth state. Although Niza and Coronado had explored the country in 1539 and 1540, the Spanish had virtually ignored Arizona in favor of the less brutal land of the present New Mexico.

The most important of the pioneer Jewish merchant families in Arizona—perhaps even of all the pioneer families of whatever religion or none—was the Goldwater clan. They are to Arizona what the Adams family is to Massachusetts, the Mellons to Pittsburgh, and the Biddles to Philadelphia, which may say quite as much about Arizona as about the Goldwaters.

The founder in America was Michael, who also came to be known as Michel, Mike, Big Mike, Don Marcus, and Don Miguel. He was the eldest of twenty-one or twenty-two children of publican Hirsch Goldwasser and his wife, Elizabeth, innkeepers in Konin, Poznan Province, Poland. Michael was born in 1821, and at about fifteen set out alone for Paris, where he worked as a tailor until he moved to London in 1848. In 1850 he anglicized his name when he married a native English Jew, Sarah Nathan, in London's Great Synagogue on March 6; but on their marriage contract (ketubah), written in Aramaic, his name is given as Jehiel ben Zvi Hirsch.

In 1852 the 6–3, boldly mustached Big Mike—as he would usually be called in America—came to California via the Nicaraguan Isthmus and brought with him his younger brother Joseph, short, fat, and so-named Little Joe in America.

By working as a peddler, Mike was able in two years to save enough money to bring over Sarah and their two children born in London, Caroline (Carrie) and Morris. The family operated a saloon *cum* poolroom *cum* general store at Sonora, California, on the first floor of a brothel whose girls, according to Senator Goldwater, loved to dress little Carrie up and play with her when they were not otherwise engaged.

After two difficult years, Mike declared himself "an insolvent debtor," a turn of events quite common for these marginal merchants in the villages and mining camps of the West that were boom towns one day and ghost towns almost the next. Sarah had taken advantage of an 1852 act authorizing a married woman to transact business in her own name as a sole trader once she had set forth before a notary the nature of her business and her intention to pay her just debts. But the Sonora mining community was playing out. In about 1858 Mike moved himself and his family (there were now four children) to Los Angeles. There he and Joe operated a pool hall, saloon, tobacco shop, and Yankee notions store in the Bella Union Hotel.

In addition to minding this store, Mike and Joe bought a wagon and a four-mule team, and peddled knives, tobacco, army epaulets, and whatever else fetched a good price in Arizona. But in 1862 Mike was again declared bankrupt, losing not only the store but also the wagon and mules in the sheriff's sale held the day after Christmas for the benefit of the creditors.

Although scarcely an honor, bankruptcy was not a disgrace either. It was a common disaster, like a flood or a business depression, from which the strong, over a period of years, could expect to recover. A man was judged not by his bankruptcy but by how he took it.

Ten years after this bankruptcy, the credit rating of the Goldwater brothers in the Mercantile Report of Hope, McKillop & Company of San Francisco had risen to 2½. This was not quite as good as 2 ("Safe for Business Wants") and still a considerable remove from 1½ and 1 ("Undoubted Credit" and "Highest Commercial Rating"), but it was adequate and improving.

To get credit, businessmen had to be honorable within the meaning of that word in the morals of the marketplace—a standard considerably less stringent than the one at least urged by clergymen for the guidance of others. But like other businessmen in other times and places, Mike and Joe were not, for example, given to overestimating the value of their property for tax purposes—indeed, a Board of County Commissioners in 1870 assessed their property at $1,500, three times the value given by the brothers. And in 1873 Joe was accused of selling large quantities of merchandise stolen from the United States government, although he was never indicted.

When men in the business of extending credit said that they were interested in a man's *character,* they were not really concerned as to whether he coveted his neighbor's wife or manservant or maidservant or ox or ass or, in fact, whether he kept or broke the other commandments. What they meant by character was that a man be scrupulously truthful to his creditor and put his promise to a creditor first among his obligations. Just such a man of character was another pioneer Arizona merchant, Hyman Goldberg, who had, like the Goldwaters, declared bankruptcy before he eventually became one of the most successful storekeepers in the Territory. That he kept his promises to those who extended him credit, even when he didn't have to, was best proved when he was captured by Apaches who released him only because he promised he would later give them certain provisions. He did so some days later when the Indians came to his store in Yuma.

In 1862, after the second bankruptcy, Mike and Joe had begun again. Leaving Sarah and the children in Los Angeles, Mike moved to La Paz, Arizona, a village on the Colorado River, where he went to work in the tiny adobe store of a friend, Bernard Cohn, whom he eventually bought out. When Joe joined them, they expanded into freighting and served as sutlers for the nearby army posts.

When Mike contracted with an army quartermaster to deliver 400,000 pounds of shelled corn or barley at 7.35 cents and an additional 500,000 pounds at 8.39 cents, he did not drive the ox carts himself; he hired others to collect and deliver what he bought and sold. But his were the potential for profit and the risk of loss. These were considerable—a quarter of a cent difference on half a million pounds, $1,250, was a small fortune in 1870.

Despite the success the brothers were having in La Paz, the strong-willed Sarah refused to bring either herself or her children to Arizona. She had had enough of the primitive and violent life of mining camps and did not propose to raise her children in the dangerous, lonely, and ignorant atmosphere of a frontier village. After ten years of roughing it in Los Angeles, she moved back to the civilization of San Francisco early in 1867, and is only known to have visited once in Arizona—and that, briefly.

Mike visited her regularly in San Francisco, where he bought most of the store's merchandise and where the last six of their eight children grew up.

The violence to which Sarah Goldwater refused to expose her children was a constant of frontier life well into the twentieth century, not only for the few swaggering gunmen but for the peaceful merchant as well. On June 15, 1872, Mike, Joe, and a third man named Jones were suddenly attacked near Granite Mountain west of Prescott by some thirty Indians—either Apaches or Yavapais. Badly outnumbered, they decided to make a run for it. In the chase, Mike's hat was pierced by two bullets and Joe received two bullets in his back. They were lucky to escape with their lives, and two weeks later Mike wrote to thank both "General Crook for the promptness with which signal aid was furnished my brother," and Dr. Ensign, who removed the lead balls that Joe wore ever after attached to his watch fob.

It was not Joe's only gunshot wound. He had a disagreement in a saloon that was resolved by a shotgun blast that cost Joe one of his eyes. When the mail-order glass eye he received turned out to be blue rather than the brown he had requested to match his surviving eye, Joe kept it, explaining: "What the hell's the difference. After all, variety is the spice of life."

In May 1880, Mike and Joe dissolved their partnership. Mike continued to run the business with the help of his sons. Joe tried storekeeping in southern Arizona, where he went broke for a second time in 1881. After a dozen more years of the rigors of storekeeping, he moved back to Los Angeles. There, with his son Lemuel and one Morris Cohn, he manufactured "Boss" overalls, a brand that for many years was at least as famous as the competitive brand made in San Francisco, Levi Strauss.

Just as most small frontier merchants did not grow into great department-store princes like Mike Goldwater and his heirs, so many of them did not survive the frontier's chronic violence. They were scalped by Indians or murdered by robbers and laid in obscure graves, if any. Violence had always been a factor in the merchant's life. As Karl Marx pointed out regarding the four-teenth-century Hanseatic, Levantine, Genoese, and Portuguese merchants: "This original rate of profit was necessarily very high. The business was very risky, not only because of widespread piracy; [but] the competing nations also permitted themselves all sorts of acts of violence." Marx also recognized the merchant as a revolutionary in the stable society of the Middle Ages whose peasant and serf, artisan and aristocrat kept his inherited place from generation to generation with little regard for money and profits. "Into this world entered the merchant with whom its revolution was to start. But not as a conscious revolutionary; on the contrary, as flesh of its flesh, bone of its bone."

American merchants must share a significant part of the blame for causing revolution in this country—long before television worked the same revolution in Europe and South America. In this revolution, secretaries and clerks, carpenters and day laborers ceased "to know and keep their proper places" and to accept their spartan lives and instead came to feel that a life including the fashions and luxuries they saw in the store's windows and advertisements were theirs by right.

For Southwestern storekeepers, dealing with bandits was noth-ing unusual, whether the bandits came to the store to buy or to rob or whether the meeting took place on the long lonely trails between settlements.

In 1878 a group of Mexican merchants from Chihuahua came to Spiegelberg's in Santa Fe to buy 100,000 Mexican pesos worth of merchandise. They said they were willing to send their own Mexican freighters for the merchandise, but they were too fearful of Billy the Kid to send up the payment—the Spiegelbergs would have to pick up the money themselves in Chihuahua and bring it back to Santa Fe.

A German-Jewish clerk of the Spiegelbergs, one Sam Dittenhoffer, whose name was usually simplified to Navajo Sam, volunteered that he was a friend of the Kid and so believed he could bring back the money safely. He rode to Chihuahua, where he had the merchants make up two barrels with double heads and bottoms, stamped: "Extra Fine Chihuahua Flour for Spiegelberg Bros., Santa Fe, New Mexico." He then carefully supervised the rolling of the heavy silver pesos, first in paper and then in muslin. He packed these tightly between the false head and bottom so that they would make no noise. The false compartments were filled with flour and the barrels put into an ordinary *carreta* pulled by one mule.

On the second morning of the five-day trip back to Santa Fe, he ran into the Kid, who greeted him cheerfully, dismounted, tied his pony to the back of the *carreta,* and climbed up into the cart to sit next to Sam. They exchanged whiskey flasks and tales of their adventures since they last met. Sam discouraged the Kid's terrifying request for a few cups of flour—it would get Sam in trouble with his bosses, the Spiegelbergs, and the flour wasn't that special. After what seemed forever, they parted. Sam delivered the silver safely to Santa Fe.

Solomon Bibo had an even more extraordinary experience. Only a few days after he had been held up and robbed on the trail, Bibo met the same Mexican bandit again and this time got the drop on him. The bandit, certain that Bibo would kill him, fell to his knees and begged to be spared, swearing he would return permanently to Mexico.

In his *Reminiscences,* Bibo wrote: "I could not kill a man in cold blood . . . who promised he would leave the country and never come back to the Rio Grande. I am sorry to say we let him go because we could have saved the lives of nearly a dozen people who were killed by this one desperado within two years after this before he was killed. . . ."

In addition to the problems of outlaws and Indian violence, freight costs in Arizona in the early days were very high, which meant that prices in the stores had to be high too, whether at Wormser's, Goldwater's, Jacobs's, Ilfeld's, Rosenwald's, Drachman's, Goldberg's, Zeckendorf's, or Steinfeld's. A bar of soap that cost the merchant 6.5 cents in San Francisco sold in Arizona for 25 cents, coffee costing 60 cents a pound brought $2, and a $5 100-pound barrel of flour was $25 in the Territory.

There were many factors that made this high markup mandatory. Most merchandise came from San Francisco and was sixty to ninety days in transit. Therefore, a merchant needed at least two inventories—the one in his store and the one en route. And because most of his customers bought on credit and paid him at best once a year, he had several more inventories sold but unpaid for, although he was of course paying interest on the money he had borrowed to finance himself.

His merchandise usually came from San Francisco by steamer around Baja California up the Gulf of California to the mouth of the Colorado River. It then had to be transferred to a shallow-draft, flat-bottom steamer and moved upstream to Yuma, where it was again unloaded and reloaded on wagons for its final journey. The freighters generally had a main wagon with two trailer wagons attached behind it. Pulled by twelve- to twenty-mule teams, these made about 15 miles a day barring storms and Indian attacks, less when pulled by ox teams.

The various transporters demanded to be paid in gold on delivery at every point and many San Francisco wholesalers also demanded payment in gold. The Arizona merchant was lucky if a third of his sales were for cash, and even these were usually for Mexican silver or greenbacks.

Despite the resulting high prices and the occasional anti-Semitic comments they inspired (although of course the non-Jewish storekeepers charged the same prices), there was usually more demand than merchandise on the frontier, so that selling was not a problem most of the time. But there were exceptions.

In 1854 Hanover-born Louis, Aaron, and William Zeckendorf had come to Santa Fe from Independence. They clerked for their cousins the Spiegelbergs, then with the Spiegelbergs' help opened their own store in Albuquerque. In 1865 they rewarded the Spiegelbergs' kindness by opening a competing store in Santa Fe, but the city was becoming overstocked and in the recession following the Civil War the Zeckendorfs found themselves with too much merchandise.

Having heard that the village of Tucson was booming, Louis set out with twelve wagonloads of excess inventory. After four months of driving through unfriendly Apache territory, he arrived at Tucson and sold out almost immediately from the wagons without even having to rent a store. The brothers decided to repeat the coup, this time with sixteen wagonloads; but by now the demand had lessened, and they had to open a store in Tucson, A. & L. Zeckendorf.

.Western merchants' experiences with outlaws were not all violent and were sometimes profitable. One of the more valuable customers of my grandfather's store in the very first years after he had come to Dallas from Houston was Belle Starr, whose parents had moved to Dallas in 1864. Until she was shot in 1889, she came down from the Indian Territory to do her shopping. Like the Dallas prostitutes, she was an especially valuable customer because she had no charge account and paid cash, whereas the rich society women in Dallas charged what they bought and paid their accounts once a year, if that frequently.

The Goldwaters were as mobile as all the other successful merchants in the West. When in 1870 the Colorado River had changed its course, leaving La Paz high and dry, Mike had moved to the town he subsequently named Ehrenberg, after a friend; and at one time or another there were Goldwater stores in Prescott, Parker, Seymour, Lynx Creek, Phoenix, Bisbee, Fairbank, Contention, Tombstone, Benson, and Crittenden. But it was in Prescott, twice the territorial capital, that the Goldwaters first achieved the success that put them on their way to becoming the most important merchant family in Arizona.

In 1877 the Arizona *Weekly Miner* described "Goldwater and Bros' New Mammoth Store" as "certainly the finest in Arizona." In fact, it was at best a miniature mammoth, a two-story, 60- by 30-foot brick building at the southwestern corner of the Plaza. But it offered its customers a comfortable porch 10 feet wide along the front and northern side, and an elegant high-ceilinged first floor with four fine chandeliers and fixtures painted white and trimmed in gold, as were the cornices and moldings. The office at the left of the entrance was a platform raised four feet and surrounded by a low railing. From it the Goldwaters had an unobstructed view of the whole floor—salespeople, customers, shoplifters, or visiting competitors—for they knew, probably in Yiddish as well as in Spanish, that *El ojo del amo engorda al caballo* (Under the master's eye, the horse fattens).

This raised and open office also enabled the customer, as was intended, to admire the carved black walnut desk, elegant calendar clock, artistically decorated gold scales, and celebrated Macneale & Urban safe. He or she could easily interrupt the boss's work to complain, praise, or just pass the time of day.

An advertisement for the new store makes clear that even this early on, the Goldwaters were determined to have the "nobby" store: "The attention of epicures is called to a fresh supply of Cheese, Caviar, Dutch Herrings, Olives, Sea Moss, Farina, Maple and Rock Candy, Syrop, Broma, Isinglass, Shelled & Bitter Almonds, Boneless Codfish, Citron & Lemon Peel, Chutnee, Mushrooms, Salmon Bitters & Mackerel. Coffee Ground Fresh Every Day."

The local newspaper stories about stores and storekeepers were usually as glowing and hyperbolic as the stores' own advertisements; indeed, there was often a remarkable similarity between what the merchant professed in his advertisement and what was reported in the story that appeared in the paper's news columns. But what advertisers say about themselves and what journals say about their advertisers are—like lapidary inscriptions—not given under oath. "Go to Goldwater's gorgeous two-story brick store," the Arizona *Enterprise* urged its readers in a breathless news story, "and see the dazzling array of goods. Be sure and get Morris to show you the magnificent set of buggy harness that is to harness the firm's fast-going horses. It takes the palm from any harness in the territory."

The Goldwaters and their "mammoth" store played an important role in the social life of the city. Mike was in charge of the 1879 Christmas Ball at the new Masonic Hall that occupied the upper floor of his Prescott store. More than 100 guests waltzed to the music of the 12th Infantry band, dined at midnight, then danced again until three o'clock in the morning.

The *Daily Miner* advised its readers: "Mr. Sam Goldwater, son of Michael Goldwater, became 'a man amongst men' today having attained twenty-one years. With his birthday came also valuable presents. From his father . . . a beautiful stem-winding gold watch, chronometer. . . . From his mother a solid gold chain . . . from brothers and sisters gold sleeve buttons, ivory match and cigarette case, delicately embroidered handkerchiefs."

These social notes, like the Christmas season advertisements suggesting such chic gifts as "Wine, delicacies, a 'nobby' Hat, mirrors, bird cages, Engravings or Chromos, a piano or fine sad- dlery, &c, &c," gave the store "tone." Most of what it sold was far more utilitarian and plebeian, but customers found it more exciting to buy a bit of new oilcloth for the kitchen table at such a "posh" establishment than at a more ordinary one. It was at the Prescott store that Mike adopted what was to remain the Goldwaters' motto and to a remarkable extent their policy, "Al- ways the Best."

Even (perhaps especially) on the frontier, women and men as well were sometimes given to emulating what they knew about the pretensions of the East Coast and of Europe. It was to appeal to this need that the Western merchant named his store The Bos- ton Store, The New York Store, or even The City of Lyons or The City of Paris. But as the social notes about the Goldwaters indicate, the West had not yet taken up what in the East was already a fashionable form of snobbery—anti-Semitism.

That is not to say that no anti-Semitism existed. If a man drove a hard bargain he was surely referred to, at least behind his back, as "that son-of-a-bitch," and if he was a Jew, the reference was "that Jew son-of-a-bitch." But in this difficult land where survival occupied most people's energy most of the time and there were very few Jews and many more Indians and Mexicans to abuse and exploit, there was very little anti-Semitism. How little was repeatedly demonstrated when Jews were elected to public office, as was Morris Goldwater, on whose career his nephew Barry would frankly model his own.

As Mike's oldest son, Morris had gone to work early in his father's La Paz store while Mike and Joe concentrated on getting army grain contracts. At twenty, he was sent in 1872 to run the brand-new Phoenix branch. There he learned that the army's proposed telegraph line to Prescott would bypass Phoenix; he proceeded to convince the army to run a branch line to the Goldwaters' store in Phoenix by promising to provide a free telegrapher. He thereupon taught himself the Morse code but transmitted his first message so badly that the answer suggested succinctly: "Get the hell off the wire!"

Each merchant competed intensely to get for his store the post office, telegraph office, stagecoach stop, Wells Fargo station, or anything else that brought customer traffic and made his store the news and social center of the town. These meant that whoever wanted to know the election results or commodity prices back east or in New Orleans or San Francisco could learn them first at the store. When in 1869 Joe Goldwater had been appointed postmaster at Ehrenberg, it not only meant that citizens came to the store to get their mail but also logically led the Goldwater brothers into becoming forwarding agents (6 cents per pound to Prescott, 3.5 cents to Wickenburg, *in gold*), and subsequently storage agents (2 million pounds of barley on July 11, 1873).

When the telegraph office in Phoenix was removed from Goldwater's to Michael Wormser's store in 1874, Morris was furious and did his very best to get it back. But despite Morris's energy, the Phoenix store was proving unprofitable. Soon he closed it and moved to Prescott, where he was both a business and a social success.

He helped to organize a volunteer fire company known as "The Dudes," and also the "Prescott Rifles," whose purpose was allegedly to protect the citizenry from marauding Apaches and Yavapais but who happily spent far more of their time as a drinking, marching, and chowder society.

Just before Christmas in 1878, at the age of twenty-six, Morris was nominated for mayor by the Democrats. Until his nephew Barry vitalized the Republican Party in Arizona a half century later, the Democratic nomination was tantamount to election, and Morris was elected in January 1879 by 208 votes to 144. Thereafter he was referred to in the newspapers (and by those seeking favors) as "Hon.," a state of affairs very pleasing to his mother in San Francisco. And he was in the papers constantly: as welcoming General W. T. Sherman to Prescott; as the owner of an elegant buggy and a fleet team of "sparkling bays, 'Mary' and 'John' "; as attending a *Bal Masqué* in the guise of the "Prince of Paradise"; or when he and his brother Sam "had a fine new carpet laid in their counting room."

Morris was elected mayor—at no salary—ten times, serving on and off for forty-eight years, and he served as well on the town council and in the territorial legislature. A convivial, witty, and self-deprecatory man, he enjoyed strong spirits and good friendships until he died at eighty-seven in 1939, as full of fun as when he had moved at Arizona's Constitutional Convention: "Mr. President, the pages will receive $5 per day. I propose that I resign from the convention as a member serving for $4 per day and be hired as a page." His motion failed to carry.

Morris's much less convivial father, Big Mike, ran for mayor only once and was elected; but before completing his term, he resigned in 1885 in a pique when the council insisted on assessing him and the other downtown property owners for the cost of building wooden sidewalks—this prefiguring his grandson Barry's long fight against similarly profligate big government.

Mike's reason for agreeing to run for mayor in the first place may have been to vindicate his good name after his embarrassing connection with a questionable public lottery. The purpose of the lottery was first to raise the money necessary to construct a capital at Prescott, and then to build public schools throughout the Territory.

Mike Goldwater, in his role of president of the Bank of Arizona, was treasurer of the lottery—$5 for a full ticket and $2.50 for a half ticket—whose 282 prizes were to distribute $31,250, including a first prize of $10,000. But when the date announced for the drawing arrived, not enough tickets had been sold and the drawing was postponed and finally never held at all. Arizona's Democratic politicians and newspapers had a field day with Governor Frémont and Goldwater. The "bogus lottery scheme," declared the Arizona *Citizen,* intended only to provide its promoters with "grand wine dinners at the Fifth Avenue Hotel, in New York, at the expense of the rusty looking miner (poor soul)." According to the *Weekly Miner,* the lottery's promoters were the last thing "needed in a young Territory which has been cursed with everything, from the murderous Apache down to the parasites with which we are infected, compared to whom the Indians are respectable people."

Horrified and hurt by the unjust criticism and scorn heaped on him for performing what he had considered another public service, Mike advertised in the territorial newspapers that he would personally refund the price of every sold lottery ticket offered to him, which he did. Many years later his grandson, Barry, characterized the lottery as part of "a responsibility that often was repaid—as public life can be today—with criticism as much as with appreciation for honest efforts."

Shortly after Mike's resignation as mayor, he sold the store to his sons and moved back to San Francisco and Sarah. He died there in 1903.

Not until two years later, when Sarah died, did her sons, Morris and Baron, dare to marry the Christian fiancées they had long kept secret from the matriarch. Perhaps it was Sarah herself who had driven the boys to marry Christian girls by her unrelenting practice of providing an endless stream of "nice Jewish girls" for them to take to parties when they came up to San Francisco.

Baron Goldwater, the youngest of Mike and Sarah's eight children, had been brought up comfortably in San Francisco and had not come out to Arizona until 1882 when he was eighteen. He was something of a playboy and a dandy, sporting matching suits and ties, pince-nez glasses, and carefully parting his hair in the middle. Whereas his older brother Morris believed that Prescott would continue to be Arizona's most important city, Baron believed in Phoenix, despite the family's two false starts there. When the federal government moved the territorial capital to Phoenix in 1889 and a railroad finally joined Phoenix and Prescott six years later, the trend seemed clear, and in 1896 another Goldwater's store opened in Phoenix with Baron in charge.

On New Year's Day, 1907, Baron married a trained nurse from Nebraska, Josephine Williams, who had come to Arizona because of her supposedly incurable tuberculosis. Their son, Barry Morris, was born two years later on New Year's Day; Robert Williams was born eighteen months later on the Fourth of July; and Carolyn arrived two years later, and perhaps because she was only a girl, not on a holiday.

Josephine—called "Jo Jo" by her friends and "Mun" or "Mungie" by her children—was an Episcopalian. She brought up her children in Phoenix's Episcopal Cathedral. Although Baron, whose bar mitzvah had been lavishly celebrated in his parents' home in 1879, never abjured his Jewish religion, his descendants all became Christians, as did those of other pioneer Jewish merchants including the Drachmans of Tucson—Philip Drachman had come over in 1852 in the same steerage as Michael and Joseph Goldwater.

"Mun" Goldwater's paternal great-great-great grandfather was Roger Williams. Her great-great grandfather, Ephriam Foster, had served the Continental Army as an artificer and lieutenant for four years and taken part in the Battle of Stony Point—which enabled Barry to join the Sons of the American Revolution. The patriotism that was a constant of the children's upbringing is as difficult for many to feel today as would be Barry's boyhood recollection of the thrilling day in 1912 when his mother stitched to the family's American flag the forty-seventh and forty-eighth stars for New Mexico and Arizona.

Baron was away in New York much of the time, and even when he was home he spent little time with his rambunctious children and much at the card tables of the Maricopa Club playing "paganini." Nor did he spend an excessive amount of his time minding the store; but he enforced the policy that it was to be the fashion store of the city, handling exclusive and expensive lines of merchandise and not merely competing for the cheaper business with the city's two bigger department stores, Korrick's and Diamond's.

In her own way and for her time, "Mun" was no less colorful a parent than Baron. She smoked cigarettes in public, played golf in knickers, and set an athletic example for her children by winning the state and Southwestern woman's golfing championships—an example followed best by Bob who is a championship golfer.

Baron never learned to drive an automobile—the Goldwaters' rented two-story brick home at 710 North Central was only a few blocks' walk from the store. But "Mun" drove all three of her children in the various family cars—a Chalmers, a Pierce-Arrow, a Packard—all over the state to see Indian dances, monuments, natural wonders, or anything else she considered educational or interesting. She camped out with them on the side of the road on these trips or on the four-day drive to Los Angeles. Despite the bad health that had brought her to Phoenix, "Mun" lived to the age of ninety-two and until she died in 1966 was an important influence in her children's lives.

For Barry and Bob, growing up in Phoenix was fun. They knew everybody and everybody knew them. Baron was a silent partner in Riverside Park, which had the only swimming pool in town, and in the local movie business, so the boys had "party passes," good not only for themselves but for all their friends as well.

They went to public school, the only one in a town of some 10,000 except for the segregated Indian School whose big Thanksgiving Day football game against Phoenix Union High was the holiday's most important event. For the Goldwater boys, sports and school politics, in which they both excelled, were much more important than scholarship, in which they did not.

To keep his active, noisy sons out of the house as much as

possible, Baron converted the second floor of the garage into a clubhouse and gymnasium. Here the boys put on six-bout boxing cards and charged two bits' admission. Because they also sparred at a downtown gym with, among others, the son of their father's black masseur, young John Henry Lewis, who would become the world light-heavyweight champion in the 1930s, they suffered countless broken noses—in Bob's case so frequently that for the rest of his life he could bend the tip of his nose and it would stay bent. But both remained almost startlingly handsome and popular with the girls.

As was then the case throughout the West, society in Phoenix was relaxed to a degree difficult to imagine now. Houses were not locked. If unexpected guests came to the Goldwater house and found no one at home, they let themselves in, fixed themselves drinks at an open bar, and made themselves comfortable.

Morris and his political cronies were of course frequent guests in Baron's home, where young Barry took part in their discussions and arguments, addressing his elders on a first-name basis.

When the Phoenix Country Club was founded in 1904, the Goldwaters were as automatically among the first members as they were among the supporters of a library or the directors of a bank. Neither Barry nor Bob remembers a single anti-Semitic incident in his youth. But by the 1930s, when their best friend, jeweler Harry Rosensweig, was proposed for the country club, there were objections. In the course of the struggle that followed, "there was blood on the floor," but the Goldwaters finally got their boyhood chum in.

As new rich Easterners poured into Arizona, they brought with them their prejudices and pretensions. Slowly the state began to change from what it had been when the University of Arizona was first organized in 1890 and two of its first three regents were Jews, Abraham Frank and Jacob Mansfield, while the third was José Maria Redondo.

"Putting on the dog and keeping up with the Joneses were unheard of in Phoenix then," Bob remembers. "Dad spent money like he had it and we ate *pâté de fois gras* and used fancier china and crystal than a lot of our friends because that's the way he enjoyed living. But the only thing he and my mother stressed to us about ourselves was how good Arizona had been to our family and that we were obligated by that—we had a lot to live up to."

Because so much of young Barry's life was devoted to mischievous fun—such as firing off his homemade cannon on Sunday morning during services at the Central Methodist Church—he was sent to Staunton Military Academy in Virginia. He took to the discipline, repeated his freshman year, and was elected president of his class just as he had been at Phoenix Union High. When he graduated in 1928, he won the award for best all-around cadet.

Equally popular at the University of Arizona in Tucson, where he turned up with a 1925 balloon-tire Chrysler roadster, he was elected president of his freshman class and joined the Sigma Chi fraternity. But when his father died in March 1929, Barry finished his freshman year and then went to work at the store: "The greatest mistake I ever made."

Five years later he married Margaret ("Peggy") Johnson, a Muncie, Indiana, heiress of the Borg-Warner fortune. He won her away from G. Mennen Williams, who would become "Soapy," the Democratic governor of Michigan and a presidential hopeful.

Although during the 1964 presidential campaign, many people who did not know Barry Goldwater characterized him as a monster, among those who knew him well—including those of us who voted for his opponent—there has never been any doubt that he is absolutely honorable, candid, and frequently witty at his own expense, characteristics not invariably associated with presidents and presidential candidates before, during, or since his campaign. "I'm not even sure that I have the brains to be president of the United States," he once said—a doubt apparently shared by a great majority of the voters in 1964. But that he had the moral character is beyond question and his character, like his principles, was formed by his family and his southwestern environment.

As his relatives had stood up to the violence of the Arizona frontier, so Barry, for example, stood up to the pandering pornographer who during the 1964 campaign published the long-distance diagnoses of hundreds of shabby psychiatrists stating that Goldwater was "homosexual, latent or overt, doubted his manhood, was emotionally unstable, paranoid, was, like Hitler, a sadist, immoral, and amoral."

Nothing but heroic courage and an unyielding sense of his duty ("If you can say that kind of thing about a man who is running for public office, then decent people are going to stop running for public office") induced Goldwater to bring the libel action that resulted in a jury awarding total punitive damages of $75,000. He was well aware that even if he won the suit, it would cost him more in money, time, pain, and widespread repetition of the obscene and untrue charges than he could possibly hope to be compensated for. But he believed that if he and his wife had been given fortunes and positions of leadership, there came with them often unpleasant duties impossible for others. In the trial, Peggy had testified in answer to the allegations that Barry was homosexual that her husband had always been "very ardent."

Barry's response to libel derived from his background, as did his view of how to help his less fortunate fellow citizens. When Big Mike had returned to San Francisco from the frontier, he had continued to follow the centuries-old Jewish tradition to be his brother's keeper. In the years he served as president of San Francisco's First Hebrew Benevolent Society—founded in 1849 to share the blessings of the Gold Rush—Mike stressed to its members that "unless old age or incapacity for work demanded such a course," he did not insult or corrupt his fellow Jew by a regular dole that would make him dependent on the Society, but instead performed the Society's "bounden duty to offer him all the reasonable assistance toward earning, by his own exertions, sustenance for himself and family. . . . able-bodied heads of families I have furnished with horse and wagon wherewith they have been placed in a position to earn a livelihood."

It was Barry's sense of obligation that finally took him from the rich man's hobbies of collecting and traveling to the rough and tumble of full-time professional politics. He wrote an apology to his brother Bob and the store manager Bill Saufley both for leaving the store on their shoulders and for involving it in the animosities that he knew politics would inevitably generate. But he reminded them that earlier Goldwaters had also felt the call to service. "Don't cuss me too much," he begged. "It ain't for life and it may be fun."

He had obviously overestimated the painfulness of the duty and underestimated the pleasures of power, for it seems evident now not only that his decision is for life but also that he loves it, as he now willingly admits. Unlike most duty-ridden people, he has a sense of humor even about his strongest feelings of duty and principle—he was the first to joke that he would rather be Right than President.

To many native-born Americans who came to the Southwest before the turn of the century, it was a purgatory where one stayed only as long as absolutely necessary, made as much money as possible, and then fled: a "deformed and wretched featus of creation . . . a half-finished work from the mighty hand of Jehovah, thrown aside in utter disgust at its worthlessness," or as another mid-nineteenth-century observer put it more simply, "this rectum of the world."

Many of the immigrant pioneer Jewish merchants also went back east as soon as they could afford to; but a surprising number stayed on and worked to improve their communities. Although a century later it would become fashionable to condemn what they did as "exploitation," in fact these men succeeded because in the main what they did was the opposite of exploiting. They earned the trust of the Anglo as well as of the Mexican, Indian, and Oriental. The citizens, Catholic and Protestant, repeatedly elected them to local and state offices as evidence of this trust— for they had no constituency of fellow Jews, who numbered only a small fraction of 1 percent of the population.

To an extraordinary degree, the local feeling that these Jews were among each community's best citizens derived not only from their fair dealing with everyone and their comparative civility to minority groups, but from their repeated efforts to improve the community with "culture." This impressed their fellow citizens, whether it took the form of lining the streets with cottonwood trees, supporting schools and libraries, or making the city feel more civilized and like the cities back east, as in 1873 when the *Daily New Mexican* (after first recovering from shock) expressed pride that Willi Spiegelberg had initiated the practice of putting female mannequins in the store's windows.

The merchant's support of performances by a visiting opera company of course helped to sell evening dresses and "boiled" shirts, just as the merchant's children benefited when he served on the school board and saw to it that teachers had some competence and were not appointed merely because they had powerful political friends and despite the fact that they were alcoholics who could beat the children more easily than they could teach what they did not know themselves.

But even the most skeptical recognized that the merchant's contributions to "culture" and to the beginnings of interracial understanding, like his political service, usually cost him more than it directly benefited him. Often when he had first arrived in his community, saloons, brothels, monte banks, and faro tables had offered the only relief from work. He had become a prime mover in bringing to town such patents of civilization as Edwin Booth's *Julius Caesar* and Lily Langtry's *She Stoops to Conquer*.

But the chief wonder was the country itself—not only its phenomenal physical and economic growth but especially its growth in tolerance. It says something significant about America that 110 years after a Polish immigrant began peddling here in 1852, his store sold for more than $2 million to the chain that owns Lord & Taylor and Joseph Horne. But what a country where, two years later, the grandson of that "Jew peddler" is the Republican nominee for president.

9

The Jewish Argonauts
of San Francisco

In the ninth century Jewish merchants surpassed not only
Christian but also Muslim merchants in the scope of their
trade. . . . [They] spanned the whole known world . . .
from the farthest west to the farthest east . . . to Bulgaria
to purchase slaves whom they later sold in Venice; to Prague,
the great city of stone where Arab coins circulated side by
side with cloth which the Baltic peoples used as money.
—*The Cambridge Economic History of Europe*

Only one American storekeeper became so world famous that,
like a pope or king or emperor, he is known everywhere by his
first name. That storekeeper was Levi Strauss.

The Bavarian-born Strauss came to America at fourteen. At
twenty, in 1850, he became one of the Argonauts who sailed
round the Horn to California. He did not come to be a gold miner—
hoping to survive in the desert heat and mountain cold on sow
belly, sourdough, jack rabbits or, as a last resort, by eating his
own burro. Strauss came to sell merchandise.

In San Francisco, "eggs laid on the other side of Cape Horn
sold for ten dollars a dozen and a drink of whiskey cost a pinch
of gold." In this seller's market, Levi Strauss began as a peddler

in the mining camps and soon earned enough to open a tiny store on J Street in Sacramento.

At this same moment, four other men started behind the counters of pioneer stores in Sacramento but quickly left storekeeping for bigger games, including banking and railroading. They were the "Big Four" of California history: Collis P. Huntington, Charles Crocker, Mark Hopkins, and Leland Stanford.

The Auerbach brothers were another storekeeping family that started out in the California gold-mining camps—in a tent store at Rabbit Creek. When in 1864 they moved to Salt Lake City, Utah, Brigham Young himself selected the site for their store, and after studying their success, Young opened his own store four years later. But the Auerbachs survived that as well as the indignity of being called "Gentiles," the epithet applied by the Mormons to all non-Mormons.

After only a few months in Sacramento, Levi Strauss had put aside enough money to move to San Francisco. There he opened a dry-goods and clothing business on California Street, selling— at retail and wholesale—everything from corsets and petticoats to umbrellas. Not until the 1860s did he come upon the opportunity that would eventually make his name as well known as that of Suleiman or Napoleon.

At least according to legend, a miner named Alkali Ike was given to getting drunk and roaring his complaint that his work pants, bought from a tailor named Jacob W. Davis, didn't hold up worth a damn. The problem was that, like all miners, Ike jammed his pockets full of mining tools and rock samples until they tore off. Tired of Ike's complaints, Davis one day sewed on new pockets and then had a local harnessmaker rivet the pocket corners with copper. It worked.

Strauss, who had by now built a considerable business making and selling work clothes, put Davis in charge of his overall factory. In 1873, the two of them received a seventeen-year patent on the use of copper rivets to strengthen work clothes at the points of strain. By the time a seventeen-year patent renewal ran out in 1908, the reputation of "Levi's" was established.

Strauss had originally made pants from a roll of tentmaker's canvas that he had brought with him around the Horn. Thereafter he used whatever fabric he could lay his hands on, including the sun-bleached, often arrow-pierced coverings of Conestoga wagons that had crossed the continent, or the wind-torn, worn-out, salt-stiffened sails of abandoned ships in San Francisco Harbor. But as soon as he could, he assured himself of a supply of the strongest denim (the name probably derives from *serge de Nîmes,* of which the French workingman's blue clothes have traditionally been made). Strength was what the miners, muleskinners, cowpunchers, stage drivers, lumbermen, and just plain dirt farmers wanted—and strength was what Strauss gave them. On his increasingly familiar leather label was the boastful trademark that showed two horses trying in vain to pull apart a pair of pants. A century after Strauss began making these trousers, an occasional farmer still hitches up two horses and pulls a pair of Levi's apart. Strauss's heirs always send him a new pair.

In 1847, a year before gold was discovered in John Sutter's millrace in the Sacramento Valley, San Francisco was an unknown adobe village of 500 residents. Only twenty-three years later, in 1870, its population was 233,000 and it had become one of the largest and most sophisticated cities in America. French immigrants played a significant role in this transformation, non-Jews such as the Verdier brothers, as well as Jews.

When Felix and Émile Verdier arrived in 1850 in a chartered ship, *La Ville de Paris,* full of merchandise with which they planned to open a store of the same name, the gold-rich miners bought out everything right at the dockside and the brothers returned immediately to Paris for more merchandise. They and Felix's descendants built a store that became such a city landmark that when, in 1974, the Carter Hawley Hale chain tried to demolish it in order to build a Neiman-Marcus branch, San Francisco citizens rose and stopped the "desecration."

The most colorful of these early French pioneer merchants was Raphael Weill, a Jew from Lorraine, whose life in San Francisco began when he was shipwrecked at Coronado on his arrival. The sixteen-year-old boy grew into the city's best-known merchant prince, boulevardier, club man, arts patron and connoisseur, gourmet chef, and perennially eligible bachelor. His department store, the White House, was long the city's best. And part of the reason for success was clearly Weill's ability to obtain adequate credit.

In a country as enormous as America, with so many tens of thousands of businesses, it was of course difficult for lenders to separate the sheep from the goats, to determine who was worthy of credit and who was not. To answer this need, agencies such as R. G. Dun & Company and later the Bradstreet Company were developed, to supply purportedly pertinent data on applicants for credit.

Dun almost invariably pointed out if a merchant was a "Jew" or "Israelite." Unless this was qualified positively as "White Jew" or "Israelite of the better classes," the implication clearly intended was "poor credit." Not only Jews but also other moral degenerates—who were therefore poor credit risks—found themselves exposed in Dun's reports. One merchant was reported to be a frequent visitor to San Francisco's "numerous Chinese flesh palaces," and another merchant's "moral character is considered bad, has a wife and children, has been accused of keeping for a long time past a mistress and of having a child by a servant girl."

Jewish merchants were often forced, therefore, to borrow from other Jews. Levi Strauss at first relied on the credit of his brothers, Jonas and Louis, in New York. Successful local merchants such as the Seligman brothers made loans to smaller merchants. In February 1849, only a few months after the very first rumors of Sutter's gold, Ben Davidson had arrived in San Francisco to serve as an agent of the Rothschilds of London.

But for Raphael Weill there had never been credit problems. His brother Alexandre was a member of Lazard Frères; as a result, Raphael had all the credit he wanted in New York, London, and Paris. Weill spent six months a year in San Francisco and the other six in Paris, equally and outspokenly loyal to both cities. He explained San Francisco to Sarah Bernhardt and Anatole France and explained them to his friends in San Francisco. The cross-fertilization of cultures between civilizations accomplished by Jewish merchants over the centuries continued well into this one, calling to mind Saki's comment, "the people of Crete unfortunately make more history than they can consume locally."

Both in Paris and in San Francisco, Weill was constantly interviewed because he was a reporter's delight—always willing and usually equipped to give strong opinions on virtually any subject, often outrageous, original, and surprising. In 1919 he declared that the achievements of France's women in the World War had been at least the equal of those of its men, and had been accomplished "in the face of conservatism, of male egotism, of male jealousy, of poverty and of prejudice."

Weill was never more lyrical than when interviewed on the subject of food and its proper preparation. For forty-four years he was perhaps the most popular member of San Francisco's Bohemian Club, where his portrait shows him in the traditional chef's cap and apron and where he prepared his famous Sunday morning breakfasts for hundreds of his friends.

Despite his popularity, however, he never became a member of the exclusive Burlingame Country Club, although for years his "Frogs' legs à la Raphael Weill" was a staple of its menu, causing a waggish friend to remark: "At least he made it as an entrée." After the Civil War, San Francisco began to suffer from the same "hardening of the social arteries" as appeared back east. Not until after World War II were a few Jews admitted to the Pacific Union Club and the Burlingame.

Prominent Jews resented their own and their families' exclusion from the best clubs not because of any misconception that they were thereby deprived of a higher level of culture and intellectual intercourse. They knew it was a matter of business disadvantage: that they and their children would have greater difficulty in getting promoted in business; and that, as *Fortune* magazine reported the situation in New York City: "At the Metropolitan or the Union League or the University . . . you might do a $10,000 deal, but you'd use the Knickerbocker or the Union or the Racquet for $100,000, and then for $1 million you'd have to move on to the Brook or the Links."

There was only one subject that Raphael Weill always refused to discuss with reporters—his Jewishness. He was unwilling even to tell his parents' names. "No, no, I do not care to give that. No, not that. You cannot get anything out of me about my parents. I do not see that it matters whether they were Jews or Mohammedans or Christians. We all came out here as adventurers and without a family—we were the Argonauts."

When Raphael died in 1920, he was buried in Paris. His Paris-born nephew, Michel David Weill, who had come to San Francisco in 1904, assumed the direction of the White House. He was president of San Francisco's de Young Museum, until replaced in 1953 by Grover Magnin. Michel, like his uncle, was a famous gourmet, and was dedicated to broadening the cultural and social outlook in San Francisco. But as I observed when buying with him in Europe in the 1950s, his chief study was women. At seventy-five in 1963 he protested to a San Francisco *Chronicle* reporter against the injustice of the double standard. "Non, non, non. I see no reason why a man should feel justified in having affairs and expect his wife to remain faithful. Women have needs and emotions just like men, and if men feel they are entitled to sexual freedom, they should recognize the same right for women."

A number of San Francisco women had not found it necessary to wait for Michel's approval but had always lived precisely as they pleased—not the least blatant of these being another famous figure of the French-Jewish community, Ernestine Roos. Her first husband, Alsace-born Adolphe Roos, with his brother Achille founded in 1866 what would become the city's best men's store, Roos Brothers.

Whether because he was following the biblical injunction that a man marry his brother's widow, or for more personal reasons, Achille, when Adolphe died, wedded the high-spirited, *"épater le bourgeois"* Ernestine. She had always, the gossips whispered, been at least as fond of Achille as of Adolphe, and one of the many

"Roos stories" that circulated in San Francisco society was that when any of her sons, George, Leon, or Robert, was asked at school, "Who is your daddy?" he immediately replied, "Roos Brothers."

When she married her brother-in-law, a number of women who envied Ernestine's *je m'en foutisme* quite as much as her great and frequently displayed jewels, purred, "Keeping it in the family has scarcely been her usual practice." Equally ungenerous suggestions about keeping it in the family were heard when Arabella Huntington, the widow of Collis P. Huntington, married her nephew, Henry E. Huntington, whose Gutenberg Bible, Gainsborough's *Blue Boy*, and Lawrence's *Pinkie* had the same baleful effect on many San Francisco society ladies as Ernestine's jewels.

Whether "Madame Roos," as she was always called, was spending a week at the fashionable Tahoe Tavern in Lake Tahoe, or was elaborately satin-and-point-de-Venise gowned and jeweled at 3:30 in the afternoon as she served "a refection" to President Taft when he visited San Francisco in 1911, or was receiving guests as a very old woman propped up by dozens of lace pillows in bed in her suite at the Mark Hopkins Hotel, invariably as covered in gems as the Virgin of the Macarena during Holy Week—she set the pattern for vulgarity for all of San Francisco.

But the Jewish storekeeping family that most obviously set the fashion for San Francisco's *nouveaux riches*, who ordained how they decorated their Nob Hill palaces and what they collected, was that of the Gumps.

Solomon Gump, the seventeen-year-old son of a Heidelberg linen merchant, arrived in New York in 1850. At thirty he went out to San Francisco to work in his brother-in-law's shop making gilded cornices for the palaces of the city's multiplying millionaires as well as mirrors for its myriad saloons. The demand for Gump's saloon mirrors was constant because they were such irresistible targets for the bottles and bullets of miners, sailors, and drunks whose opposing views on the respective vices and virtues of the Union and the Confederacy offered a gratifying opportunity for violence.

After Solomon Gump bought out his brother-in-law, he expanded the business, selling marble statues and oil paintings of toothsome nudes to the same saloons that repeatedly bought his mirrors. The Grand Hotel Bar bought a life-sized Aphrodite whose nakedness was minimally disguised by flying doves. There was no shortage of art lovers who threw corn at her feet to tempt the doves. Among their many salubrious—indeed salutary—services, these saloons served as the first art galleries of the West.

The same bourgeois houses that needed Solomon's gilded cornices could not of course display nudes—which was what made the nudes so desirable to the saloons. But these homes needed decoration and even "art," which Solomon bought on his now annual trips to Europe. He offered increasingly enormous canvases in elaborately hand-carved frames, on such socially acceptable subjects as praying peasants, frolicking tots, noble animals, and inspiring landscapes.

To these Solomon soon added European *objets d'art,* including vases, porcelains, bronze and china figures—as well as American works such as the perennially popular and profitable John Rogers groups. He became the exclusive agent in the Far West for Currier and Ives prints that sold for $4 each.

While Solomon's fourth and smartest son, Abraham Livingston, was still young, Solomon took him to the homes of such rich customers as Leland Stanford. This taught Abe how to sell, how to decorate, and, at the sixty-room mansion of the sugar king Claus Spreckels, for example, how *not* to laugh at vulgarity. There were and are in San Francisco those unkind enough to say of Claus and his heirs: "The Spreckels are the Rooses of the Gentiles."

As a result of this training, Abe was able without a hint of a smile to wait upon the enormously fat millionairess for whom his workshop made and gilded a toilet seat 5 inches wider and 10 inches longer than standard.

When Abe waited on such great heiresses, his manner was precisely the same as when he waited on the madames of San Francisco's legendary brothels, Louise Smith, Tessie Wall, Jessie

Haman, and May Stuart, or when he sold Collis P. Huntington a painting of the nude Empress Josephine.

It was Abe who turned the store's attention to oriental art. Despite the fact that he was nearly blind, he built the store's international reputation for Chinese, Japanese, Korean bronze, ceramic, and jade masterpieces. Sarah Bernhardt, Otto Kahn, Andrew Mellon, Mary Garden, Sir Phillip Sassoon, and Ellen Terry came, admired, and bought his treasures of the East. So did such shrewd experts as Avery Brundage, whose collection is the chief splendor of San Francisco's de Young Museum. Other of Gump's oriental objects are in museums from New York's Metropolitan to Basel.

From Nathan Wildenstein and Joseph Duveen through today's greatest art dealers, both in America and in Europe, Jews have constituted a disproportionally large percentage of that trade. This concentration of Jews in art and antique dealing had the same historical bases as in money-lending, peddling, and shopkeeping, and all of these tended to complement one another. Excluded in Christian Europe from most businesses and professions, Jews were permitted to lend money. Secondhand clothes and furnishings were frequently pawned as pledges against small loans. When these were forfeited because of nonpayment, the moneylender had to sell them and so the refurbishing and repairing of old furniture and paintings, like the mending and dyeing of old clothes, became Jewish specialties.

The same peddlers and shopkeepers who were permitted to sell secondhand merchandise were perforce also permitted to buy rags and junk. And a few of the ablest *chiffonniers* and *brocanteurs* of France, the *strazzaiuoli* of Italy, and their counterparts in Central and Eastern Europe, developed from these beginnings into successful specialists in antiques and art.

Similarly in America today, the several billion-dollar scrap-metal and waste-products business is still dominated by Jews because Jewish immigrants earlier in the century got into the business when it required no capital and had no status.

It was in the role of internationally famous fine art dealers that the Gumps civilized (some said sybariticized) the rich of San Francisco and so also, to some degree, the rest of the citizenry. They had helped to change the local conviction that all Orientals were "lesser breeds without the law" into a recognition of their ancient and glorious civilization. Gertrude Stein had complained about Oakland, "When you get there, there isn't any there there." The Gumps put a lot of there there.

When Abe Gump died at his desk on August 29, 1947, he had built a store whose name across America was better known than those of the city's two art museums. His sons gave the name additional fame—and for the first time notoriety.

San Francisco's papers delighted in Richard, the younger son, a best-selling writer, much in demand both as a lecturer and as a wildly costumed conductor of his creation Dr. Fritz Guckenheimer's Sour Kraut Band—"My musicians may no longer play with the San Francisco Symphony. I do not want them to spoil their style."

His divorces gave San Franciscans even better reading; for example, when Richard vigorously denied in court that he had resumed marital relations with the German screen actress Hala Linda, but a witness testified that she had served coffee in bed to Miss Linda while Gump slept soundly at her side. A third wife attempted suicide, leaving a note to "Daddy Darlingest."

Richard now spends most of his time in his South Seas home on Moorea overlooking Cook's Bay. His older brother, Robert, was the subject of a *Life* magazine picture story when he married former brothelkeeper Sally Stanford, who "admits having run the most exclusive establishment of its kind in the U.S." Her business was conducted at 1144 Pine Street, in a house designed by Stanford White and built in 1907 for Anna Held by an admirer. Here, surrounded by carefully selected, fine antiques, including a Roman bath 9 feet in diameter, Sally's no less carefully selected young helpers entertained visiting princes, shahs, movie stars, and well-known business executives. Her greatest fame came when she and her girls served as San Francisco's unofficial but much-loved hostesses to the delegates attending the United Nations Charter Conference in 1945. Having divorced Robert only a few months after the wedding, Sally moved to Sausalito where she runs a restaurant and also serves as mayor.

Employed at Gump's soon after he came to America in 1876 with his wife, Mary Ann, and six children was a red-bearded Dutch Jew named Isaac Magnin. He was a skilled woodcarver and was equally expert at the tedious work of applying gold leaf—a talent for which San Francisco's myriad millionaires created an enormous demand in what Mark Twain had in 1873 christened The Gilded Age.

But the genius of the family was Mary Ann, whose exquisite needlework brought a steady procession of carriages from Nob and Telegraph Hills to the Magnin's uncomfortably modest home. The ladies—and some females who were not ladies—came to buy Mary Ann's embroidered, lace-trimmed lingerie (chemises, drawers, nightgowns, teddies), baby clothes (from long elaborate christening dresses to diapers of Canton flannel at $1 per dozen), and, most spectacular of all, her bridal gowns.

By 1888, I. Magnin & Co. on Market Street was the carriage-trade store of the city. Although Mary Ann made the Victorian wifely gesture of naming it for Isaac, he never had any significant say in the running of the store. She alone wielded all the power until reluctantly, bit by bit as old age weakened her, she shared some of it. Her store served in its early days as the school for all four of her sons—John, Joseph, Sam, and Grover. "I remember," Joseph reminisced in his eighties, "there were always a lot of pretty women around there and the Magnins always loved pretty women. We made a good many costume dresses then for girls in the Barbary Coast district. One day my father asked me to deliver a C.O.D. package. When I got to the address, two women in negligees answered the door and asked if I'd like to come in. Next thing I knew I was in bed between the two of them and really having a heck of a time. Finally, when I had to leave, I reminded my new-found friends that the delivery was C.O.D. They ran me out of that house fast. I didn't have the money to pay my father, and I knew he'd skin me alive. Fortunately, I told my story to a tailor who owned a shop on our block, and he loaned me the cash. But it took two and a half years before I'd saved enough to pay him back for those dresses."

There were also less exciting lessons, as when Mary Ann made Grover (her American-born son) stand with his hands behind his back and learn to identify different kinds of lace entirely by touch.

She made John president of the store, but in 1905 he moved permanently to New York. Here he was able to make certain that Magnin's was always first with the best and the newest. That he was also several thousand miles away from his mother's iron hand had perhaps not been an inconsequential factor in his decision to move.

Although Grover was the youngest, he was also clearly the most effective and was therefore soon in charge in the store—except, of course, for Mary Ann. This did not sit well with Joseph, and was one of the reasons that he left his mother's store in 1913. He founded his own, the Joseph Magnin Company, which successfully built a fashion business for young women who could not afford to pay I. Magnin & Co.'s increasingly high prices.

In the opinion of resolutely anonymous members of the Magnin family, however, Joseph did not leave only to found his own store. Despite his mother's strict prohibition against having social relations with young women who worked in the store, Joseph—who at an earlier age had dallied in the Barbary Coast brothel—now so far forgot himself as to fall desperately in love with an employee in the store's millinery department, one Charlotte Davis. Ignoring Mary Ann's disapproval, he married the girl, which led to his departure from the store. Eventually, however, the two women became good friends.

That parental disapproval constituted such a serious problem seems today as archaic as Romeo and Juliet's similar mischance, but this does not mean that it was then less real or less heartbreaking—although there were sometimes happy endings for the courageous. When Eli Sanger married Claudia Meader, a beautiful but undeniably Christian salesgirl in the glove department of Sanger

Brothers, he hid his new bride at my grandparents' house while he went, trembling, to announce the *fait accompli* to his family. They forgave him and it proved to be a long and happy marriage.

When twenty-eight-year-old Andy Goodman (of Bergdorf Goodman in New York) announced to his father his intention to marry Consuelo Mañach, a penniless Cuban girl, Edwin Goodman unequivocally refused his permission. Nena, as she was called, was not only foreign but also divorced, had a child by her first husband, and lived in a one-room apartment by the Third Avenue el. It was obviously too long a reach from the Plaza.

When the usually timorous and obedient Andy would not this time be dissuaded, Edwin had a contract drawn by Bergdorf Goodman's lawyers that limited to $100 any alimony that Andy would have to pay this gold digger when the divorce that Edwin assumed was inevitable came to pass. Only after Nena had signed the humiliating document were she and Andy married.

After years of happy marriage and the birth of five children, Nena on her birthday received from her parents-in-law a large, violet, Bergdorf Goodman gift box. As she drew from it a handsome fur, there fell from the fur a snowstorm of bits of paper— the tiny pieces into which the contract had been torn.

Like all the first-generation storekeepers, Edwin Goodman was adamant that everything connected with his establishment be absolutely *comme il faut.* On a walk through his store one day, he noticed that a male customer seemed to be hypnotized by a young and well-endowed saleswoman whose décolletage, when she leaned over to bring forth handbags from a drawer under the counter, revealed much more than Goodman thought appropriate to the place and occasion. When the young man left, having bought a bag several times more expensive than he had originally asked to see, Mr. Goodman suggested: "Miss, please don't show what we don't have in stock."

Like his counterparts across America, however, the usually stiff and formal Edwin Goodman was nothing if not adaptable and he knew when to put aside his customary pomp and pretension. He built a lavish sixteen-room penthouse apartment above his

store and when he learned that city regulations forbade anyone
except a superintendent to live in a building where manufacturing
took place (in this case, custom clothes and furs), the usually
stuffy Edwin immediately listed himself as "janitor."

Edwin and later Andy used the glorious apartment not only
as a family home but also as a sumptuous place to dine and
entertain famous designers and no less famous customers. The
rhapsodic reports in newspaper gossip columns and fashion magazines of these elaborate and expensive entertainments and their
glamorously gowned and jeweled guests contributed to the reputation and mystique of Bergdorf's, just as the similarly reported
revels of the Stanley Marcuses and the Grover Magnins fascinated
their customers.

Not until 1931, when he was forty-six, had Grover Magnin
married his shockingly beautiful model, Jeanne Melton, formerly
of Arcadia, Louisiana. The wedding took place in Mary Ann's
apartment at the St. Francis Hotel. At eighty-two the matriarch
had finally, in family as in store matters, resigned the role of
absolute autocrat. She died at ninety-five in 1943, only a few
weeks before the sale of her store to Bullock's of Los Angeles,
unaware of the impending sale.

But, even after the sale, Grover and Jeanne's social life remained
an important part of the store's publicity. When they gave a party
in Paris that progressed from the Ritz to Maxim's to Monseigneur,
every enviable detail from Jeanne's "single jewel, her famous shell
of diamonds" to the "astonishing crescendo of Monseigneur's
fourteen wild Hungarian violinists" found its way into San Francisco's newspapers.

No less passionately reported were the dinner guests at the
St. Francis Hotel apartment where Grover and Jeanne lived for
the almost forty years of their marriage—an elegant two-story
apartment that now rents for over $1,000 a day. Here, as the
press described in delicious detail to insatiable readers, Jeanne
and Grover entertained such foreign and local luminaries as Captain Edward Molyneux, Mrs. Ailsa Mellon Bruce, and United
States Ambassador to Italy James David Zellerbach (whose San

Francisco-pioneer-Jewish grandfather had preferred paper supplies to shopkeeping).

Living in a downtown hotel rather than one's own house has been a tradition for some of San Francisco's rich since the 1850s. It would have been difficult to find more luxury in the 1870s than was offered at the Palace Hotel and Lick House (whose dining room, roofed over by an immense elliptical cupola, was reputed to be the most elegant in the United States). The Social Register of 1910 reveals that Mrs. Henry S. Crocker as well as Mr. and Mrs. Charles Crocker and children lived at the St. Francis Hotel. Mr. and Mrs. Jerome A. Hart lived at the Fairmont Hotel where Achille and Ernestine Roos lived until she moved, after his death, to the Mark Hopkins. In 1978 the white-haired, handsome, seventy-nine-year-old Cyril Magnin, Joseph and Charlotte's son, and generally considered to be "Mr. San Francisco," had for many years been living in an all-white, ultra-contemporary apartment, high up in the Mark Hopkins, surrounded by his catholic collection ranging from African tribal art to antiques to Rodin's bust of Victor Hugo.

In Grover and Jeanne's apartment, not only in the high-ceilinged, wood-paneled drawing room and dining room but also in the upstairs galleries was displayed their collection of Impressionist and Post-Impressionist paintings, including two Renoirs, a van Gogh, a Pissarro, a Boudin, and a Bonnard. After Grover died at eighty-three on March 17, 1969, just seven of his paintings sold for almost $2 million at a special auction at Parke Bernet in New York. His "Dancer on Point" by Degas set a new record of $550,000 for a Degas sold at auction.

The publicity value of world record prices paid at public auction had not been lost on Grover during his lifetime. He had frequently instructed his fur buyer that "regardless of cost" he was to buy the very finest bundles of sable, mink, or fisher skins at the widely reported international fur auctions. When the Neiman-Marcus and the Bergdorf Goodman buyers received the same instructions, it sometimes led to grotesquely inflated prices being paid; but this was often not a bad thing. A rich customer seeking the psychological comfort and the social status of a Magnin's, Neiman's, or Bergdorf's label was at least as often reassured as resentful in knowing that she was paying a world's record price.

The proceeds of the auction of Grover's paintings are to be held in trust for Jeanne during her lifetime and then divided equally between San Francisco's California Palace of the Legion of Honor and the city's de Young Museum.

Grover had been among the first to understand the value of branch stores. Beginning in 1912 at Santa Barbara, he opened the first of a series of small shops in chic resort hotels where bored rich women from all over America quickly learned that Magnin's was a pleasant place to relieve their ennui by spending money. In the optimistic pre–World War I atmosphere that prevailed at such fashionable watering holes as Del Monte, Coronado, and Pasadena, Grover opened similarly therapeutic stations, a pattern that the store's future owners would continue to follow at La Jolla, Carmel, and Phoenix.

In 1939 Grover built a sumptuous store on Wilshire Boulevard in Los Angeles despite the outspoken pretensions of his fellow San Franciscans that Los Angeles was nothing but a social and cultural backwater. That store for years was the most fashionable spot in the city, but the most famous Magnin in Los Angeles was located in fact a few blocks away, also on Wilshire Boulevard. He was Rabbi Edgar F. Magnin—Sam's son—whose Wilshire Boulevard Temple was reckoned by many to be the richest synagogue in the world. "Edgar is an even greater promotional genius than Grover," declares a longtime friend of both men. "It was not by accident that he gave the invocation at President Nixon's first inauguration, but because he has carefully and persistently made himself into America's premier token Jew."

In Los Angeles, the wealthiest and most powerful Jews were not storekeepers but such movie and radio figures as Louis B. Mayer, Jack Benny, and Jack Warner, whom Edgar had on his board. "I have always believed in quality, like the store," Edgar confides, proudly pointing out his temple's enormous green columns, extravagant stained-glass windows, heavy gold leaf—most of these glories accomplished during the country's worst depression and all of them reminders of the Rose de Brignolles marble and expensive bronze fixtures that give the Magnin stores their ambiance of lavish luxury. This sense of solid luxury in the most exclusive stores provides the comforting feeling of security once found in houses of worship, a calming atmosphere that gives a surcease from the tensions and terrors of contemporary life. "It calms me down right away," says Holly Golightly in *Breakfast at Tiffany's,* "the quietness and the proud look of it; nothing very bad could happen to you there."

Because like ancient Greece, America is polytheistic and because Mammon has not been our least important god, future anthropologists and historians may learn more of what Americans really cared about—as opposed to what they professed to care about— by digging in Bloomingdale's rather than in St. Patrick's Cathedral or St. James's or Temple Emanu-El. In the department store they will discover what we wore, read, listened to and ate, how we cooked, the things that amused and beguiled us, from children's toys to sports equipment to sex manuals.

In some American cities—Atlanta, Columbus, Phoenix, Hartford—a single Jewish family of storekeepers was unquestionably dominant. In others—Memphis, Dallas, New Orleans—not one but several such storekeepers' families predominated. In Los Angeles, as in St. Louis and Cincinnati, the most important Jewish families were not those of storekeepers. And in San Francisco, although there were important Jewish storekeepers, there were also other Jewish civic leaders—lawyers, manufacturers, and even bankers—whose families' influences on the city were sometimes greater than those of the storekeepers. These included families that, at least in their own view, ceased to be Jews, such as the Sutros and the de Youngs.

Such significant San Francisco pioneer families included the Haases, who were wholesale grocers, and the Brandensteins, who were tea and coffee importers and of whom, when they were transmuted into the Branstens, some said that they had "circumcised their name" and others that the younger generations were "less stimulating since they had the caffeine removed." There were also the Koshlands, wholesale wool merchants, and the Gerstles, for whom Alaska's Gerstle River is named and who touched off the Klondike Gold Rush in 1897 when one of their steamboats reached San Francisco with $750,000 in Alaskan gold.

Half a century before the Gold Rush, San Francisco Jews had been fur traders with Alaska's Russian-American Company, just as from central Canada—in the sod houses and wooden shacks of Medicine Hat and Red Deer—all the lonely way up to the Yukon, ubiquitous Jews were peddlers, shopkeepers, traders, trappers, ranchers—survivors.

After San Francisco's 1906 earthquake and the fire that followed it, Jewish bankers such as the Hellmans (Wells Fargo Bank) and the Lilienthals, Steinharts, and Fleishhackers (Anglo-Californian Bank) financed much of the city's rebuilding, including Magnin's, the White House, Gump's, and Roos Brothers. Although the stores' credit records were destroyed, most customers nevertheless came in and paid what they owed. This pattern of customer honesty and regard for the storekeeper was the same across the country, as when Brandeis's burned in Omaha in 1894 and Hartford's G. Fox in 1917. Such fires were much more common in the past than today, but when a store had more than one—Lowenstein's in 1883 and 1906, Neiman-Marcus in 1913 and 1964—local wits were given to good-natured inquiries about insurance and such infrequently heard anthropological arcana as "of all animals only humans possess the use of fire."

In 1887 the San Francisco *Daily Examiner* had advised its readers: "Were it not for the large Jewish patronage we should seldom see a first-class tragedy or famous opera rendered in our Thespian temples." Almost a century later, Yehudi Menuhin in his autobiography pointed out that support of the arts had also meant support of individual San Francisco artists. To sponsor young Menuhin's training in Europe, a rich lawyer, Sidney Ehrman, had supported the entire family there with "modesty and authority, the splendor which rejected *éclat* and the patronage which made no claim upon the protégé."

The heirs of Levi Strauss, who died a bachelor in 1902—Sterns, Koshlands, Haases—were perhaps the greatest supporters of the arts and certainly the richest. When shares of Levi Strauss went public in 1971, "the offering created at least 28 instant million-aires," according to *The New York Times*. "The Bay Area is honey-combed with cultural contributions from members of the compa-ny's founding family. . . . Levi Strauss & Co. says that it now earmarks 3 percent of its net income to social responsibility pro-grams, including charitable contributions."

In terms of social effect, of influence on society, from San Fran-cisco to the Côte d'Azur to Moscow, more than any charitable gift that derived from them, Levi's britches have themselves made such a mark that countless sociologists interpret the ubiquitous Levi as everything from a medium of political protest to "a declara-tion of sensuality."

In San Francisco's Jewish aristocracy, as in most aristocracies, intermarriage led toward one-big-but-not-always-happy family that worked and played and strayed together—"If you don't com-mit incest you've made a bad marriage." When Dan Koshland married his first cousin Eleanor Haas, he went to work for the Levi Strauss Company. It was, declared the experts, "a perfect match." When brothers Jacob H. and David Neustadter married sisters Dora and Josephine Dannenberg, they even lived together in the same gloriously gingerbreaded mansion on the northwest corner of Van Ness Avenue and Sacramento Street. Its ballroom easily accommodated meetings of the Philomath Club, the exclu-sive Jewish women's club, "conservative but progressive, to pro-mote the general culture of its members by the discussion of educational, moral, and social topics." Across the street, the David N. Walter mansion had no ballroom but boasted a small theater with footlights and a Green Room in the tower. In the Philip N. Lilienthal home, the circular tower room served instead as a playroom for the children.

Most such mansions were of wood and in Queen Anne, Italian-ate, Gothic, Renaissance, or Tudor style—or often some uninhib-ited mixture of these. The number of turns and landings of the grand staircase in each house was an important indication of the wealth of the family, as were ornate onyx mantels and the presence or absence of a conservatory, library, or wine room. But nothing else in a San Francisco house so revealed its owner's position in the economic pecking order as the view—the higher up and the better the views of the Bay, the Coast Range, the city itself, the more important the family. One reason that collections of expensive paintings were rare among the rich was that big bay windows with splendid views were more important patents of social position.

Only marginally if at all less grand than the Nob Hill mansions of the railroad and Comstock kings is the "Petit Trianon" at 3800 Washington Street, built by Marcus Koshland in 1904 for his wife, Cora. So solid that it suffered only minor damages in the earthquake, it is a replica of its eighteenth-century namesake in the park of Versailles. All twenty-six main rooms open on the marble, two-storied, central atrium. A concert hall is in the basement.

Cora's younger son Robert, like the scions of so many of these rich Jewish families, remembers his boyhood as often embarrassingly exotic compared to those of his school friends. "Dan [his elder brother] and I were ashamed of the elaborate house, the chauffeur and footman who brought us to school and picked us up in the Locomobile, the long curls and stiff 'ping-pong' collars and the music lessons and French lessons and other endless 'improving' things like dressing for dinner that made us appear esoteric or weird. On the other hand, the lessons from Captain Dillon at the Riding Academy were fun and after Mr. Wienowski had finished giving us our fencing lesson at home, Jim Ransohoff and I would throw the foils from the second floor down into the fountain in the center of the atrium in always unsuccessful attempts to spear the goldfish. But I preferred my grandmother Koshland's house—it was less pretentious, and Hong Koshland, the Chinese cook she had for thirty-six years and sent on three trips home to China, was the finest cook in town."

Who had the finest cook, like who had "come first," was, as

in all aristocracies, a matter of endless argument. But according to the director of the Bancroft Library, James D. Hart, who is the city's wittiest observer and whose family is one of the oldest: "Nobody came first. And now half the prominent Gentiles are Jews and the best San Francisco Jews are Gentiles."

But not quite all. In San Francisco as elsewhere, to quite a number of Jews, when their religion became meaningless, abandoning it for another one had little more significance than giving up a dress that is passé for one that is in fashion. When a young, rapidly rising businessman or doctor took his family from the Baptist to the more socially acceptable Episcopalian Church, adverse comment, if any, was soon forgotten. When a Jew did the same thing, the change was less quickly forgotten.

For many of the rich Jews who did not convert, their religion had also become largely symbolic, consisting of no more than a minimal concern with a few religious holidays, the welfare of other Jews, and the occasional nostalgic use of certain Yiddishisms and foods. But these they refused to give up, whether out of sloth or fear of appearing opportunistic, or because of a genuine if vague feeling that they wanted to remain, however peripherally, a part of a courageous and humane tradition.

What made Cora Koshland celebrate Hanukkah at her "Petit Trianon" was that she could have her Christian friends join the celebration and so presumably make them understand better what Jews are. To the Haases and Koshlands and Slosses, how they appeared to San Francisco's Christian society—whether or not they or other Jews were members of the Pacific Union Club or the boards of directors of the Bank of America and AT & T and Stanford—were matters of serious concern, not merely evidences of social ambition and vanity.

The conviction held by many Jews that each of them bears a personal responsibility for what non-Jews feel toward Jews has often been an important factor in their lives. They know that what many Christians feel about all Jews often derives from experiences with a very few Jews or even with just one. This Jewish feeling of responsibility appears at all levels, high and low, and its justification is regularly reconfirmed—not only in San Francisco. Perhaps as important for Jews as any other single decision was President Harry S. Truman's in 1948 to see Chaim Weizmann and then to support the establishment of the State of Israel. The president was not brought to this view by a Straus or Rosenwald or other great merchant prince. Nor did it come from having worked with many Jews. It was the result of his experience and friendship with one Eddie Jacobson. The two men had briefly been partners in a small haberdashery store in Kansas City until they went broke, and Truman had found Jacobson to be a man of honor.

10

The Meiers and Franks
of Oregon

A Jew is a man other men call a Jew.
—Jean-Paul Sartre

For many years while the great center of what would be the
United States was still virtually unknown to any except the Indians and wild animals, there were already whites on the Pacific
coast. In 1578 Francis Drake had anchored not only in what was
later called San Francisco Bay but also probably as far north as
Oregon. Two hundred years later, Drake's heirs, the American
ship captains, found in Oregon the key to the sea trade with
China of which Columbus had dreamed.

To bring back the tea, the silks, the porcelains from China
for which America's merchants had a ready market, it was necessary to find something the Celestial Empire did not have and
wanted. Briefly, ginseng provided such a cargo, until its Chinese
purchasers finally accepted the fact that it was just as ineffective
as powdered rhinoceros horn as a restorative of virility.

What Oregon offered in abundance that the mandarins wanted
was furs—especially sea otter—and those furs, along with the

sandalwood the ships picked up in the Hawaiian Islands, were for years essentials of the China trade.

The United States's claim to the American Northwest was established by the Boston merchant ship *Columbia,* which became the first American vessel to sail round the world after her initial trip to Canton. On her second voyage, in 1792, the *Columbia* entered the mouth of the great river of the Northwest, and gave her name to the river.

The merchant who developed a virtual monopoly of the fur trade in America was John Jacob Astor. Like so many American department-store founders, he was an immigrant from Germany. Born in the village of Waldorf near Heidelberg in 1763, he came to America in 1784. Although he was not Jewish, he began here as most Jews did, peddling. He first peddled tea rusk, cookies, cakes, and doughnuts—as his sister, Mrs. Michael Miller, once angrily recalled in the accent she never lost: "Yacob was noting put a paker poy, und solt preat und cake."

Astor later became a pack peddler between Schenectady and Utica, bartering cheap jewelry and novelties to the Indians for furs. Before going on his own, Astor learned the fur trade from one of New York's most successful pre-Revolutionary Jewish merchants, Hayman Levy, for whom Astor began by beating furs "at the wage of one dollar per day."

Soon after the Revolution, Astor's American Fur Company, chartered in 1808, became the most important in America and much of its merchandise came from Astoria, on the south bank of the Columbia River.

The demand for furs, like the supply, then seemed endless: marten, muskrat, raccoon, rabbit, wildcat, fox, and especially beaver, the "hairy banknotes" from which were made the elegant tall hats essential to all gentlemen.

In the millions of square miles of this continent between the East and the Hudson Bay Company's or Astor's primitive trading post on the Pacific, there were a very few fur trappers and traders, including the "mountainy men" of the Great Plains and the Rocky Mountains. And a few of these few were Jews.

One such was Berlin-born Ezekiel Solomon, who went to Fort Michilimackinac (Mackinac), Michigan, in 1761. He was captured there by the Indians during the 1763 massacre but was later ransomed. Another Jewish trader, Nathan Chapman, was ransomed from the Hurons and Potawatomis during Pontiac's siege of Detroit that same year, but there is no evidence that another Jewish trader named Levy, held at that moment by the Miamis, was saved.

For more than a century—from before the United States had become a nation until after the Civil War—such adventures with the Indians were often repeated by Jewish traders. As late as 1870 the Apaches captured a Jewish peddler named Adolph Kohn, who was on his way to the Indian Territory of Oklahoma. The Apaches traded him to the even fiercer Comanches, with whom he rode the warpath until he was released in November 1872.

All over Oklahoma, traders such as Julius Haas in Atoka and Joseph Sondheimer at Muskogee, who married a Cherokee woman, traded with the Creek and other Indian nations in buffalo hides that brought from $1 to $3 each—a trade that reached its peak in 1883, when perhaps as many as 13 million buffalo had been slaughtered.

If Jewish traders played an important part in building commerce and culture in America, they were also part of the destruction of the Kansa and Crow, Blackfoot and Pawnee, Sioux and Cheyenne. To the Indian, the buffalo had been "a galloping department store" that supplied everything he needed: fresh meat in summer, pemmican in winter, clothing, tipi, bowstring, and arrowhead. And there is no comfort in the fact that the Indian cooperated with white traders in his own destruction, trading buffalo skins for guns, ammunition, and whiskey.

Similarly, the few mountainy men on their own could never have supplied the world's demands for furs without the help of the Indians; but with that help, by the early 1840s the beaver was virtually exterminated in the Rockies. Then suddenly there was new work for the mountainy men who knew every stream and mountain pass: serving as guides for the thousands of Americans who had caught "Oregon fever" and were determined to cross an entire unmapped continent to reach the fertile valleys of the Clackamas and the Willamette, and to enjoy the teeming, tumbling salmon of the Columbia.

Led by James Bridger, "Kit" Carson, and other guides who were as dirty and illiterate as they were canny and courageous, the pioneers followed the Platte over the Great Plains. There were no paths and no markers until enough weather-bleached wagons and skulls, animal and human, helped to show the way. The Oregon Trail was 2,000 miles of freezing cold, blistering heat, and usually hostile Indians. Along it, according to a cultured Eastern tenderfoot who would survive and become a great historian, Francis Parkman, there "shouldered heavily along, inch by inch, on their interminable journey" clumsy Conestoga wagons, some weighing as much as 7,000 pounds and requiring as many as twelve horses or oxen, averaging only 15 to 20 miles a day. Lucky the survivors of a train that left Independence or Council Bluffs in May if by December most of them finally saw the glorious peaks of Mount Hood and Mount Rainier.

The few Jews who chanced these dangers were not all peddlers and storekeepers but a mixed bag of adventurers, fortune hunters, and failures. For example, Solomon Nuñes Carvalho was the daguerreotypist on John Charles Frémont's last exploratory expedition across the Rocky Mountains in 1853. Even more than his photographs, paintings, and sketches, Carvalho's book about that expedition offers affecting pictures—of herds of buffalo numbering 200,000, of Brigham Young's beautiful young wives, of angry and bitter Indian chiefs. ("I am for war. I will never lay down my rifle and tomahawk. Americats have no truth. Americats see Indian woman, he shoot her like deer.")

Carvalho astounded the Cheyennes with his photographs, with the effect of his "quicksilver" on their bracelets, with his "lucifer matches" and alcohol "firewater," so much so, indeed, that: "They wanted me to live with them and I believe if I had remained they would have worshipped me."

Life on such an expedition did not allow for the limitations of a kosher cuisine. In fact, it included meals of horse, mule, and buffalo meat cooked, Carvalho explained, over dried buffalo manure that "burns like peat and makes a very hot fire, without much smoke . . . a peculiar smell exhales from it while burning, not at all unpleasant."

Equally oblivious of the dietary laws was nineteen-year-old Sigmund Schlesinger—one of the numberless Jewish adventurer-peddler-jack-of-all-trades who did not become merchant princes—who noted in his diary on September 22, 1868, "Killt a Coyote & eat him all up." Schlesinger must have been exceptionally hungry because for the previous nine days he had been one of fifty mounted scouts fully occupied in fighting desperately to hold off seven hundred Sioux and Cheyenne braves under Chief Roman Nose in the Battle of Beecher Island, Colorado. During the battle, Schlesinger had "scalpt 3 Indians which were found about 15 feet from my hole concealed in grass."

The Hungarian-born boy had come over in 1864 and followed the Kansas Pacific Railroad west, where he tended bar, baked bread, brewed beer, or took whatever work would keep him alive. He was briefly a partner in a store in Hays City, Kansas. The value of its entire inventory was only $5, but its customers included General George Custer, Buffalo Bill, and the town marshal, Wild Bill Hickock. Had Schlesinger been successful at storekeeping or any of his many other early attempts in business, he would not have hired on temporarily as one of those fifty civilian scouts who were each paid $35 per month plus 45 cents a day to bring along his own horse.

The man who began what would become the greatest department store in the Northwest got there not over the Oregon Trail but via the Isthmus of Panama. And he was not an adventurer, but followed the typical hard-working German-Jewish peddler-to-merchant-prince pattern.

Born in the Bavarian village of Ellerstadt in 1831, Aaron Meier came to America at twenty-four and went to work in the store of his two older brothers in Downieville, California. According to Ellin (Mrs. Irving) Berlin, in her biography of her glamorous grandmother, Marie Louise Antoinette Hungerford, it was a typical village general store: "Its shelves were piled with an interestingly varied assortment of goods—cigars and playing cards, miners' tools and revolving pistols and cans of fruit. Apricots gleamed in brandy. A big glass jar was bright as a rainbow with candies, glistening black licorice and red and white peppermints and multicolored fruit balls. Best of all on the counter Louise liked the scale that waited to weigh the gold dust."

Marie Louise was anything but typical. As a child she began by playing in the California village with the Meier children, but she grew up to marry John Mackay, who promised her "the whole damn world on a silver platter" and delivered it—the heart of the Comstock Lode.

Aaron Meier was anything but glamorous. After two years of typically long hours in his older brothers' store and long peddling trips north into the Oregon Territory, he decided in 1857 to open his own general store in Portland. It was a village of over one thousand souls, but its future seemed to some to be less than promising as the fur trade and the California Gold Rush boom times diminished. Before Aaron added one more, Portland already had forty-two dry-goods and grocery stores.

Aaron experienced the typical bad luck that either tempered or destroyed small merchants: his partner bankrupted the store in 1863, while Aaron had returned to Germany to get a wife, and the store was again wiped out in the great fire of 1873.

Typically, the store's ledgers show that in the early days bills were paid not by specie but "by eggs," "by potatoes," "by pickles," "by salmon," and "by furs."

For many years as the store grew and additional hands were needed, Aaron's wife, the former Jeannette Hirsch, brought over from Germany brothers, half brothers, nephews, and cousins. After the great flood of 1894 these young relatives built a false sidewalk above the submerged sidewalk in front of the store; raised the counters inside the flooded store; built walkways around some counters and paddled customers in small boats around others.

Many of the store's best customers were farmers and their wives, who came by boat up or down the river once or twice a year just as Goldsmith's customers came up to Memphis by wagon. The men were offered free tobacco and clay pipes; the women, coffee, candy, gossip, and fashion news from the East. The young Hirsches worked quickly and late to wrap and label the purchases and deliver them to river steamers.

As was customary, their salaries were sporadic and small. Vacations were unheard of. When young Max Hirsch was invited on a trip to nearby Wilhoit Springs and requested a few days off, he was asked: "What do you want a vacation for? You just came!" He had then been at the store for seven years.

Typically, the rich supply of relatives helped the store to grow. The dumber ones were reliable in small positions and the smarter ones played more important roles. Some of the smartest left to form their own businesses, an important wholesale drug company and the White Stag Company (named for its partners Weis and Hirsch) that started by making canvas sails and tents for Alaskan gold prospectors, but changed with the times into sportswear and skiwear manufacturers.

The one untypical thing in Aaron's life and for thirty-six years after his life ended in 1889 was his wife. She was the most important force in building the great store and in preventing its destruction by the ambitions, lusts, rivalries, and enviousness of a growing and increasingly rich family.

The short, stout, heavy-bosomed, firm-jawed "Shannet" (as the German accents had it) was eleven years younger than her husband, but she was, from the beginning, completely in charge. She went to the store every day of her life and although she never had an office or a title, every package boy and ribbon clerk knew she was the boss. Every Sunday, at first around the stove at the back of the store and later in the upstairs sitting room of her home, she reigned.

The predinner court she held was brief and absolute. The family sat stiffly on the formal furniture upholstered in frise, a particularly harsh and hot plush whose discomfort was somewhat lessened in summer by tan and brown striped linen slip covers. If her dicta were objected to by so much as a cough or a sigh, they were repeated just once, slowly, and with her cane pounding the floor to emphasize the most essential points. One such repetition was always enough.

When her children and grandchildren fell out with one another over store or private matters, Shannet knocked their heads together. No question was too small to receive her attention and her absolute final answer. For example, dust cloths were to be used in the store as opposed to feather dusters that "chust move dust from vun place to another."

She expected a dutiful telephone call every morning from her daughter, daughters-in-law, and later from each of her adult granddaughters and granddaughters-in-law. After these, she would schedule her chauffeur, Norcross, to do some of their errands and all of her own, including delivering checks to pay bills, thereby saving the postage.

Of course, she and she alone determined which marriages were suitable and which were not. Her husband, on a buying trip to San Francisco in 1872, had met a charming, recently arrived, German-Jewish music teacher, Sigmund Frank. Meier offered him a job "clerking" at the store and when, after long and careful observation, Shannet's sharp eye certified that Frank would make a proper spouse for her oldest daughter, Fannie, Frank became a partner and the store name changed to Meier & Frank.

On the other hand, Shannet was not a bit impressed when on June 12, 1922, the front page of Portland's morning newspaper announced that her nineteen-year-old granddaughter, Jean Meier, who was on a nine-month trip around the world with her family, had become engaged in Paris to a young Englishman, one Daryl Klein. Mr. Klein was forthwith summoned to Portland to appear before "Grandma Meier," as her grandchildren called her.

Mr. Klein came. He was adjudged quite as insubstantial as his first name and immediately disappeared without a trace. ("I really believe that Shannet may mistakenly have equated too little luggage with too little breeding," recalls a family member who was present but who insists upon absolute anonymity even though she has now been for over half a century presumably beyond the reach of Shannet, who to her relatives' surprise finally died at eighty-two in 1925.)

A year after Daryl's dismissal, Jean married Joseph Ehrman in a ceremony so splendid that it required almost a full newspaper page of text and photographs to describe. "The elite of the city" were present at the ballroom of the Hotel Portland, which had been transformed into an "exotic woodland floral bower with masses of woodwardia interwoven with Darwin tulips of orchid shades and white Easter lilies, entirely covering not only the walls but the ceiling and columns."

Sumptuous displays of luxury were not reserved for such relatively rare occasions as weddings. After every Sunday evening council, the entire family descended to a prodigal dinner at which the favorite main course was *Gänsebraten.* The goose's skin had been removed and rendered into crisp, crackling *grieben.* The legs and wings, good only for stew, had been cut off and with the enormous roasted bird came an endless supply of apple sauce and potatoes, as well as half a dozen "extra things for the children," such as a Lucullan loaf made of the local Olympia oysters. The meal usually ended, to the delighted squeals of the children, with several mountains of at least two flavors of butter-rich, home-churned ice cream and a suitable selection of ornately decorated cakes.

Ostensibly in order to educate the children to "the better things," these meals were always served on the "real" rosepoint lace tablecloths with the "good" china, the "heavy" silver, and the "best" crystal. The relative importance of the various "better things" about which the children must learn was sometimes striking. Linens, china, silver, glass, and such other things as were sold in "the store" were unquestionably of the first rank of importance. But as the almost-Mrs.-Daryl-Klein remembers: "Papa was not big for museums. In Paris we 'did' the Cluny, the Luxembourg, and the Louvre all in one morning."

Shannet never disapproved of spending money on luxurious

living. Indeed, she seemed to enjoy if not encourage competition among her grandchildren in this area. Lloyd Frank, a fat dandy who was the older son of Sigmund and Fannie, considered himself "artistic," and as with certain other of his activities he refused to tell his wife, Edna, a word about their proposed country place until the plans were completed.

"Fir Acres," as he called it, was an enormous English Tudor manor. The house was of salmon-pink brick, rough side out and set in patterns. It had bronze window casements, leaded windows of tinted glass, antiqued lead gutters and downspouts, and a golden brown slate roof set unevenly with the greatest care to look as though it had withstood centuries of English winters. In addition to dozens of bed, dressing, dining, drawing, sitting, living, play, storage, butler, cold, breakfast, and waiting rooms for the family, guests, and staff, there were rooms now seen less frequently: a conservatory, a library, a ballroom, an ironing room, and a room set aside especially for a White Russian second maid to arrange flowers.

There were outbuildings for wood, vegetables, refrigeration, greenhouses, potting shed, dovecotes, garages, gatekeeper's house, two bath houses (one for either sex), and two gazebos. In addition to the cutting gardens, there were formal, terraced English gardens with reflecting pools, culminating in a view of Mount Hood. Smith, the head gardener, was from Kew Gardens and had thirty-four full-time gardeners under his direction.

When third-generation Meier and Frank children brought home their non-Jewish playmates from Portland Academy and Miss Catlin's school, their family estates were provided with better swimming pools, croquet lawns, tennis courts, and stables than the Waverly Country Club, to which no Jews belonged. Although compared to the East and Middle West there was relatively little anti-Semitism at the top of the social scale, there was some. Two of Shannet's granddaughters belonged to the Junior League in the 1920s. But it is not until recently that a very few Jews have become members of the Waverly or the best downtown club, the Arlington.

Even among the lower social orders, with a few ugly exceptions, anti-Semitism took relatively harmless and often humorous forms that included commonly referring to the store as "Murphy and Finnegan."

At "Fir Acres" there was no detail too small for Lloyd's attention: the perfectly mortised and pegged oak mill work, the height at which to hang the Aubusson tapestries and oriental screens, the superb Art Deco designs for the tops of the swimming pool ladders, the pure white sand brought as ballast from Belgium, the patterns and colors of rugs specially woven in Spain. While some of Lloyd's friends and family considered such obsession with decorating details effeminate, doubts on this score were resolved when his wife quite inadvertently one evening walked into one of the gazebos to find Lloyd *in flagrante delictu* with a young woman who in addition served as his secretary.

Before the beautiful and brave Edna could decide whether or not to forget the incident, Lloyd ran off to Europe with the doubly talented young woman, who there presented him with a child. In the divorce arrangements, Edna allowed her brother-in-law, Aaron Frank, to be appointed trustee of the Meier & Frank stock settled on her and her children—a move understandable in the days when well-bred women were not supposed to know or care about money, but one that she would regret bitterly.

Short, short-tempered, sharp-tongued, and vindictive, Aaron Frank was a man who never forgot or forgave an injury, great or small, real or imaginary. He cherished and nurtured his grudges as he did his fine string of show horses at his Garden Home Farms. The extravagance that his older brother Lloyd expressed through his home, Aaron lavished on his stables—quilted, padded stalls, expensively tiled floors, the very finest tack—and when any of his worldwide network of scouts sent word from the Dublin Horse Show or Madison Square Garden of a splendid possible addition to his string, the otherwise often frugal Aaron invariably cabled the same two-word answer: "Buy it."

But in the 1930s he lost half his horses in a fire at the Oakland show barns, and a year later most of the rest in a train wreck.

"Those were the only times I ever saw him weep," an intimate remembers. "But he recovered, got out of the horse business entirely, and never again showed any love for anyone or anything—except power."

It seemed to some amateur analysts in the family that what poisoned Aaron's life and his personality in addition to his shortness was his envy of his mother's youngest brother. Julius Meier was a man easy to envy. He was tall, handsome, given to Falstaffian humor and Rabelaisian practical jokes. He was as charismatic to men as to women. Even his mother, the notoriously autocratic Shannet, found his charm so irresistible that she could refuse him nothing. Early on, Julius learned not to ask permission to do what she might find difficult to approve. Instead, he went ahead and (with some circumspection) did it, in the knowledge that Shannet would make a point of not noticing.

There was perhaps no more important essential of Victorian morality than that some breaches of it be studiously ignored. When my father was six years old, he had to accompany his mother who was going to visit a sick friend out in the country. To get there she had to drive her buggy through Dallas's red-light district where my father saw his father's friend, the newspaper publisher, come staggering out of one of the houses.

"Hello, Mr. Kiest," my father shouted, waving.

"That's *not* Mr. Kiest!" my grandmother snapped.

"Of course it is," my father answered, waving again and calling, "Afternoon, Mr. Kiest."

"I *told* you, that's *not* Mr. Kiest!" his mother insisted, slapping him sharply across the mouth.

In later years my father would explain when he told the story: "I was not a very bright child and it was not until I was eight or nine that I learned why, when, and where Mr. Kiest was not Mr. Kiest."

Julius Meier planned not to be a storekeeper. He received his law degree from the University of Oregon at twenty-one in 1895 and formed a law partnership with his best friend, George William Joseph. But after a few years he went to work at the store.

When Sigmund Frank, who had succeeded Aaron Meier as president of the store, died in 1910, Julius's older brother, Abe, became the senior male member of the clan. He was handsome, graceful, sweet-tempered, and universally liked, but he was an idiot. He had never had an office in the store but had instead played the traditional role for such figures in the great Jewish storekeeping families—he stayed on the selling floor greeting customers, many of whom he knew by name, who were flattered to tell friends that they had been "served by the boss, Mr. Meier." When Sigmund Frank died, Abe was made president of the store and Julius became general manager. Although there was no discussion of it, there was also no doubt as to whose role was ceremonial and honorific and who really made the important decisions.

Julius, somewhat less after his marriage than before, was given to quite strenuous forms of merrymaking, including philandering, but unlike Lloyd he was relatively discreet. When he was in a car accident in which a woman died, there was a newspaper reporter there, but no account appeared in the papers; the reporter was given a lifetime job at the store, and Julius's wife, Grace, remained resolutely ignorant of this potential scandal as she did of all others.

It is frequently still said in the Northwest that the moral and conservative New England types who came over the Oregon Trail settled in the Oregon Territory. Supposedly they brought with them and practiced a strict code of conduct, whereas the sinners followed the Oregon Trail only to a point near the present Wyoming–Idaho boundary when they took a fork that turned southwestward and formed the California Trail.

Despite this myth of strict New England virtue, if Portland (named for Portland, Maine) was no less sinful than other frontier towns, it was also no more so except for the relative ease in finding the Chinese community opium dens there. The incidence of saloons and brothels was about the same as anywhere else, although perhaps the periodic public objections to the latter were a bit more peevish and pious.

As usual, the chief purveyors of piousities were the newspapers.

In 1852 *The Oregonian* pontificated on "the very difficult question" raised when ladies lifted their long skirts because of mud puddles. The paper suggested that proper Portland women should avoid the problem by staying home—this in a place where it rains an average of 150 days a year. More than half a century later, the same problem still existed when in 1910 a group of Portland ladies petitioned the mayor to require the streetcars to lower their steps in order that they could "ascend and descend without being subjected to the leers of male loiterers."

That more serious sins were prevalent was indicated by the Vice Commission Report of 1912. It revealed that more than one of every five cases of disease treated by Portland doctors were venereal—presumably none of them caught by ogling ankles.

Another revelation in the Report was that the city's brothels were profitable tenants of real estate owned by many of the city's most prominent pioneer families, including such names as Corbett, Ainsworth, Henry Wemme (who when he died two years later left half his fortune to found a home for wayward girls), and Hirsch. In an effort to embarrass these "good families" out of their wicked profits, the city council passed the first "Tin Plate Law" in America. It required the owners to affix and maintain on each building a conspicuous sign detailing the owner's name and address. But families had not grown rich and powerful because they were dumb and unobservant. They quickly noticed that there was no requirement that the signs be in English and therefore wrote them in Arabic, Hebrew, Chinese, and Urdu.

Like most sinners, contrary to the often envious fantasies of the virtuous, Julius Meier spent most of his time working. He built his law practice and later the store while also devoting much effort and time to the city's booster projects. These included Portland's 1905 World's Fair, which celebrated the centenary of the Lewis and Clark expedition. Its purpose, of course, was to encourage immigration to and investment in Portland, especially *vis-à-vis* Seattle which, since the arrival of the railroads in 1884 and the Alaska Gold Rush in 1897, had become a boom town and was outdistancing Portland. The fair was a great success. Such fairs usually lose money, but Portland's made money and it "put the city on the map." In 1900 the population had been 90,000; by 1910 it was well over 200,000.

Julius was less successful in two other enterprises. He invested in a newspaper that failed, and in 1929 he bought with others a controlling interest in the Pacific Bancorporation that held ten banks in Oregon including Portland's American National Bank. When the bank was threatened with failure, Julius felt that because he was its chairman and therefore the name Meier was involved, he must use his own funds to save it. In 1893, when there had been a threatened run on Henry W. Corbett's bank, Sigmund Frank had in the dead of night wheeled over bags of gold coin from the store and so saved the bank. But nobody offered, secretly or publicly, to help Julius. To get the needed money, he borrowed it from his nephew, Aaron Frank, putting up his shares of store stock as collateral and so giving Aaron the control for which he lusted.

Between 1928 and 1930, George Joseph, Julius's friend, former law partner, and the lawyer who got Julius out of various scrapes, had gotten into some of his own. With the help of private detectives and public scandal, Joseph had brought about the disbarment of one Thomas Mannix because of irregularities in the Wemme estate cases. Joseph had also fought the proposed merger of the corrupt and insolent private electrical power interests. Joseph was then himself disbarred for his fiery attacks on judges who were creatures of the power company and he thereupon decided to vindicate himself by running for governor. In the May primaries, Joseph secured the Republican nomination and was well on his way to election when, a few weeks later, he died.

Julius, like many prominent Jewish merchants in America, had at least publicly always stayed out of politics. But he felt morally obligated to continue the vindication of his friend's name, as he had felt morally obligated to protect his own family's name at the bank. On the night of August 7, 1930, at the Portland municipal auditorium, Julius was nominated not as the Republican but as an independent candidate pledged to Joseph's platform.

It was a heated and bitter campaign. Julius was continuously attacked by *The Oregonian* and during his speeches he would hold up a copy, point to the Meier & Frank advertisement on the back page, and declare it was the only thing in the paper worth reading. When in November, Julius won handily, he refused to be sworn by any member of the state supreme court that had treated Joseph so shabbily.

He was a good governor. He formed a state police force. He began a new system for a nonpartisan, nonpolitical judiciary, old-age pensions, free school textbooks, and conservation programs to reduce the exploitation and pollution of the state's forests, rivers, and sea beaches. He reduced the state's spending by 10 percent by the end of his first year and reduced taxes on real property by 15 percent. He issued pardons to all unemployed owners of cars who had been arrested because they were unable to pay taxes on them and he commuted all sentences to the electric chair.

Other Jews in America were elected state governors—store-keeper Moses Alexander in Idaho, Arthur Seligman in New Mexico, and Simon Bamberger, the first non-Mormon, the first Democrat, and the only Jew ever elected in Utah. That Herbert Lehman could be elected governor of New York was less remarkable, given the large number of Jews there, than the fact that a Jew won the office in a Western state such as Idaho that even today numbers its Jews only in hundreds.

The South, too, where the Jewish population was small, elected Jewish congressmen and senators, including Florida's first senator, David Levy Yulee. As chairman of the Senate Naval Committee in 1846, Yulee was strong in advocating ironclad ships and in opposing the abolition of flogging in the navy, proving that you don't have to be a Goldwater from the Wild West to be a conservative and a patriot. Bamberger, Alexander, and Yulee were foreign-born, as were the majority of American Jews until about 1940.

Most American Jews and virtually all the rich ones were Republicans until the social snobbery of rich non-Jews drove them away from the Grand Old Party and the humanitarian and liberal policies of Wilson and Franklin Roosevelt drew most of them, their brains and their money, into the Democratic fold.

Despite Julius Meier's success as governor, he refused to run for a second term or for the office of United States senator, either of which he could probably have won. Since 1912 he had been the chief force behind the Columbia River Highway, one of the most beautiful scenic routes in the world. Along it, some 20 miles east of Portland, he had built "Menucha" (pronounced "Menu-shay"), his summer home. To some friends he joked that it was a Hebrew name, and to others, an Indian one. Here, surrounded by his family and friends, he loved to entertain, and he never lacked for excuses—including that he had been born on New Year's Eve in 1874 and had married on Christmas Day, 1901, the only times, he pretended, that the store was closed. Here at sixty-two he died on Bastille Day in 1937.

Aaron Frank was as tyrannical and bad-tempered as Julius was friendly and generous and merry, but Aaron, too, continued to build Meier & Frank into the greatest store west of Chicago, and he helped to build Portland as well. To some of his gifts and supposed sacrifices, however, there was, in fact, a good deal less than met the eye. He made much of the fact that during the years of World War II he devoted most of the store's newspaper advertisements and all thirty of its Christmas windows not to merchandise but to promoting war bonds, the Red Cross, blood donations, and such worthy causes. But during that war the problem for large stores was not selling merchandise but rather getting enough merchandise to sell.

As cool as he was cold, Aaron remained calm when a terrorist set off a bomb on the store's third floor because Aaron had refused a demand for $50,000, and he fearlessly helped police to capture another unsuccessful extortionist.

He was equally cool toward the increasing demands of dozens of stockholder relatives that he either run the store more profitably and pay larger dividends or sell it. As with most of these family-run department stores, Meier & Frank's merchandising and cus-tomer-service policies had as their chief purpose to keep it dominant rather than maximally profitable. And of course all of the important chains were anxious to buy a store that dominated the entire state.

Aaron flirted with prospective buyers, including Fred Lazarus, Jr., whose Federated Department Stores was considered by many to be the best of the chains. But Aaron treated Lazarus like a whore whose services he wanted but with whom he would be ashamed to be seen. Lazarus was forbidden to come to Portland. He went instead to secret meetings at the Olympic Hotel in Seattle. There he was met not by Aaron but by his attorney. No secretaries were allowed; the two men wrote out by hand the terms of a proposed letter of intent.

Fred was quite accustomed to such shabby back-street treatment and as always refused to let it get in the way of what he wanted.

After the merger terms were worked out, however, Aaron told his surprised board of directors that he was going to refuse the offer. The only reason for his decision that he deigned to give to the board was: "The Lazari are personally too unattractive."

This kind of arrogance was unanswerable so long as he controlled a majority of the store's stock. But in 1964 that control suddenly ended. The trusts of his brother Lloyd's children ended, and to Aaron's surprise they ceased to be as meekly acquiescent as they had been when they had no other choice. Making common cause with Julius's widow and children and others who had long chafed under Aaron's imperious rule, they exploded in a palace revolution led by Julius's son Jack.

The revolt shocked the city of Portland as much as it did Aaron. Under the headline: HEIRS' STOCK STRUGGLE IGNORES M & F MATRIARCH'S HARMONY WISH, the newspapers quoted from Shannet's will: "It is my earnest wish and prayer that my children and their children and their children's children and so on shall remain together and harmoniously carry on and continue such great enterprise commenced by my husband and their father, and to this end I wish to bestow and do hereby pronounce my blessing upon them for the success and endurance of such enterprise."

But her children's children were finally out of her control, and indeed some were out of their own as years of suppressed humiliation, self-doubt, envy, and rage burst forth.

Each stratagem and confrontation was watched and discussed by a fascinated Oregon citizenry, endlessly curious about what could have caused such an explosion in what had always appeared to be a monolithic family.

Despite the fact that Aaron and his immediate family now controlled only just over 20 percent of the company's stock, there were not many citizens willing to bet that the shrewd and feral Aaron would lose the fight. For some observers this was especially true after he sold his family's 200,000 shares for $50 apiece to the Broadway-Hale Stores chain, acquiring thereby along with $10 million the cunning and the financial power of the chain's president, Edward William Carter.

On the other hand, some curbstone pundits declared: "Aaron has just outsmarted Ed Carter. He's promised Carter that Jack is a weakling whose allies will desert him and that then he can deliver the whole store instead of just a piece of it."

Other observers doubted that even so shrewd a man as Aaron could outsmart Carter who was not—they insisted—a man to buy only a piece in the hope of getting the whole unless he saw a profitable use for just the piece. And to at least one spectator it appeared that Aaron's anger had foolishly led a small fox to ally himself with a large and hungry lion.

To many, Jack seemed a reincarnation of his father. A longtime store employee and a popular sportsman, Jack had put together a family alliance that controlled more than twice as many shares as Aaron controlled, in fact, a majority of all the common stock. The largest stockholders in this group were angry women, including Lloyd Frank's widow and daughters who for so many years had been required by Aaron to beg for anything they needed. Julius's widow and his two daughters were just as delighted to join in depriving Aaron of his only comfort, power, in revenge for what they considered his long abuse of Jack. But their majority stockholdings were not enough to accomplish their purpose—a tax-free merger with May Department Stores that required legally the approval of at least two-thirds of the common stock. So Jack's group maneuvered to control or buy that magic fraction while Aaron, with Carter's help, sought to buy enough shares to cause a stalemate.

Jack's group sold rights to purchase its shares for $56 apiece to the May chain, the rights to expire on December 1, 1966. The war, therefore, was now national as well as local, and involved egos, reputations, and stock values far from the limited arena of the Northwest.

In 1937, some 20 percent of the store's common stock had been sold to the public. Now suddenly the price of these shares skyrocketed from $20 to $60 and an increasingly small number of shares became more and more essential to the combatants.

The bitterness and infighting were of course titillating to local spectators. Jack's group was powerful enough to remove Aaron and his son Gerry from the store's board of directors and the two resigned from their store jobs as well before they could be fired. In a sad imitation of Aaron's own vengeful pettiness, his opponents took away his employee's discount card, his free parking space in the store's garage, and the keys to his handsomely paneled twelfth-floor office. All of this was reported in detail not only in the local press but a continent away in *The New York Times,* whose headlines announced: FAMILY WINGS WAGE BITTER BATTLE FOR STORE CONTROL.

By spring of 1965 the giant chains had reached a stalemate. Ed Carter had no chance of controlling the store, but having got possession of only 301⅓ shares more than the necessary one-third, he made the proposed tax-free merger with May Company impossible. The battle of press releases escalated into law suits and countersuits.

Then, as the December 1, 1966, deadline approached, Carter suddenly sold all his shares to the May Company for $63 apiece, a net after-taxes profit of almost $2.5 million. The fox's fury had cost him dear.

An essential element of "Oregon fever," of the settling and

growth of the West, indeed of the growth of America, was the attitude called Manifest Destiny. In addition to its imperialism and its "all too evident jingoism," it represented a quite genuine, idealistic expression of "the chosen-people, beacon-to-mankind interpretation of America's mission and duty." Whether settling Oregon or stealing the Philippines, Americans were following "the decrees of the Almighty who has evidently raised up this nation to become a lamp to guide degraded and oppressed humanity."

After disillusioning experiences from World War I through Vietnam, it is more difficult than it once was to smile at the youthful optimism, the callow insolence of a republic that believed it could bring the arts to China and rescue it from "barbarism" by dividing it up with Russia. Missouri's great Thomas Hart Benton in an 1848 oration on Oregon declared: "A Russian Empress said of the Crimea: Here lies the road to Byzantium. I say to my fellow-citizens: Through the valley of the Columbia lies the North American road to India."

It is scarcely surprising that the Jewish immigrants who built the great temples to American material progress and optimism, the department stores, should share this messianic delusion. That in later generations the delusion had ended, that the dream was dead, was one of the reasons for the sellout of these stores to the large, impersonal chains whose managements prided themselves on having no missionary morality and no religion except a worship of profits.

11

Sears, Roebuck and the Rosenwalds

[The] scrupulous attachment to the Mosaic religion, so conspicuous among the Jews . . . becomes still more surprising
if it is compared with the stubborn incredulity of their forefa-
thers. When the law was given in thunder from Mount Sinai,
when the tides of the ocean and the course of the planets
were suspended for the convenience of the Israelites . . .
they perpetually relapsed into rebellion against the visible
majesty of their Divine King. . . . As the protection of
Heaven was deservedly withdrawn from the ungrateful race,
their faith acquired a proportionable degree of vigour and
purity.

— Edward Gibbon, *The History of the Decline and Fall
of the Roman Empire*

Sears, Roebuck and Company was not started by Jews.

Richard Warren Sears was the son of a Minnesota blacksmith
and wagonmaker. As a boy of eight in 1871, he was constantly
writing off for catalogues and samples. "The quantity of mail
he received was a family joke," his sister remembered. "He ordered
trinkets and notions and traded them to the boys."

More than fifty years later, pulp magazines, as well as *Health
and Strength* and *Popular Mechanics,* still ran advertisements offering

for "Payment in coin or stamps" an extraordinary variety of merchandise that a boy who needed money (and what boy did not?) might sell at a profit.

My own greatest commercial triumph as a child was selling Catholic medals that I had bought by mail. These sold very briskly for a while not only to my Protestant and Jewish contemporaries but also to adult blacks. My Catholic friends would not buy them because they already had them or at least knew what they were, and so could not be flimflammed by my assurances of their miraculous powers carefully tailored by me to the particular miraculous needs of each customer—a black cook who hoped the neighbor's chauffeur might fall in love with her, a school friend who wanted desperately to become a yo-yo champion. It was never considered too early in America to instill in its young the morals of the marketplace.

I had considerably less success, however, with a correspondence course from a school that promised to make me a medical doctor.

But neither profit nor self-improvement, I suspect, was the chief motive for all of us who constantly wrote off for free samples of fabulous new garden seeds, free catalogues of prosthetic devices, and Charles Atlas's surefire method for turning 97-pound weaklings into Greek gods. Rather it was, like carving your name in a tree (or spray-painting it today on a subway car), a method of establishing your identity. If a letter came in the mail with your name on it, that proved who you were and if many letters came, you were really *somebody.*

As a teen-ager, Sears learned telegraphy and became a freight and express agent, but he constantly continued to buy and sell on the side for his own account. At twenty he took a consignment of pocket watches that had been refused by the local jeweler in Redwood Falls, Minnesota, and sold them by letter to other railroad express agents on the line. He sold them so cheap that the agents could resell them at a profit and still substantially undersell the local jewelers.

Within six months Sears had made a profit of $5,000. He went into watch-selling full time, first in Minneapolis and then in Chicago, where he hired a self-taught watchmaker, Alvah Curtis Roebuck. There were then some 20,000 express agents in America to whom Sears wrote offering to sell watches at wholesale, and in 1887 and 1888 he also began experimenting with mail-order advertisements in country newspapers. He was soon selling general merchandise as well as watches, and by 1896 his annual sales were almost $250,000.

Sears was not the first to see the opportunity to sell merchandise by mail in a still rural America that had become too big, too rich, and too diverse in its demands for peddlers to supply. Aaron Montgomery Ward at twenty-seven had just set up his mail-order business in Chicago in 1871 when he was wiped out by the great fire that killed several hundred people and destroyed a city built of wood, making way for a lusty, vibrant, cruel new city of steel and stone.

By the following spring, Ward was back in business, circularizing farmers, and by 1875 he was sending out a seventy-two-page catalogue that guaranteed satisfaction or the customer's money returned. Soon Ward was operating a private railroad car with minstrels and vaudeville entertainers. It toured from whistle stop to whistle stop, where after the free show the audience received free catalogues and a speech on the reasons to buy by mail—no middlemen, cheaper for cash, open your package on delivery and if you're not satisfied, refuse the shipment.

Chicago is one of the cities (others include Detroit and Minneapolis) that proves you don't have to be Jewish to build the dominant department store. Field's and Carson's have long been the city's most significant fashion stores, although such Jewish concerns as Mandel's and Goldblatt's built large, low-priced businesses and Schlesinger & Mayer had Louis H. Sullivan design the most beautiful store building in America.

Marshall Field started life as a Presbyterian farm boy in Pittsfield, Massachusetts, and like so many of the greatest nineteenth-century tycoons, from James Jerome Hill to Junius Spencer Morgan, he began his business career "clerking" in a dry-goods store. He arrived in Chicago in 1856 at twenty-one and before he was fifty had made a fortune by following his own motto: "Give the lady what she wants."

When in 1907, the year after Field died, the thirteen-story, 73-acre store at State, Washington, Randolph, and Wabash was completed, it was the biggest store in the world—bigger even (for the moment) than Macy's. One significant and continuing difference between Field's and Macy's was that under Field himself and under his successors, Field's did not hire Jews. Which did not mean, of course, that it did no business with Jews, even such a Jew as Aaron Nusbaum.

Nusbaum was the son of a poor upstate New York peddler who moved to Chicago where he just eked out a living. With such a background, Aaron, handsome, adored, and spoiled by his six sisters, was ready for the main chance when it came.

Learning that Marshall Field had lost a trainload of merchandise, he set about to find it. He succeeded, and brought it to Chicago. He was taken to Marshall Field's office, where the millionaire asked how he could express his gratitude.

Faced with the mythic, fairy-tale problem, If-you-had-just-one-wish-what-would-you-ask-for, Aaron with a cool shrewdness unusual at any age but especially in youth, dared to refuse the bird in the hand and asked whether he might not come back and claim a favor at some time in the future.

Field agreed.

A few years later, as plans for Chicago's 1893 Columbian Exposition began to be revealed, Aaron thought he saw his chance and went back to see Marshall Field and collect his favor—unless the older man chose to have forgotten it.

Field remembered and obtained for Nusbaum the favor he asked: the soda-pop and ice-cream concession for the Exposition. From that concession of a few months, Nusbaum made a profit that constituted a sizable fortune in those days, $150,000. He was resolved not to invest it foolishly.

One of the businesses with which Aaron became connected was the Bastedo Pneumatic Tube Company. He sold to department stores systems of tubes that transmitted sales slips and cash from a store's many sales areas to its central cashier, a safer system than allowing each salesperson to keep cash and make change. (Young Barry Goldwater was on occasion given to sending a live mouse through his store's tube, thereby causing terror and havoc in the cashier's office.)

Nusbaum had heard of the enormous success of Sears, Roebuck's mail-order business and called upon Richard Sears in the summer of 1895 to sell him a system of tubes, but also to see if he could buy into the business.

Precisely because Sears's headlong success demanded more capital for the booming business, Sears offered Nusbaum a half interest for $75,000, writing the terms in pencil on the stationery of the restaurant of the Chicago Stock Exchange. For years these two framed pieces of paper have hung in the boardroom of Goldman, Sachs in New York (bankers to Sears, Roebuck's later owners, the Rosenwalds) because they represent perhaps the greatest single investment opportunity in America's history.

But Nusbaum was nothing if not careful and he was unwilling to risk half of his soda-pop profits in even so obviously thriving an enterprise as Sears's. He therefore offered half of his half to various relatives and friends, who, to their lifelong regret, turned down the offer. But when Nusbaum offered it to his sister Augusta's husband, Julius Rosenwald, he accepted.

Unlike Nusbaum, Rosenwald had never been poor. His German-born father had progressed in the traditional way from foot peddler to horse and wagon peddler, and when in 1857 he married Augusta, the sister of the rich Hammerslough brothers, they put him in charge of their "Baltimore Clothing House" in Peoria, Illinois. He managed other stores for his brothers-in-law in Talladega, Alabama, and Evansville, Indiana, until in 1861 he moved his family to Springfield, Illinois. There in his home at Seventh and Jackson streets, one block west of Abraham Lincoln's home, Julius was born on August 12, 1862. The twenty-two other dry-goods stores in this town of only 9,300 people provided strong competition, but Samuel and his family worked hard enough that in 1868 he was finally able to buy out his brothers-in-law and

change the name of the store from "Hammerslough Brothers"
to "S. Rosenwald, the C.O.D., one-price clothier." Julius earned
his share however he could, pumping the organ in the Congregational Church, peddling chromo lithographs from door to door,
and of course selling in "the store."

He was bright and observant. "I remember as a boy watching
the wagons of the early pioneers going through Springfield on
their long journey west," he later recalled. And he was thrilled
at the age of twelve by shaking hands with President Grant who
was visiting Springfield. "I was particularly impressed because
he had on yellow kid gloves. He was the first man I ever saw
who wore kid gloves."

For those with enough money it was a happy and optimistic
time to grow up in America, but then as now for Jewish children
it was impossible to avoid being marked by some experiences
of prejudice. As Julius's father wrote to relatives in Germany,
"although there is not much *Riches* [the Yiddish word for anti-
Semitism] here, yet we are not on the same level with the Christians. . . . In business one hardly ever hears anything like that,
but the children often hear about it, and that is unpleasant
enough."

After only two years of high school in Springfield, Julius in
1879 went to work for his Hammerslough uncles, who had moved
to New York and become important manufacturers and retail merchants of men's clothing. He worked as a stock boy for $5 a
week and earned an extra $2 in the Rogers, Peet store at Broome
and Broadway on Saturday nights. But his life was not all hard
work. He had fun with other rich boys who were learning their
business "from the ground up." These included the future banker
Henry Goldman and the future lawyer Henry Morgenthau.

In less than five years, with the help of money from his father,
credit from his uncles, and the arrival in New York of his younger
brother Morris, Julius opened his own clothing store. It was not
very successful, but the observant Julius kept his eyes and ears
open. While he was at a manufacturer's showroom buying summer
suits for his shop, "One of the partners remarked to me that

they had received over sixty telegrams for goods that day which they were unable to supply and that the demand was increasing constantly. . . . I did not give it much thought at the moment, but during the night I awakened and thought of what he had told me and the opportunity entered my mind of embarking in the same sort of business. The idea took such hold of me that there was no more sleep that night for me. . . . "

His uncles, too, thought it a good idea for Julius to go into the summer-clothing business making seersucker and alpaca suits that were especially dashing when set off by a white piqué vest and straw boater. They suggested that he open a factory in Chicago, and they again supplied the necessary credit. With $2,000 from his father and another $2,000 from the father of his cousin and new partner Julius E. Weil, Rosenwald began the enterprise in a second-floor loft on Market Street in October 1885. It flourished.

Julius was successful enough that his father sold the store in Springfield and moved the family to Chicago. Five years later, on April 8, 1890, Julius married Augusta Nusbaum.

In 1895, Rosenwald disposed of his interest in the clothing business to join his brother-in-law, Aaron Nusbaum, at Sears, Roebuck. Although the two of them together owned a half interest, Richard Sears was the most important figure in the business. In that same year Sears wrote virtually the entire 527-page catalogue himself, as well as the thousands of mail-order advertisements the company ran in monthly magazines and rural weekly newspapers. He understood farmers and farm life and was a genius at writing copy that created in a farm family a desire for the object he was describing, a desire sufficiently strong to make that family give up hard-earned money to an unseen merchant for an uninspected object.

Often the advertised object did not exist. Sears would decide that there was—or that he could create—a demand for something and would write an advertisement for it. If he was right, as he usually was, it then fell to Nusbaum and Rosenwald to find someone who could produce the object at the proper cost and instantly.

"Costs Nothing—for $4.95 we will send C.O.D. subject to examination, etc. a fine black cheviot suit," Sears advertised, with not a single suit in stock. Then as some 25,000 orders flooded in, his partners had the suits manufactured and sent out to the impatient customers.

To Sears it was the most exciting game in the world: creating a demand for carloads of something. Indeed, the excitement of it had in earlier days led him to risk imprisonment. In 1889 he had run in various country newspapers an illustrated advertisement showing a couch and two chairs and promising:

AN ASTONISHING OFFER

This beautiful miniature UPHOLSTERED PARLOR SET of three pieces (for the next 60 days) will be sent to any address on receipt of 95 cents to pay expenses, boxing, packing, advertising, etc. This is done as an advertisement and we shall expect everyone getting a set to tell their friends who see it where they got it and to recommend our house to them. This beautiful set consists of one sofa and two chairs. They are made of fine, lustrous metal frames, beautifully finished and decorated, and upholstered in the finest manner with beautiful plush (which we furnish in any color desired). To advertise our house, for 60 days, we propose to furnish these sets on receipt of 95 cents. Postage stamps taken. No additional charge for boxing or shipping; order immediately. No attention paid to letters unless they contain 95 cts. R. W. Sears, & Co. Minneapolis, Minn.

When the customers received only a set of doll furniture instead of something to sit on in their parlors, they complained furiously to the Post Office Department, which finally decided not to prosecute Sears in court. In later years Sears was given to telling Rosenwald, "Honesty is the best policy—I know because I've tried it both ways." But the temptation of selling masses of something continued always to pull Sears at least to the far edge of hyperbole.

Advertising, as Daniel J. Boorstin warns, is the characteristic rhetoric of democracy, with "the temptation to allow the problem of persuasion to overshadow the problem of knowledge"—a dan-

ger because "Democratic societies . . . tend to become more concerned with what people believe than with what is true." Similarly, storekeepers are concerned with what people can be induced
to buy rather than with what people need.

Rosenwald was a scrupulously honest man; he disagreed with
Sears about the morality as well as the necessity and practicality
of overstatement. But he was also a good-natured and well-mannered man, whose criticism was never on the personal level, and
so he never offended Sears.

Nusbaum, on the other hand, delighted in dwelling at length
on Sears's inevitable errors while ignoring his successes. Handsome, dapper, arrogant, spoiled, acerbic, and pathologically stingy,
Nusbaum finally succeeded in permanently alienating Sears, who
in 1901 told Rosenwald that he was willing to be bought out
by the brothers-in-law or was equally willing to join Rosenwald
in buying out Nusbaum, but that he refused absolutely to stay
in business with Nusbaum any longer.

For Rosenwald the choice was distressing when he finally realized that his role of peacemaker between his two partners would
no longer work. He did not want to fight with his wife's only
brother, the man who had brought him into Sears, Roebuck in
the first place. Yet he knew that Richard Sears's genius was what
had built the company, and his own relationship with Nusbaum
had been made increasingly trying by Nusbaum's sarcasm and
insolence.

Rosenwald decided to join with Sears. Together they offered
Nusbaum $1 million for his interest—twenty-six times the $37,500
Nusbaum had invested just six years earlier. When Nusbaum
refused the offer and demanded $1.25 million, they paid his price.

Although Rosenwald had hoped thereby to avoid any estrange-
ment from his brother-in-law, it was inevitable and, in fact, became so bitter that Augusta never again spoke to her beloved
brother. Nusbaum took the untaxed fortune and invested it well—
in Inland Steel, among other companies. But even as his fortune
multiplied, he became more and more convinced that he had somehow been cheated by his former partners.

Perhaps because they contrasted so with Nusbaum's conduct, Rosenwald's simple straightforwardness, his insistence on honesty, his modesty, and his generous good nature seemed more and more to Nusbaum to be only disguises for guile. And the story grew in his family—especially after Rosenwald's fortune outstripped his—that there had been in the sale a secret or implied buy-back arrangement never honored by Rosenwald.

Of such are the best family feuds made; but there is no evidence whatsoever that Nusbaum's charges were true, and endless evidence that Rosenwald was scrupulously, indeed unbelievably, fair. When in 1909, after Sears had retired from the company, he sold his half interest to Goldman, Sachs for $10 million, Henry Goldman offered Rosenwald an option on part of it. Despite the fact that Rosenwald was a constant buyer of his company's stock, he refused Goldman's offer because he said he wanted no one to be able to say someday that he had profited at a partner's expense.

Which is not to say that the $1.25 million he and Sears had agreed to pay Nusbaum did not turn out to be a great buy. Just two years later, on December 31, 1903, the company had made such profits that it paid Rosenwald and Sears a special dividend of $2.5 million, enabling them to pay off Nusbaum with no difficulty. And only three years later Goldman, Sachs arranged an underwriting of some $40 million for the company.

Small wonder, then, that Nusbaum grew increasingly bitter at having sold his quarter interest. He was a man who cared more about money than most people, as was best demonstrated when he took his family or friends to dinner. He either left no tip for the waiter or one so small that as the party was leaving the restaurant, a guest usually found an excuse to return to the table to remedy the situation. This pathological thrift seemed to increase rather than diminish as his fortune grew, and no saving was too small to matter, including steaming uncanceled (or nearly so) postage stamps off envelopes.

There was an example of poetic justice at the end of Nusbaum's life. He was a diabetic, and one day he read a mail-order advertisement for insulin at a cut-rate price. He immediately ordered some and when it came—it killed him.

Especially in the first generation of department-store riches this exaggerated thrift was evident and was justified to later more profligate generations—including my own—by the tale of Baron Rothschild and the coachman. The first Baron, so the story went, came home in a hack and tipped the driver a few sous.

"But, Monsieur le Baron," the coachman complained, "your son always gives me a louis."

"Yes, of course, my man, but unlike him, I do not have a rich father."

Whether because of Nusbaum's unpleasant reputation or because the late radio comedian Fred Allen's comic character "Mrs. Nusbaum" made the name (German for "nut tree") laughable to many Americans or for entirely different reasons, Aaron Nusbaum's male descendants have the family name "Norman."

Once Nusbaum had been bought out, Rosenwald was completely in charge of handling the constantly rising flood of business that Richard Sears brought in. Now that he had a free hand, he reorganized it and made it more profitable by making it more efficient. But first he had to build a big enough plant to combine all the operations that had grown up and spread out haphazard all over Chicago.

In 1906, when the new plant was completed, Rosenwald returned full time to what was his primary contribution to Sears, Roebuck—devising and endlessly improving its systems. These had to handle the deluge of orders, averaging 20,000 a day, with a peak of 100,000 a day at Christmas. His purpose was to reduce the hundreds of thousands of dollars lost when orders were not filled or (even more costly) filled late or incorrectly so that the customers returned the merchandise. One customer who ordered a baby carriage later wrote asking that the order be changed to one for chewing tobacco and a shotgun because while waiting for the baby carriage his little boy had grown to manhood.

Another perhaps apocryphal story concerned the millions of dollars of merchandise returned by customers. Purportedly a teamster working for Sears, Roebuck was in a saloon arguing with a Montgomery Ward teamster about which firm did more business when the Sears teamster snorted: "Hell, we have more goods *returned* than Montgomery Ward ships!"

More than most businessmen, Rosenwald enjoyed repeating these stories at his own expense; but he realized that for the business Richard Sears was building so rapidly to be properly profitable, it had to be much better organized. It was an enormous undertaking. Hundreds of thousands of different pieces of merchandise and many thousands of different recurring problems had to be dealt with in a systematic manner. It required a kind of creativity foreign to Richard Sears, to whom the whole problem was boring. But to Rosenwald, a man whose love of thrift and hatred of waste approached passion, it presented the greatest challenge of his life.

Merchandise returned by customers was a primary cause of lost profits because all the expense of buying, storing, advertising, selling, and sending out that merchandise was wasted, and the returned merchandise was often less saleable than when it was new. When a customer in the South returned what was obviously a heavy-weight suit and complained that he had ordered a 16-ounce suit, Rosenwald asked why the heavy one had been sent and was told that there was no lighter one in stock. "Why didn't you send a watch?" Rosenwald snapped.

The bad fit of suits and unsatisfactory workmanship in many items sold by Sears, Roebuck led Rosenwald to devise and then enforce standards of manufacture, both in its own factories and in those from whom it bought. And in 1911 he had a testing laboratory set up in Chicago to improve further what Sears, Roebuck offered its customers.

But the two main means of cutting down returns were, first, to make certain that the catalogue descriptions were accurate, so that the customer would not be disappointed when he received the merchandise he had never seen; and second, to fill orders quickly and correctly.

In executing the second task, Rosenwald had a free hand. With

the help of others, he worked out a schedule and developed mechanical aids to speed order filling. Incoming mail was weighed.
This soon revealed that there were usually forty orders per pound,
and helped in scheduling each day's work.

The first automatic mail openers were developed and female
order clerks then took out the money, typed and numbered each
order form, stamped on it its scheduled time of shipment, then
shot it to the proper stockroom in a pneumatic tube system like
the one Nusbaum had suggested to Richard Sears. Conveyor belts
and gravity chutes were designed to satisfy Rosenwald's demands
for faster customer service, and his timetable approach soon had
orders for a single item opened, filled, and sent out in a single
day, multiple orders in two. Because Rosenwald required a differ-
ent-colored order form for every day of the week, late orders
were easy to spot.

If a multiple order was not completed within the time the schedule called for, the partial order was shipped out anyway and late
items shipped later by express at the company's expense. These
charges plus a 50-cent penalty against the offending department's
profits stimulated speed, as did the hiring of fleet-footed boys
and girls who could also be paid lower salaries than adults.

Young Henry Ford studied Sears, Roebuck's scheduling system
and based his "assembly line" on it, thereby reducing the time
it took to assemble every Model T chassis from twelve and a
half hours in 1913 to one hour thirty-three minutes in 1914.

When a later president of Sears, Charles Kellstadt, was asked
to compare Rosenwald to General Motors's organizing genius,
Alfred P. Sloan, he pointed out that Sloan had built on the system
devised by Durant, but that "What Rosenwald did was pioneer.
He did something that hadn't been done before."

But no system, however brilliantly designed, could avoid those
returns whose basis was in the catalogue itself. Richard Sears
was a dry-goods Barnum. He knew how to inspire the farmer
and rural villager to order, but when his description was more
tempting than the object was on arrival, that was self-defeating.

Sears was a genius at recognizing, stimulating, and creating

desire, indeed he may have inspired more and happier fantasies
than all the pornography in America's history. He understood
the enormous range of hopes and fears of the average American
at the turn of the century as perhaps no one else did and as his
catalogue repeatedly revealed. It assured readers unsure of their
penmanship, grammar, and arithmetic: "Don't be afraid you will
make a mistake. We receive hundreds of orders every day from
young and old who never before sent away for goods. Tell us
what you want in your own way, written in any language, no
matter whether good or poor writing, and the goods will be
promptly sent to you." The catalogue also, of course, repeatedly
stressed safe arrival and money back if the customer was not
pleased; but because Sears understood quite as well as a Magnin
or a Marcus the uses of status and snobbery, his catalogue also
promised that "the neighbors would admire it once they were
permitted to inspect it."

As the nonpareil American historian S. J. Perelman has pointed
out, the 770-odd-page 1897 Sears catalogue not only outcirculated
virtually all other books published that year but will also prove
more useful to a twenty-fifth-century archeologist "attempting
to adumbrate a vanished civilization." Only some seventy years
after its first publication, Perelman declared that "the Sears catalogue exercised an effect on me not unlike Marcel Proust's made-
leine and limeflower tea."

It is not only the seemingly impossibly low prices that fascinate
us, but Richard Sears's knowledge that if local stores are the primary source of entertainment and education in their community,
his catalogue must also offer these in abundance to compete successfully. He turned everything from politics to sex to the dual
purpose of entertaining and selling. If William Jennings Bryan
could whip America into a frenzy over what Carlyle had called
"the dismal science," economics, Sears could turn that to his advantage: "You can talk about free silver and free gold. Wherever
high prices prevail there is little freedom of any kind of money.
It is such prices as are named in this book that loosens the money
market." And for the simpler and often wiser folk who distrusted

and ignored economics and banks, he promised: "We are naming such prices as will bring out many a dollar that has been hidden away in a stocking."

Like his contemporaries Hearst and Pulitzer, and like today's television producers, Sears recognized that violence, especially in its ultimate expression, war, always appeals to the human heart: "These circulars are worth as much to you as most newspapers you get. They tell of War on Prices. They tell of Killing Competition. If you want news of War, Sensation, Science, and Art, read our circulars." More clearly than many psychoanalytic disquisitions, Richard Sears's catalogue reveals that Victorian women were no more ignorant of sex and no less interested in it than any women of any age. "If nature has not favored you with that greatest charm, a symmetrically rounded bosom, full and perfect," Sears offered a swift and certain solution to the problem, his Princess Bust Developer, that looked like nothing so much as a plumber's friend. With each $1.46 Bust Expander came a FREE jar of Bust Cream or Food. There was also a per dozen price of $15.60, but no suggestion as to who might need that many.

In those days when young men had far fewer opportunities to see the female form displayed, the catalogue pages illustrating Ladies Union Suits drawn on toothsome and provocatively posed models were much thumbed and last used in the outhouse for the catalogue's ultimate role, as toilet paper. And it seems not unlikely that men's underwear, drawn on well-muscled and generously mustached male models, may have secretly served an equally useful function for American women.

Catalogue illustrations were sometimes whimsical rather than erotic when, for example, Richard Sears put the head of Teddy Roosevelt on a sketch illustrating suits for stout men. But for both male and female customers, beautiful women were usually the most effective models, and in later years when photographs replaced drawings as illustrations, anonymous Sears, Roebuck catalogue models who outgrew their anonymity included Gloria Swanson, Norma Shearer, and Susan Hayward.

The cover of the catalogue might be a George Inness landscape, and America's favorite versifier, Edgar Albert Guest, was once commissioned to write a poem called "The Catalog." In keeping with the Victorian injunction to "improve each shining hour," the catalogue was dotted with useful and improving bits, and the company also offered pamphlets free of charge, such as *Tips to Trappers* by "Johnny Muskrat," for which the demand eventually exceeded 7 million copies.

Even in the area of customer relations where Rosenwald was supposed to be the expert, Richard Sears knew how to get the greatest mileage at the cheapest cost. When Sears was still in the watch business, years before he met Rosenwald, a customer came to his office one day with a broken, mud-covered watch he had dropped in a puddle in the street. Sears handed him a brand-new watch. When the customer explained that he had come in only for a joke, Sears told him: "We guarantee our watches not to fall out of people's pockets and bounce in the mud." The widespread repetition of this story was one of the things that established Sears's reputation. It was the best kind of free advertising.

Whatever the customers needed, the catalogue offered: a "ventilated" false beard, a wig ("To measure for a toupee cut a piece of paper the exact size and shape of the bald spot"), stereopticon slides of humorous and edifying subjects (dentist drawing teeth, bull tossing dog, parson carrying pig, man swallowing rats), as well as infallible cures from the Drug Department (Hair Restorer, Liquor Habit Cure, Obesity Powders, The Great Consumption Cure, Sure Cure for the Tobacco Habit).

Sears's ability to create and stimulate a market was perhaps best demonstrated when on a trip in 1902 he saw a dairy farmer using a centrifugal cream separator for which he said he had paid over $100. Sears thereupon offered one for $24.95, spent a fortune advertising it, and could not keep up with the orders. In the depression that came five years later, he conceived the notion of asking farmers who had bought the separator for names of other farmers who might buy one, and for every one who bought, the farmer who suggested his name was sent merchandise premiums. This single idea accounted for almost one-third of the company's profits in 1908. In that same year some 3.6 million copies of a catalogue were sent out, so the company had a more than passing interest in the mail service.

By 1901, there were some 77,000 post offices in America performing for Sears's and Ward's many of the functions that big-city department stores performed for themselves. An even greater windfall came when catalogues were classed as second-class "educational" matter, so that the Post Office was subsidizing Sears, Roebuck's advertising as it now subsidizes *Playboy* and *Atlantic Monthly*.

In 1891 Postmaster General John Wanamaker, the Philadelphia department-store millionaire, had proposed a system of rural free delivery (RFD), and by 1903 the mail was being delivered directly to the farmers. When parcel post finally went into effect on January 1, 1913, and farmers no longer had to drive into town to the freight depot for every package, it was only after a long and bitter fight had been waged by the thousands of small-town dry-goods merchants. But these anti-chain-store activities, although intense and acrimonious, were rearguard actions and could not save "the dying past of the general store, the village post office, the one-room schoolhouse, and the friendly corner drugstore." Within fifteen months after parcel post began, Sears, Roebuck became its single biggest user, flooding the Chicago Post Office with 20,000 pieces a day and paying the bargain price of $6,000 a day for postage.

Under Rosenwald's guidance, the company had become too big and too regulated for its creator. Richard Sears's "Baltic Seal" or "Electric Seal" were now (albeit in fine print) exposed in his own catalogue as dyed rabbit. His Vegetable Cure for Female Weakness, his great Hay Fever Remedy ("Siberian Snuff"), his French Arsenic Complexion Wafers, and his Electricating Liniment ("It Never Fails for Man or Beast"), that had for years rivaled the raising of Lazarus in their miraculous curative powers, were now being proven ineffective in his own company's testing laboratory.

Sears had always had a free hand both as to how much and what kind of advertising was best for his company, and he spent from 9 to 13 percent of sales on promotion. In 1908, he proposed to raise this to 17 percent. When his own merchandising executives agreed with Rosenwald that this was too much, he resigned.

Rosenwald, now in absolute control, built up a cadre of executives to whom he could leave the day-to-day management while he spent more time at other pursuits. He enjoyed building what he always called "the store" into the greatest retailing operation in the world. But even more, he enjoyed giving away money.

After he had become one of the half-dozen or so best-known philanthropists in America—and before he died he would give away $63 million—reporters frequently asked him, "What is the largest gift you ever made?" Rosenwald invariably replied, "Two thousand five hundred dollars." When he had set up as a clothing manufacturer in Chicago but was still far from rich, he had gone to a meeting where money was being raised for Russian Jews suffering under the czarist pogroms. He was so moved that he pledged $2,500. Given Rosenwald's financial situation at the time, it was an enormous sum, perhaps more than he would earn in that year. He was very worried, therefore, as he walked home from the meeting, as to what his wife would say.

But Augusta assured him, "It will work out," and throughout their life together she enthusiastically encouraged his philanthropy.

As a young man Rosenwald had told a friend that his ambition was someday to have a yearly income of $15,000, so that he could spend $5,000 on his family, put $5,000 away for a rainy day, and have another $5,000 to give away.

Julius and Augusta's commitment to charity was in the Jewish tradition. The Bible is full of injunctions to love, feed, clothe, assist, dower, ransom, and otherwise comfort those in need and not only one's own family and tribe but the outsider as well. "Love ye therefore the stranger: for ye were strangers in the land of Egypt."

As with everything else in the Bible, charity is discussed and defined in endless detail in the Talmud, that accumulation of centuries of rabbinical analyses, although in fact there is no word in Hebrew for charity, and the word most often used, *zedakah,* means righteousness. Helping others was a *mitzvah,* a duty, and far from being a favor to the recipient was something he or she had a right to.

How much charity is enough (in terms of grains of barley or measures of silver) is no more exhaustively discussed in the Talmud than the proper manner of giving, with special emphasis on avoiding any embarrassment or shame for the recipient. The twelfth-century Jewish physician-philosopher Maimonides listed, in order of increasing virtue, the eight ways of giving charity. To give: 1) but sadly; 2) too little, but with good humor; 3) only after being asked; 4) before being asked; 5) so that the donor does not know who the recipient is; 6) so that the recipient does not know who the donor is; 7) so that neither donor nor recipient knows the other's identity; 8) help to the unfortunate not in the form of a gift but rather a loan or a job or whatever means are necessary for him to help himself and so to maintain his self-respect.

Rosenwald's enormous charitable gifts were influenced both by this Jewish tradition and by the American tradition as well, a tradition he in turn failed to influence. As Daniel J. Boorstin points out, one of the most important and least recognized American contributions is the notion of community. In Europe every person was, after the days of the early adventurers, Aeneas or Beowulf or Siegfried, born into a fixed society with no choice in the matter and lived in the adversary position defined in 1884 by the title of Herbert Spencer's book *The Man versus the State.*

By contrast, in America, from its beginning into the twentieth century, excepting blacks and Indians, almost everyone here (or his father or grandfather) had come by choice and had helped to form a new community before there was formal government or where its writ ran rarely if at all. Unburdened by the obsolete political machinery of Europe, there was first voluntary community collaboration, a kind of do-it-yourself government that slowly became more formal and until relatively recently was viewed by citizens as their servant, not their master.

In Europe everyone paid taxes to the state and its ancient partner, the church. Some part of these funds the two institutions purportedly spent on philanthropic activities. Private charity, if any, was a personal and often secret matter—personal not only in the sense that it was directed to individuals but also that "The almsgiver was less likely to be trying to solve a problem of this world than to be earning his right of entry into the next."

Americans rejected Jesus's promise that "The poor ye always have with you," and changed the focus of philanthropy "from the giver to the receiver, from the salving of souls to the solving of problems, from conscience to community." Like water supply or sewage disposal or educating the young, philanthropy was a prudent social act and Benjamin Franklin's example taught that any useful undertaking, from a police department to a circulating library, should be supported, if not by government then by a group of individuals.

Although it had begun as a traditional Jewish commitment, Julius's own pattern of giving, evolving with his explosively expanding riches, became less and less traditional. Indeed, it offered several new, or at least rare, patterns of charity, some of which were copied, but others unfortunately not.

Initially he had simply given money to whatever Jewish causes were suggested by his Chicago rabbi, Emil Gustav Hirsch. Then in 1905, as increasing thousands of Jews were murdered and driven from their homes in Russia, Rosenwald began, on his own, giving larger sums to help them resettle. At first he supported segregated agricultural communities within Russia; but as it became obvious that there was no hope for Jews in Russia, he helped them to emigrate through the Baron Maurice de Hirsch's organization to resettle abroad in Argentina and Brazil.

Unlike the Baron Edmond de Rothschild, who for more than twenty years had been supporting the resettlement of Jews in Palestine, Rosenwald was an anti-Zionist. Like the Strauses and many other rich American Jews, he feared that a Jewish homeland would increase anti-Semitism and substantiate charges that the first loyalty of Jews was not to America.

In 1914 Julius took Augusta to visit Palestine, where they had contributed money to particular enterprises but had consistently refused to support the Zionist cause. He believed that a Jewish homeland there could never be economically self-sufficient and would exist only so long as massive transfusions of American and European funds supported it—a view yet to be proven incorrect. He also believed that such a homeland would bring into question the patriotism of all Jews living elsewhere in the world.

Similarly, he was strongly opposed to separate relief for Jewish victims of the world war. He believed it would cause non-Jewish victims in the war zones to attack Jews so singled out and would cause existing agencies to ignore Jewish victims or help them last, if at all. Theoretically, of course, he was right. But when the increasingly terrible actual suffering of Jews in Palestine and elsewhere was made clear to him by such distinguished Jewish American leaders as Louis D. Brandeis and Louis Marshall, his heart overruled his logic. Sending Marshall a check for $10,000 for special Jewish war relief, Rosenwald wrote: "While I have not changed my mind in the least concerning the wisdom of the plan for raising a fund for the relief of distinctly Jewish sufferers . . . I desire, out of respect for the judgement of yourself and your co-workers, to contribute, anonymously, the amount of the enclosed check. Making anonymous contributions is contrary to my policy, since I have always urged that, as a rule, the personality behind the gift is far more valuable than the gift itself, and should be known, but in this case I can see no other means of accomplishing the desired end."

But in his philanthropy as in his business, Rosenwald was able to admit when he was wrong and to change his mind when presented with the facts. Three-quarters of a million Jews in Russia were made refugees by the war, and 300,000 Jews fled from Galicia to Vienna. By 1917 the plight of Europe's Jews was so desperate that American-Jewish leaders such as Jacob H. Schiff and Felix M. Warburg determined to try to raise $10 million—twice as much as ever before. To give their drive the push he believed it had to have, Rosenwald announced that he would donate 10 percent of every $1 million raised up to the $10 million. The effect in Jewish communities all across America was electrifying: rich local Jews were urged to "Be the Julius Rosenwald of Your City," and more than fifty of them, including Governor Simon Bamberger of Utah and Adolph S. Ochs, formerly of Tennessee, each pledged 10 percent of the funds raised in his community.

Jacob Schiff, who two years earlier had been unable to convince Rosenwald to give any support to separate Jewish relief, now declared: "I believe there is no one who has done so much to make the name of Jew respected, to raise it, not only in the eyes of our countrymen, but everywhere, as Julius Rosenwald!"

President Woodrow Wilson said that Rosenwald served both democracy and humanity, and throughout this period Rosenwald made certain that with his time as well as his money he supported his country and the Jews. With others (including Bernard Baruch and Samuel Gompers) Rosenwald served on the Advisory Commission of the Council of National Defense, and in 1918, when he was invited to go to France to tell "our fighting boys" that America was proud of them, he accepted immediately. Offered an army commission by Secretary of War Newton D. Baker, Rosenwald refused it.

In France, when he was presented to American soldiers along with high-ranking generals and field officers, he often introduced himself as "General Merchandise." As he was boarding the S. S. *Aquitania* with crate after heavy crate full of Sears, Roebuck catalogues, the troopship's officers at first refused to load them since they far exceeded the ship's allowance for personal baggage. But Rosenwald insisted, and as he anticipated, nothing presented to the military hospitals in France and England gave the patients more comfort than these reminders of home.

Although Rosenwald was not himself minding the store, and although his executives tried scrupulously to follow his strict instructions to lean over backward in their efforts to avoid profiteering from the war, the net profits for Sears, Roebuck in 1917 were almost $20 million. In the immediate postwar years the enormous profits continued. In 1920 a common stock dividend brought its par value to $105 million, of which Rosenwald and his family reputedly owned some 40 percent. But like most very rich men, he never knew exactly how rich he was and habitually said, and meant, "Whatever it is, it's too much."

Beginning in 1920, the high wartime prices for agricultural and manufactured products declined drastically. In 1921, wheat fell from $3.45 to $1.42 a bushel and corn from $2.17 to 59 cents. Sears, Roebuck stock that had sold for $243 a share in 1920 fell to a low of $54 a year later. Rosenwald stopped his own salary, reduced others, and pared employee rolls. His markdowns on merchandise were higher than they would have been had he allowed Sears, Roebuck simply to cancel its outstanding orders at high prices as many merchants were doing; instead, he insisted on honoring his company's orders, even when they were not legally enforceable. In February 1921, instead of paying the usual cash dividend on the common stock, he paid it in scrip bearing interest at 6 percent and payable before August 15, 1922. But because he worried about small stockholders who needed their cash dividends to meet their monthly bills and who would therefore have to sell their scrip to speculators at a discount, Rosenwald offered personally to purchase it from any stockholder who owned fifty shares or less.

At the end of 1921 the company was faced with a loss of $16.5 million and another $500,000 was coming due in preferred stock dividends. Rosenwald personally made a gift of $5 million to the company and in a complicated arrangement also made it a loan of $16 million. Financiers including John D. Rockefeller, Jr., and C. W. Barron, as well as editorial writers all over America, praised him for saving his stockholders with his own money; but despite these eulogies his example was not widely followed in that financial crisis or subsequent ones.

By once again addressing himself virtually full time to the management of the company and so temporarily cutting down his philanthropic activities, Rosenwald whipped Sears, Roebuck into such shape that in 1922 there was a net profit of $5.4 million and by 1924 of over $14 million. He then brought in new management and was soon spending most of his time again giving away money.

The largest beneficiaries of the millions of dollars that Rosenwald gave away were not Jews but American blacks. When I asked his daughter Marion why this was the case, she suggested only half facetiously: "Because my mother had the Jews, my father needed a people of his own."

What in fact turned Rosenwald's attention to the blacks in America was Booker T. Washington's book *Up from Slavery*, one of the two books he claimed had most influenced his life. (The other was John G. Brooks's *An American Citizen, the Life of William H. Baldwin, Jr.)*

Rosenwald himself was unsure whether his interest was "because I belong to a people who have known centuries of persecution, or whether it is because I am naturally inclined to sympathize with the oppresssed." But to an important degree it was Washington's up-from-slavery example of courage and practical view of individual responsibility that moved him. "The individual who can do something that the world wants done," Washington wrote, "will, in the end, make his way regardless of race."

Decades later, some blacks would scoff at Washington's limited goals and at his refusal to demand complete social equality for blacks or to indulge in the exciting joys of invective and vengeance. To them, his wisdom smacked of Uncle Tomism: "No race can prosper till it learns that there is as much dignity in tilling a field as in writing a poem. . . . Nor should we permit our grievances to overshadow our opportunities."

But the practical Rosenwald agreed that until the overwhelmingly illiterate American blacks could read and write and use numbers, education must have priority. As Washington told a white audience in Atlanta in 1895: "The opportunity to earn a dollar in a factory just now is worth infinitely more than the opportunity to spend a dollar in an opera house."

In 1910, the year before Rosenwald met Washington, he was

approached for a donation toward building a YMCA in Chicago
for blacks. Not only would the "Y" serve for the health and
education of Chicago blacks, but in those days when no black
could eat, much less spend the night, in a decent hotel in most
of America, it would also provide a place where blacks and whites
could meet together and where prominent visiting out-of-town
black artists, scientists, and educators could spend the night. Rosenwald's reply to the committee that called upon him shocked
its members: "I will give you $25,000 for a YMCA building for
colored people in any city in the United States where an additional
$75,000 is raised among white and colored people."

Reminded by the committee that no Jew was allowed to serve
on the national or local boards of any Young Men's Christian
Association, he said he nevertheless wanted to help and to encourage other rich Jews to help, too. When the Negro "Y" in Chicago
opened, Rosenwald said: "The man who hates a black man because
he is black has the same spirit as he who hates a poor man because
he is poor. It is the spirit of caste. I am the inferior of any man
whose rights I trample under my feet.

"Men are not superior by the accident of race or color; they
are superior who have the best heart, the best brain. Superiority
is born of honesty, of virtue, of charity, and above all, of the
love of liberty."

Rosenwald's offer attracted national notice and the praise of
many including President Taft—who wanted a similar "Y" for
Washington, D.C.

Rosenwald soon expanded his offer to include contributing a
quarter of the cost of buildings for black women as well as men.
In the next ten years in twenty-five communities he donated
$712,000, and in response to his challenge some $6 million was
raised for this work.

In far less lavish ways, too, Rosenwald set a personal example.
In 1911 he gave a lunch for Booker T. Washington at Chicago's
Blackstone Hotel. It was the first time the hotel had admitted a
black guest.

Prior to Washington's visit, Rosenwald's white chauffeur had complained at the prospect of driving a black. Rosenwald did not object and said he would get a substitute driver. The reluctant chauffeur then asked if Rosenwald himself planned to ride in the same car with Washington, and Rosenwald assured him that he did. "Well, if you can stand it to ride with him," the chauffeur declared, "I guess I can stand it to drive him."

In 1912 Rosenwald was elected a trustee of Booker T. Washington's Tuskegee Institute. He served for the rest of his life, gave generously, raised money from others, and visited the black Alabama college regularly, often bringing with him a private railroad car full of friends, relatives, and other supporters. But like Washington, Rosenwald was a practical man and he realized that education for American blacks was needed on a much more basic and widespread level.

At the turn of the century, Alabama spent an average of $3.10 annually for each child attending school—less than one-tenth the average spent in North Atlantic states. No Southern state spent as much as one-half of the national average of $21.14. The average in the South was $4.92 for each white child; in the "separate-but-equal" schools for blacks, the average was $2.21.

In his famous Atlanta speech in 1895, Washington had warned his white audience: "Nearly sixteen millions of hands will aid you in pulling the load upward, or they will pull against you the load downward. We shall constitute one-third and more of the ignorance and crime of the South, or one-third of its intelligence and progress; we shall contribute one-third to the business and industrial prosperity of the South, or we shall prove a veritable body of death, stagnating, depressing, retarding every effort to advance the body politic. . . ." Or, as he repeatedly pointed out more simply, "You can't hold a man down without staying down with him."

Rosenwald set about to stimulate the building of rural schoolhouses for blacks in the South with much the same careful and detailed planning that he had used to create an orderly system out of the chaos of filling Sears, Roebuck's mail orders.

First he had Tuskegee design a simple architectural plan and specifications for a standard one-teacher schoolhouse that could be built inexpensively anywhere in the South. Compared to the leaking, unheated, drafty shacks with no inside plumbing that served most black children as schools, it was luxurious.

Then, in accordance with his seed-corn theory, he offered to donate half the cost of such a new black school to any community whose citizens would raise the other half.

Witnesses of the local "arousement meetings" often described moving scenes, as in Boligee, Alabama, in the winter of 1916–17, when "You would have been over-awed with emotion if you could have seen those poor people walking up to the table, emptying their pockets for a school. . . . One old man, who had seen slavery days, with all of his life's earnings in an old greasy sack, slowly drew it from his pocket, and emptied it on the table. I have never seen such a pile of nickels, pennies, dimes, and dollars, etc. in my life. He put thirty-eight dollars on the table, which was his entire savings."

Rosenwald himself was usually the first to point out that it was not *his* generosity that was extraordinary, but rather the generosity of its beneficiaries, who in proportion to their means were giving much more than he.

By the time he died, Rosenwald had contributed to the construction of 5,357 schools, shops, and teachers' homes in 883 counties of fifteen Southern states. These had cost a total of $28,408,520, of which Rosenwald's seed-corn $4,366,519 was only 15 percent. Some 64 percent came from tax funds; the blacks had spent 17 percent. Whites had provided the other 4 percent, but whites had also reaped an enormous reward from the program in terms of improving their own schools.

In 1901, schoolhouses in the Southern states cost an average of $276 each; the average annual teaching salary was $25 per month; the children who actually attended school received an average of 5 cents worth of education a day for an average of eighty-seven days per year. The Rosenwald Fund gave its school plans free of charge to anyone who asked for them, and they were used for more than 15,000 white schools, many of these in communities incensed at the prospect of "niggers" having better facilities than whites.

Despite Rosenwald's strong preference for helping groups rather than individuals, his Fund also gave $2 million in educational fellowships for particular Southerners. These too benefited mainly blacks, some 600 of them, including Langston Hughes, James Baldwin, Marion Anderson, and Katherine Dunham. Some 250 fellowships went to whites, including Lillian Smith and the Atlanta *Constitution* editor Ralph McGill, who in 1962, 100 years after Rosenwald's birth, said: "It is my studied judgment, expressed many times in recent years, that the human and spiritual values created by the Fund have been among the major reasons why so much of the South managed to begin acceptance of the United States Supreme Court's school desegregation decision without violence, and why, when defiance did appear, there were Southerners ready and willing to combat and help defeat it."

From many of these tiny Southern schoolhouses, as from many of Rosenwald's big gifts—$2 million to the University of Chicago, $3 million to build Chicago's Museum of Science and Industry—there came requests that his name be put on the resulting buildings or programs; but he almost always refused. Rosenwald was given to making fun of the vanity that often prompts such gifts. He would explain that even in those very rare cases when immortality is achieved, it is often not as the subject might have wished, for example, "with Nesselrode, who lived as a diplomat but is immortal as a pudding."

Many important Chicago institutions were named for storekeeper donors. The Adler Planetarium was established by Rosenwald's brother-in-law Max Adler, a Sears executive. The John G. Shedd Aquarium was named for a president of Marshall Field and Company, and for many years the Chicago Natural History Museum was called the Field Museum.

But in addition to his natural modesty, Rosenwald knew that there were practical reasons for his point of view. Important private art collectors, for example, are frequently disinclined to give their collection to an institution called the Carnegie Museum or the Frick Museum lest their own name be forgotten, and even money contributions are sometimes influenced by such considerations, which are, of course, no problem for an institution called the Boston Museum of Fine Arts or the Los Angeles County Museum.

A friend once told him he had heard it said that Rosenwald's philanthropy was merely self-advertisement. "I'm too good a businessman for that," Rosenwald said, laughing, "and I know how to buy publicity much cheaper, if that's what I wanted." But he also knew that publicity was an important part of fund raising and he was therefore, as he had written to Louis Marshall, opposed to anonymous benefactions. These lost, he insisted, the important multiplying factor of example. Just as seed-corn gifts should stimulate gifts by other donors and government support, so publicity about a giver should inspire other givers and thus get the most for every charitable dollar.

But the thing that differentiated Rosenwald most clearly from virtually all other philanthropists was his strong objection to perpetuities. He explained this in his article "Principles of Public Giving" in the *Atlantic Monthly* of May 1921. Anticipating the opposition felt today by many voters and their congressmen to charitable foundations, Rosenwald reminded his readers of the early struggle between the state and the dead hand: when England's monasteries held, purportedly for philanthropic uses, from one-third to one-half of the country's wealth, Henry VIII resolved this problem by the simple expedient of expropriation, because a country, as Sir Arthur Hobhouse has explained, "cannot endure for long the spectacle of large masses of property settled for unalterable uses."

Even the most brilliant minds, Rosenwald went on to explain, cannot predict the future. He cited, for example, Benjamin Franklin's assumption that there would always be apprentices, that they would need money to start their own businesses, and that his irrevocable trust to lend them a maximum of $300 at 5 percent would forever solve the problem. Rosenwald poked fun at other trusts, including one that he said provided a baked potato at each meal for each young woman at Bryn Mawr College and another that paid one-half the cost of a loaf of bread delivered each day to the door of every student in one of the colleges of Oxford.

But he was serious about his subject, pointing out the millions of dollars of endowment restricted to supporting orphanages all over America, even though it was now accepted that keeping orphans in institutions was worse for the children's physical and mental health (as well as more expensive) than placing them in private homes.

Endowments that cannot be invaded, he wrote, prevent museums from buying important objects that will never again be available. They are useless to any institution for extraordinary and unforeseen opportunities. "And nothing serves more successfully to discourage additional gifts than the knowledge that an institution already possesses great endowments.

" . . . Wisdom, kindness of heart, and good will are not going to die with this generation. . . . Perpetuities are, in a measure at least, an avowal of lack of confidence in the trustees by the donor. . . . More often, probably, perpetuities are set up because of the donor's altogether human desire to establish an enduring memorial . . . [but] I am certain that those who seek . . . to create for themselves a kind of immortality on earth will fail."

In order to be sure that the trustees of his own Fund of many millions of dollars would not lose sight of its goal in attempts to preserve or increase its capital, Rosenwald not only gave them the right to add sums of principal to any gift, if the income was insufficient, but also stipulated that all the principal *must* be spent within twenty-five years of his death. In 1928 Rosenwald gave an additional gift of 20,000 shares of Sears, Roebuck to the Fund, bringing its total to over 200,000 shares with a pre-1929 Crash value of some $40 million. With the gift came a letter stressing his conviction that by using up the Fund within this generation, "we may avoid those tendencies toward bureaucracy and a formal or perfunctory attitude toward the work which almost inevitably develop in organizations which prolong their existence indefinitely."

Rosenwald's *Atlantic Monthly* article stirred up so much interest that the magazine asked him for another, which ran in December 1930: "The Trend Away From Perpetuities." It was an excessively hopeful title. Rosenwald influenced a number of rich men and their lawyers to be careful that their foundations should not be too limited in purpose. But in terms of self-liquidation, he was far less successful. Influenced by Rosenwald, John D. Rockefeller, Sr., released for current expenditure funds he had given to the University of Chicago, and Andrew Carnegie released some to Tuskegee. Although non-Jewish millionaires including the Rockefellers and Pierre S. Du Pont publicly praised Rosenwald's self-liquidating idea and his professionalism in philanthropy, appointed him to the boards of their funds (Rockefeller Foundation in 1917), and even gave substantial sums to Jewish causes in his honor, very few followed his example of spending principal.

It would be unfair to assume that all the gigantic investment losses of the Ford Foundation, among others, as well as its choice of which undertakings to support or ignore, are due to the trustee timidity Rosenwald often spoke of, when the roles played by arrogance, ignorance, or sloth are in many instances no less significant. But it is difficult to study the conduct of many present-day foundation executives without recalling Rosenwald's dictum: "Endowed cats catch no mice."

Rosenwald's fund practiced what he recommended to others. In 1948, only sixteen years after his death, having spent in thirty-one years every cent of its many millions of principal and income, the Julius Rosenwald Fund went out of business.

When Rosenwald died in 1932, New York's most distinguished rabbi, Stephen S. Wise, compared him to the other two great American-Jewish philanthropists, the banker Jacob Schiff and the storekeeper Nathan Straus. "Schiff gave more widely, Straus gave with tenderer compassion, but Julius Rosenwald, for the most part, gave more constructively and, therefore, more enduringly." Rosenwald would have asked for no better eulogy, especially given that Schiff and Straus were members of Wise's congregation.

Despite Rosenwald's extraordinarily generous public philanthropy, he was not, early on, guided by any strong conviction that charity begins at home, at least in the sense of his ordinary employees. As a clothing manufacturer his use of sweatshop labor was no different than that of such local competitors as Harry and Max Hart, Joseph Schaffner, Marcus Marx, and Bernard Kuppenheimer and his sons. And when Rosenwald moved over to Sears, Roebuck, his salaries and labor practices were no more exemplary. Ironically, this was revealed and widely publicized because of his public-spirited fight against white slavery in Chicago.

Not even its slaughterhouses have brought Chicago as much international fame as its criminals, and their leaders have usually been Italians such as "Scarface" Al Capone. Only rarely has an Irishman such as George "Bugs" Moran risen to eminence in Chicago's underworld. And although it would be an egregious effrontery to pretend that Jews played a decisive role in Chicago's or America's organized crime, a few exceptionally talented Jews— from Capone's treasurer, Jake "Greasy Thumb" Guzik, to Meyer Lansky in our own days—have occasionally made a not entirely insignificant contribution.

If Chicago was the Second City overall, its reputation in several areas was unmatched, and in none more so than in crime. It was known to have a large local and national traffic in girls from which its politicians as well as the white slavers themselves derived generous profits. Therefore, when in 1908 the Illinois legislature passed a Pandering Law, the first law of its kind in America, skeptics assumed it was in fact only another welfare bill for politicians. But they reckoned without the Chicago *Tribune.* The paper, well aware that prurience is no less a stimulus to circulation than to charity, helped to finance a committee to study the problem, as did Rosenwald and other rich businessmen.

The report of this Chicago Vice Commission was so sensational that it was forbidden distribution through the United States mails. It revealed that more than $15 million a year was derived from vice in Chicago and that more than 5,000 women practiced prostitution. The report indicated that not Eros but economics seemed best to explain the problem.

Even without a day's sickness or a week out of work, the report asked, how could single girls who did not live at home exist on what it found to be their average salary, $6 a week? It answered its own question: "It is impossible to figure it out on a mathematical basis. If the wage were eight dollars per week, and the girl paid two and a half dollars for her room, one dollar for laundry and sixty cents for carfare, she would have less than fifty cents left at the end of the week. This is provided she ate ten-cent breakfasts, fifteen-cent luncheons and twenty-five-cent dinners."

No less aware than the Chicago *Tribune* and Illinois clergymen of the keen public interest in sex and in rich men—an interest much more than doubled when the two are combined—the Illinois Senate in 1913 provided for a committee of four senators to investigate white slavery. Its chairman was Lieutenant Governor O'Hara, who called as the first employer of women to appear on the witness stand Julius Rosenwald. O'Hara learned from Rosenwald that for the week ending March 8, 1913, Sears had employed 4,732 women for an average weekly wage of $9.12, and that the lowest wage, $5, was paid to girls under sixteen, but raised to $5.50 if they lasted three months.

O'Hara asked his witness if low wages had anything at all to do with the immorality of women and girls, to which Rosenwald replied: "I think the question of wages and prostitution has no practical connection."

O'Hara then elicited from Rosenwald the fact that the net profits of Sears, Roebuck in 1911 had been over $8 million, but Rosenwald refused to reveal what salary and dividends he had received in that year.

"Could you, Mr. Rosenwald, live on $8 a week?" wondered committee member Senator Juul.

"That is pretty hard to tell without trying."

"Have you ever tried?"

"No, I don't think I ever tried."

O'Hara continued to see a possible relationship between a girl's low wages and her need to supplement them by prostitution, as well as a possible connection between wages and profits. "Well, would you say," he asked Rosenwald, "that taking $8,500,000 as the earnings for the stockholders, would you say that in using $260,000 to pay one thousand girls an additional $5 a week, to keep the girls off the streets and to give them a good living, would you say that would be reasonable?"

"I would say it would be entirely in our province to give all our earnings to our help."

"That isn't the question, Mr. Rosenwald. Let us be fair with one another. I mean to be fair with you."

"I shall try to be fair."

If Rosenwald was initially as insensitive to the needs of his employees for higher wages as most employers of his time, unlike many of them he was able to learn from criticism.

His friend Jane Addams chided him for permitting Sears, Roebuck to buy merchandise manufactured by prison labor because such forced labor depressed the wages of free workers. Rosenwald was never angered by the candid criticism of this banker's daughter who had founded Hull House. Indeed, when she left after dining at the Rosenwalds' house one night, Rosenwald told his Gussie, "One feels that it is a benediction to have her in the home."

In 1916, Rosenwald instituted one of the first and most generous profit-sharing and savings plans for employees in America. As *The New York Times Magazine* pointed out, 90 percent of his tens of thousands of employees voluntarily joined the plan, by which Sears, Roebuck obligated itself to contribute to the fund 5 percent of its net earnings, without deducting stockholders' dividends.

Rosenwald was the first to insist that he was no intellectual— only an extraordinarily lucky man. This modesty, as unchangeable as his naïveté, had seemed to Nusbaum at worst a ruse, at best a pose. But it was absolutely genuine. Rosenwald told a newspaper reporter in New Orleans: "I believe that success is 95 percent luck and 5 percent ability. I never could understand the popular belief that because a man makes a lot of money he has a lot of brains. Some very rich men who made their own fortunes have been among the stupidest men I have ever met in my life. There are men in America today walking the streets, financial failures, who have more brains and more ability than I will ever have. I had the luck to get my opportunity. Their opportunity never came. Rich men are not smarter because they are rich. They didn't get rich because they are smart. Don't ever confuse wealth with brains. They are synonyms sometimes, but none too often."

Six months before the stock market crash of 1929, Rosenwald suggested that economic growth in America and its consequent enormous personal fortunes might not continue forever. "We must remember that many of the great fortunes in America have been made in part at least simply by taking advantage of the great natural resources of this new country and by reaping the almost inevitable rewards of developing these resources in the presence of a rapidly growing population. . . .

"As we pass the pioneering period in America, and as the great natural resources of this new country become more nearly balanced by increasing population, it may not be so easy to build up huge fortunes by these relatively simple means."

Even more than his public statements, his private conversation revealed his essential modesty. One day while wandering as he loved to do through his great wooded estate at Ravinia, he remarked with wonder to one of his daughters: "Who am I to live in a park?"

Self-deprecatory good humor has not invariably been the hallmark of great capitalists, nor have men whose beliefs were strong usually been able to joke about them. But because Rosenwald had such firm ideas about the uses and abuses of charity did not mean that he was humorless on the subject. His favorite story concerned a Pullman porter on whose car he was traveling to New York. The porter spread the word to other porters during the night that the famous millionaire was his passenger and there was much speculation as to the size of an anticipated generous tip. But after the train's arrival in New York, the porter revealed sadly that the tip had been only average and explained: "I guess Mr. Rosenwald is really more for the race than for the individual."

He loved, too, telling his children and grandchildren in confidence about a very well-known Christian millionaire from one of Chicago's top social families, who came to see Rosenwald, as many did, seeking advice from the famous money raiser on how to be successful in a money-raising campaign. Only a very few minutes after he had entered Rosenwald's office, he burst out of it, his face crimson, and fled without a word to anyone. "When he told me he wanted to raise five million dollars," Rosenwald said, laughing, "I asked him what he planned to give himself and he said, 'Twenty-five thousand.' I suggested that he would find it easier to raise the sum if he were able to say that the first million was already in hand and that I would give half a million if he would. That's when he started to choke so badly I feared for his life until he ran out of my office and, I'm told, didn't stop running until he was safely back in his limousine."

If Rosenwald was often generous to his causes, to his employees, to his executives, and to his Gussie, he was often not so to his children.

According to his youngest son, William, who at seventy-six is still in the psychoanalysis he began almost fifty years ago, "Busy as he was, Father decided he should nevertheless sit with my sister Marion and me ten minutes a day when we were small. And whenever he was in town, he usually managed to do it. But he invariably sat holding his watch in his hand.

"Recently," William said to an interviewer in December 1977, "I told my analyst I thought they had been too busy even to name me. There was at the beginning of this century a popular expression or vaudeville number, 'Hello Bill,' and I thought they chose that in order to be able to remember my name.

"When I went into analysis with Dr. Herman Nunberg in 1930 at the age of twenty-seven, I was unhappy and impotent. After only a few months of experiencing for the first time someone who was genuinely interested in my thoughts and my feelings and my fears, I became normally or even a little over-sexed. That was in Philadelphia, and the reason I moved to New York from Philadelphia was because Dr. Nunberg moved there and I didn't want to lose him. Now I still go to his son, Dr. Henry Nunberg.

"It was only through analysis I learned that it was understandable and normal to have been so terribly unhappy as a child despite all the luxury and toys and servants. Lessing was more of a father to me than my father."

Lessing, the oldest of Julius and Augusta's five children, was born in 1891 in Chicago and knew his parents before Sears, Roebuck had made them so very rich. His childhood recollections are of the modest and cosy house at 4239 Grand Boulevard, before the home at 49th Street and Ellis Avenue and the grandeur of the great country estate at Ravinia. "I remember Father as rather nice-looking, with pince-nez glasses and carefully dressed, five-foot-eight or nine, prone to anger but usually able to hold it under control. I was never afraid of him and thought of him as good-humored. I can never remember his punishing me. He was not very expressive—reticent about giving praise or blame. When at twenty I preferred going to work at Sears instead of going back to Cornell, he didn't object.

"My mother was the same size but a great deal merrier. She had a deep gentle voice and a sensitivity and understanding he lacked or at least never showed his children.

"I wanted to succeed him as the boss at Sears. I had begun at the bottom and worked my way up and I had done an obviously first-rate job in running the Philadelphia operation as well as serving for years on the board of directors. I learned that Father was planning to pass me by and hand over the reins to General Wood. I went to see Father and told him why I thought I should be president of the company and that if I was not given the post I would resign. He listened, but said nothing.

"Then Mother had a long talk with me. 'Dad told me about your ultimatum,' she said, 'and he's very upset about the pressure. He would like to be able to make his choice on a free basis. And I think you would be very wrong to come out here and run the company even though you are unquestionably equipped to do it. Here you would be constantly under his eye, and the reason you went to Philadelphia was to avoid that. And more important, you have not considered the terrible cost to your family. Your children would have to leave their school and their friends and make a whole new life for themselves out here. And so would Edith who, like you, has made an important contribution to Philadelphia and would have to give up the life she has made there and start all over again. And you would have to give up your print collecting and book collecting and much of the time you now spend with your family and spend it working instead— just as your father has always had to. You don't need more money and you don't need to prove yourself. I think you're doing this to satisfy your ego and haven't weighed what you would have to pay for it—what it would cost those who love you.'

" 'I agree with you,' I told her, and I withdrew my ultimatum. She could have put it another way and I would have resisted."

The leadership of Sears, Roebuck went, therefore, to Robert Elkington Wood, who was almost a parody of a turn-of-the-century American hero. A graduate of West Point, he made his mark in the Panama Canal Zone. There he became General George Washington Goethals's quartermaster and did a superb job, scheduling and getting the mountains of supplies necessary to build the Canal.

But after Panama, regular army life was a bore and he resigned to work first for DuPont, then for General Asphalt. He reenlisted for the world war and at thirty-nine was called to Washington and made a general by Goethals. For the rest of his life Wood insisted on being addressed and referred to as "General."

After the war he went to work for Montgomery Ward, where he opened retail stores as a method of unloading the excessive inventory build up in the boom war years. These retail stores were so successful that Wood wanted to build more. Roads were getting better, farmers were acquiring cars, and the migration of rural America into the cities was increasing. In Wood's view this meant that the growth of retail stores would be greater than that of mail-order sales, but he was unable to convince his superiors at Ward's. So in 1924 he moved over to Sears, where he was made vice-president in charge of the company's factories and retail stores. The first retail store opened in February 1925, and that same year stores were opened in Seattle, Dallas, and Kansas City.

The success of the retail stores was so enormous that in 1926 and 1927 a new store was opened every other business day. Montgomery Ward never caught up with Sears's head start. In only six years, retail-store sales became more important than mail-order. And they were more flexible. Prices could be marked down, or up, quickly and were not frozen as in the catalogue.

During his twenty-six-year reign at Sears from 1928 to 1954, Wood did not allow Jews to be hired as buyers or at any executive level. His was only marginally, if at all, the social-climbing kind of anti-Semitism. It was visceral, and its bedrock was the same Middle American, Populist, Know-Nothing, anti-East Coast tradition that made unquestioning anti-Semites of Henry Ford and Charles Lindbergh.

In the 1950s he gave not only money but the enormous publicity and prestige value of his name to Senator Joseph McCarthy's "crusade" against the Communist-Jewish-eastern-liberal conspiracy.

When asked how his father could support such an anti-Semite so uncritically, Lessing answered sadly: "It is just as difficult now as it was then to explain. You know Wood was not overt, not explicit. It was basic and subconscious so that he could deny with the greatest conviction and sincerity that he was in the slightest degree anti-Semitic.

"You know he asked me to come on the America First board and I did. Then when Lindbergh made his famous attack on the Jews, I asked Wood to repudiate it and he said, 'Give me one week.' Then when nothing happened I called him again and he asked for another month. And finally I understood that he would never repudiate it and I resigned from the America First board and ceased to be his friend. We continued as business associates for many years, but no longer as friends."

Cynics then and since have suggested that like Wood's great business ability, his anti-Semitism was an important asset to Sears, Roebuck and that the Rosenwalds realized it. Today it is almost impossible to understand the hatred felt all across America for the mail-order merchants and the great chain stores, including not only Sears, Roebuck and Ward's but also J. C. Penney, the A & P, Woolworth, Walgreen, Newberry, and W. T. Grant. Democratic National Chairman Robert Strauss, whose father was a shopkeeper in various West Texas villages, remembers: "My daddy hated J. C. Penney worse than the Czar! After all, Penney's was *selling* overalls and sheets at retail for less money than Daddy could *buy* them for on credit at wholesale."

The local dry-goods merchant, grocer, drugstore owner, along with their banker and friends, fought mail-order and chain stores doggedly. Local newspapers often refused or overcharged for their advertising, and printed stories about shoddy merchandise and shady business practices along with numberless jokes about "Rears and Soreback" and "Monkey Ward." Often the local storekeeper was also postmaster, so he knew what local "Judas" received mail-order catalogues and packages—until Sears learned to ship in a "plain, brown, unmarked wrapper," like the purveyors of naughty books and birth-control materials.

In some localities children received a dime or a free movie ticket for every mail-order catalogue they brought in—no questions asked. But sometimes these attacks backfired. When a local storekeeper was solicited for a contribution toward a new church and instead suggested that the committee solicit Sears, Roebuck, "who are taking a fortune out of this community and contribute *nothing,*" the members did so and immediately received $10.

Although much of the hatred of the chains was whipped up by angry and envious small merchants and their allies whose profits were hurt by the chains, much was also the result of sharp practices by the chains themselves. Using their power to place enormous orders, they brutally squeezed down the prices of their suppliers, who often made no profit, or even lost money, but didn't want the orders to go to a competitor. Numbers of A & P store managers have in the past been accused of short-weighting, short-changing, and a variety of other dishonest practices such as "selling the broom"—propping a broom against the checkout stand, adding its price to every customer's check, and apologizing for the "error" whenever a customer noticed it.

Local merchants pressed their fight in every way they could from local, state, and national laws, including "fair trade," down to campaigns of slander that included spreading the story that Frank Winfield Woolworth was a "nigger." With Rosenwald, such invention from whole cloth was unnecessary. He was widely known to be Jewish and even in the rare places where that might be unknown, he was recognized as the greatest "nigger lover" in the country. To combat allegations that both Sears and Roebuck were black, their pictures were run in the catalogue.

Clearly it was no disadvantage in this climate of fear and hatred to have as the president of Sears the great Protestant hero of Panama.

Pressed as to whether or not his father was aware of Wood's anti-Semitism, Lessing said: "It was obvious. During Wood's administration every Jew in an important position was relieved and not one was hired. My father really believed that if you hired a man to do a job you should let him do it and not interfere and to some extent he may unconsciously have hidden behind that."

Like some of the Strauses and other rich American Jews, Rosenwald was sometimes ambivalent in his reactions to explicit anti-Semitism.

In 1923 Rosenwald gave $100,000—and raised more—to feed starving German women and children. Because Hitler, Ludendorff, and others were fanning anti-Semitism there, Jews asked Rosenwald why he did not at least send with his gift a protest against such activities. "The fact that Jews are 'giving more than their share toward helping all the different creeds in Germany' is known," Rosenwald answered, "and, to my mind it is more helpful to give *without protest* which would make it appear that the money was given for the purpose of having the Jew-baiting stopped. My opinion is that this disagreeable thing will subside of its own accord as rapidly as it would if any form of propaganda were resorted to."

In 1930 German president Paul von Hindenburg wrote to thank Rosenwald for his continuing gifts, and to "assure you not only in my own behalf but also in behalf of the German people of my sincerest gratitude." But this "disagreeable thing" was not subsiding.

Perhaps the greatest single contributor to the spread and legitimizing of anti-Semitism in America was Henry Ford, the quintessential American hero. Ford attacked Rosenwald in his virulent newspaper, the Dearborn *Independent.* But Rosenwald opposed a Jewish boycott of Ford products because "revenge is never justifiable." And when Ford, after five years of flooding the country with anti-Semitism whose effect is still felt, finally apologized under severe pressure, Rosenwald said: "I congratulate Mr. Ford that he has at last seen the light. He will find that the spirit of forgiveness is not entirely a Christian virtue, but is equally a Jewish virtue."

Looking back from an era when "confrontation" is esteemed by many as the most effective way to achieve social progress, the measured, even timid response to anti-Semitism offered by Rosenwald and Jesse Straus and many such storekeepers may seem to lie somewhere between insensitivity and cowardice. But their contribution to the now generally favorable view of American Jews by their fellow citizens is not inconsiderable and whether the final appraisal of more strident voices presently in fashion will be more favorable remains to be seen.

After Julius Rosenwald died on January 6, 1932, Lessing succeeded him as chairman of the board at Sears. He and his brother and sisters were the dominant Sears stockholders, but they never spoke to Wood about his anti-Semitism. "He was powerful and popular and was doing a superb job running the company for the stockholders in terms of profits and dominance," says Lessing, who was only forty-nine when Wood reached Sears's retirement age of sixty in 1939, but who then resigned Sears's board chairmanship in Wood's favor.

Four years later, Lessing, called by *Time* magazine "shy and esthetic," donated his well-known collection of some 6,500 prints and drawings (including 236 Rembrandts) to the National Gallery of Art in Washington, D.C., and his important collection of books to the Library of Congress.

It is rare enough for children of an extraordinary and powerful man or woman to be even average. For the second or third generation to produce strong and useful citizens is rarer still, but not unknown. The Rockefellers did it and so did the Rosenwalds.

Like all Rosenwald's children, Lessing followed the pattern set by Julius; but the father cast a long shadow. From Los Angeles, where he was at the moment of the stock market collapse in 1929, Lessing immediately wired every Sears store that he would personally guarantee the brokerage account of any company employee who might need help. Julius was delighted at his son's generous response, so much so in fact that he took over.

A witness described the scene with wonder. "He had been ill; nevertheless he was at the office promptly at 8:30 on that memorable blue Thursday of late October. As thunders and lightnings began to threaten the financial structure of America he placed two telephones before him, squared himself at his desk, opened the three doors to his office, and began to 'do business.'

"Streams of callers poured through those doors making three long lines right up to his desk. He took them in order from the heads of each line, snapping out decisions and clearing the business of the callers as fast as the lines could move forward. He periodically called Washington and New York and answered a hundred telephone messages.

"In the course of one attempt to get an order through to a broker, the report came back that the telephone exchange for the whole LaSalle Street section had suddenly gone out of order; he burst into a gale of laughter at the absurdity of such an accident on such a day.

"In the collapse which culminated this day, he saw his own fortune reduced by $100 million. He saw his business and his personal affairs plunging inevitably into the most troubled waters. It was one of the happiest days of his life."

In order to save so many employees and friends, Rosenwald personally borrowed $7 million from the Chase National Bank, a debt he had not paid when he died two years later.

When the wire services picked up the story and sent it around the world, the comedian Eddie Cantor telegraphed Rosenwald: "Understand you are protecting your employees on their margin accounts. Can you use a bright industrious boy in your office? I am ready to start at the bottom."

Having had the time of his life, Julius finally realized that he had stolen Lessing's idea. Typically, he wrote to every department manager in the company explaining that: "The favorable comment which came to me as the result of the newspaper publicity was due almost entirely to Mr. Lessing Rosenwald."

According to her brothers and sisters, the star of the five Rosenwald children was Adele, a luminous lady who was generous and loving not only in the public spotlight but in the privacy of her family. "She *did* more, not just talked about but actually *did* more, than any of the rest of us," says her sister Marion, "and yet she never took herself too seriously and no matter how busy she was she telephoned me every day."

Her first marriage, at nineteen, to a childhood Chicago friend, Armand Deutsch, ended in divorce after the birth of two sons. In 1927 she married the handsome, witty child psychiatrist David Mordecai Levy, who first described and named phenomena such as "sibling rivalry" and "maternal overprotection" that are now part of the language.

Her own work was in a variety of causes, but none was more important to her than that for the welfare of children. She was horrified by tales of abused and exploited children, and through the Citizens' Committee on Children of New York she served as a watchdog in their behalf. Because of who she was and because of her money, she had instant access to the politicians—Mayor Robert Wagner, Governor William Averell Harriman, President Harry S. Truman—who could press for the legislation and funding she wanted for children's protection, health, and education. But her warmth (the word that was most often repeated by eulogists and editorial writers when she died) got her even more of what she wanted. "If this city is bankrupted," New York's mayor Abraham Beame once said to her sister, Marion Ascoli, "one reason is because none of us knew how to say no to that lovely sister of yours."

"She was like Mrs. Roosevelt," her friend Freida Lash remembers, "she wanted to be certain she was not being used just for her money and her name and, of course unlike Mrs. Roosevelt, she was hypersensitive to the slightest nuance of anti-Semitic discrimination. On the board of the Museum of Modern Art or in any milieu, she was anxious that no one else be preferred to her, that if there was a significant committee she be on it or at least be offered the refusal of it, and she did not propose in any sense to be a second-class or merely decorative board member, nor like the dilettantes of both sexes who abounded on many of her boards.

"Most of all she wanted fun in her work. For herself and for those who worked with her she was determined it not be dreary but fun."

Adele kept a photograph of her mother on her piano and she was very close to her father, but at least part of her love of fun and of great luxury was a reaction to their insistent training in the virtues of thrift. She reveled in buying beautiful and expensive clothes at Bergdorf's, in being surrounded by great art, and especially in the comfort of too much room and too many servants, if indeed these exist. But in fact her greatest and most extravagant luxury she had learned from her father—the joy of a royally lavish generosity. Unlike his, it extended as often to individuals as to institutions. Quietly, compassionately, secretly, she indulged herself in the fun of giving serious sums of money to friends in need.

Her longtime friend, Eleanor Roosevelt, remembering Adele's spirit of zestful, warm-hearted fun, wrote that she wanted her daily newspaper column, "My Day," on March 14, 1960, two days after Adele died, not to be sad but rather "a song of triumph," because "how few people leave this world with as triumphant a record!"

"No one living in New York can dominate and transform the

entire city the way Edith has New Orleans," Adele remarked, referring to the next younger of Julius and Augusta's children.

"I think that one thing we children each learned from our parents," says Edith Rosenwald Stern, "was the importance of the example we set. And I don't mean a snobbish sort of fashion setting like the Warburgs or the Lehmans—just the opposite in fact.

"My mother never ceased telling us with pride about the calluses she wore on her hands as a child scrubbing floors and helping to raise her sisters and brother. And after my father made so much money and they went east, where they were entertained at the feudal estates of the Schiffs and the Strauses outside New York, my mother was more than ever resolved never to become like that, never if she had a country place to have statues or anything else she considered pompous or stiff. Mother was very naïve, but she was a very great lady—very sensitive, in the good sense of being sensitive to the feelings of others and not just her own. And when she built Ravinia, she insisted that it be kept natural, using the ravines and local flowers and only tanbark trails and gravel roads—nothing forbidding.

"That's why she had a Japanese butler. When my father asked why in the world she wanted a *Japanese* butler, she told him she had been put off by the English butlers of his rich New York friends and would not allow that same thing to happen to her old friends in Chicago, none of whom she was sure could find a Japanese forbidding.

"Adele and I adored our mother and were more than a little frightened of our 'Prussian' father. He had a phobia about virginity and I remember he once shook me so violently I thought my teeth would break when I came in from a date ten minutes late.

"He often made a point of coming home on the streetcar and of taking just an upper or lower berth in the Pullman to New York, not a drawing room. My Uncle Morris, who was his 'poor' younger brother, offered to pay for a drawing room, but JR wouldn't let him—it smacked of self-indulgence.

"And when his children, especially his three daughters, wanted to marry, he didn't care about the 'background' of prospective sons-in-law in the snobbish way that the Goldmans or the Sachses did—were they German Jews and were they socially prominent? He wanted to know if they were rich enough and hard-working enough to afford to support his daughters. He was very much against divorce—all three of his daughters divorced—and his objections, I think, were not on moral grounds but because he didn't want to have us back on his hands again to support."

After divorcing Germon Sulzberger, Edith selected for her second husband Edgar Bloom Stern of New Orleans, who although he was not Rosenwald rich was rich enough and whose earlier marriage proposal to Jesse Isidor Straus's daughter Beatrice had been refused.

"We tried to set a pattern here, Edgar and I," Edith explained in 1977. "We hoped to change the local way of life, but I think we failed. Among New Orleans men, there was simply no tradition of generous giving. Jews usually, but not always, gave more than the others, but no one gave seriously. And women gave nothing at all. Southern women are brought up to be decorative not forceful, modest not vital. I must have seemed a monster to them, but if that pattern has been broken here, it's we out-of-town women who've done it.

"The focus of the rich here is on Carnival. They're entirely absorbed in Mardi Gras. And Jews are excluded from that, so those who can afford to, find reasons to leave town at Carnival time.

"Whatever we've achieved here, we had to do ourselves. When the New Orleans Country Club was organized we and the Godchauxs and a few other Jews were charter members (unless the Godchauxs are considered Episcopalian rather than Jews), but the membership never again opened for Jews.

"There were no good progressive children's schools, so we started Newcomb Nursery School for our own children and then about 1929 the Metairie Country Day School."

In addition to the schools Edith organized that continue to benefit New Orleans, so does the gift of her estate at 11 Garden Lane, including its (contrary to her mother) splendid formal gardens.

Like many if not most second-generation rich German Jews, Edith Stern is not religious; indeed she is, at least in private, mildly mocking about Jewishness. "My father insisted when we were children that we go down to the ghetto in Chicago and serve food to the Jewish orphans. I once raised a great furor there because I 'unkoshered' the kitchen by serving soup and sausage in cups and saucers reserved for milk and cocoa or vice versa and a rabbi had to be called to 'rekosher' the china. I thought at first I would be punished severely but when I got home, Father laughed about it."

In the days of the Inquisition, Spanish Jews who had converted to Catholicism were often accused of making a great show of public piety by attending masses and taking communion on every possible occasion, but in the privacy of their homes secretly worshipping in the Jewish tradition. With Julius Rosenwald's children the opposite was true—although frankly agnostic in private, they made a public show of their Judaism, most especially, perhaps, Edith Stern.

Although there is in her private life nothing of the observing Jew, and although she did not send her children to religious school, when her daughter Audrey planned to marry *The New York Times* art reporter Tom Hess in a lay ceremony, Edith Stern was furious. She absolutely insisted that the public ceremony had to be performed by a rabbi, and it was. But when the rabbi naturally proposed the symbolic breaking of a wineglass, traditional at Jewish weddings, Mrs. Stern was again outraged and refused. Jewish, yes—too Jewish, no!

And yet standing beneath a Waterford chandelier of museum quality, looking up at an oil portrait of her grandmother, Augusta Hammerslough Rosenwald, hanging in the place of honor in Edith Stern's splendid living room, the undisputed doyenne of New Orleans grows wistful. "The passage of time is no guarantee of progress. On my seventy-second birthday I stood in front of that painting in my slacks and dyed hair and thought—I wish I could look like *that*. My father visited his mother every morning and every afternoon. It was part of the tradition, the duty all Jewish families felt toward parents. Now it's sunk, without a trace.

"Of course it worked both ways. My father used to accomplish tender miracles when we were children. We would wake up to find by our beds long-wanted toys from the store. And the same after we were grown. When Edgar was building this house for me, Father would visit and Edgar would find his bookmark had been replaced by a large check. Father was anything but grandiose. He never wanted to embarrass the receiver of his generosity."

In terms of public reputation, the best-known member of the third generation is probably Edith's younger son, Philip, a writer whose books on such subjects as taxes and national security are rather the opposite end of the stick from his grandfather's conservatism. "But I loved him wildly although he died when I was only six. My parents tell me that the moment he walked in the front door if I was upstairs in my crib I began screaming until I was in his arms. The only interesting Freudian slip I made in a psychoanalysis of many years was when I said to my analyst about JR, 'He was only six when I died.'

"It seems to me after observing all the many members of our family for some fifty years that the strongest and least beneficent influence JR had on his family resulted from his penury with his children and—excepting Adele—their's with their children."

This typical Victorian emphasis among the rich that their children must be made to "learn the value of money" led sometimes to comic and sometimes to tragic results. Adele's older son, Armand, now a Hollywood movie producer, recalls his experience at the family compound on Lake Michigan where: "I had no way of knowing that these summers were being lived in a somewhat unusual atmosphere. One year, when I was eight or nine, I decided I wanted a lemonade stand. This entrepreneurial desire, filtering upwards, met with considerable enthusiasm, and Kiku was put in charge of the project.

"Kiku was my grandparents' butler whose wardrobe—or the only part of it I ever saw—consisted of a severely tailored morning coat, starched white shirt, and black tie for informal daytime occasions; a dinner jacket for normal wear; and, if the assemblage exceeded six people, white tie and tails for evening.

"He named his eldest son Julius Rosenwald Yohamino and upon my grandfather's death, returned to his homeland. During World War II, it sometimes occurred to me that Julius Rosenwald Yohamino may well have been the oddest name in the entire Imperial Armed Forces of Japan.

"In any case, the date for the grand opening of the lemonade stand was set; I was to meet Kiku at 10:00 A.M. at our family entrance on Sheridan Road. Our stand consisted of a table covered by a beautiful damask cloth, a dozen large crystal glasses, two silver pitchers, pails of ice, and other pails filled to the brim with pure lemonade.

"Kiku had wisely opted for his morning coat. It was a hot, lazy Midwestern day, and although we had only the most discreet sign advertising our presence, we were a hit from the beginning. When a customer stopped on our side of the road, Kiku filled a glass with ice and lemonade. I served it and collected the five cents. If the customer was going the other way, Kiku served it. That was because one of the hard and fast rules of the compound was that no one of my generation was allowed to cross Sheridan Road.

"Like any other enterprise, this one had a few bugs to be ironed out. Several cars, for instance, departed with the crystal glasses, and we made a mental note to bring paper cups for those who were pressed for time. In spite of minor problems, the enterprise was a bonanza. I kept all the nickels. It seems too bad that I was never indoctrinated in the cost of doing business—i.e., Kiku's prorated salary, the price of pure lemonade, and so on.

"It was a joyous experience, but it was to be short-lived. A lady down the way had run a soft-drink stand for years. After one week she issued a plaintive plea that we were not only hurting her business but ruining it. My grandfather instantly decided that the Good Neighbor Policy should prevail, and we were ordered to close down forthwith. My grandmother was delighted since she had been far from pleased with Kiku's long daily absences."

Almost like do-it-yourself grandchildren were Julius and Augusta's last two children, Marion and William, born in 1902 and 1903. "No one's childhood is entirely happy," says Marion at seventy-five, "and ours was a mix of happy and unhappy, regardless of what my brother Bill may tell you. It's true we didn't get to see our parents much, but when we did it was often fun and games. Father loved fun and he loved to laugh. To celebrate Mother's birthday we always did skits on December 27 and after we grew up and married, husbands and wives took part too. If Mother came in while we were planning the production, we told her, 'Get out! We're busy.' She was always jolly and loved it when we teased her and made fun of things she'd preached to us. Or we would base a rhyme or song on something Father had said, such as, 'Edith suffers from nervous prosperity,' or, 'Where shall we send the mushrooms?' The mushrooms were always a problem. As a part of thrift and not wasting time or space or darkness or whatever, we raised mushrooms and with Father's organizational supervision our crops were so terribly big that we always had more than we could eat or sell or give away.

"That thrift business *was* awful. They were so terribly stingy with us that we had the smallest allowances in our crowd and our friends got sick of treating us. I think it was insane and why we all ended up on the couch. My brother Bill, for example, is even more eccentric than a Warburg. I know you don't believe it's possible for anyone to be more eccentric than the Warburgs, but you'll see.

"Mother kept a closet full of scraps and old clothes and odds and ends of fur and made our clothes at home from that junk. On my wedding trip I looked appalling in those homemade dresses. But the older children fought for us. Dellie and Edith would say, 'Don't do this dress over again,' and, 'Don't make her go to the dance with a maid,' or, 'If she goes to college give her decent clothes.' My parents didn't, so Edith did. She bought me the first pretty clothes I ever owned.

"I was an ugly duckling. I only went to parties because I was too proud not to and because my parents wanted me to. I remember Edith bought me such a beautiful long yellow dress of silk petals and decided to do me over. 'Sit down!' she ordered, and I sat and she did my hair herself.

" 'Take off those glasses,' she commanded, snatching them off.

" 'I can't see,' I complained.

"You don't have to see! Just keep time to the music and let them see you.'

"Dellie and Edith were both surrogate mothers and there were good governesses as well as bad. Luthera M. Nickerson was a hateful, a dreadful woman. My father decided that a governess for just Bill and me was wasteful, so he organized a kindergarten under Miss Nickerson in the ballroom. We had fourteen or sixteen outside children, including our black chauffeur's child who had been named Renault after one of the cars. On the other hand, we loved one governess, Fräulein Marta, so much that Bill and I both learned German just to please her.

"Later, when we went to the children's school of the University of Chicago, there were problems, too, even though Father was on the board. One of the Caldwell kids would stick out her foot and trip me and whisper under her breath, 'Dirty Jew!' And when I told my father about it, he asked how many kids there were in the class and suggested that I play with kids who liked me.

"Except about thrift, he was easygoing. He didn't get upset or lecture us when we got mediocre report cards or had dirty hands or holes in our socks. He was only obsessive about money. When I hated Wheaton and wanted to change to Wellesley, he was perfectly agreeable.

"I'm sympathetic that Mother neglected me. She had three teenagers and on top of that two small kids. I know the problem because my own sons are twenty years apart. She had been a fine mother to Lessing and Dellie and Edith, who grew up in a nice middle-class house on Grand Boulevard with a nice middle-class mother and father and a happy home life. But when Bill and I came along, everything had changed. It was no one's fault. Father had become enormously rich and was the leading spirit in American-Jewish life, and Mother was too busy too.

"I hope this doesn't sound like one long complaint because of course there were wonderful times. Ravinia was Paradise—so much freedom, such a beautiful big beach, the ravines to explore. But no parents. When I decided to divorce my first husband, Alfred Stern, it never occurred to me to discuss it with my parents. Alfred was from Fargo, North Dakota, and had left me and fallen in love with Martha Dodd. She was a really glamorous figure—her father was a famous American ambassador and she was becoming a flaming liberal. (That's why he had to live in Prague and couldn't come back to America for so long.)"

In 1940, Marion married her second husband, Max Ascoli, who according to the Washington *Post,* was "given to moments of stunning insight and as temperamental as a typhoon." An Italian Jew, he was born in Ferrara, although presumably his ancestors had once lived to the south at Ascoli, from their choice of a last name, just as Modigliani's had taken the name of the nearby village of Modigliana.

An early opponent of fascism, Ascoli fled to America in 1931, taught at New York's New School, and in 1949, with Marion's money, founded *The Reporter.* During its nineteen-year life, the magazine had an influence in America quite out of proportion to its tiny circulation. Before "investigative journalism" had been so christened, let alone become chic, *The Reporter* exposed the China Lobby, the obscene pattern of wiretapping, and in addition it provided a rostrum for such later-to-be-famous figures as Henry Kissinger, James Schlesinger, and Daniel P. Moynihan.

To one observer it seemed: "He brought Marion real excitement, ardent love, and for the first time in her life, power. From her first taste of it, Marion loved power. And she loved Max. To please him she learned Italian and bought the beautiful Tintoretto self-portrait that Adele said had sex appeal. Through his magazine she got Kissinger and lesser lions to decorate the dinner table in her really splendid home at 23 Gramercy Park South, just as at her father's table she had met great and powerful people.

"It's a mistake to think that Marion was Max's creature or his victim. She has all the wit and humor that Adele lacked.

She's a good friend and a really great enemy. And when Max's flirtations or pontifications became excessive, her 'Max! Basta!' brought him into line immediately."

The interests of William Rosenwald, Julius's youngest child, contrast with those of his father and of his older brother, Lessing, who, even more strongly than Julius, believed that the creation of a nation in Palestine, a "Jewish homeland," would increase anti-Semitism. Lessing became, therefore, the first president and a generous supporter of the American Council for Judaism, founded in 1942 to disseminate as widely as possible the view that "Judaism is a religion of universal values—not a nationality . . . nationality and religion are separate and distinct. . . . Israel is the homeland of its own citizens only and not of all Jews."

Another prominent Jewish department-store figure who became an outspoken member of the Council was Stanley Marcus. But once Israel was a *fait accompli,* and especially after the Six-Day War of 1967, much of the Council's support quietly disappeared.

In contrast, William Rosenwald's support of Zionist causes has always been at least as strong as Lessing's support of the Council, but neither brother has allowed even this political difference to affect their warm family affection or their joint family investments. In 1939, when William was thirty-five, he was one of the three signers of the document establishing the United Jewish Appeal, and although he has also supported such relatively non-Jewish enterprises as Tuskegee and the Philharmonic Symphony Society of New York, his chief focus is on the UJA.

Most second- and third-generation descendants of the great Jewish storekeepers were not so obsessed with their charities, their collections, or their vices as to ignore the essential that supported all these—money. Bill Rosenwald, despite his endless efforts for the UJA, does not fail to address himself to making money, both through the family corporation, "Starwood," and through his American Securities Corporation.

Educated at MIT, Harvard, and the London School of Economics, the once painfully shy and still incredibly soft-spoken Bill has forced himself to become an excellent public speaker and major money raiser. "The multiplier effect of example, especially early in a campaign, is difficult to overestimate," he explains. "It was only possible for me to convince the UJA in 1946 that we had to raise the then unheard-of sum of $100 million because Adele, Edith, Marion, and I each had agreed to give $250,000, so that I was able to say in that speech, 'My family will give the first million.' What a lucky thing to be able to say to your children, 'I made a speech that in a small way may have changed history.'

"But in addition to money, what many Jewish businessmen have been able to give their favorite causes is the kind of organizational skill my father gave to Richard Sears's business, that changed it from merely another very profitable business to a giant enterprise. In the early 1950s, for example, Israel had poor credit and was borrowing money any and everywhere at interest as high as 12 to 20 percent. Some of us were able to convince the New York banks that to consolidate these into a single loan at low interest (prime plus a half percent) was a matter of public interest. And we convinced them to do this without collateral but payable from the first UJA receipts. And when the New York banks came in for $20 million, banks across the country followed suit to a total of $100 million and what we saved in interest over five years was the same as $25 to $40 million more in capital contributions.

"Perhaps Father's rages if we left a light burning did good as well as harm. It may be part of why Edith is so efficient she's called 'Effie.' But Mary and I—there were no children from my earlier marriage to Renée Sharf—have tried to be less money-obsessed with our children."

Whatever his shortcomings as a father, Julius Rosenwald as a husband was close to ideal and Augusta was no less ideal a wife. She was in Europe on April 9, 1911, the twenty-first anniversary of their wedding, when he wrote that she had "multiplied many times the love I felt for you twenty-one years ago. . . . What I am of Jew or Citizen or any honors which have come to me would not have come but for your co-operation and helpfulness."

Beginning in 1927, Augusta underwent several serious operations for cancer and suffered great pain. After Dr. William James Mayo came to Chicago to examine her, he wrote Rosenwald asking for permission to charge no fee, requesting that "you would let us consider that such service as I was able to be to you was a slight token of esteem and sympathetic recognition of your work for a better America." In accepting this and other tributes, Rosenwald showed himself as gracious at receiving as at giving.

On May 23, 1929, Augusta died at the age of sixty and Julius conducted the simple funeral service himself. As so often happens with the survivor of a happy marriage, he soon remarried. On January 8, 1930, he married his son Lessing's mother-in-law, Mrs. Adelaide R. Goodkind, in Lessing's home in Philadelphia.

Some eighty years after Rosenwald joined Richard Sears in 1895 and began building "the store," it has achieved superlatives that would have shocked even a man as gifted in hyperbole as Sears himself. It is the largest retailing organization in the world. Its headquarters in Chicago is the tallest building in the world. It is the biggest publisher in America and the biggest user of newspaper advertising space. It employs 1 out of every 204 employed Americans. One in three adult Americans buys at Sears, and one in four has an account there. Sears's sales, over $17 billion, constitute 2 percent of the gross national product.

12

Legions of Lazari, or How Fred Lazarus, Jr., Ate Up Everybody Else

Speaking against the Mexican War, Abraham Lincoln said it reminded him of the Illinois farmer who claimed: "I don't want all the land there is—I only want what jines mine."
—Carl Sandburg

In the summer of 1929 at Charlevoix, Michigan, nine-year-old Richard, the youngest son of Fred Lazarus, Jr., and his first wife, Meta, was struck by an automobile and killed. Immediately after the tragedy and for the rest of that summer, whenever Fred was there, he insisted that every evening Meta take a walk with him up and down fashionable Dixon Avenue to prove that they were not defeated. This demonstration was unnecessary. For many years no one who knew him at all doubted that Fred was tough.

Or perhaps no one doubted it except Fred himself. He was tiny, a little over five feet tall. At the age of three he had contracted both scarlet fever and the measles, with the result that he had a permanent tremor in his hands, and when he became excited, his body seemed to shake uncontrollably.

These handicaps only made him more competitive and more "feisty." On his eighty-eighth birthday on October 29, 1972, when he had long been the most successful storekeeper in America, he still could not resist boasting that when he and his older brother, Simon, were boys and walked through a tough section of their native Columbus, Ohio, "Si carried a loaded revolver and I a blackjack and neither of us would have hesitated to use them."

The story of the Lazari, as they were often called, began no differently from that of the other Jewish merchant families. Immigrant Simon Lazarus opened a men's clothing shop in Columbus in 1851, and with his sons built from that small start a department store that dominated his area quite as completely as the Riches' store dominated Atlanta. The elements of success were the same as everywhere else. "Ohio's great one price house, that price the lowest, and the same to one and all!" The premium for the purchaser of a man's suit was a free pair of suspenders; with a pair of shoes came a punch ticket worth fifty free shoeshines; with a boy's suit, a free baseball and bat. In 1888 during the four-hour parade celebrating the Encampment of the Grand Army of the Republic, "free barrels of ice water and lemonade were placed on the sidewalks as a courtesy to the visitors," and for eighteen years a large live alligator attracted adult and young gawkers into the store.

In 1908, the twenty-six-year-old Si Lazarus and three friends made a splash in the papers by driving a carriage and four-mule team over the mountains to Washington, D.C., to attend the inauguration of William H. Taft. A less colorful but more lasting reminder of the store's existence was its twice-daily deafening whistle blasts that signaled the predicted weather and temperature for city dwellers and farmers in the countryside.

Of course in addition to alligators and whistles there was the usual good service, generous returns policy, and concern with the quality of the goods. The Lazari made certain that it was true when they advertised that a fabric was "all wool and a yard wide," and they distributed a warning booklet to their customers explaining how to detect clothing that contained shoddy: "Shoddy is a fibrous material obtained by deviling or tearing into fibers refuse woolen goods, old stockings, rag druggets, etc. To detect shoddy, shake the clothes hard, and the shoddy dust will fall out. Rub your hand on the clothes and the shoddy will black your fingers. When you get humbugged, always try to avoid such clothing stores and bear in mind that Lazarus, the square-dealers and strictly one price clothiers is the place to get full value for the amount spent."

But the essential difference between the Lazari and all other storekeeping families, was what *Fortune* magazine called "the driving, ambitious, little man," Fred Lazarus, Jr. Although he was not the oldest son, he had been in charge of family affairs since shortly after he quit his first term at Ohio State to go into the store. Despite the shaking, he had learned to copy his father's handwriting and was allowed to write checks and borrow money, signing his father's name.

Fred planned and supervised the expansions of the Columbus store and the purchase in 1928 of the Shillito department store in Cincinnati, which had once been the leading store of the city but had fallen to fourth or fifth place. In only a decade Fred whipped it back into first place.

By his mid-forties, Fred was not one to be satisfied merely by making himself the biggest merchant in Ohio. The Standard Oil trust had been born in Ohio, and in the years since Fred was born in 1884, many similar consolidations had followed. Railroads and other fruits of technology, along with the ambition of men, had combined America's many communities into one country and many of its localized industries into monopolies or at least into nationwide corporations. So why not department stores?

At the end of 1929, the same year that little Richard had been run over at Charlevoix, Fred joined his family's store with Filene's and Abraham & Straus to form Federated Department Stores.

Two months later, Samuel J. Bloomingdale brought his store into the holding company.

In the years that followed, it was the cause of some wonder in the East how this—in their view—uneducated little fellow from the dim reaches of Middle America took over control of Federated from the "older families." But to the careful observer there was no mystery. Fred did not suffer from the disadvantages that burdened his Eastern partners. He had not "daughtered out" like Sam Bloomingdale. He was not married to a Warburg and so did not think about, let alone worry about, his social position. He felt no obligations of time or money to sports, hobbies, education, the arts, his family, or any other distraction. He could, therefore, focus his entire attention, his relentless ambition, his insatiate curiosity and intensity on what *Fortune* said was his major characteristic and the word to describe him, "dominance." He must dominate his family and his corporation just as each of his stores and every individual department in them must dominate its community.

Like the other great American storekeepers from the Strauses to Stanley Marcus, Fred was not a creator—he was an observer, a questioner, an improver, an organizer, an enforcer, and, of course, an acquirer. On a trip to Paris as a young man, he noticed that the Printemps department store was grouping dresses by size rather than by price as had been traditional. Back in Columbus his buyers objected to the crazy idea, but when he forced the underwear department to try it, the success was instantaneous. Instead of having to search through a table of $1.95 slips to find her size 34, a customer could go to a single table of size-34 slips and find many different slips to fit her. Whereas formerly she had gone to the $1.95 slip table because that was all she wanted to spend, now she was exposed to higher-priced slips and of course she so frequently succumbed to the $2.95 or even $5 slips she had never seen before that the department's volume soared. Other departments quickly followed suit.

Fred questioned similar traditional practices not only in merchandising but in every aspect of storekeeping, from customer credit to architecture. In his youth the store had required a chattel mortgage on whatever it sold for only a down payment. But reclaimed merchandise usually sold for less than the cost of repossessing it, so Fred dropped the mortgages, steadily reduced the percentage of down payment required until it reached 20 percent, and then declared: "If we're willing to trust people for 80 percent, we might just as well trust them for all of it." Fred always claimed that his was the first store in America that sold merchandise on the installment plan with no down payment, and that this put such additional pressure on his credit department to make certain of the customer's trustworthiness that his credit losses actually dropped rather than increased.

No matter how time-honored and universally accepted, no tradition was sacred to Fred. From behind rimless glasses, his bright, skeptical eyes noticed, questioned, examined every aspect of storekeeping. There were few aspects that he did not improve—at least from the standpoint of profitability—and few people he did not infuriate by his insistent iconoclasm.

In 1939, Thanksgiving Day, then traditionally the last Thursday in November, would fall on November 30, leaving only twenty-four shopping days until Christmas. Fred decided that the holiday should be changed permanently to the fourth Thursday in November so that it would fall on November 23 that year and never any later than November 28, thus ensuring an earlier beginning of Christmas shopping.

He mounted a program that convinced President Franklin Roosevelt to make the change in a holiday proclamation from Campobello on August 14. Long-standing plans across the entire country, traditional Thanksgiving Day football-game weekends, railroad timetables, all were upset by this sudden and unanticipated change. Conservative traditionalists were furious that a "holy day" had been moved merely to profit "greedy merchants."

In fact, unlike other countries, the United States had no national holidays, the formal legalizing of holidays having been left to the states. But the President's power to give federal employees the day off on such holidays as he proclaimed was an important force.

This was neither the first nor the only time that the needs of merchants and causes other than divine revelation influenced holidays in America. In early New England the fear of "popish idolatry" so moved the General Court of Massachusetts that in 1659 it passed an act authorizing a fine of five shillings for "anybody who is found observing by abstinence from labor, feasting, or any other way, any such days as Christmas day." For the next two centuries, Christmas had little commercial significance. Then, after the Civil War, as Daniel J. Boorstin points out, there was constantly increasing evidence that Christmas was becoming "a spectacular nationwide Festival of Consumption." In 1874 Macy's had its first exclusively Christmas windows, although as late as 1880 F. W. Woolworth only reluctantly gave a $25 sample order to a maker of Christmas-tree ornaments—a business that soon gave Woolworth tens of millions of dollars of sales every year.

Essential to the Christmas explosion was a "patron of a nationwide Saturnalia of consumption. The department store was the proper habitat of *Santa Claus Americanus,*" who evolved from an unknown fourth-century bishop of Myra in Lycia into the patron saint of Russia, sailors, virgins, children, pawnbrokers, merchants, and whores.

Similarly "Mothering Sunday," the fourth Sunday before Easter, had served in Europe as a day to honor the Mother of God and to give servants the day off to visit their own mothers. There was no counterpart in America until 1907, when one Anna Jarvis of West Virginia discussed the possibility of a national Mother's Day with the Philadelphia storekeeper John Wanamaker. "Pious John," who left the office of Postmaster General under a cloud of scandal because he had exceeded even the generous limits of that day for pork barrel, was not a man to fail to see the opportunity in such a celebration of motherhood. Nor did such other selfless sentimentalists as evangelists, newspaper writers, and politicians fail to understand them and climb on the bandwagon.

When Postmaster General James A. Farley in an effort to help business in 1934 issued a Mother's Day stamp showing "Whistler's Mother," the stamp included a vase of carnations not in

Whistler's painting, presumably to help the unimaginative giver. "Like other American festivals which had originated in church," Boorstin observes, "Mother's Day too ended in the department store."

Fred had been neither embarrassed nor frightened by the widespread attacks inspired by his Thanksgiving Day change. Indeed, he thrived on controversy and attack, both in his business and his family affairs.

"When various Lazari began moving to Cincinnati from Columbus, they were looked down on by the best Jewish families here, the Wachtmans and Seasongoods and Stixes," says Mrs. David Weston, doyenne of the city's Jewish society, "and they still are. None of them knew or cared anything about art or music. I can't ever remember even one of them giving a penny personally— only through their store. Up at Charlevoix too, they were not a blessing to the community."

Typically, rather than being defeated by this snobbery, Fred determined that he would mix instead with Cincinnati's rich non-Jewish families, those whose Kroger or Procter & Gamble fortunes gave them the same powers in the city as he so enjoyed exercising.

"Fred, of course, had to have a substitute for the athletic activity of which he was physically incapable," explains a longtime associate, "and it sometimes took the form of absolutely terrifying rages directed against members of his family and Federated executives— who were often the same person. His round cupid's face would turn beet red and along with the most gross obscenities he snarled the most cruel and sarcastic criticisms imaginable. That these publicly delivered criticisms were usually accurate only made them more cruel, but the rages seemed always to have a marvelously tonic effect on Fred and I am certain that they contributed to his long life."

One of the most often heard clichés of retail gossip was that Fred Lazarus, Jr., had *had* to build America's largest department-store chain in order to have enough jobs for his incompetent relatives. Certainly the only thing as obvious at Federated as Fred's genius had been, and still is, is its nepotism, characterized by

Fortune as "the somewhat alarming geometric progression that produced one Lazarus merchant in the first American generation, two in the second, and four in the third. . . ."

Among Fred's own children, the only unmixed blessing was his delicious daughter, Ann. "We were all terrified of him," she recalls, "but of course it was worse for the boys. I was only a girl and so not worth much bothering about so long as I did absolutely everything I was ordered to do by Cele [Celia Kahn Rosenthal, whom Fred married in 1935 after Meta died in 1931] and always gave in to Andy [Andrew Rosenthal, Celia's child by an earlier marriage] on whatever he wanted. Even after I married [Dr. Stuart Schloss] I was supposed to be like a servant, at Cele's orders, until my husband put a stop to that. But all my brothers were scared to death of their father until the day he died."

The oldest son, Frederick Lazarus III, was given big titles but little authority of Shillito's, close to home where his father could keep him out of trouble and use him as a target for his fury when no better target was at hand. Fred's second son, Ralph, was chosen as the heir apparent, and so was the chief victim of Fred's brutal training methods. Maurice, or "Mogie," as everyone called him, was the third son, whose longings to escape from storekeeping were savagely suppressed until Fred finally died on May 27, 1973.

Fred's New York publicity agent was the late Ben Sonnenberg. A public relations genius whose work, in his own unbuttoned phrase, consisted of "diapering rich men," Sonnenberg succeeded in getting stories about Fred into *Time, Fortune, Saturday Evening Post,* and other journals in the 1940s and 1950s—stories that were an important part of building Fred's reputation for being the shrewdest retailer in America. "In what seemed like the middle of the night, Fred once telephoned me and insisted that I immediately come over to his New York apartment," Sonnenberg remembered. "Of course I was angry, but Fred sounded genuinely distressed and besides, the annual retainer I charged Federated was very substantial. On the way over I tried to imagine what was disturbing him so, but nothing I had heard from my friends in Wall Street gave me any clue.

"When I got to his apartment, he did not even greet me but burst out immediately, 'A terrible thing has happened, Ben, just terrible, or I would not have disturbed you at this hour or at least I would have been willing to discuss it on the telephone.'

"Braced for a business tragedy of considerable proportions, I listened without saying a word and suddenly Fred exclaimed, 'It's Mogie! Mogie wants to quit the business. He wants to be a *writer!'*

"If Mogie had wanted to be a jockey or a pimp, Fred could not have been more horrified. I managed not to laugh and explained that wanting to be a writer and actually becoming one were two different things—that the aberration would probably pass—which it did."

Traditionally among Jews, writing and studying the 2.5 million words of the Talmud ranked higher than anything else—the scholar was more honored even than the rich man. But there had always been exceptions to this rule and in America where the score was kept in dollars, the exceptions increased. Fred often boasted that neither he nor his father had had a college education and that none of his family had wasted any time on hobbies.

That the Lazari did not become the Jewish Kennedys is not Fred's fault. He was at least as tough and as talented as old Joe Kennedy, but he was working with inferior materials. But if he was less successful in his dynastic ambitions than he had hoped to be, even his rapacious ambitions as a storekeeper must finally have been satisfied by the empire he built.

As World War II ended, Fred, already in his sixties, decided to assemble a national chain of department stores. It was not a new idea. B. Earl Puckett, a former bookkeeper at Loeser's in Brooklyn, had already assembled Allied Stores into a big nation-wide chain, and Macy's had played at the idea.

Some of Fred's Filene–A & S–Bloomingdale associates in the East objected to his ambitious plans, but when Fred issued an ultimatum that if they would not go along with his plans he would break up the holding company and go it alone, they backed down. From that moment, the man some of them considered a tiny little barbarian from the Midwest was in full command, although there were increasingly rare resentful challenges as when, for example, the no-less-bellicose Sam Bloomingdale took Fred to court, charging that Fred was giving himself excessive stock options.

Other descendants of the family founder, Lyman Gustavus Bloomingdale, had discovered more amusing pastimes than storekeeping. Sam's brother, Hiram C. Bloomingdale, an unashamed playboy, was, said Sam, "usually just getting home in the morning as I was going to work." Hiram developed an interest in showgirls no less intense than Fred's interest in power and profits. Hiram's love for theatrical affairs was transmitted to his son, Alfred. As a backer of shows, Alfred may be the only Bloomingdale to achieve immortality and that as the result of a George S. Kaufman quip never uttered by Kaufman but more often repeated as his than many genuine Kaufmanisms. A show Alfred backed was in trouble out of town and purportedly Alfred brought Kaufman in to save it. His advice to Alfred after seeing a performance was: "Close the show and keep the store open nights."

Even Fred's worst enemy—and there were many who yearned for the title—would have to admit that under Fred's supervisors, Bloomingdale's changed from a profitable department store of no particular distinction into the fashion setter for New York, the most exciting place to shop in America. When England's Queen Elizabeth came to New York, like millions of other tourists she might or might not have visited the city's many other stores and sights, but had she not seen Bloomingdale's, she would not have seen New York.

Fred built a chain that was better than any of the others by a very wide margin. He bought stores chiefly in what would later be called the Sun Belt, from Burdine's in Florida to Bullock's and Magnin's in California. Wherever he could, he bought the dominant store in its community, such as Goldsmith's in Memphis. Where he could not, he bought stores that had much fallen in reputation, such as Sanger Brothers in Dallas, but that had the potential to be built into the dominant store.

In Cincinnati, he assembled a team of experts that no individual store could afford: a real estate expert who specialized in nothing but department-store sites and the financial details, large and small, necessary in order to negotiate the optimum deal for a store; a tax expert to advise local store managers on how to pay the lowest possible *ad valorem* and other taxes, and how to manipulate local politicians in tax matters; as well as experts on architecture, store fixtures, and customer credit.

For years each local merchant had tied up millions of dollars, a large percentage of his personal fortune, in his store's banking and real estate functions. When his customers owed millions for stoves and refrigerators bought on the installment plan, the storekeeper was in fact in the money-lending business, and as he built a bigger and bigger downtown store as well as branches, he found more and more of his money tied up in the real estate business.

Fred freed his stores of these burdens, selling his customers' accounts to banks and selling the real estate to insurance companies and foundations—from whom he leased back the stores. This reduced his debt and enabled him to expand explosively in the field he knew best, buying and selling merchandise. He was following with a vengeance the advice of Mark Twain's Pudd'nhead Wilson, "Put all your eggs in one basket and—*watch that basket.*"

In this area of merchandising, Fred refused to be distracted by vanities that might cost him profits, for example, by demanding that his stores be the high-fashion leader in each locality. In fact, in the most vulgar language imaginable he made absolutely clear to his local store managers that their function was not to elevate the local taste level, not to be the first with the newest, but to make the maximum profit by dominating the center of the middle-class trade. There was to be no egotistic competition on a fashion-first level with Lord & Taylor or Neiman-Marcus. "You can't be a dominant store the Lord & Taylor way," declared Fred.

Instead, the essential was to dominate the middle area, even if this meant pricing work clothes and bed linens at a loss in order to be competitive with Penney and Sears.

By making each local Federated store dominant—having the largest selections and competitive prices in every merchandising area in which he chose to compete—Fred convinced the local shopper to go to his store first, since she would eventually have to go there anyway to be certain that what she'd tentatively selected elsewhere was the best. Once the local customer believed that Fred's store was dominant, it could avoid such costly expenses as excessive advertising and underselling its competitors.

Fred made the ultimate use of the figure exchanges instituted so many years earlier by Lincoln Filene. Fred demanded that every local glove buyer, delivery department manager, and alteration department supervisor should study the best job being done—and whoever could not quickly reach close to this level of excellence was fired.

Asked again and again why, in his sixties, he had undertaken such a Herculean job, Fred always gave the same answer: "Because it's fun!"

Unlike his father, Fred found the exercise of power much too much fun to give or share with any of his sons. When at eighty-one Fred gave Ralph the presidency, Ralph in a moment of unguarded candor admitted to *The New York Times*: "Actually this is only a change of title."

In this Fred was like the founding storekeepers, who because it was such fun kept minding the store long after they should have given over its management to younger men. These pioneers continued to pretend that they knew personally every single piece of merchandise in the store, long after their stores had grown so immense that such a knowledge was patently impossible. Gilbert Lang, who later became the president of Frost Brothers in San Antonio, had been trained by such a founder, Julius Joske, an immigrant who had begun in San Antonio with a bag over his back until he could afford a pushcart. From that beginning he built the largest department store in Texas, Joske's. "When I was merchandise manager of the first floor at Joske's," Gilbert remembered, "we were taking inventory one Sunday in the cosmetics department and had boxes of Kotex piled high on the counters. Old Mr. Joske passed by and asked, 'Vat's dat, Gilbert?' and I answered, 'That's Kotex, Mr. Joske.' He looked confused for a moment and then snapped with authority, 'Kodeks? Kodeks? Mark it down, clear it! Nobody vill take dat many pictures!' "

After Fred died, his sons were finally free. Now the actual as well as the titular head of Federated, Ralph seemed to some a considerable comedown from his dynamic, dominant father; to others he appeared as a figure of fun, more concerned with the trappings of power than the imaginative use of it. Perhaps to bolster his yearning for importance so little satisfied during his father's life, Ralph was anxious for the cachet of membership on other important corporate boards. A retired chairman of General Electric came on Federated's board and Ralph got a seat on GE's board. Such board memberships have replaced the dozens of honorary degrees that half a century ago served as symbols of a corporate executive's success and power. Another such current symbol, the corporate private plane, may project an image of absurdity instead of authority when the plane—as was reported— was sent to pick up a Smith College girl and bring her to a Dartmouth weekend for Ralph's son—a trip more expeditiously made by automobile.

But since Ralph would surely have been blamed if Federated had deteriorated despite the momentum generated by Fred, so he must be credited because it has not. "Ralph ought to have learned *something* sitting on Mr. Fred's lap for twenty-five years," says Jack Goldsmith.

"All three of Fred's sons must have something not readily visible to the naked eye," declares another observer, "to have won and kept such superior wives."

Although Federated has become the largest of the department-store chains, with some $5 billion in sales in 1978, there are other giants as well. Dayton Hudson is about half as big, with the May Department Stores (including Famous-Barr, G. Fox, and Hecht Co.) close behind. Allied Stores' sales exceed $2 billion, with Carter Hawley Hale and Macy's almost at that figure. The "white shoe" Associated Dry Goods, as usual, trails badly, but even the sales of the mini-chains are not unimportant: Marshall Field (including Frederick & Nelson and Halle's) at over $700 million, and Garfinkel Brooks approaching $400 million. None of these, including Federated, even approaches Sears's $17 billion or Penney's at half that total.

In storekeeping as in government and elsewhere, bigger has not invariably meant better in every respect. Often it means worse.

The department store had put the door-to-door peddlers out of business. Ironically, today's traffic congestion, at shopping centers as well as downtown, combined with the at best indifferent salespeople now typically associated with shopping in the chain-owned department store, has brought back the peddler. "Your Avon lady," with her little gift, her solicitous service, her return visit with special orders just for you, is the old-time peddler *redivivus* and the sales run to over $500 million.

Similarly, the department store had once replaced so much of the mail-order business that Sears, Roebuck and Montgomery Ward were forced to open local retail stores. But today there is an important revival of mail-order catalogue business, not only at the level of staples and inexpensive merchandise but even in high-fashion and expensive wares. Many of the rich and formerly pampered customers of such stores as Saks Fifth Avenue and Neiman-Marcus now prefer the hazards of ordering sight-unseen to the myriad difficulties and indignities of big-store shopping.

And for those who want to see, touch, and try on expensive high-fashion things, there are once again in every city small specialty stores, whose owners are in the store, on the selling floor, and so provide the same kind of excellent service that absentee ownership cannot at the very stores originally built by just such superb service.

In the past, one of the disadvantages suffered by such small specialty shops *vis-à-vis* the big department stores was that they did not have the capital to offer sufficient credit to their customers. In recent years this problem has virtually disappeared with the ubiquitous national credit cards. One credit card company, Diners

Club, was founded by a department-store heir, Alfred S. Bloomingdale, who decided that in addition to his theatrical adventures, this was a better way to spend his time than minding the family store.

As it always has, technology continues to play a significant role in department stores. Television, an expensive advertising medium, is more appropriate for the national chain than it was for the individual home-owned store. However, television has diminished the power of the store *vis-à-vis* the manufacturer, who uses TV to increase the demand for his brand name at just the same moment when the authority of the store with its local customers is diminishing under absentee management. The revelations of the new consumer-protection agencies, private and governmental, have also recently lessened the credibility of the department store.

Just as modern shopping difficulties have revived peddling and mail order, so the modern shopping mall has in another way turned back the clock. Whereas the original department stores and their "one-stop shopping" were built on the corpses of individual specialized stores—the stationer, the gift shop, the corset shop—now the air-conditioned shopping mall has revived the specialized shop. Only a few steps away from the mall's department store, the specialized shop often offers within its specialty a larger and better selection than the department store's corresponding department, and almost invariably the service is better.

Will any of these little shops grow into a big store as Filene's glove shop and Lazarus's men's clothing store did? Most, of course, will not. The days when Gimbel or Kaufmann or Goldsmith could open almost literally with a shoestring and grow into a giant seem to have passed. The dollar investment required for a new department store is too large for an individual, but easy for the chain that merely opens another branch of an existing store. And yet, a new insight into the public's needs, coupled with courage, can still triumph. The discount-store revolution, of which the end is not yet in sight, was to a large extent begun only a few years ago by E. J. Korvette, an acronym for "Eight Jewish Korean Veterans."

"Big Mike" Goldwater, like other founding merchants, could repeatedly go broke and start all over again. But the heirs of these founders felt that they had too much to lose and so wanted to ensure their security by spreading their risks and joining a chain.

Unfortunately, a much greater price than the poor service now usual in department stores has been paid by virtually every local community in America for the takeover of local department stores by the national chains. In the 1920s and 1930s, when Sears, Roebuck, A & P, and other chain stores were putting small local dry-goods stores and grocers out of business—dramatically and irretrievably changing the villages and cities of America—various politicians condemned these giants for "sapping the lifeblood of prosperous communities and leaving about as much in return as a band of gypsies."

The chains replied that precisely because they were so big and rich and powerful, the local communities would in fact benefit from bigger stores, more jobs, bigger payrolls, health and retirement benefits. However, as Senator (later Supreme Court Justice) Hugo L. Black of Alabama warned in 1930: "The local man and merchant is passing and his community loses his contribution to local affairs as an independent thinker and executive."

Today, the top local store executive put in charge by Federated or Allied or Carter Hawley Hale knows that if he does a suitably profitable job in his store, he will only live in that community for perhaps five years. Then he will be promoted to a bigger store in the chain, or to its corporate management, or will be snapped up by a competing chain.

The competitive bidding among department-store chains for top professional retail executives has driven the total remuneration—including salaries, tax-free perks, deferred compensation, capital gains opportunities, and uncancelable retirement benefits—to geometrically increasing highs. One reason for this is that even corporate financial executives whose only interest is profit figures have come to understand that, in order to be profitable, a fashion store must have an identity. And for the supposed restorers of damaged or lost identities, corporate owners of stores seem willing to pay almost any price.

To lure Robert J. Suslow from the presidency of St. Louis's Famous-Barr department store to run Saks Fifth Avenue, the British-American Tobacco Company gave Suslow a package of remuneration and fringe benefits worth some $2.5 million. About the same prize was purportedly needed to bring John Schumacher from the chairmanship of I. Magnin's to the top post at New York's Bonwit Teller.

That such retail altitudes may be damaging to your health is indicated by the fact that Bonwit's owner, the conglomerate Genesco, Inc., summarily dismissed Schumacher less than two years after hiring him and after photographs and articles appeared in *The New York Times* describing his lavish Park Avenue triplex and reporting that "Bonwit Teller employees spent an inordinate amount of time in helping Mr. Schumacher plan, build, and decorate his showplace apartment."

With such prizes, the competition is deadly—the storekeepers' executive offices have revolving doors. Suslow was Saks's third president in three and a half years; Schumacher was the fifth top executive to leave Bonwit's in seven years.

Those men who are selected to fill these top jobs come from among the hired hands who run the various chains' department stores all across America. It is, therefore, easy to understand why such a store manager's interest in the local ballet or the plight of local blacks or migrant workers might be, at best, short-lived, and why his own best economic interests are served by producing maximum profits and skillfully avoiding all controversial matters, whether these are in the field of politics, pollution, the arts, or civil rights.

This is precisely the opposite of what was the case with most local, independent Jewish merchants. They took the long view. Most of them literally *loved* their store and their city. Of course, making money was an important part of it, but the love was based on more than that. Many had begun life in a place where they might reasonably expect suddenly to be brutally maimed or murdered, where they were forbidden to own land, forbidden to appear after sundown outside the pale of the ghetto, forbidden to practice most professions and trades, or where they at the least had been subjected to daily humiliations. In America their stores made them not only safe but *respected.* Not only did they own land; it was frequently the most valuable piece in town, and often the biggest building in town was their store built on that land. They were passionately concerned with *their* city and *their* state, where they expected that their sons and grandsons would live and prosper. Their best interest, therefore, was served not by avoiding controversial problems but by helping to solve them, privately if not publicly.

The chains, of course, pay at least lip service to local and national social concerns, but too often their efforts run to "image" rather than substance—such as the pretense that each store is "a local institution with local control," and attempts to disguise the fact that absentee managers review and so control all substantive decisions.

In the 1960s, Ralph Lazarus was making public pronouncements about the department store's responsibility to face up to the black/white problem. Simultaneously, his experts were carefully surveying to see whether or not an area in which they had a store was likely in the years ahead to become "too black"—in which case they would close the store.

One of Ralph's favorite, frequently repeated pieties has been: "Federated expects its executives to spend one whole day a week working for the good of the local community." The inside joke goes: "Our store principals all know that Ralph means Sunday, on their own time, because if they don't work six full days a week on getting higher profits, he'll fire them."

In the chain department stores, if the local manager (or his wife) is sufficiently interested to want to contribute serious sums of money to the local museum or symphony orchestra, that, like an expensive company car, is a permissible and mildly encouraged perk; but such activity is insignificant in terms of his promotion within the company, and there is a risk that it may harm rather than help him.

Corporations, like individuals, are allowed in preparing their income taxes to deduct specified percentages given to charities, educational and religious institutions, hospitals, museums, and the like. Formerly, many privately owned stores—including Goldwater's, Neiman-Marcus, and A. Harris & Company—regularly gave contributions that amounted to more than their allowable deduction. Today, the gift totals of major department-store chains, like those of most American corporations, do not even approach their allowable gifts, and there are few more carefully guarded secrets than just how little these department-store chains actually contribute in total, even though particular gifts on both the local and the national level are often the subject of lavish self-congratulation in the press and in the companies' annual reports to their stockholders.

More typical, sadly, are the gifts in a recent year to the Heard Museum in Phoenix, Arizona. Federated's local stores, like Carter Hawley Hale's, gave nothing at all. Dayton Hudson and Saks Fifth Avenue each contributed $100. Goldwater's, which under the Goldwater family management had generously supported virtually everything in the state, under the present ownership of Associated Dry Goods gave $250—the same sum that Bob Goldwater gave personally. "The store has no voice in the community anymore," says Goldwater, with obvious sorrow.

In every community, hospital and educational services are essential, and the leadership and support for them once supplied by local merchants and manufacturers will now probably come from other sources. Whether or not the lost support for less obviously essential organizations—orchestra, opera, ballet, art museums—will be replaced is much more doubtful.

As the twentieth century draws to an end, few people doubt that American innocence has ended already, that like the "agrarian myth," the optimism traditional in the United States for almost two centuries has been replaced. The great Jewish department-store barons were both formed by and themselves formed the earlier optimistic point of view that expected not-one-but-two-chickens-in-every-pot and two-cars-in-every-garage.

Traditionally, Jews have not been so sanguine. Tevye, the milk-man created by a storekeeper's son, Sholem Aleichem, remarked that when a Jew eats a chicken, at least one of them is very sick. This kind of essentially pessimistic "Jewish humor" is today popular enough in a variety of forms among non-Jewish Ameri-cans to be common fare on television, the stage, and in movies.

Even thirty years ago, although fewer and fewer Jews believed the messianic promise any longer, most Americans still thought that with enough of W. K. Kellogg's cereals and Henry Ford's motorcars would come the New Jerusalem. Those who have this faith today are as hard to find as an independently owned depart-ment store. More and more Americans, whether or not they actu-ally read Bellow or Roth, Malamud or Mailer, have a more "Jew-ish" view—that is, a more skeptical expectation of life's possibilities and problems. The long-famous Jewish malaise, the once-thought-to-be-atavistic sense of exile and alienation, is now an increasingly evident fraction of general American culture. Many Americans, like the Jews of the Diaspora, feel estranged and helpless in the hands of big government, big business, big unions, and modern technology.

Quite as irretrievably a part of past history as the feudal system in Europe is the superb service once commonplace in the stores of these early merchants. In large measure this loss is attributable to the improved social conditions for which some of these mer-chants worked. The fear of starvation in this world and the fear of hellfire in the next were once strong influences toward hard work and obedience in America; but no longer. Few people would dispute that if today's widespread poor service is the price paid for free education, unemployment compensation, health insur-ance, and the other common social benefits in America, it is a bargain price—the kind of real bargain these Jewish storekeepers loved to offer.

Vanished along with good service is the enormous influence in their communities that these department stores and their owners once exercised, not only over how citizens dressed themselves and their houses but over their city as well—its streets, its schools, its symphony orchestra.

Today, the local department store is no longer the arbiter of fashion; it is only a conduit. The tastemakers now are not local. They are the national media—movies, magazines, but perhaps more than all the others combined, television.

America's department stores are bigger and more profitable than ever, crowded with customers come to buy their dreams. But what they come to buy—what they hope will enrich their lives, solve their problems, attract or retain their lovers—is no longer determined primarily by the store's selections, its newspaper advertisements, and its windows. The customer wants what is shown on national television—in the programs themselves as well as in their commercials—and that, therefore, is what the store must buy.

Similarly, what Americans want in art, architecture, music is increasingly determined not so much by local example and support as by national television. This is a mixed curse. The objects in a great museum exhibition, the dancers in a ballet, are sometimes much better seen on television than in a museum packed with pushing people or from the twenty-ninth row of an opera house.

Whether all local arts institutions can survive the transition from local private supporters to state and national public support is less than certain. Perhaps national corporations will eventually more than replace Benjamin Altman, who donated all his Rembrandts to the Metropolitan Museum, the Strauses, who helped to build Harvard. And perhaps they will not.

Most uncertain of all is who, if anyone, will have both the public stature and the courage to exert the power for moral leadership that Stanley Marcus did in Dallas or that Julius Rosenwald did nationally. These men owned their stores and so were not answerable to others for the public uproars that they provoked— a protection not enjoyed by hired chief executives. It now appears that, for better and worse, political leadership in its broadest sense will be exercised across the country by professional politicians rather than jointly with prominent private citizens.

From 1850 to 1950, many American merchants were an important part of an optimistic sense of community, of melting pot, of *E pluribus unum,* and of joining together to build Beulah Land here and now. If much of this was pietistic rhetoric, much of it also was genuine, effective, and glorious.

*   *   *

On January 14, 1935, two days after my father died, the arts
critic John Rosenfield wrote in the "Passing Parade" column of
the Dallas *Morning News:*

Although he served on no committees and was officer in no fine
arts group, the late Leon Harris was of vast importance to the
things that pass for art, music, and drama in Dallas. He was almost
our best critic. He had been everywhere and seen and heard everything. His diversions were the fine arts because he liked and loved
them. He was so sound and secure in his good taste that he felt
free to enjoy what should be enjoyed whether it wore the local
or imported label. As a result he had a keen eye and ear for local
art and musical endeavor. These he backed with the full force of
his business and social prestige. We think he did it unconsciously.
In an acquaintanceship dating from the time of our birth, we never
knew Leon Harris to pat himself on the back for a protégé who
made good. And, as his friends were aware, Mr. Harris was a singu-
larly articulate and vividly human person. Before his death he
was never mentioned as a patron of the arts. During his lifetime
there was never an indication that he, our very best patron of
the arts, felt that he had been slighted in the journalistic kudos.
It was the grandest sort of modesty—a lack of self-consciousness
on the subject of achievement.

Now that we think of it, a fine standard of Dallas taste was
formulated in the Harris drawing room on Lakeside Drive with
the host as almost supreme arbiter—and a most provocative dispu-
tant if questioned. Painters and musicians who really did things
were generally in his social circle. His presence at exhibitions and
concerts was the cue that the thing might be good. His absence—
when he was not out of town—meant the contrary; although he
was the last man in town to realize that by staying away he was
damning the event. His friends will miss him keenly and for many
months. The rest of the city, without quite knowing it, will miss
a salutary influence.

Acknowledgments
and Notes

Although I am grateful to them, I cannot remember, let alone list, the hundreds of storekeepers and their families I have known over the last half century. I thank those who in the last three years have contributed to the writing of this book and I have listed most of them below with the notes for that chapter with which each was most helpful—although many so listed were also of great help in other chapters.

Chapters I had hoped to include were finally dropped to avoid too long a book. This means, of course, that there are many—Richard Ernst and Walter N. Rothschild, Jr., in New York, Martin B. Kohn and Mrs. Albert Hutzler, Sr., in Baltimore, Arthur Phillips and Sam Strauss in Little Rock, to name only half a dozen (to use a merchant's sum) of the several dozens—who were most helpful but whose kind contributions will have to await another occasion.

Librarians all across America, from the Widener to the Bancroft, including those at newspapers and historical societies, have made a greater contribution that I can possibly describe. Most I have thanked in the notes for the chapter where their greatest contribution was made, but here I thank especially Decherd Turner and Page A. Thomas of the Bridwell Library, Lorna M. Daniells at the Baker Library of the Harvard Business School, Nathan Kaganoff of the Brandeis University Library, John George of the Dallas Public Library, and the staff of the library of the Hebrew Union College in Cincinnati.

My greatest and most obvious debt is to the work of historians, especially to Daniel J. Boorstin, as well as to Henry Steele Commager, Frank Freidel, Oscar Handlin, Rabbi Jacob R. Marcus, the late Samuel Eliot Morison, Albert Outler, Moses Rischin, and most of all to the late Wilbur J. Bender. But as the notes make abundantly clear, there are many other historians whose works make this work possible.

Readers will find that for many subjects merely touched upon in this book, the best first step toward more information and a bibliography is the *Encyclopedia Judaica.* I make this recommendation with the strong caveat that this may be habit-forming to anyone not already an *EJ* junkie. No one should look up anything in the *EJ* unless he or she is prepared to give up the next several hours or days. Like the proverbial one peanut, one reference in the *EJ* is virtually impossible—it leads to the next and the next and . . .

There is no way for me adequately to express my affection and admiration for my friend and editor of many years, Simon Michael Bessie. My thanks as well go to those who helped with the manuscript, especially Janet Balch, Yvette von Hartmann, and Bernard B. Skydell.

The abbreviations used in these notes and in the bibliography as well are:

AJA   *American Jewish Archives* magazine
AJHQ   *American Jewish Historical Quarterly* (and its predecessor publications)
INT.   Interview by Leon Harris
NYT   *The New York Times*
WSJHQ *Western States Jewish Historical Quarterly*

Printed sources cited here in abbreviated form are fully identified in the bibliography; page numbers cited in the works of others refer to the edition listed in the bibliography.

Introduction

ix Aristide Boucicaut's Bon Marché: Pasdermadjian, *Department Store,* pp. 3–5.

xiii "ethnocentric schmoose": Int., Rabbi Jacob Marcus.

xiv Boorstin has explained: *Democratic Experience,* p. 106 (hereafter referred to as Boorstin).

xx St. Augustine: Bk. 1, Sec. 15.

xx "I think shopkeeping": Johnson, *Liberal's Progress,* p. 79.

1. The Filenes of Boston

The standard written sources on the Filene family are Gerald Johnson's biography of E. A. Filene, *Liberal's Progress;* E. A. Filene's own published work and manuscripts; and the Filene and Kirstein materials in the Baker Library at the Harvard Business School and at the Boston Public Library. In addition to these, I found especially useful the manuscript material of the late Robert Cantwell, kindly lent to me by Justin Kaplan, to whom I am most grateful. Cantwell was recommended to E. A. Filene by Lincoln Steffens, who had refused Filene's offer to write the merchant's biography for a fee. Steffens had first offered the job to Whittaker Chambers, who turned it down. Cantwell was summarily fired by Filene just after he had moved to Boston and begun his research. Nevertheless, Cantwell continued to work on the material in various forms—fictional, biographical, and as Filene's autobiography—the various versions reflecting a fury considerably justified by his mistreatment.

I also thank George Collins and Richard Ockerbloom at the Boston *Globe,* who were generous with their files.

The oral sources for this chapter (extending back more than forty years to the day I met Louis Kirstein in Boston) are too many to list, but those to whom I am most obliged include: Edward L. Bernays, Thomas Dudley Cabot, Mr. and Mrs. Philip Eisman, Virginia Harris, Harold D. Hodgkinson, Stacy Holmes, George Kirstein, Lincoln Kirstein, Maurice Lazarus, Malcolm P. McNair, Sidney R. Raab, Frank Vorenberg, and particularly to Rabbi Malcolm H. Stern regarding family names taken by Jews.

PAGE

2 Jews are not: Commager, *Empire of Reason,* p. 77.

2 "was generally operative": Rischin, "The Jews," p. 5.

2 painted by Gilbert Stuart: See London, *Portraits of Jews.*

3 Boston's "Aunt Rachel": Kligsberg, "Jewish Immigrants," pp. 295–296.

4 All his life Edward Filene: Cantwell manuscripts, pp. 138–139.

5 "Kindergarten!" . . . or rent or medicine: *ibid.,* p. 152.

5 "Ugly Duckling": *ibid.,* p. 43. (See also Boston *Globe,* Sept. 8, 1934.)

8 On October 12, 1883: *ibid.,* pp. 69–175.

8 "I wonder if Socrates": *ibid.,* p. 174.

11 "My brother and I": *ibid.,* p. 53.

13 "How to Make a Poet": *ibid.,* p. 89.

13 "knowledge is rapidly": Commager, p. 42.

PAGE

15 After various evolutionary changes: Holmes, *Brief History of Filene's,* p. 17.

16 Joseph Kennedy's children, Harvard presidents: *Time,* Sept. 27, 1963.

18 of his picaresque adventures: Ints. Harold D. Hodkinson, George Kirstein, Lincoln Kirstein, and others.

18 Nathan Stein: Wile, *Jews of Rochester,* pp. 73–74.

19 "Advertising pays" . . . "attend to it": *Women's Wear Daily,* Dec. 10, 1942.

21 "Vunce already, Lou": Ints., Maurice Lazarus and George Kirstein.

21 given and sold 12 percent: Int., Hodgkinson.

23 "Filene is forever": Steffens, *Autobiography,* p. 601.

23 "to muckrake Boston": *ibid.,* p. 598.

23–24 mother-in-law, servants, dog . . . "as municipal physician": Kaplan, *Lincoln Steffens,* p. 168.

24 "New England . . . of hypocrisy: *ibid.,* p. 167.

24 "So, Mr. Filene!": "An Open Letter to E. A. Filene and the Progressive Capitalists," Lenin, *Collected Works.*

24 "I told them": Steffens, pp. 601–602.

25 He kept . . . in the world: Int., Hodgkinson.

26 "there has been a tacit": Cantwell, pp. 199–200.

27 paid $15,000: Bernays, *Biography of an Idea,* p. 438.

27 "The Filenes' real family name": Int., Bernays. Sidney R. Raab confirms that Lincoln Filene told him the family name had been Katz.

27 This practice prevailed: Int., Rabbi Malcolm H. Stern. See Stern's *Americans of Jewish Descent.*

29 "We know perfectly well": McWilliams, *A Mask for Privilege,* pp. 138–139. See also Lipset and Ladd, "Jewish Academics in the United States," in Sklare, ed., *The Jew in American Society,* p. 261. Re anti-Semitism in education, see also Glazer and Moynihan, *Beyond the Melting Pot.*

30 "excellent warm friends" . . . "before coming here": Perry, *Higginson,* p. 125.

31 In czarist Russia: Alston, *Education,* pp. 122, 130–132. See also Dubnow, *History of the Jews in Russia,* Vol. 3, p. 158, and Kochan, *The Jews in Soviet Russia,* pp. 145–148, 154–157.

32 "It was a cowardly sellout": Int., Lincoln Kirstein.

32 "Please, Lincoln, don't": Int., George Kirstein.

32 "harbored vengeful fantasies": Taper, *Balanchine,* p. 159.

PAGE

32   "We never saw Father" . . . "in the store": Int., Lincoln Kirstein.

33   "life, if you had money" . . . "to fight McCarthy": Int., George Kirstein.

33   "At lunch at": Int., Frank Vorenberg.

34   even as he lay dying: Int., Stacy Holmes.

34   E. A. had died . . . Otis Place home: Boston *Globe,* Oct. 7, 1937.

35   "The modern business": quoted in the anticipatory obituary of Associated Press dated Feb. 26, 1932.

35   the Fund had investments: Twentieth Century Fund, Annual Report, 1975.

35   "The Story of an Unsuccessful Millionaire": Johnson, *Liberal's Progress,* p. 33. See also Steffens, p. 603.

2. The Strauses of New York—Five Generations

All the members of the Straus family whom I interviewed were generous with their time and private papers. They were both forthcoming and candid. Not one of them suggested, even by implication, the change or elimination of ideas or material with which he or she disagreed. I am especially grateful to Barbara Levy, Gerald Levy, Donald Blun Straus, Jack I. Straus, Ralph I. Straus, and Robert Kenneth Straus. Other interviews particularly helpful to this chapter were those with C. Douglas Dillon and Benjamin Sonnenberg.

PAGE

36   At the end of the eighteenth century: Material on the Strauses living in Europe is based on Isidor Straus's *Autobiography;* on Oscar Straus's recollections (as set down in his books) of his parents' words; and on interviews with Robert K. Straus as well as his privately printed research. The material on Lazarus Straus and his family's early decades in America and on Isidor Straus's adventures as a Confederate agent is based on Isidor's *Autobiography* and Oscar's writings. Most material on Isidor's sons, unless otherwise noted, is from Kauffman's *Jesse Isidor Straus.*

39   "By adopting one price": Howar, *Macy's,* photograph opposite p. 20.

39   George Fox: Boorstin, p. 108. Captain Macy was in fact paraphrasing Fox, who had explained: "they might sende any childe and be as well used as themselves at any of these [uaker] shopps."

40   Its price wars with: Howar, p. 288.

PAGE

41 known thereafter as Abraham & Straus: Isidor Straus, p. 54. For a contrasting and unfriendly view of this transaction, by Henry Morgenthau, the attorney for the seller, see Morgenthau's *All in a Life-Time,* pp. 34–36.

41 But Lazarus Straus: Isidor Straus, pp. 35–39.

42 "Straus farm": Kauffman, pp. 46–49.

42 Great Blizzard of '88: *ibid.,* p. 59.

44 When Alva Bernheimer: Int., Alva Bernheimer Gimbel.

44 Nathan led: Nathan Straus, *Diseases in Milk.* Also *NYT,* Jan. 12 and 13, 1931.

45 a $1 bill: Golden, *The Right Time,* pp. 56–57.

45 Oskar, the Viennese composer: Robert Straus, *Straus Genealogical Miscellany.*

45 Emil Straus in Paris: *ibid.*

46 Isidor's youngest brother, Oscar: The best understanding of Oscar S. Straus emerges from his own memoir, *Under Four Administrations.*

47–48 "the question of the condition": Adler, *Jacob H. Schiff,* Vol. II, p. 129.

48 In a long, rambling speech: Schiff repeatedly denied the gaffe, *ibid.,* pp. 71–72; but there had been too many witnesses and the story, involving the most powerful Jew in the country, was too delicious and has been repeated endlessly since. Birmingham, *"Our Crowd,"* pp. 341–342; "An Intimate Portrait," *AJA,* Apr. 1973, pp. 21–23.

48 five years before he died: *NYT,* May 4–6, 1926.

49 they died together: *ibid.,* Apr. 15–21, 1912. See also Lord, *A Night to Remember.*

49 written letters of advice: Isidor Straus, pp. A–1 through A–10.

51 "For Heaven's sake": Kauffman, p. 60.

51–52 "The tassels belong": *ibid.,* p. 80.

52 "Isidorsyncrasy": *ibid.,* p. 44.

53 same Cabinet post: Freidel, *Franklin D. Roosevelt,* pp. 145, 152, 153.

53 Jew as ambassador to Hitler's Germany: *ibid.,* p. 361.

54 "As my brothers have": Kauffman, p. 205.

54 "surly and resentful" . . . "clean-minded, clean-bodied": Kauffman, pp. 262–263.

54 "flowers always": *ibid.,* p. 303.

54 "avoided the Fourth of July": *ibid.,* p. 305.

PAGE

54–55   "Untermeyer keeps on" . . . "in which they live": *ibid.*, p. 354.

55   "America became his religion": *NYT*, May 6, 1926. Oscar Straus's patriotic and religious feelings were better described by Naomi Cohen, *A Dual Heritage*, who wrote, as her title implies, that he "wove his religious heritage inextricably into his secular activities."

60   the wedding guests: O'Conner, *The Guggenheims*, p. 169.

60   Ralph was sent: Int., Ralph I. Straus.

60   "Get back on": Int., Robert K. Straus.

61   "Why couldn't Junior": *ibid.*

61–62   "My parents both" . . . "wanted to go on Sunday": Int., Donald B. Straus.

65   "Your father will speak": Birmingham, *"Our Crowd,"* p. 415.

65   "Regretfully, I said": Warburg, *The Long Road Home*, pp. 32–33.

67   "a sect with a minimum": Clarence Day, *God and My Father*, from *The Best of Clarence Day*, p. 5, quoted in Baltzell, *Philadelphia Gentlemen*, p. 226.

67   His son "Doug": Int., C. Douglas Dillon.

68   "only on the solemn assurance": *NYT*, Jan. 16, 1962. Also quoted in Baltzell, *Protestant Establishment*, p. 86.

68   "Straightening Out the Straus(s)es": Mar. 21, 1953, pp. 33–35.

3. *The Gimbels, Albert M. Greenfield, and Other Brotherly Lovers*

Particularly helpful with this chapter were Alva Bernheimer Gimbel and Arthur C. Kaufmann, as well as Mildred Custin, Mrs. Benedict Gimbel, Mrs. Richard Gimbel, Gordon K. Greenfield, Walter Hoving, Mrs. Isidore Kahn, Rabbi Bertram W. Korn, Charles Martyn, Dan Rottenberg, Mr. and Mrs. Milton H. Snellenberg, Mrs. Rose Gimbel Stecker, and Edwin Wolf II.

PAGE

69   In colonial Philadelphia: Int., Edwin Wolf II. Wolf and Whiteman, *History of the Jews;* and Morais, *Jews of Philadelphia.*

70   rich Jewish merchants were: Int., Edwin Wolf II. Also Baltzell, *Philadelphia Gentlemen*, pp. 276–282, and *Protestant Establishment*, pp. 138–139. Burt, *Perennial Philadelphians*, pp. 564–571.

70   less important . . . more snobbish: Baltzell, *Philadelphia Gentlemen*, pp. 282–291, and Burt, pp. 571–573.

PAGE

70 New York banks: What moved the financial capital of the United States from Philadelphia to New York was President Andrew Jackson's victory over the insolent Nicholas Biddle in the matter of the Bank of the United States. Jackson wrote Biddle: "Ever since I read the history of the South Sea Bubble, I have been afraid of banks." The fear and hatred of Eastern banks common in America's West was for a century a cause of at least rhetorical anti-Semitism because it was said that they were in the control of "Rothschild and the Jews," whereas in fact most would not even employ Jews.

72 invaded Milwaukee: Swichkow and Gartner, *Jews of Milwaukee,* p. 99.

72 "encircled by huge mirrors": *ibid.,* p. 100.

72 "servants [who] think much": *ibid.,* p. 30.

73 first full-page newspaper advertisement: Boorstin, p. 106.

74 the main meeting place: McCormick, "Meetcha at da Iggle," *Philadelphia,* Dec., 1970, pp. 110–167.

74 young David Sarnoff: Boorstin, pp. 391–392.

74 "When Uncle Daniel opened": Int., Mrs. Rose Gimbel Stecker.

75 "One of the Gimbel brothers": Sinclair, *Brass Check,* pp. 227, 283–284.

77 "Who's he kidding?": Int., Alva Gimbel.

77 "I'm delighted": Davis, *The Guggenheims,* pp. 293–294.

77 " 'Never heard of getting' ": Gunther, *Taken at the Flood,* p. 191.

78 decided to marry him: Int., Alva Gimbel.

79 "most costly lease": *NYT,* Apr. 29, 1909.

80 transatlantic liner: *ibid.,* Feb. 16, 1922.

80 "colored wigs more brilliant": *ibid.,* Mar. 17, 1914.

80 indoor golf tournament: *ibid.,* May 22, 1913.

80 $5,000-prize airplane race: *ibid.,* May 22 and Aug. 2–6, 1911.

80 Miss Ruth Morgan: *ibid.,* Mar. 9, 1920.

80 Mrs. O. H. P. Belmont: *ibid.,* Nov. 18, 1913.

80 William Randolph Hearst's art collection: Swanberg, *Citizen Hearst,* pp. 499–500, and Considine, *Armand Hammer,* pp. 80–89.

80–81 Harry Chandler: *Time,* Mar. 13, 1939.

81 many of the greatest bargains: *NYT,* June 30, 1942.

81 "Dear Sirs": Considine, p. 86.

82 the impression that he was crazy: Int., Mrs. Rose Gimbel Stecker.

PAGE

82 As an undergraduate . . . Rosenwalds: Int., Mrs. Richard Gimbel.

82 Morton went downstairs: Ints. Mrs. Rose Gimbel Stecker and Arthur C. Kaufmann.

82–83 When Joseph N. Snellenburg married: Int., Mrs. Isidore Kahn.

83 the most powerful man in Philadelphia: The best account to date of Albert M. Greenfield is Dan Rottenberg's witty and telling "Once There Was a Greenfield," *Philadelphia,* May 1976, pp. 166–194. See also *Fortune,* "Philadelphia," June 1936, pp. 67–208.

83 failed to pay $1 million: Yaffe, *American Jews,* p. 267. Annenberg's oversight was only a fraction of the more than $3 million that the United States Attorney General demanded of Andrew Mellon for back taxes and penalties in 1934. But Mellon had bought more than $20 million of art from the consummate Jewish merchant Joseph Duveen, and forthwith gave much of it to Uncle Sam as a pourboire to forget the tax evasion (see Behrman, *Duveen,* pp. 239–302). Presumably Moe Annenberg's children have profited from this lesson, for they collect art—though of course on a considerably less than Mellonesque scale.

85 "The deal had all": Rottenberg, p. 171.

88–89 However, when he and Hoving: Int., Walter Hoving.

89 more than 1,400 people: Philadelphia *Inquirer,* Jan. 9, 1967.

89 "Of those who are truly": *ibid.,* Jan. 6, 1967.

89 "Albert made me president": Int., Mildred Custin.

4. The Kaufmanns of Pittsburgh

Those most helpful included Arthur C. Kaufmann, Oliver M. Kaufmann, the late Al Palmer, Virginia Charles Trimble, Mr. and Mrs. Irwin D. Wolf, Jr., Mr. and Mrs. John Wolf, and the librarians of the Pittsburgh *Press* and the *Post-Gazette.* An enormously valuable source throughout this chapter is Stefan Lorant's *Pittsburgh: The Story of an American City,* a handsome book subsidized by Edgar Kaufmann. I have noted below much but not everything taken from Lorant, including those things from Henry Steele Commager, Oscar Handlin, and others who contributed to Lorant's book.

PAGE

91 *Belle Rivière . . . La Demoiselle:* Commager in Lorant's *Pittsburgh,* pp. 9–19.

PAGE

92 *"Resit fun Kornel Bon":* Int., Rabbi Jacob Marcus.

92 Morris Kaufmann always recalled: Int., Arthur C. Kaufmann.

93–94 barefoot boy . . . invested shrewdly: Handlin in Lorant, p. 104.

94 "folly of soldiering": *ibid.,* p. 233.

94 *Fortune* magazine would estimate: *ibid.,* p. 406.

94 "Hell with the Lid Off": Steffens, p. 401.

94 Karstadt store . . . Galeries Lafayette in Paris: Int., Oliver M. Kaufmann.

96 very first shampoo: Holbrook, *Age of the Moguls,* p. 154.

96 "They bought paintings" . . . could play the instrument: In Lorant, pp. 297–301. Also Holbrook, p. 155.

97 Florenz Ziegfeld: Int., Irwin D. Wolf, Jr.

99 "dogs, women, Democrats": Nicolson, *Mary Curzon,* pp. 12–13.

100 on East 74th Street: Pittsburgh *Press,* Sept. 24, 1935.

101 Tudor Hall . . . Josephine Bennett Waxman: *Bulletin-Index,* Sept. 28, 1933.

101 "horrible menace": In Lorant, p. 254.

101 "A sadistic pervert": Amory, *Who Killed Society?,* p. 367.

101 Evelyn Nesbit: See Mooney, *Evelyn Nesbit and Stanford White.*

102 The lawsuit brought by Horne's: Int., Arthur C. Kaufmann.

102 Horne's had a summer camp: Int., Al Palmer.

103 Scholarly art and architecture books are about equally divided about whether the correct spelling is "Fallingwater" or "Falling Water," but because Edgar Kaufmann, Jr., has opted for the former (in Donald Hoffmann, *Frank Lloyd Wright's Fallingwater: The House and Its History,* New York: Dover, 1978) as has Frank Lloyd Wright (*A Testament.* New York: Horizon Press, 1957), and that is the spelling on the printed material offered at the site, I have followed that spelling.

104 "a scene so dreadfully": In Lorant, p. 328.

104 "the blackest place": *ibid.,* p. 168.

104 that Herbert Spencer: *ibid.,* p. 272.

104–105 "Pittsburgh . . . nor public library": *ibid.,* p. 205.

105 "It would be cheaper": *Post-Gazette,* Apr. 9, 1959, "City Built All Wrong, Wright Said."

106 merchant prince of the Hanseatic League: *Bulletin-Index,* July 31, 1941.

106 "great quantity of smoke": In Lorant, p. 93.

107 Mellon "called the president": *ibid.,* p. 392.

PAGE
107 "the Mellons' fire escape": *ibid,,* p. 348.
107–108 "The Cathedral of Learning" . . . "The Cathedral of Earning": *ibid.,* pp. 416–417.
108 "He usually appeared": Int., Oliver M. Kaufmann.
109 "Oh, don't worry": Int., Irwin D. Wolf, Jr.

5. The Goldsmiths of Memphis

For their kindness and assistance I thank Elias J. Goldsmith, Jr., Jack L. Goldsmith, Robert T. Goldsmith, Abram Schwab, Rabbi James A. Wax, and the Memphis Publishing Company for access to the library of *The Commercial Appeal* and the Memphis *Press-Scimitar.*

PAGE
113 Sir Alexander Cuming: Davidson, *The Tennessee,* Vol. I, pp. 82–93.
113 began as foot peddlers: See Friedman, "The Problems," pp. 1–8.
114 One Memphis woman: Mrs. Harriet Schroyer, Memphis *Press-Scimitar,* Sept. 4, 1967.
115 astounded by Benedict's generosity: Memphis *Press-Scimitar,* Sept. 1, 1955.
115 largest inland cotton market . . . racetrack: Capers, *Biography of a River Town,* pp. 102, *et seq.;* Wax, "Jews of Memphis," pp. 56, 62, 72, and *passim.* See also Korn, "Jews and Negro Slavery," *AJHQ,* pp. 151–201.
116 in Memphis, as in Nashville: Folmsbee, *Tennessee,* p. 289.
116 "the Jews as a class": *War of the Rebellion—Official Records of the Union and Confederate Armies,* Series I, Vol. XVII, pt. II, p. 424.
116 Dead mules . . . "family graveyards": McIlwaine, *Memphis Down in Dixie,* p. 124.
116 salt essential: Parks, "Confederate Trade Center," pp. 293–296.
117 "indulging in a little fisticuff" . . . "for infamous purposes": Memphis *Daily Bulletin,* Dec. 17, 1862, and Aug. 19, 1862; Wax, p. 71.
119 "The number of sick": Wingfield, "Dr. William J. Armstrong," p. 108.
119–120 "whole families down sick": Keating, *History of the Yellow Fever,* p. 417.
120–121 It usually took all day: Int., Abram Schwab.
123 This new store: Int., Jack L. Goldsmith.

PAGE
124   "In the early days": *ibid.*
126   "Mr. J.," complained Uncle Robert: Int., Robert T. Goldsmith.
129   Jacob Goldsmith's favorite daughter-in-law: Int., Jack L. Goldsmith.
132   he bought it immediately: *ibid.*

6. The Riches of Atlanta

Many of the happiest days of my youth were spent in Atlanta and St. Simons with my uncle and aunts. There I knew Walter Rich, Frank H. Neely, Richard H. Rich, their wives and families and Standard Club friends—Haases, Elsases, Regensteins, and Montags. In the preparation of this chapter I was aided by Cecil Alexander, Miles J. Alexander, Joseph F. Asher, Howard Hoffman, the late Sinclair Jacobs, Albert Mayer, Mr. and Mrs. Louis Montag, Louis Regenstein, and Michael P. Rich, as well as the librarians of the Atlanta *Constitution* and the Atlanta *Journal.*

PAGE
137   Regenstein's was the first: Garrett, *Atlanta,* p. 887.
139   cotton fell . . . nor their grandchildren: Baker, *Rich's,* pp. 131–132, 149, 205. A subsidized history, this is nevertheless full of revealing and accurate facts.
139–140   Some activities . . . but not scandal: Baker, pp. 138, 162, and *passim.*
140   "Why trouble": Atlanta *Constitution,* May 18, 1879.
141   Jack Straus ingenuously: Int., Robert K. Straus.
143   "Frank is an engineer": Int., Joseph F. Asher.
144   Sex has historically: Hofstadter, *Paranoid Style,* pp. 34–35.
144   sexually desirable and desiring Jewess . . . "lunges of desire": Bitton, "Jewess as a Fictional Sex Symbol." Handlin has also discussed the role of the beautiful, desirable, mean-fathered Jewess in such late nineteenth-century popular American novels as Noel Dunbar's *Jule the Jewess* (1881): Harriette Newell Baker's *Rebecca the Jewess* (1879); Edward Payson Berry's *Leah of Jerusalem* (1890).
145   Leo Max Frank: Dinnerstein, *Leo Frank Case.*
145   Tom Watson: President Jimmy Carter and his parents have expressed enthusiastic praise for Watson, "the No. 1 demagogue," according to the historian Samuel Eliot Morison. As would happen later to Alabama's governor, George Wallace, Watson suffered an early defeat at the polls for being some-

PAGE

what liberal on the race issue and thereafter was careful never again to be "outniggered."

The Atlanta *News,* on Sept. 10, 1879, editorialized that it was "time to meet brute-force with brute-force" to keep the "half-barbarous negroes" in subjugation and many newspapers in the South and Midwest such as Watson's *Jeffersonian* praised lynching. The murder of Frank, "the Jewish sodomite," Watson called "the triumph of law in Georgia." A few American editors away from the Eastern seaboard such as William Allen White condemned the Klan as "a cheap screw outfit," but most hunted with the hounds or at best ignored the problem. See Woodward, *Tom Watson.*

148 first plate-glass: Garrett, p. 764.

148 electric lights . . . by machine: Baker, p. 49.

148 Depression . . . air-conditioned: *ibid.,* p. 207.

148–150 "democratized luxury" . . . to shop and work: Boorstin, pp. 107, 389–390, 101–105.

150 Running water . . . the store as well: *ibid.,* pp. 351, 437–438.

150 "O mamma": *ibid.,* p. 359.

152 he continued . . . liberal credit: *Business Week,* July 23, 1955, ". . . Rich's has perhaps the slowest collection rate of any department store in the country, but by the same token its losses are very low."

153 Invited to join: Birmingham, "The Club Griffin Bell," *NYT Magazine,* Feb. 6, 1977, p. 68.

153 "I am considering": Int., Michael P. Rich.

153 his death at seventy-three: Atlanta *Journal,* May 1, 1975.

154 The Piedmont Driving Club: Although at least one Jew, Aaron Haas, was an early member, the pattern in Atlanta as elsewhere as the nineteenth century ended, had become to exclude them. Hertzberg, "Jewish Community of Atlanta," pp. 270–271.

155 "Will it stay the same?": Charlotte *Observer,* Aug. 5, 1976.

7. Dallas and the Marci

The best book on Dallas is still the late Sam Acheson's *35,000 Days in Texas,* and I am forever in his debt for many decades of friendship. Much of the material on the Sangers not otherwise identified below comes from the 1967 doctoral dissertation at NYU of Leon Joseph Rosenberg, "A Business History of Sanger Brothers 1857–1926." This, in somewhat altered form, has just been published as a book, *Sangers': Pioneer Texas Merchants.*

Among those most helpful to me in personal interviews were Herbert Gambrell, A. C. Greene, the late Lucile Harris, the late William Kittrell, Mr. and Mrs. Ben Lewis, Joseph S. Linz, the late Edward Marcus and Mrs. Edward Marcus, Stanley Marcus, Frances Sanger Mossiker, Rabbi Levi Olan, Mrs. John Rosenfield, Mr. and Mrs. Leo Rothouse, Dr. Bertram J. Sanger, Elliott M. Sanger, Morton Sanger, and Ruth Potts Spence.

PAGE

156   Ned, his pony Neshoba Tenva: Rogers, *Lusty Texans,* p. 25.

157   "We soon reached": *Handbook of Texas,* Vol. I, p. 456.

157   "These fairs were always": At the age of seventy, Lehman Sanger set down his recollections. These are available in twenty-one pages of typescript at Temple Emanuel in Dallas and are quoted in Leon Rosenberg's book. (The memoir is cited hereafter as Lehman.)

158   Archbishop Agobard: "Agobard, an anti-Semitic bishop, claimed that the Jews stole children in France." *Cambridge Economic History,* p. 262.

158–159   "went to New Haven": Lehman.

159–160 $5 a month . . . "your brother Philip": *ibid.*

160–161   "The goods for which" . . . "as a matter of precaution": *ibid.*

161   "Late in the summer": *ibid.*

162   Philip's home: Int., Joseph S. Linz. See also "Sanger Home Built," Dallas *Morning News,* Nov. 19, 1951.

164–165   At a cock-fighting . . . dresses in the audience: Acheson, *35,000 Days,* pp. 124–130.

165   Alex Sanger's three story: Int., Frances Sanger Mossiker.

166   *Beau Monde:* Rogers, pp. 179–189.

170   AND YET ANOTHER HORROR": Acheson, pp. 122–123.

171   best local dressmakers: Rogers, pp. 318–319. There were, of course, fine private dressmakers as well from Miss Waller to Mrs. Hanson.

174   "I should like": letter from Walter McKittrick, Sept. 1, 1919.

174   "I intend to": letter from Thomas H. Hall, Sept. 2, 1919.

174   "One salesperson, alone": Stanley Marcus, *Minding the Store,* p. 31.

176   "If you do decide": *ibid.,* p. 179.

178   "many a day": *ibid.,* pp. 18–19.

178   "Oy-yoy, sheeny!": Ferber, *Peculiar Treasure,* pp. 40–41.

178–179   "In my senior" . . . "my first overwhelming success": Stanley Marcus, pp. 19–20.

PAGE

179–180   "Playing with other children" . . . "experiences of my life":
          ibid., pp. 13, 23.

180   Ben Sonnenberg: Bowen, "Reputation by Sonnenberg," and
          Hellman, "A House on Gramercy Park."

183   *Fortune* in a 1937 article: Nov. 1937, pp. 112–120.

183   "the most exciting experience" . . . in Stockholm: Stanley
          Marcus, pp. 149–150, and 147.

185   Bergdorf Goodman . . . "borrowed": *ibid.,* pp. 161, 262.

186   made them so hugely successful: Another reason for their
          failure elsewhere was a different priority. What their next
          employer usually required was substantial profits, whereas
          with Stanley, profits were always secondary. What he had
          demanded was that they be first in terms of style, fashion,
          publicity, splendor.

186   "egotistical, opinionated": Stanley Marcus, p. 36.

187   "Stanley was always" . . . undisguised preference for Stanley:
          Int., Edward Marcus.

187   "unhappy tensions": Stanley Marcus, p. 47.

188   "vitiated" . . . "imbibe": *ibid.,* pp. 30, 64.

191   "Collectors like Stanley": Int., David Randall.

193–194   Just after World War II: Int., Ruth Potts Spence.

194   "was not a grandstand play": Stanley Marcus, p. 263.

196   multimillion-dollar penalties: United States District Court,
          Southern District of New York, Dennis et al. *v.* Saks & Com-
          pany, Bergdorf Goodman, Inc., Genesco, Inc., No. 74 Civ.
          4419, etc.

196   Shefferman ran: "Shefferman's 400 Clients," *Business Week,*
          Nov. 2 and 9, 1957; Bell, "Nate Shefferman, Union Buster,"
          Fortune, Feb. 1958; *NYT,* Feb. 5, 1968.

197   "Say what you want": Int., Stanley Marcus.

199   "Specialty-store retailing": Stanley Marcus, pp. 44–45.

8. The Wild Southwest

To Barry M. Goldwater and Robert W. Goldwater, with whom I kept
buying offices in this country and in Europe and who were as helpful
to me when I was storekeeping as they were when I was writing this
book, my thanks. Others also helpful include Bert M. Fireman of the

Arizona Historical Foundation at Tempe, Alvin M. Josephy, Jr., Norton B. Stern, and Albert J. Schwartz.

PAGE

202 "from the cradle to the grave": Goldwater, "Three Generations," p. 141.

204 *extranjero . . . manifesto:* Fierman, "The Spiegelbergs," p. 373.

204 Leitensdorfer and Albert Speyer: Parish, "The German Jew," pp. 4–8.

206 special gubernatorial message: *ibid.,* p. 34.

207 Emanuel Spiegelberg became: Fierman, "The Spiegelbergs," pp. 417–418.

207 Hernando Alonso: Liebman, "Hernando Alonso," pp. 291–296.

208 Lamy saw a train: Horgan, *Lamy of Santa Fe,* pp. 163–164.

208–209 willow saplings . . . taken from her: *ibid.,* pp. 412, 415–416.

209 John B. Lamy, Jr.: Fierman, "The Spiegelbergs," pp. 434–435.

210 the Bibo brothers: Fierman, "The Impact," pp. 460–522.

211 Freudenthal-Lesinsky-Solomon clan: Fierman, "Samuel J. Freudenthal," pp. 353–435.

214 "One morning just after": *ibid.,* p. 388.

215 "quite an imposing city": *ibid.,* p. 360.

216 "a big book" . . . "official red tape": *ibid.,* pp. 374–375.

217 In 1850 . . . Aramaic: Letter, Bert M. Fireman to Rabbi Floyd S. Fierman, Mar. 13, 1964. See also Krawet and Stern, "Early California," p. 174.

217 the first floor of a brothel: Like many others, I have frequently heard Barry tell this story with relish. During and after his presidential campaign, he continued to tell it, so horrifying some of his advisors that they tried what is usually impossible—to prove a negative. "My former historical associate and myself were in Sonora on two different occasions and carefully studied official records at the Tuolumne County courthouse . . . and whether it was on the ground floor beneath a bordello. We could not find factual evidence or documentation on the issue . . ." Letter, Bert M. Fireman to Leon Harris, Mar. 18, 1976.

218 Sarah had taken advantage: Sacks Collection, Arizona Historical Foundation, Tempe, # 9510, copy of Vol. VIII, pp. 14–15, Tuolumne County, Jan. 4, 1855.

218–219 value of their property: Ehrenberg Board of County Commissioners, July 8, 1870.

PAGE

219 Hyman Goldberg . . . his store in Yuma: Fierman, "The Goldberg Brothers," p. 9.

220 "What the hell's": Stocker, *Jewish Roots,* p. 9. See also, Jensen, "We Are All Descended," p. 10.

221–222 one Sam Dittenhoffer: Fierman, "Billy the Kid," pp. 98–106.

222 Solomon Bibo had: Fierman, "The Impact," p. 460.

222–223 freight costs: Stanley, "Merchandising in the Southwest," pp. 90–98.

223 Louis, Aaron, and William Zeckendorf: Fierman, "The Impact," p. 463.

224 "New Mammoth Store": Sacks Collection, # 9380.

225 "The attention of epicures": May 25, 1877.

225 "Go to Goldwater's": Nov. 27, 1878.

226 1879 Christmas Ball: Arizona *Enterprise,* Dec. 26, 1879.

226 "Mr. Sam Goldwater": *Daily Miner,* July 6, 1877.

226 not to say that no anti-Semitism: As everywhere else, there were some Jews who deserved the contempt and hatred they inspired. Possibly the worst of these in early Arizona was Michael Wormser, a tight-fisted, litigious, peevish bachelor of whom the Arizona *Weekly Miner* wrote: "Had it not been for the high cost of freight, our old friend, Mr. Wormser, would have brought a wife from the East." He only once delighted those who knew him—when he was shot in the ass in an Apache ambush. Wormser appears in Clarence Budington Kelland's novel *Sugarfoot.* Also Goldberg, "Michael Wormser, Capitalist," p. 181.

230 Baron, whose bar mitzvah: *The Jewish Progressive,* San Francisco, May 23, 1879, p. 4.

230 Drachmans: Fierman, "The Drachmans of Arizona."

231 "Mun" was no less colorful: Int., Robert W. Goldwater.

232 When the Phoenix Country Club . . . "there was blood on the floor": Int., Bert M. Fireman.

232 "Putting on the dog": Int., Robert W. Goldwater.

233 "I'm not even sure": *Time,* July 24, 1964.

234 "homosexual, latent or overt": William F. Buckley, Jr., "The Case of Goldwater vs. Ginzburg," Cincinnati *Inquirer,* June 1, 1968.

234 "unless old age": Kramer, "Some Further Notes," pp. 37–39.

235 "deformed and wretched" . . . "of the world": Parish, "The German Jew" pp. 46, 48.

9. The Jewish Argonauts of San Francisco

Among those who helped me most on San Francisco were Joseph Ehrman, Richard Gump, Walter A. Haas, James D. Hart, Louis H. Heilbron, Daniel E. Koshland, Robert J. Koshland, Cyril Magnin, Rabbi Edgar F. Magnin, Moses Rischin, Helen Salz, Frank H. Sloss, Mrs. Louis Sloss, the late Paul Verdier, and Reg Murphy of the San Francisco *Examiner.* I am also grateful to Ruth Rafael and Suzanne Nemiroff of the Western Jewish History Center of the Judah L. Magnes Memorial Museum at Berkeley, and to the Bancroft Library staff, as well as to Lynn Donovan at the California Historical Society.

PAGE

237 "eggs laid on": Morison, *The Oxford History,* p. 569.

238 The Auerbach brothers: See Watters, *Pioneer Jews of Utah,* and Dressler, *California's Pioneer Mountaineer.*

239 Strauss's heirs always send: *Time* magazine, "Fashions," Feb. 27, 1950.

239 stopped the "desecration": San Francisco *Chronicle,* July 19, 1977.

240 "Jew" . . . "poor credit": Decker, *Fortunes and Failures,* pp. 99–100.

240 "numerous Chinese flesh palaces" . . . "by a servant girl": *ibid.,* pp. 100–101.

240 Ben Davidson . . . Rothschilds: Wilson, "Pioneer Jews," pp. 8–9.

240 His brother Alexandre: Pusey, *Eugene Meyer,* p. 8.

241 "in the face of": San Francisco *Chronicle,* July 15, 1919.

241 Bohemian Club: O'Day, "Varied Types."

241 "hardening of the social arteries": Decker, p. vii. On the West Coast as on the East, the pattern was often the same—clubs at the moment of their founding admitted Jews, but subsequently excluded them. Los Angeles's California Club had no fewer than 12 Jewish members out of the first 125 when it began in 1887, but later admitted no Jews. See Vorspan, p. 81.

241–242 "At the Metropolitan": This quotation from *Fortune* appears again and again to explain the business disadvantage of what superficially appears to be merely social discrimination: in Goldman, *Rendezvous with Destiny,* p. 69; in Elliott, *Men at the Top,* p. 163; in Baltzell, *Protestant Establishment,* p. 140; in Morris, *Better Than You,* p. 44.

242 "No, no, I do not": Weill, typescript, pp. 1–2.

PAGE

242   "Non, non, non": "Monique's Daily Male," San Francisco *Chronicle,* June 19, 1963.

243   Solomon Gump: Most material about Solomon, Abe, and the store is from Carol Wilson, *Treasure Trade.*

246   His divorces: San Francisco *Examiner,* May 4, 6, June 23, 1938, and Mar. 15, 1944.

246   *Life* magazine: May 7, 1951.

246   built in 1907 for Anna Held: San Francisco *Chronicle,* Apr. 25, 1951.

247   "I remember": Colen, "The Store That Made."

248   He founded his own: Int., Cyril Magnin.

249   twenty-eight-year-old Andy Goodman: Herndon, *Bergdorf's,* pp. 112–116.

250   a party in Paris . . . James David Zellerbach: San Francisco *Examiner,* July 18, 1954, Dec. 27, 1956, Apr. 19, 1961.

251   Living in a downtown hotel: Decker, pp. 221–223.

251   his paintings sold . . . a special auction: San Francisco *Chronicle,* Oct. 16, 1969.

252–253   "I have always believed: Int., Rabbi Edgar F. Magnin.

253   "It calms me down": Capote, *Breakfast,* pp. 39–40.

254   "Were it not": "California's Hebrews, 1887," *WSJHQ,* p. 198.

254   "modesty and authority": Menuhin, *Unfinished Journey,* p. 58.

255   "the offering created" . . . "including charitable contributions": *NYT,* Aug. 6, 1972.

255   "a declaration of sensuality": Reich, *Greening,* p. 236.

255   "conservative but progressive": Meyer, *Western Jewry,* p. 57.

255   Most such mansions: See *WSJHQ,* Oct. 1972, pp. 15–23, and Oct. 1973, pp. 43–47.

256   "Dan [his elder brother] and I were": Int., Robert J. Koshland.

257   "Nobody came first": Int., James D. Hart.

10. The Meiers and Franks of Oregon

Those most helpful to me include Gerald W. Frank, Harold Hirsch, Mrs. W. H. Holmes, Jack L. Meier, Mrs. Irving Reichert, Mrs. Louis Sloss, Mrs. Harold Wendel, as well as Ms. Sandra Macomber and Jack Meyers at the *Oregonian,* Gordon Manning at the Oregon Historical Society, and the staff of the Multnomah County Library.

PAGE

259–260   American ship captains . . . gave her name to the river: Morison, pp. 284, 538–539.

PAGE

260   John Jacob Astor . . . "one dollar per day": Barrett, *Old Merchants*, pp. 32–33, 165–166, 194–195, 285–288; Second Series, pp. 81–82, 125; Fourth Series, pp. 5–11.

261   Ezekiel Solomon: "Jewish Beginnings." See also Heineman, "The Startling Experience."

261   Nathan Chapman: Heineman, pp. 31–35.

261   Adolph Kohn . . . had been slaughtered: "Trail Blazers," pp. 122–124.

261–262   part of the destruction . . . usually hostile Indians: Morison, pp. 539–547.

262   Solomon Nuñes Carvalho: *Incidents of Travel.*

262   "I am for war": *ibid.,* p. 257.

262   "quicksilver" . . . "would have worshipped me": *ibid.,* p. 129.

263   "burns like peat": *ibid.,* p. 126.

263   Sigmund Schlesinger: J. R. Marcus, "The Quintessential," p. 18.

264   "Its shelves were piled": Berlin, *Silver Platter,* p. 41.

265   "What do you want": Int., Harold Hirsch.

265–266   She went to the store . . . saving the postage: Int., Mrs. W. H. Holmes. Saving pennies was fashionable among Portland's rich, though scarcely necessary when, in 1910, fresh beef, pork, and ham were 20 cents per pound, and skilled workers, painters, plumbers, and plasterers were paid $3.50, $5, and $5.50 per day, respectively.

267   "Papa was not big": Int., Mrs. Irving Reichert.

272   "the very difficult question" . . . "of male loiterers": O'Donnell, *Portland,* pp. 13, 49. See also MacColl, *The Shaping,* p. 234.

272   Vice Commission Report: *Report of the Vice Commission of the City of Portland,* Oregon Historical Society. See also MacColl, pp. 401–412, and O'Donnell, pp. 49–50.

272   *vis-à-vis* Seattle: Kirkland, *American Economic Life,* p. 343.

273   wheeled over bags of gold coin: MacColl, p. 101.

275   terrorist set off a bomb: Oregon *Journal,* Nov. 29, 1968.

276   Aaron flirted with: Int., Jack L. Meier.

278   took away his employee's discount: *NYT,* Apr. 17, 1965.
      profit of almost $2.5 million: *The Oregonian,* May 29, 1966.

278–279   Manifest Destiny: When John L. O'Sullivan in 1845 put the phrase into circulation, it was the very time that these German-Jewish future storekeepers were starting to arrive in America. Manifest Destiny was both a mood that fitted their own and a process in which they took part.

PAGE
279   "all too evident" . . . "and oppressed humanity": Clark, "Manifest Destiny," pp. 1–17, reprinted in Freidel, *Builders,* pp. 173–180.

11. Sears, Roebuck and the Rosenwalds

For giving me their time, their recollections, and their insights, I am especially grateful to Mrs. Max Ascoli, Mrs. Freida Lash, Lessing J. Rosenwald, William Rosenwald, Mrs. Edgar B. Stern, Philip M. Stern, and Frank A. Weil.

PAGE
283   Field's did not hire Jews: Until after World War II there were many great department stores that at least on the level of buyer and above would not hire Jews. These included Hudson's, Dayton's, and Wanamaker's as well as Field's. When Oscar Webber hired Norman Wechsler to be Hudson's token Jew, he made it plain to the brilliant young merchandiser that there was to be no other exception.

283   Learning that Marshall Field: Int., Frank A. Weil.

285   "I remember as a boy" . . . "wore kid gloves": Werner, *Julius Rosenwald,* p. 10. Much of the material in this chapter not identified in these notes is from Werner, a remarkably accurate and balanced biography despite the fact that it was subsidized by the Rosenwald family.

287–288   "the temptation to allow" . . . "what is true": Boorstin, *Democracy and Its Discontents,* pp. 28–29.

293   S. J. Perelman: Israel, *1897 Sears, Roebuck Catalogue,* Perelman's introduction, pp. ix–xiv.

298–299   As Daniel J. Boorstin points out . . . "entry into the next": "Transforming the Charitable Spirit," *Julius Rosenwald Centennial,* pp. 5–33.

310   "Schiff gave more widely": *NYT,* Jan. 7, 1932.

313   *The New York Times Magazine:* Dec. 31, 1916.

315–316   "Busy as he was" . . . "than my father": Int., William Rosenwald.

316   "I remember Father": Int., Lessing J. Rosenwald.

318   "It is just as difficult": *ibid.*

320   "It was obvious": *ibid.*

322   "He had been ill": Embree, *Julius Rosenwald Fund,* pp. 3–4.

324   "She was like Mrs. Roosevelt": Int., Freida Lash.

324   "My Day": New York *Post,* Mar. 14, 1960.

PAGE
325 "I think that one thing": Int., Mrs. Edgar B. Stern.
326 whose earlier marriage proposal: Int., Robert K. Straus.
328 "But I loved him": Int., Philip M. Stern.
328 "I had no way": Deutsch, "Days of Lemonade."
330–332 "No one's childhood" . . . "couldn't come back to America for so long": Int., Mrs. Max Ascoli.
332 "given to moments": "Max Ascoli," Washington *Post,* Jan. 3, 1978.
334 "The multiplier effect": Int., William Rosenwald.

12. Legions of Lazari

Those most helpful to me in researching the materials for this chapter include Lyman Bloomingdale, Richard Ernst, Robert Fuoss, John H. F. Hoving, Mrs. Fred Lazarus, Jr., Mr. and Mrs. Robert Lazarus, Jr., the late Simon Lazarus, Jr., Rabbi Jacob R. Marcus, Marc Lee Raphael, Mrs. Jessie Ross, Mrs. Stuart Schloss, Murray Seasongood, the late Ben Sonnenberg, Mrs. David Weston, and Charles Isetts at the Ohio Historical Society in Columbus.

PAGE
337 "Si carried a loaded revolver": Gottschalk, *Fred Lazarus, Jr.,* p. 17.
338 "the driving, ambitious, little man": "Mr. Fred of the Lazari," *Fortune,* Mar. 1948.
340 In 1939, Thanksgiving Day: Boorstin, pp. 157–158.
341–342 In early New England . . . "in the department store": *ibid.,* pp. 158–164.
342 "When various Lazari": Int., Mrs. David Weston.
343 "We were all terrified": Int., Mrs. Stuart Schloss.
343–344 "In what seemed": Int., Ben Sonnenberg.
345 Sam Bloomingdale took Fred: "How Much Is Enough?," *Time,* July 16, 1945, pp. 74–76: " . . . birdlike, aging (73) Samuel Joseph Bloomingdale . . . In high dudgeon . . . minced no words saying . . . that Federated's $100,000-a-year bigwigs had all the incentive they need. The plan . . . is actually a device to give executives a salary increase 'not subject to ordinary income taxes.' "
345 "Close the show": Teichmann, *George S. Kaufman,* pp. 117–118, and Meredith, *George S. Kaufman,* pp. 1–2.
351 "sapping the lifeblood" . . . "thinker and executive": Boorstin, pp. 111–112.

352 "Bonwit Teller employees spent": Barmash, "Lavish Apartment Is Said to Cost Bonwit Teller Chairman His Job," *NYT,* Nov. 1, 1977.

352 executive offices have revolving doors: The headline of Isadore Barmash's front-page story, *NYT,* Oct. 29, 1977, was "Bonwit Ousts $200,000 Chairman Who Was Hired to Revamp Store." Continuing on p. 33, Barmash noted: "Bonwit, in particular, has had more than half a dozen chief executives in the last dozen years. . . . Among those who have left Bonwit's chairmanship or presidency in the last seven years are William Smith, Mildred Custin, William F. Fine, and George Baylis."

Bibliography

AJA	*American Jewish Archives* magazine
AJHQ	*American Jewish Historical Quarterly* (including its predecessor publications)
NYT	*The New York Times*
WSJHQ	*Western States Jewish Historical Quarterly*

Acheson, Sam. *35,000 Days in Texas.* New York: Macmillan, 1938.

Adler, Cyrus. *Jacob H. Schiff: His Life and Letters.* New York: Doubleday, Doran, 1929.

Agristi, Olivia Rossetti. *David Lubin: A Study in Practical Idealism.* Berkeley: University of California Press, 1941.

Alston, Patrick L. *Education and the State in Tsarist Russia.* Stanford: Stanford University Press, 1969.

Amory, Cleveland. *Who Killed Society?* New York: Harper & Brothers, 1960.

"Anti-Jewish Sentiment in California—1855." *AJA,* 12, 1 (Apr. 1960), pp. 15–33.

Bachmann, Lawrence P. "Julius Rosenwald." *AJHQ,* 66, 1 (Sept. 1976), pp. 89–105.

Baker, Henry Givens. *Rich's of Atlanta: The Story of a Store Since 1867.* Atlanta: University of Georgia School of Business Administration, 1953.

Baltzell, E. Digby. *The Protestant Establishment: Aristocracy and Caste in America.* New York: Random House, 1964.

————. *Philadelphia Gentlemen: The Making of a National Upper Class.* Chicago: Quadrangle Paperbacks, 1971.

Barrett, Walter. *The Old Merchants of New York City.* New York: Carleton Publisher, 1863.

————. *The Old Merchants of New York City.* Second Series. New York: Carleton Publisher, 1863.

————. *The Old Merchants of New York City.* Fourth Series. New York: Carleton Publisher, 1866.

Behrman, S. N. *Duveen.* New York: Random House, 1952.

Bell, Jack. *Mr. Conservative: Barry Goldwater.* New York: Doubleday, 1962.

Berg, Louis. "Peddlers in Eldorado." *Commentary,* 40 (July 1965), pp. 63–67.

Berlin, Ellin. *Silver Platter: A Portrait of Mrs. John Mackay.* New York: Doubleday, 1957.

Bernays, Edward L. *Biography of an Idea.* New York: Simon & Schuster, 1965.

Birmingham, Stephen. *"Our Crowd": The Great Jewish Families of New York.* New York: Harper & Row, 1967.

————. *The Grandees: America's Sephardic Elite.* New York: Harper & Row, 1971.

————. "The Club Griffin Bell Had to Quit." *NYT Magazine,* 6 Feb. 1977, pp. 20–21, 68–71.

Bitton, Livia E. "The Jewess as a Fictional Sex Symbol." *Bucknell Review,* 23 (Nov. 1971), pp. 63–86.

Boorstin, Daniel J. *Democracy and Its Discontents: Reflections on Everyday America.* New York: Random House, 1971.

————. *The Americans: The Democratic Experience.* New York: Random House, 1973.

Bowen, Croswell, and George R. Clark. "Reputation by Sonnenberg." *Harper's Magazine,* Feb. 1950, pp. 39–49.

Breck, Allen duPont. *The Centennial History of the Jews of Colorado, 1859–1959.* Denver: University of Denver Press, 1960.

Bregstone, Philip P. *Chicago and Its Jews: A Cultural History.* Privately published, 1933.

Brooks, John Graham. *An American Citizen: The Life of William Henry Baldwin, Jr.* Boston: Houghton Mifflin, 1910.

Broun, Heywood, and George Britt. *Christians Only: A Study in Prejudice.* New York: Vanguard Press, 1931.

Burt, Nathaniel. *The Perennial Philadelphians: The Anatomy of an American Aristocracy.* Boston: Little, Brown, 1963.

Business Week. "Shefferman's 400 Clients." 2 Nov. 1957, p. 41.

————. "Employers' Turn on the Stand." 9 Nov. 1957, pp. 32 & 34.

The Cambridge Economic History of Europe. Vol. II. Eds. M. Postan and E. E. Rich. Cambridge: The Syndics of the Cambridge University Press, 1952.

Cantwell, Robert E. Manuscripts, courtesy of Justin Kaplan.

Capers, Gerald M. *The Biography of a River Town.* Chapel Hill: University of North Carolina Press, 1939.

Capote, Truman. *Breakfast at Tiffany's.* New York: Random House, 1958.

Carey, Charles H. *A General History of Oregon.* 2 vols. Portland: Metropolitan Press, 1935.

Carvalho, Solomon Nuñes. *Incidents of Travel and Adventure in the Far West.* Philadelphia: The Jewish Publication Society of America, 1954.

Cather, Willa. *Death Comes for the Archbishop.* New York: Knopf, 1927.

Chyet, Stanley F., ed. *Lives and Voices: A Collection of American Jewish Memoirs.* Philadelphia: The Jewish Publication Society of America, 1972.

_____. "Moses Jacob Ezekiel: A Childhood in Richmond." *AJHQ,* 62, 1, (Mar. 1973), pp. 286–305.

Clark, Dan E. "Manifest Destiny and the Pacific." *Pacific Historical Review,* 1 (Mar. 1932), pp. 1–17.

Cogan, Sarah G. *Pioneer Jews of the California Mother Lode, 1849–1880: An Annotated Bibliography.* Foreword by Moses Rischin. Berkeley: Western Jewish History Center, Judah L. Magnes Memorial Museum, 1968.

_____. *The Jews of San Francisco & the Greater Bay Area, 1849–1919: An Annotated Bibliography.* Foreword by Moses Rischin. Berkeley: Western Jewish History Center, Judah L. Magnes Memorial Museum, 1973.

Cohen, Henry. "Settlement of Jews in Texas." *AJHQ,* II, 1894, pp. 139–156.

_____. "The Jews in Texas." *AJHQ,* IV, 1896, pp. 9–19.

_____. "Henry Castro, Pioneer and Colonist." *AJHQ,* V, 1897, pp. 39–43.

Cohen, Naomi W. *A Dual Heritage: The Public Career of Oscar S. Straus.* Philadelphia: The Jewish Publication Society of America, 1969.

Colen, Bruce David. "The Store That Made California Fashionable." *Town & Country,* Aug. 1976, pp.48–57, 98, 100.

Commager, Henry Steele. *The Empire of Reason: How Europe Imagined and America Realized the Enlightenment.* New York: Anchor Press/Doubleday, 1977.

Considine, Bob. *The Remarkable Life of Dr. Armand Hammer.* New York: Harper & Row, 1975.

Curtiss, Mina. *Other People's Letters: A Memoir.* Boston: Houghton Mifflin, 1978.

Davidson, Donald. *The Tennessee.* Vol. I. *The Old River.* New York: Rinehart & Co., 1946.

Davis, John H. *The Guggenheims: An American Epic.* New York: William Morrow, 1978.

Decker, Peter R. *Fortunes and Failures: White-collar Mobility in Nineteenth-Century San Francisco.* Cambridge: Harvard University Press, 1978.

Deutsch, Armand S. "Days of Lemonade & Crystal." *Chicago,* June 1977, pp. 153–154.

Dinnerstein, Leonard. *The Leo Frank Case.* New York: Columbia University Press, 1968.

———. "A Neglected Aspect of Southern Jewish History." *AJHQ,* 61, 1, (Sept. 1971), pp. 52–69.

Dinnerstein, Leonard, and Mary Dale Palson, eds. *Jews in the South.* Baton Rouge: Louisiana State University Press, 1973.

Dressler, Albert. *California's Pioneer Mountaineer of Rabbit Creek.* San Francisco: n.p., 1930.

Dubnow, S. M. *History of the Jews in Russia and Poland.* Vol. 3. Philadelphia: The Jewish Publication Society of America, 1920.

Elliott, Osborn. *Men at the Top.* New York: Harper & Brothers, 1959.

Embree, Edwin R., and Julia Waxman. *Investment in People: The Story of the Julius Rosenwald Fund.* New York: Harper & Brothers, 1949.

Emmet, Boris, and John E. Jench. *Catalogues and Counters: A History of Sears, Roebuck and Company.* Chicago: University of Chicago Press, 1950.

Encyclopedia Judaica. 16 vols. and supplements. Jerusalem: Macmillan, 1971–.

Evans, Eli N. *The Provincials: A Personal History of the Jews in the South.* New York: Atheneum, 1976.

Fein, Isaac M. *The Making of an American Jewish Community: The History of Baltimore Jewry from 1773 to 1920.* Philadelphia: The Jewish Publication Society of America, 1971.

Feldman, Abraham J. *Remember the Days of Old.* Hartford: n.p., 1943.

Ferber, Edna. *A Peculiar Treasure.* New York: Doubleday, Doran, 1939.

Fierman, Floyd S. *Some Early Jewish Settlers on the Southwestern Frontier.* El Paso: Texas Western Press, 1960.

———. "Reminiscences of Emanuel Rosenwald." *New Mexico Historical Review,* 37, 2 (Apr. 1962), pp. 110–131.

———. "The Drachmans of Arizona." *AJA,* 16, 2 (Nov. 1964), pp. 135–160.

———. "The Goldberg Brothers: Arizona Pioneers." *AJA,* 18, 1 (Apr. 1966), pp. 3–19.

———. "The Spiegelbergs: Pioneer Merchants and Bankers in the Southwest." *AJHQ,* 56, 4 (June 1967), pp. 370–435.

——. "Samuel J. Freudenthal: Southwestern Merchant and Civic Leader." *AJHQ,* 57, 3 (Mar. 1967), pp. 353–435.

——. "The Impact of the Frontier on a Jewish Family: The Bibos." *AJHQ,* 59, 4 (June 1970), pp. 460–522.

Fierman, Floyd S., and John O. West. "Billy the Kid, the Cowboy Outlaw: An Incident Recalled by Flora Spiegelberg." *AJHQ,* 55, 1 (Sept. 1965), pp. 98–106.

Filene, Abraham Lincoln, with Burton Kline. *A Merchant's Horizon.* Boston: Houghton Mifflin, 1924.

Filene, Edward A. *The Way Out: A Forecast of Coming Changes in American Business and Industry.* New York: Doubleday, Page, 1924.

——. *The Model Stock Plan.* New York: McGraw-Hill, 1930.

——. *The Consumer's Dollar.* New York: John Day, 1934.

Flexner, Abraham. *An Autobiography.* Rev. ed. New York: Simon & Schuster, 1960.

Folmsbee, Stanley J., with Robert E. Corlew and Enoch L. Mitchell. *Tennessee, A Short History.* Knoxville: University of Tennessee Press, 1969.

Fortune. "Philadelphia." 13, 6 (June 1936) pp. 66–75, 175–176, 179, 181–182, 185–186, 188, 190, 192, 194, 201–202, 205–206, 208.

——. "Dallas in Wonderland; Neiman-Marcus Company." 16, 5 (Nov. 1937), pp. 112–120, 200, 202, 204, 206, 209–210.

——. "Mr. Fred of the Lazari." 37, 3 (Mar. 1948), pp. 108–115, 162, 165–166, 168–170, 173–174, 176, 178.

——. "Nate Shefferman, Union Buster." Daniel Bell. 57, 2 (Feb. 1958), pp. 120–121, 204–209.

Freidel, Frank. *Franklin D. Roosevelt: Launching the New Deal.* Boston: Little, Brown, 1973.

——. See Williams, T. Harry.

Freidel, Frank, and Norman Pollack, eds. *Builders of American Institutions: Readings in United States History.* Chicago: Rand McNally, 1963.

Freudenthal, Samuel J. *El Paso Merchant and Civic Leader from the 1880's.* El Paso: Texas Western College Press, 1965.

Friedman, Lee Max. *Early American Jews.* Cambridge: Harvard University Press, 1934.

——. *Jewish Pioneers and Patriots.* New York: Macmillan, 1942.

——. *Pilgrims in a New Land.* Philadelphia: The Jewish Publication Society of America, 1948.

——. "The Problems of Nineteenth Century American Jewish Peddlers." *AJHQ,* 44, 1 (Sept. 1954), pp. 1–8.

Garrett, Franklin M. *Atlanta and Its Environs.* 3 vols. New York: Lewis Historical Publishing Co., 1954.

Gaston, Joseph. *Portland, Its History and Builders.* 3 vols. Portland: n.p., 1911.

Gibbons, Herbert Adams. *John Wanamaker.* 2 vols. New York: Harper & Brothers, 1926.

Glanz, Rudolph. *The Jews in American Alaska, 1867–1880.* New York: n.p., 1953.

——. *The Jews of California from the Discovery of Gold until 1880.* New York: n.p., 1960.

——. *The German Jew in America.* Cincinnati and New York: Hebrew Union College Press and Ktav, 1969.

Glazer, Nathan. *American Judaism.* Chicago: University of Chicago Press, 1957.

Glazer, Nathan, and Daniel P. Moynihan. *Beyond the Melting Pot.* Cambridge: M.I.T. Press, 1970.

Goldberg, Richard B. "Michael Wormser, Capitalist." *AJA,* 25, 2 (Nov. 1973), pp. 161–206.

Golden, Harry. *The Right Time.* New York: G. P. Putnam's, 1969.

Goldman, Eric F. *Rendezvous with Destiny.* New York: Vintage Books, 1956.

Goldwater, Barry M. "Three Generations of Pants and Politics in Arizona." Speech delivered to the Arizona Historical Society at Tucson, Nov. 3, 1962, and printed in *The Journal of Arizona History,* pp. 141–158.

——. "The West That Was." Address to the Western History Assn. at Tucson, Oct. 18, 1968, and published in *Journal of the West,* Oct. 1968, pp. 445–455.

Goodspeed's History of Hamilton, Knox, & Shelby Counties of Tennessee. Goodspeed, 1887; rpt. Nashville: Charles & Randy Elder, 1974.

Gordon, Milton M. *Assimilation in American Life: The Role of Race, Religion and National Origins.* New York: Oxford, 1964.

Gottschalk, Alfred. *Fred Lazarus, Jr.* Cincinnati: n.p., 1973.

Greene, A. C. *Dallas: The Deciding Years: A Historical Portrait.* Austin: Encino Press, 1973.

——. *A Place Called Dallas.* Dallas: Dallas County Heritage Society, 1975.

Gunther, John. *Taken at the Flood: The Story of Albert D. Lasker.* New York: Harper & Brothers, 1960.

Handbook of Texas. 2 vols. and supplement. Walter Prescott Webb, ed. Austin: Texas State Historical Assn., 1952.

Handlin, Oscar. *The Uprooted: The Epic Story of the Great Migrations That Made the American People.* Boston: Little, Brown, 1951.

——. *Jewish Life in America.* New York: McGraw-Hill, 1954.

——. *Adventure in Freedom: Three Hundred Years of Jewish Life in America.* New York: McGraw-Hill, 1954.

―――. *Race and Nationality in American Life.* New York: Doubleday, 1957.

―――. *Immigration as a Factor in American History.* Englewood Cliffs: Prentice-Hall, 1959.

Handlin, Oscar, and Mary F. Handlin. *Danger in Discord: Origins of Anti-Semitism in the United States.* New York: Anti-defamation League of B'nai B'rith, 1959.

Harriman, Margaret Case. *And the Price Is Right.* Cleveland: World Publishing, 1958.

Hart, Jerome A. *In Our Second Century: From an Editor's Notebook.* San Francisco: Pioneer Press, 1931.

Heineman, David E. "Jewish Beginnings in Michigan Before 1850." *AJHQ,* 13 (1905), pp. 47–70.

―――. "The Startling Experience of a Jewish Trader During Pontiac's Siege of Detroit in 1763." *AJHQ,* 13 (1905), pp. 31–35.

Heller, James G. *As Yesterday When It Is Passed: A History of Isaac M. Wise Temple.* Cincinnati: Isaac M. Wise Temple, 1942.

Hellman, Geoffrey T. "A House on Gramercy Park." *The New Yorker,* 8 Apr. 1950, pp. 40–61.

―――. "Straightening Out the Straus(s)es." *The New Yorker,* 21 Mar. 1953, pp. 33–35.

Herndon, Booton. *Bergdorf's on the Plaza: The Story of Bergdorf Goodman and a Half-Century of American Fashion.* New York: Alfred A. Knopf, 1956.

Hertzberg, Steven. "The Jewish Community of Atlanta From the End of the Civil War Until the Eve of the Frank Case." *AJHQ,* 62, 3 (Mar. 1973), pp. 250–285.

―――. *Strangers Within the Gates: The Jews of Atlanta, 1845–1915.* Philadelphia: The Jewish Publication Society of America, 1978.

Hoffmann, Donald. *Frank Lloyd Wright's Fallingwater: The House and Its History.* New York: Dover, 1978.

Hess, Sarah Straus. See Straus, Isidor.

Hofstadter, Richard. *Great Issues in American History: A Documentary Record.* Vol. II. New York: Vintage Books, 1958.

―――. *The Paranoid Style in American Politics and Other Essays.* New York: Vintage Books, 1965.

Holbrook, Stewart H. *The Age of the Moguls.* New York: Doubleday, 1954.

Holmes, Stacy. *A Brief History of Filene's.* Rev. ed. Boston: Wm. Filene's Sons Co., 1972.

Horgan, Paul. *Lamy of Santa Fe.* New York: Farrar, Straus & Giroux, 1975.

Howar, Ralph M. *History of Macy's of New York, 1858–1919: Chapters in the Evolution of the Department Store.* Cambridge: Harvard University Press, 1946.

Hungerford, Edward. *The Romance of a Great Store.* New York: Robert M. McBride, 1922.

"An Intimate Portrait of the Union of American Hebrew Congregations." *AJA,* 25, 1 (Apr. 1973), pp. 21–23.

Isaacs, Stephen D. *Jews and American Politics.* New York: Doubleday, 1974.

Israel, Fred L., ed. *1897 Sears, Roebuck Catalogue.* Introd. S. J. Perelman and Richard Rovere. New York: Chelsea House, 1968.

Jensen, Oliver. "We Are All Descended From Grandfathers." *American Heritage,* June 1964, pp. 9–10.

Johnson, Gerald W. *An Honorable Titan: A Biographical Study of Adolph S. Ochs.* New York: Harper & Brothers, 1946.

———. *Liberal's Progress.* New York: Coward-McCann, 1948.

Josephs, Ray. "Mr. Fred's Dream Store." *The Saturday Evening Post,* 18 Nov. 1950, pp. 42–43, 143–144, 146, 148–150.

The Julius Rosenwald Centennial. Intro. George Wells Beadle. University of Chicago Press, 1963.

Kallison, Frances Rosenthal. "Was It a Duel or a Murder? A Study in Texan Assimilation." *AJHQ,* 62, 3 (Mar. 1973), pp. 314–320.

Kaplan, Justin. *Lincoln Steffens: A Biography.* New York: Simon & Schuster, 1974.

Karp, Abraham, ed. *The Jewish Experience in America.* New York: Ktav Publishers for the American Jewish Historical Society, 1969.

Katz, Irving I. *The Beth-El Story with a History of the Jews in Michigan Before 1850.* Detroit: Wayne State University Press, 1955.

Kauffman, Reginald Wright. *Jesse Isidor Straus: A Biographical Portrait.* Introd. Robert K. Straus and Jack I. Straus. New York: privately printed, 1973.

Keating, J. M. *A History of the Yellow Fever Epidemic of 1878 in Memphis, Tennessee.* Memphis: Harvard Association, 1879.

Kirkland, Edward C. *A History of American Economic Life.* 3rd ed. New York: Appleton-Century-Crofts, 1960.

Kligsberg, Moses. "Jewish Immigrants in Business: A Sociological Study." *AJHQ,* 56, 3 (Mar. 1967), pp. 283–318.

Kochan, Lionel, ed. *The Jews in Soviet Russia Since 1917.* Alec Nove and J. A. Newth. "The Jewish Population: Demographic Trends and Occupational Patterns." London: Oxford University Press, 1970.

Korn, Rabbi Bertram W. "Jews and Negro Slavery in the Old South, 1789–1865." *AJHQ,* 50, 3 (Mar. 1961).

———. *The Early Jews of New Orleans.* Waltham: American Jewish Historical Society, 1969.

Koshland, Daniel E., Sr. "The Principle of Sharing." Berkeley: Bancroft
    Library. Ms.
Kramer, William M., and Norton B. Stern. "Early California Associations
    of Michel Goldwater and His Family." *WSJHQ,* July 1972, pp.
    175–196.
———. "Some Further Notes on Michel Goldwater." *WSJHQ,* Oct. 1972,
    pp. 36–39.
LaDame, Mary. *The Filene Store.* New York: The Russell Sage Foundation,
    1930.
Lenin, Vladimir Ilyich. *Collected Works.* Moscow: Progress Publishers, 1972.
Levy, Daniel. *Les Français en Californie.* San Francisco: Gregoire Tauzy cie.,
    1884.
Levy, Harriet L. *920 O'Farrell Street.* New York: Doubleday, Doran 1947.
Liebman, Seymour B. "Hernando Alonso: The First Jew on the North-
    American Continent." *The Journal of Inter-American Studies,* 5 (Apr.
    1963), pp. 291–296.
Lockley, Fred. *History of the Columbia River Valley.* 3 vols. Chicago: S. J.
    Clark Publishing Co., 1928.
London, Hannah R. *Portraits of Jews by Gilbert Stuart and Other Early American
    Artists.* Rutland: Charles E. Tuttle, 1969.
Lorant, Stefan. *Pittsburgh: The Story of an American City.* New York: Double-
    day, 1964.
Lord, Walter. *A Night to Remember.* Toronto/New York: Bantam Pathfinder,
    1971.
MacColl, E. Kimbark. *The Shaping of a City: Business and Politics in Portland,
    Oregon, 1885–1915.* Portland: The Georgian Press Company, 1976.
Mahoney, Tom, and Leonard Sloane. *The Great Merchants: America's Foremost
    Retail Institutions and the People Who Made Them Great.* New York:
    Harper & Row, 1974.
Marcus, Geoffrey. *The Maiden Voyage.* New York: Manor Books, 1974.
Marcus, Rabbi Jacob R. "The Quintessential American Jew." *AJHQ,* 58,
    1 (Sept. 1968), pp. 15–22.
———. *Memoirs of American Jews, 1775–1865.* 3 vols. New York: Ktav
    Publishing, 1974.
Marcus, Stanley. *Minding the Store.* New York: Signet-NAL, 1974.
Marx, Karl. *A Critique of Political Economy.* 3 vols. Edited by Frederick Engels.
    New York: International Publishers, 1967.
May, Henry F. *The End of American Innocence; Study of the First Years of Our
    Own Time, 1912–1914.* New York: Alfred A. Knopf, 1959.
McCormick, Bernard. "Meetcha at da Iggle," *Philadelphia,* Dec. 1970, pp.
    110–167.
McIlwaine, Shields. *Memphis Down in Dixie.* New York: E. P. Dutton,
    1948.

McWilliams, Carey. *A Mask for Privilege: Anti-Semitism in America.* Boston: Little, Brown, 1949.

Menuhin, Yehudi. *Unfinished Journey.* New York: Alfred A. Knopf, 1976.

Meredith, Scott. *George S. Kaufman and His Friends.* New York: Doubleday, 1974.

Meyer, Martin A. *Western Jewry.* San Francisco: Emanu-el, 1916.

Mooney, Michael Macdonald. *Evelyn Nesbit and Stanford White: Love and Death in the Gilded Age.* New York: William Morrow, 1976.

Morais, Henry Samuel. *The Jews of Philadelphia.* Philadelphia: Levytype Co., 1894.

Morgenthau, Henry. *All in a Life-Time.* New York: Doubleday, Page, 1923.

Morison, Samuel Eliot. *The Oxford History of the American People.* New York: Oxford University Press, 1965.

Morris, Terry. *Better Than You: Social Discrimination Against Minorities in America.* Foreword by Andrew Heiskell. New York: The American Jewish Committee, 1971.

Nicolson, Nigel. *Mary Curzon.* New York: Harper & Row, 1977.

Nodel, Julius J. *The Ties Between: A Century of Judaism on America's Last Frontier.* Portland, Oregon: Temple Beth Israel, 1959.

O'Conner, Harvey. *The Guggenheims.* New York: Covici-Friede, 1937.

O'Day, Edward F. "Varied Types." *Town Talk,* Dec. 9, 1911.

O'Donnell, Terence, and Thomas Vaughan. *Portland: A Historical Sketch and Guide.* Portland: Oregon Historical Society, 1976.

Ohrbach, Nathan M. *Getting Ahead in Retailing.* Foreword by Kenneth Collins. New York: McGraw-Hill, 1935.

Parish, William J. "The German Jew and the Commercial Revolution in Territorial New Mexico, 1850–1900." Sixth Annual Research Lecture, University of New Mexico. Typescript, Hebrew Union College archives. See also *New Mexico Historical Review,* 35, 1 (Jan. 1960), pp. 1–29; 35, 2 (Apr. 1960), pp. 129–150.

————. *The Charles Ilfeld Company: A Study of the Rise and Decline of Capitalism in New Mexico.* Cambridge: Harvard University Press, 1961.

Parks, Joseph H. "A Confederate Trade Center Under Federal Occupation." *The Journal of Southern History,* Aug. 1941, pp. 289–314.

Pasdermadjian, H. *The Department Store, Its Origins, Evolution and Economics.* London: Newman Books, 1954.

Perry, Bliss. *Life and Letters of Henry Lee Higginson.* Boston: Atlantic Monthly Press, 1921.

Phillopson, David. "The Jewish Pioneers of the Ohio Valley." *AJHQ,* 8 (1900), pp. 43–57.

Pirenne, Henri. *Mohammed and Charlemagne.* Trans. Bernard Miall from the 10th ed., Libraire Félix Alcan, Paris. New York: Barnes & Noble, Inc., n.d.

Plaut, W. Gunther. *The Jews in Minnesota: The First Seventy-five Years.* New York: The American Jewish Historical Society, 1959.

Postal, Bernard, and Lionel Koppman. *A Jewish Tourist's Guide to the United States.* Philadelphia: The Jewish Publication Society of America, 1954.

Pound, Reginald. *Selfridge.* London: Heinemann, 1960.

Pusey, Merlo J. *Eugene Meyer.* New York: Alfred A. Knopf, 1974.

Quinn, Robert P., et al. *The Chosen Few: A Study of Discrimination in Executive Selection.* Ann Arbor: University of Michigan Press, 1968.

Reich, Charles H. *The Greening of America.* New York: Random House, 1970.

Reilly, Philip J. *The Old Masters of Retailing.* New York: Fairchild Publications, 1966.

Reznikoff, Charles. *Jews of Charleston: A History of an American Jewish Community.* Philadelphia: The Jewish Publication Society of America, 1950.

Rischin, Moses. *An Inventory of American Jewish History.* Cambridge: Harvard University Press, 1954.

———. *Our Own Kind: Voting by Race, Creed or National Origin.* Santa Barbara: Center for the Study of Democratic Institutions, 1960.

———. "The Jews and the Liberal Tradition in America." *AJHQ,* 51, 1 (Sept. 1961), pp. 4–16.

———. *The American Gospel of Success; Individualism and Beyond.* Chicago: Quadrangle Books, 1965.

———. *The Promised City: New York's Jews, 1870–1914.* Cambridge: Harvard University Press, 1977.

Rogers, John William. *The Lusty Texans of Dallas.* New York: E. P. Dutton, 1951.

Rosenberg, Leon Joseph. "A Business History of Sanger Brothers, 1857–1926." Doctoral diss. N.Y.U. 1967.

———. *Sangers': Pioneer Texas Merchants.* Austin: Texas State Historical Association, 1978.

Rosenberg, Stuart E. *The Jewish Community in Rochester, 1843–1925.* New York: Columbia University Press, 1954.

Rosenman, Kenneth. "Power in a Midwestern Jewish Community." *AJA,* 21, 1 (Apr. 1969), pp. 57–83.

Rosenswaike, Ira. "Levy L. Laurens: An Early Texas Journalist." *AJA,* 27, 1 (Apr. 1975), pp. 61–66.

Rothschild, Janice O. *As But a Day: The First Hundred Years, 1867–1967.* Atlanta: The Temple, 1967.

Rottenberg, Dan. "Once There Was Greenfield." *Philadelphia,* 67, 5, May 1976, pp. 166–192.

San Francisco Jewish Elite Directory. Ed. Emil Stoessel. San Francisco: n.p., 1892.

Shadegg, Stephen C. *Barry Goldwater: Freedom Is His Flight Plan.* New York: Fleet Publishing, 1962.

Shankman, Arnold. "A Temple Is Bombed—Atlanta 1958." *AJA,* 23, 2 (Nov. 1971), pp. 125–153.

Shefferman, Nathan W., with Dale Kramer. *The Man in the Middle.* New York: Doubleday, 1961.

Silverman, Morris. *Hartford Jews, 1659–1970.* Hartford: Connecticut Historical Society, 1970.

Sinclair, Upton. *The Brass Check: A Study of American Journalism.* New York: Arno and The New York Times, 1970.

Sklare, Marshall. *The Jews: Social Patterns of an American Group.* New York: The Free Press, 1958.

Sklare, Marshall, ed. *The Jew in American Society.* Essay by Seymour M. Lipset and Everett C. Ladd, Jr. "Jewish Academics in the U.S." New York: Behrman House, 1974, pp. 255–288.

Stanley, Gerald. "Merchandising in the Southwest: The Mark I. Jacobs Company of Tucson, 1867–1875." *AJA,* 23, 1 (Apr. 1971), pp. 86–102.

Steffens, Lincoln. *The Autobiography of Lincoln Steffens.* New York: Harcourt, Brace & World, 1958.

Stember, Charles Herbert, et al. *Jews in the Mind of America.* New York: Basic Books, 1966.

Stern, Rabbi Malcolm H. *Americans of Jewish Descent.* Cincinnati: Hebrew Union College Press, 1960.

Stern, Norton B. *California Jewish History: A Descriptive Bibliography.* Glendale: Arthur H. Clark, 1967.

———. "Report of an Interview with Mr. Jerrold Goldwater." Typescript, Cincinnati Hebrew Union College.

Stern, Norton B. See also Kramer, William M.

Stern, Norton B., with William M. Kramer. "The Sinsheimers of San Luis Obispo." *WSJHQ,* Oct. 1973, pp. 3–32.

Stocker, Joseph. "The Dynasty of Goldwater." In *Jewish Roots in Arizona,* Journal of the Tercentenary Committee of the Phoenix Jewish Community Council, Nov. 1954, pp. 7–13.

Straus, Isidor. *The Autobiography of Isidor Straus.* Foreword by Sara Straus Hess. privately printed, 1955.

Straus, Nathan. *Diseases in Milk: The Remedy Pasteurization.* New York: n.p., 1913.

Straus, Oscar Solomon. *The Origin of Republican Form of Government in the*

United States of America. New York and London: G. P. Putnam's, 1901.

————. *The American Spirit.* New York: Century, 1913.

————. *Under Four Administrations from Cleveland to Taft; Recollections of Oscar Straus.* Boston and New York: Houghton Mifflin, 1922.

Straus, Robert K. *Straus Genealogical Miscellany.* n.p.: privately printed, 1973.

————. See Kauffman, Reginald.

Suwol, Samuel M. *Jewish History of Oregon.* Portland: n.p., 1958.

Swanberg, W. A. *Citizen Hearst: A Biography of William Randolph Hearst.* New York: Charles Scribner's Sons, 1961.

Swichkow, Louis J., and Lloyd P. Gartner. *The History of the Jews of Milwaukee.* Philadelphia: The Jewish Publication Society of America, 1963.

Taper, Bernard. *Balanchine.* New York: Harper & Row, 1960.

Teichmann, Howard. *George S. Kaufman: An Intimate Portrait.* New York: Atheneum, 1972.

"Texas Merchants After the Civil War: 1871." *AJA,* 12, 1 (Apr. 1960), pp. 71–74.

Tolbert, Frank. *Neiman-Marcus, Dallas.* New York: Henry Holt, 1953.

"Trail Blazers of the Trans-Mississippi West." *AJA,* 8, 2 (Oct. 1956), pp. 59–130.

Turner, Justin G. "The First Decade of Los Angeles Jewry: A Pioneer History (1850–1860)." *AJHQ,* 54, 1 (Sept. 1964), pp. 123–164.

Twentieth Century Fund Annual Report. New York, 1975.

van den Haag, Ernest. *The Jewish Mystique.* New York: Stein & Day, 1969.

Veblen, Thorstein. *Essays in Our Changing Order.* Ed. Leon Ardzrooni. New York: Viking Press, 1934.

Vorspan, Max, and Lloyd P. Gartner. *History of the Jews of Los Angeles.* San Marino: The Huntington Library, 1970.

Warburg, James P. *The Long Road Home.* New York: Doubleday, 1964.

Washington, Booker T. *Up from Slavery: An Autobiography.* New York: Doubleday, Page, 1901.

Watters, Leon L. *The Pioneer Jews of Utah.* New York: The American Jewish Historical Society, 1952.

Wax, Rabbi James A. "The Jews of Memphis: 1860–1863." *The West Tennessee Historical Society Papers,* 3 (1949), pp. 39–89.

Weil, Gordon L. *Sears, Roebuck, U.S.A., The Great American Catalogue Store and How It Grew.* New York: Stein & Day, 1977.

Weill, Raphael. Typescript interview, n.d., Bancroft Library.

Wendt, Lloyd, and Herman Kogan. *Give the Lady What She Wants.* Chicago: Rand McNally, 1952.

Werner, M. R. *Julius Rosenwald: The Life of a Practical Humanitarian.* New York: Harper & Brothers, 1939.

Wile, Isaac A. *History of the Jews of Rochester.* Rochester: n.p., n.d.

Williams, T. Harry, Richard N. Current, and Frank Freidel. *A History of the United States.* 2nd ed. rev. 2 vols. New York: Alfred A. Knopf, 1965.

Wilson, Carol Green. *Gump's Treasure Trade: A Story of San Francisco.* New York: Thomas Y. Crowell, 1965.

Wilson, Don W. "Pioneer Jews in California and Arizona, 1849–1875." Cincinnati: American Hebrew Union College Library, typescript.

Wingfield, Marshall. "The Life and Letters of Dr. William J. Armstrong." *The West Tennessee Historical Society Papers,* 4 (1950), pp. 97–114.

Wolf, Edwin, and M. Whiteman. *The History of the Jews of Philadelphia from Colonial Times to the Age of Jackson.* Philadelphia: The Jewish Publication Society of America, 1957.

Woodward, Comer Vann. *Tom Watson: Agrarian Rebel.* New York: Macmillan, 1938.

Wright, Frank Lloyd. *A Testament.* New York: Horizon Press, 1957.

Yaffe, James. *The American Jews.* New York: Random House, 1968.

Zarchin, Michael M. *Glimpses of Jewish Life in San Francisco.* 2nd rev. ed. Berkeley: Judah L. Magnes Memorial Museum, 1964.

Zola, Émile. "Notes de travail sur les grands magazins." *Oeuvres Complètes.* Vol. 12. Paris (these for his novel *Au Bonheur des Dames).*

Index

A & P, 319–320, 351
Abercrombie & Fitch, xviii–xix
Abraham, Abraham, 60
Abraham, David, 216
Abraham & Straus, 25, 41, 43, 44, 50, 52, 339, 364*n*
Adams, Helen, 167
Adams, Sam, 22
Addams, Jane, 313
Adler, Felix, 66
Adler, Max, 307
advertising, xiv, 19, 73–74, 93, 225
  demand created by, 286–287
  honesty in, 287–288, 296
  Jewish influence in, 161
  mail-order, 282, 286–287, 293–297, 319
  politics and, xiv, 293–294
  publicity vs., 180, 184–185
  sex and, 293–294
Agobard, Archbishop, 158, 372*n*
Aleichem, Sholem, 355
Alexander II, czar of Russia, 57
Alkali Ike, 238
Allen, Fred, 53, 290
Allied Stores, 344, 348
Alonso, Hernando, 207–208

Altman, Benjamin, x, 103, 111, 356
Amherst College, 180
Annenberg, Moe, 83, 87, 367*n*
anti-Semitism, xv, 2, 45–46, 127–128, 158, 192, 226–227, 232, 318–321, 375*n*, 379*n*
  Catholic Church and, 158, 202, 204, 207–208, 327
  children and, 60, 61, 178, 268, 285, 331
  cultural separation as cause of, 30–32, 55, 61
  in educational institutions, 30–32, 65, 180
  financial dependence and, 204–205
  in Grant administration, 116–117
  Hitler's policy of, 54–55, 320–321
  immigration as cause of, 57–59, 70
  Jewish homeland and, 299–300, 333–334
  Jewish response to, 28–29, 59–60, 61, 65, 128, 143–144, 320–321
  Middle America and, 318–321
  Russian, xv, 31, 47–48, 57–58, 297, 299–300
  sex and, 143–145, 370*n*
  wealth as cause of, 57, 58–59
anti-union activities, 195, 196–197

architecture, 91, 103, 105–108, 110, 148–
    149, 163, 255–256, 268–269, 356
Arden, Elizabeth, 96–97, 182
Arlington (club), 268
Armstrong, William J., 119
art:
    auctions of, 251, 252
    collecting of, 103, 190–192, 367n
    Hearst sale of, 80–81
    Jews associated with, 192–193
    Jews as dealers in, 243–246
    Oriental, 245–246
    Pittsburgh collections of, 103, 105–106
    in saloons, 243–244
    Straus family collections of, 62–63
    television and, 356
artists, 45–46
    entertainment of, 163–164
    patronage of, 78, 254, 358
arts, Jews as supporters of, ix, xv, 29–30,
    152, 188–189, 192–193
Ascoli, Marion Rosenwald, 303, 315, 323,
    324, 330–333, 334, 379n
Ascoli, Max, 332–333
Associated Dry Goods, 197, 349, 354
Astor, John Jacob, 260
Atlanta, 135–155, 370n–371n
Auchincloss, Mrs. J. Howland, 80
Auerbach, Beatrice Fox, xvi, 94
Auerbach brothers, 238
"Aunt Rachel," 3

Backer, Evelyn Weil, 43
Backer, George, 43
Badger, Daniel, 148
Baker, George F., 64
Baker, Newton D., 301
Balanchine, George, 32–33
ballet, 32, 78, 110, 356
Bamberger, L., & Co., 152
Bamberger, Louis, 152
Bamberger, Simon, 274
bankruptcy, 218–219
banks, bankers, xiv–xv
    vs. credit unions, 11–13
    Jewish interests in, 84–86, 89, 131, 214,
        228–229, 254, 273
    in move to New York, 70, 366n
    as Protestant business, 85
    social reputation of, 44, 125, 206–207
    vs. Western storekeepers, 206
Barmash, Isadore, 381n
Barron, C. W., 302
Barrymore, John, 101
Baruch, Bernard, 301
Beame, Abraham, 323–324

Beck, Dave, 197
Beebe, James M., & Company, 10
Beecher, Henry Ward, 47
Bendel, Henri (store), xvii, 181
Beneš, Eduard, 34
Benjamin, Judah, 135
Bennet, Colonel, 216
Benny, Jack, xi, 53, 252
Bentham, Jeremy, 13
Benton, Thomas Hart, 279
Bergdorf Goodman, x, 10, 181, 185, 191,
    196, 249, 251
Berlin, Ellin (Mrs. Irving), 263–264
Bernays, Edward, 27, 261n
Bernbach, William, 161
Bernhardt, Sarah, 240, 245
Bernheimer, Grace, 77, 82
Bernie, Ben, 53
Best's, 181
Beverly, Effie, 32
Bibo, Emil, 210
Bibo, Nathan, 210
Bibo, Simon, 210
Bibo, Solomon, 210, 222
Bibo brothers, 210
Biddle, Nicholas, 366n
Billy the Kid, 221–222
Bingham, Robert W., 54
Biow, Milton, 161
Birmingham, Stephen, 176, 364n, 371n
Bizet, Geneviève Halévy, 45–46
Bizet, Georges, 45
Black, Hugo L., 351
blacks:
    chain stores and, 353
    Jewish attitude toward, 126–128, 195
    Rosenwald aid to, 303–307, 320
    service for, 127, 154
    sexual attitudes and, 144
    Southern schools and, 305–307
Bloomingdale, Alfred S., 345, 350
Bloomingdale, Hiram C., 345
Bloomingdale, Lyman Gustavus, 345
Bloomingdale, Samuel J., 64, 338–339, 345,
    380n
Bloomingdale's, 122, 253, 338–339, 345
Bogardus, James, 148
Bohemian Club (San Francisco), 241
Bon Marché, ix, 40
Bonnet, Georges, 34
Bonwit Teller (New York), xvii, 88, 89, 196,
    352, 381n
Bonwit Teller (Philadelphia), 87, 89
book collections, 82, 180, 190, 191, 322
Boone, Daniel, 92

Boorstin, Daniel J., xiv, 149, 287–288, 298, 341, 342, 360n, 363n
Booth, Edwin, 164–165, 236
Bossom, Alfred, 188
Boston, 1–35, 361n–363n
Boston City Club, 22–23, 25
Boucicaut, Aristide, ix
Braddock, Edward, 92
Bradstreet Company, 240
Brandeis, Louis D., 23, 300
Brandeis', 147, 254
Brandenstein family, 253
Brennan, Matthew, 42
Bridger, James, 262
Broadway-Hale Stores, see Carter Hawley Hale
Brook Hollow Golf Club, 195
Brooks Brothers, xviii
Brooks, John G., 303, 349
brothels, 2, 18, 41, 120, 121, 202, 270
    Billie Scheible's, 98–100
    Goldwater family and, 217–218, 374n
    in San Francisco, 244, 246–247
    social role of, 98–100, 202
    "Tin Plate Law" of, 272
Browne, Daisy, 140
Bruce, Ailsa Mellon, 94, 250
Brundage, Avery, 245
Bryan, John Neely, 156–157
Bryan, William Jennings, 293
Bullock's, 21, 122, 184, 250, 345
Burchfield, A. H., Sr., 103
Burchfield family, 102
Burdine's, 345
Burlingame Country Club, 241
buyers, 6, 14, 15–16, 19, 20, 146–147, 251

Calhoun, John C., 132
Cantor, Eddie, 323
Cantwell, Robert, 26, 361n
Capone, Al, 311
Carnegie, Andrew, 93, 104–105, 310
Carnegie, Mrs. Andrew, 60
Carnegie, Hattie, 110, 176
Carnegie Institute, 105
Carson, Kit, 262
Carson, Pirie, Scott & Co., 106, 149, 184, 282
Carter, Edward William, 277, 278
Carter Hawley Hale, 199, 239, 277, 348, 354
Carvalho, Solomon Nuñes, 262–263
Cather, Willa, 208
Catholic Church, 202, 204, 207–209, 281
Center, Australia, 166

chain stores, 344–354
    executives of, 351–354
    investment advantages of, 350–351
    social impact of, 351–354, 356
    unfair practices of, 319–320
Chamberlin's, 137
Chambers, Whittaker, 361n
Chandler, Harry, 80–81
Chanel, Coco, 16
Chapman, Nathan, 261
charity, 33, 44–45, 234, 297–299, 300, 354
Chicago:
    crime in, 311–313
    non-Jewish stores in, 282–283
Chicago Club, 99
child welfare, 309, 323–324
Chipp, 153
City Stores, 85–86, 87, 89
Clay, Henry, 132
Cleveland, Grover, 47
clubs:
    acceptance of Jews in, 22, 60, 65, 67–68, 70, 75, 99, 143, 153, 154, 195, 232, 241–244, 257, 268, 326, 376n
    brothels as, 99
    importance of, 22–23, 241–242, 257
    Jewish-founded, 22–23, 59, 75, 99, 143
Cohen, Naomi, 365n
Cohn, Bernard, 219
Cohn, Lemuel, 220
Cohn, Morris, 220
Columbia University, 46, 110
Columbus, Christopher, 202
company stores, 215–216
Concordia Club, 99
Coolidge, Albert Sprague, 29
cooperative buying, 21
copper mining, 212
Corbett, Henry W., 273
Cortés, Hernán, 202, 208
credit, xx, 40, 41, 138–139, 152, 160, 223, 224
    in company stores, 215–216
    of department vs. specialty stores, 349–350
    down payment plans and, 339–340
    merchants' character and, 37, 41, 174, 206–207, 218–219, 240
    national credit cards and, 350
credit unions, 11–13
Crocker, Charles P., 238, 251
Crump, Edward Hull, 128
Cuahtémoc, Aztec emperor, 208
Cuming, Sir Alexander, 113
Curtiss, Mina Kirstein, 33

Custer, George A., 263
Custin, Mildred, xvii, 89, 365n, 367n, 381n

Dallas, 156–200, 371n–373n
    cultural growth of, 163–165, 188–189,
        192, 194
    founding of, 156–157
    oil money in, 192–193
    violence associated with, 193–195
Dallas Opera House, 164–165
Davidson, Ben, 240
"David the Jew," 3
Davis, Jacob W., 238
Dayton Company, 20, 191, 379n
Dayton Hudson, 348, 354
Degas, Edgar, 45
de Long, James M. Maurice, 71
Dempsey, Jack, 76
Department Store Association, 195–196
department stores:
    architecture of, 91, 148–149, 253
    branch stores of, advantages in, 252
    consolidation of, 21, 25, 28, 90, 154, 275–
        278, 279, 338–339, 344–349
    deterioration of service in, 349–350, 355
    holidays as boon to, 340–342
    importance of luxury in, 252–253
    as spectacles, 73–74, 80, 170, 183–184,
        224–225, 337
    technological progress and, 148–150,
        350
"Depositor's Accounts," 40
Desjardins, Alphonse, 12
DeSoto, Hernando, 133, 202
Deutsch, Armand, 323
Deutsch, Armand, Jr., 328–330
Diamond's, 231
Dickens, Charles, 106
Dillon, C. Douglas, 67–68, 363n
Dilworth, Richardson, 89
discount stores, 350–351
Dittenhoffer, Sam, 222
Dodd, Alvin, 29
Dodd, Martha, 332
Doniphan, William Alexander, 205
Dougherty's, 137
Drachman, Philip, 230
Drake, Francis, 259
Dreyfus, Alfred, 46, 145, 148
Dun, R. G., & Company, 240
Dunkelmann, Robert, 64
Dun's credit reports, 240
Du Pont, Pierre S., 310
Duquesne Club, 99
Duveen, Joseph, 63, 245, 367n

Eastern European Jews, xvi, 75, 108
    German Jews vs., 58–59, 70, 75
Edison, Thomas A., 101
education, support of, xv, 49, 152, 190, 232,
    305–307
Ehrman, Jean Meier, 267
Ehrman, Joseph, 267
Ehrman, Sidney, 254
Einstein, Albert, 152
Eisenhower, Dwight D., 53, 176
Elizabeth II, queen of England, 345
Emanu-El, Temple (Dallas), 189
Emanu-El, Temple (New York), 66, 253
Emmanuel, David, 154
employees:
    company ownership by, 24–25
    marriage with, 110–111, 187, 248–249
    performance standards for, 347
    profit-sharing plan for (Sears), 313
    sexual advances to, 144–147
    wages of, and prostitution, 311–313
    welfare projects for, 10–13, 24, 34, 216,
        311–313, 322–323
Emporium (San Francisco), 20

fairs, 157–158, 372n
"Fallingwater," 103, 105–107, 368n
Famous-Barr, 348, 352
Farley, James A., 26, 87, 341
fashion, timing of, 191
Federated Department Stores, xiii, 21, 88,
    133, 154, 196, 197, 276, 338–339, 342,
    349, 353, 354
Fenn-Feinstein, 153
Ferber, Edna, 162, 178, 179
Field, Marshall, 34, 138, 282–283
Fields, W. C., 53, 69
figure exchanges, 20, 347
Filene, Bert, 6
Filene, Catherine, 29–30
Filene, Clara Ballin, 3–4
Filene, Edward A. (E. A.), xx, 4–33, 53
    boosterism of, 13–14
    brother Lincoln and, 8–9, 10, 21, 25, 35
    employee welfare programs of, 10–13,
        24
    illnesses of, 5, 8
    merchandising methods of, 6–7, 14–17,
        20
    personality of, 8–9, 11, 26–27, 34–35
    political interests of, 26
    reforms and social ideals of, 13–14, 19–
        20, 22–27, 34–35
    writings of, 26–27
Filene, Helen, 29

Filene, Lincoln, 5, 6, 8–10, 17, 19–20, 21, 25, 29, 34, 35, 347
Filene, Therese, 29, 31
Filene, Rudolph, 6
Filene, William, 3–4, 5, 6, 15
Filene Cooperative Association, 10–11
Filene family, 1–35, 361n–363n
Filene-Finlay system, 25
Filene's, 10–27, 31, 33–34, 122, 338
    Automatic Bargain Basement of, 14–17
    executive advancement in, 17, 21
Finlay, Gordon, 25
Fitzgerald, Geraldine, 43
Fitzgerald, Mrs. Hugh Nugent, 167
Fitzsimmons, Bob, 76
Fleischhacker family, 254
Foley's, 196
Ford, Henry, 17, 150, 292, 318, 321
Foreman, Bernard, 21
Foster, Ephraim, 230
Fox, George, 39–40, 363n
Fox, Gerson, 3
France, Anatole, 240
Frank, Abraham, 232
Frank, Edna, 268, 269
Frank, Fannie Meier, 266, 268
Frank, Gerald, 278, 377n
Frank, Leo Max, 145, 371n
Frank, Lloyd, 268, 269, 271, 276
Frank, Sigmund, 266, 268, 271
Frank & Seder's, 108
Frankfurter, Felix, 31, 56
Franklin, Benjamin, xiii, 2, 13, 48–49, 70, 299, 308
Franklin Simon, x, 88
Franks, David, 70, 92
Franks, David Salisbury, 70
Frederick & Nelson, 349
Frémont, John Charles, 262
Freudenthal, Anna, 213
Freudenthal, Fanny, 211
Freudenthal, Joseph, 211, 214
Freudenthal, Julius, 211, 213
Freudenthal, Louis (Lewin), 211, 213
Freudenthal, Samuel J., 214–216
Frick, Henry Clay, 93
Friedlander, Louis, 210
Frost Brothers, 198, 347
Fuld, Carrie Bamberger, 152
fundraising, 315, 333–334
fur traders, 260–261

Gabor, Lazlo, 109
Galeries Lafayette, 94
Garden, Mary, 188, 245
Garfinckel, Julius, x, 181, 349

Genesco Inc., 352
German Jews, xv–xvi
    as American aristocracy, 42–44, 57–60, 75, 136
    conscription and, 159
    Eastern European Jews resented by, 58–59, 70, 75
Geronimo, 212–213
Gerstle family, 254
Gest, William Purves, 85
Gibbon, Edward, 280
Gilchrist's, 19
Gimbel, Adam, 71, 72, 74
Gimbel, Adam Long, 79–80, 81
Gimbel, Alva Bernheimer, 44, 76–77, 78, 365n, 366n
Gimbel, Benedict, 71
Gimbel, Bernard, 44, 75–83, 142
    New York stores of, 75, 78–80
    personality of, 76–78
    sports interests of, 76
Gimbel, Bruce, 77
Gimbel, Caral, 76, 77
Gimbel, Charles, 71, 79
Gimbel, Daniel, 71, 74
Gimbel, David, 77
Gimbel, Ellis, 71, 75, 81
Gimbel, Frederic, 81
Gimbel, Fridolyn Kahnweiler, 71
Gimbel, Hope, 76, 77
Gimbel, Isaac, 71, 74, 75
Gimbel, Jacob, 71, 74
Gimbel, Julie Mastbaum, 82
Gimbel, Lee Adam, 75
Gimbel, Louis, 71, 74, 75
Gimbel, Minnie Mastbaum, 82
Gimbel, Peter, 77, 78
Gimbel, Richard, 81–82
Gimbel, Sophie, 80
Gimbel family, 70–83, 165, 365n–367n
    Philadelphia business interests of, 72, 74–75
    Saks acquisition by, 79–80
    scandals in, 75
    showmanship of, 72, 75, 80
    U.S. origins of, 70–71
Gimbel's, 71, 75, 77, 79, 80–82, 90, 108, 142, 181
    art sold by, 80–81
    Macy's vs., 41, 53, 75, 80
Gladstone, William, 105
Goethals, George Washington, 317
Goldberg, Hyman, 219
Goldblatt's, 282
Goldman, Henry, 285, 289
Goldman, Sachs, 43, 173, 284, 289

Goldsmith, Aimee Landman, 129–130
Goldsmith, Dora Ottenheimer, 119, 123, 129, 130
Goldsmith, Elias, 130
Goldsmith, Elias, Jr., 131
Goldsmith, Fred, 129, 130, 131
Goldsmith, Fred, Jr., 130, 131
Goldsmith, I. & Bros. (Goldsmith's), 119, 128–129, 265, 345
Goldsmith, Isaac, 117–118, 120, 123
Goldsmith, Jack L., 131, 132–133, 348
Goldsmith, Jacob, 117–133
Goldsmith, Jen, 131
Goldsmith, Joan, 131
Goldsmith, Leo, 130
Goldsmith, Wanda E., 131
Goldsmith family, 117–134, 369n–370n
Goldwasser, Elizabeth, 217
Goldwasser, Hirsch, 217
Goldwater, Baron, 229–233
Goldwater, Barry, M., 94, 202, 217, 227, 228, 284, 373n, 374n
  early life of, 230–233
  libel suit of, 234
  moral character of, 233–235
Goldwater, Caroline (Carrie), 217–218, 219–220
Goldwater, Carolyn, 230
Goldwater, Joseph, 217–220, 230
Goldwater, Josephine Williams, 230–231
Goldwater, Margaret Johnson (Peggy), 233
Goldwater, Michael (Big Mike), 136, 217–221, 224, 226, 228–230, 234, 236, 351
Goldwater, Morris, 217, 219–220, 227–228, 229–230, 232
Goldwater, Robert Williams, 230, 231–233, 235, 354, 373n, 375n
Goldwater, Sam, 226
Goldwater, Sarah Nathan, 217, 218, 219–220, 229
Goldwater family, 217–221, 224–235, 354, 373n–375n
  political careers of, 227–229, 230, 233–236
Goldwater's, 222, 224–227, 230, 354
Gompers, Samuel, 301
Gone with the Wind (Mitchell), 141
Goodkind, Adelaide R., 335
Goodman, Andy, 249, 250
Goodman, Consuelo Mañach, 249
Goodman, Edwin, 249–250
Gordon, Lady Duff, 49
Gordon, Sir Cosmo, 49
Gould, Jay, 3, 42, 164
Graham, Martha, 103
Grant, Ulysses S., 116–117, 207, 285

Gratz, Rebecca, 70
Gratz family, 69, 70
Greenberg, Hank, 77
Greenfield, Albert M., 83–90, 367n
  banking business of, 84–86, 89
  early life of, 83
  personality of, 83, 84, 88–89
  political influence of, 86–87
  real estate ventures of, 84–85, 86, 88
  reputation of, 83, 87–89
Greenfield, Edna Kraus, 84
Groton, 60, 67
Guest, Edgar Albert, 295
Guggenheim, M. Robert, 77, 82
Guggenheim family, 82
Gump, Abraham Livingston, 244–246
Gump, Richard, 246
Gump, Robert, 246
Gump, Solomon, 243–244
Gump family, 243–247
  as art merchants, 243–245
  scandals in, 246
Gump's, 254

Haas, Julius, 261
Haas family, 253, 255, 257
Haines, Granville B., & Company, 72
Haldeman, Bob, 192
Halévy, Fromental, 45
Hall, Lulie, T., 140
Halle, Walter, 125, 196
Halle Brothers, 196, 349
Halleck, H. W., 117
Haman, Jessie, 244–245
Hamburger, Nathan, 71
"Hammerslough Brothers," 285
Hammerslough family, 284, 285
Hamon, Jake, 192
Handlin, Oscar, 360n, 367n, 370n
Hapgood, Hutchins, 26
Harriman, William A., 323
Harris, A., & Company, 21, 126, 168, 169, 171, 174, 188, 196, 197, 354
Harris, Adolph, xii, 28
Harris, Leon (father), xii–xiii, xix, 56–57, 174, 206–207, 270, 358
Harris, Lucile Herzfeld, 175–176
Harris family, xii–xiii, xix, 28, 164, 175–176
Hart, Harry, 311
Hart, James D., 257, 376n
Hart, Jerome A., 251
Hart, Mrs. Jerome A., 251
Hart, Max, 311
Hartnell, Norman, 16

Harvard Business School, xv, 7, 108–109, 180
Harvard Medical School, 30, 31, 32
Harvard University, xiii, 1, 5, 6, 31, 33, 49, 51, 65, 67, 153, 180, 333, 356
Harzfeld's, xvii, 181
Haughwout's, E. V., 149, 150
Hawkes, Mrs. Howard (Slim), 184–185
Hayward, Susan, 294
Hearn's, 40–41, 88
Hearst, William Randolph, 80–81, 87, 294
Hecht Co., x, 348
Hellman, Geoffrey, 68
Hellman family, 254
Henri Bendel, xvii, 181
Henry VIII, king of England, 204, 308
Hess, Tom, 327
Higginson, Henry Lee, 30
Hill, James Jerome, 282
Hill, Napoleon, 123, 132
Hindenburg, Paul von, 320–321
Hirsch, Emil Gustav, 299
Hirsch, Baron Maurice de, 47, 299
Hirsch, Max, 265
Hitler, Adolf, 53, 54, 321
Hobhouse, Sir Arthur, 308
Hoffman, Paul, 195
Hollister, Margaret, 141
Holmes, D. H., 184
Hoover, Herbert, 53, 86
Hoover, J. Edgar, 56
Hopkins, Harry, 53
Hopkins, Mark, 238
Hopkinson, Edward, Jr., 85
Horgan, Paul, 208
Horne, Joseph, 92
Horne, Joseph, Company, 20, 92–93, 97, 101, 102–103, 108, 236
Horowitz, Louis J., 79
Horowitz, Vladimir, 163–164
Hoving, Walter, 88–89, 365n, 367n
Hudson, J. L., Company, 20, 379n
Humphrey, Hubert H., 89
Hungerford, Marie Louise Antoinette, 264
Hunt, H. L., 192, 195
Huntington, Arabella, 243
Huntington, Collis P., 190, 238, 243, 245
Huntington, Henry E., 243
Hutzler Brothers Company, x, 21, 166

immigration, xv–xvi, 15, 57–59, 70, 108
Indians, American, 91
    Catholics and, 207–208
    Jews and, 1–2, 206, 210–211, 219, 261–263

Indians, American (cont'd)
    as threat to Western settlers, 211, 212–213, 220
Ismay, J. Bruce, 49

Jackson, Andrew, 366n
Jackson, Maynard, 154
Jacobson, Eddie, 258
Jarvis, Anna, 341
Jews:
    assimilation and, 46, 54–56, 65–68, 210–211, 257
    as Confederate supporters, 38–39, 116–117, 136, 141, 159
    conversion of, 29, 46, 65–66, 112, 202, 230, 257, 327
    dietary laws of, 211, 263, 327
    European oppression of, 47, 57–58, 111, 136, 211, 299–301
    group reputation as concern of, 257–258, 327
    Indians and, 1–2, 210–211, 212–213, 219
    as linguists, 202–203, 210–211
    as nation of traders, 201, 202, 204–205, 221, 237
    nonreligious, 29, 55–56, 62, 66, 189, 230, 257
    in public office, 26, 46–48, 53–55, 143–144, 154, 227–229, 233–235, 273–275
    Russian treatment of, 47–48, 57–58, 297, 299–300
    stereotypes of, xvi, 201–202
    surnames changed among, see names, changes of
    as sutlers, 203–205, 210, 219
    Talmudic vs. materialist aspirations of, 344
    see also anti-Semitism; Eastern European Jews; German Jews
Johnson, Jack, 76
Johnson, Lyndon B., 89, 193
John Wanamaker's, ix, 72, 73–74, 90
Jordan, Eben Dyer, 9
Jordan, Eben Dyer, Jr., 10
Jordan Marsh, ix, 9–10
Jordan's 10, 19
Joseph, George William, 270, 273
Joseph II, emperor of Austria, 27
Joske, Julius, 347–348
Junior League, 195, 268

Kahn, Eddie, 179
Kahn, Otto, xv, 245
Karstadt (store), 94
Kaufman, George S., 345

Kaufmann, Arthur C., 81, 102, 365*n*, 367*n*, 368*n*
Kaufmann, Betty, 94
Kaufmann, Edgar, xiii, 94–111
  lawsuit over estate of, 110–111
  love of scandal of, 100–101, 102–103
  personality of, 95–96, 106–107, 108
  women and, 94–95, 97, 98, 110–111
Kaufmann, Edgar, Jr., 110, 111, 368*n*
Kaufmann, Grace A. Stoops, 110–111
Kaufmann, Henry, 92
Kaufmann, Isaac, 92, 95
Kaufmann, Jacob, 92
Kaufmann, Lillian Sarah (Liliane), 95–97
  business interests of, 96–97
  personality of, 95–97
Kaufmann, Morris, 92, 94
Kaufmann, Oliver M., 97, 108, 367*n*, 369*n*
Kaufmann family, 92–98, 101–111, 367*n*–369*n*
Kaufmann's, 93, 96–97, 103, 108–109, 130
Kellstadt, Charles, 292
Kelly, Grace, 185
Kilrain, Jake, 164
Kirstein, George, 33, 361*n*, 362*n*
Kirstein, Lincoln Edward, 32–33, 361*n*, 362*n*
Kirstein, Louis Edward, 17–21, 25, 30–34
  children of, 32–33
  death of, 34
  as eccentric, 17–18
  managerial talent of, 18–20
Kirstein, Mina, *see* Curtiss, Mina Kirstein
Kirstein, Rose Stein, 18, 33
Kirstein family, 17–19, 31–35
Kissinger, Henry, 332
Klein, Daryl, 266–267
Koenig, Julian, 161
Kohn, Adolph, 261
Korvette, E. J., 351
Koshland, Cora, 256, 257
Koshland, Dan, 255, 256, 376*n*
Koshland, Eleanor Haas, 255
Koshland, Marcus, 256
Koshland, Robert, 256, 376*n*
Koshland family, 254, 255, 256, 257
Kramer, Arthur, 168, 174, 188–189
  business talent of, 188–189
  collections of, 188
  as music patron, 188–189
Krock, Arthur, 68
Kronenburger, Louis, 183
Kuppenheimer, Bernard, 311

Lamy, Archbishop Jean Baptiste, 208–209
Lamy, John B., Jr., 209

Landsburgh's, 88
Lang, Gilbert, 347–348
Lansky, Meyer, 311
Lapowski, Clarence, 67
Lapowski, Jake, 67
Lapowski, Sam, 67
Lash, Freida, 324, 379*n*
Lasker, Albert, 77, 160–161
Lasker, Edouard, 160
Lasker, Edward, 77
Lasker, Morris, 160–161
Law, John, 113
Lawrence, David L., 107
Lazar, Jacob Ben, 36
Lazarus, Celia Kahn Rosenthal, 343, 380*n*
Lazarus, Emma, 36
Lazarus, F. & R., & Company, 20, 25, 122
Lazarus, Fred, Jr., 88, 122, 133, 196, 276, 338–348
  chain built by, 344–347
  credit policies of, 339–340, 346
  holidays and, 340–342
  middle-class trade sought by, 346–347
  nepotism and, 342–343
  personality of, 336–337, 342, 347
  storekeeping practices improved by, 339–340, 346–347
Lazarus, Fred, III, 343
Lazarus, John Ralph, 348
Lazarus, Maurice (Mogie), 343, 344, 361*n*
Lazarus, Meta, 336, 343
Lazarus, Ralph, 343, 347, 348, 353
Lazarus, Richard, 336
Lazarus, Simon, 337
Lazarus, Simon (founder), 337
Lazarus, Virginia, 153
Lazarus family (the Lazari), 336–348, 353–354, 380*n*–381*n*
Lehman, Herbert, 51, 274
Lehman, Sissie Straus, 43
Leitensdorfer, Eugene, 204
LeLong, Lucien, 16
Lenin, V. I., 24
Leopold, Nathan, 145
Lesinsky, Charles, 211
Lesinsky, Henry, 211–213, 215
Lesinsky, Morris, 211
Lesinsky family, 211–213
Leslie, Warren, 184
Levi's, 68, 220, 238–239, 255
Levy, Adele Rosenwald, 323–325, 330, 331, 334
Levy, Barbara, 68, 363*n*
Levy, David Mordecai, 323
Lewis, John Henry, 232
Lilienthal family, 254

Lincoln, Abraham, 117, 336
Linda, Hala, 246
Lindbergh, Charles, 318
Lindsley, Henry, 166
Linz, Clarence, 166–167
Linz, Joe, 163–164
Linz, Lois Sanger, 166–167
Lippmann, Walter, 51, 77
Lit Brothers, 85
Lit family, 72, 82
Livingston, Mary, xi
Loeb, Richard, 145
Longworth, Mrs. Nicholas, 60
Lorant, Stefan, 96, 108, 367n
Lord & Taylor, xvii, 88, 236, 346
Louis XIV, king of France, 203
Loveman's, 87
Lowell, Lawrence A., 31
Lowenstein, Abraham, 114
Lowenstein, Benedict, 114
Lowenstein, Bernard, 114–115
Lowenstein, Elias, 114, 129
Lowenstein's, 87, 114, 126–127, 254
Lubin, David, 14

McCarthy, Joseph, 33, 318
McCormick, Robert R., 96
McCreery's, 102
McDuff, Marihelen, 186
McGill, Ralph, 307
Mackay, John, 264
Macy, Rowland Hussey, xx, 39–40, 52, 363n
Macy's, ix, xii, 45, 52–53, 75, 79, 80, 88, 141, 142, 145, 283, 341, 344, 348
  Captain Macy's success with, 39–40
  Gimbel's vs., 41, 53, 75, 80
  price policies of, 39–41
  Straus ownership of, 39–42
Magnin, Charlotte Davis, 248, 251
Magnin, Cyril, 251, 376n
Magnin, Edgar F., 252, 376n
Magnin, Grover, 147, 242, 247–248, 250–252
Magnin, I., & Co. (Magnin's), 122, 181, 191, 247–248, 252, 254, 345, 352
Magnin, Isaac, 247
Magnin, Jeanne Melton, 250–251
Magnin, John, 247–248
Magnin, Joseph, 247–248, 251
Magnin, Joseph, Company, 247
Magnin, Mary Ann, xvi-xvii, 247–248, 250
Magnin, Sam, 247, 252
mail-order business, 280–297
  catalogues in, 280, 282, 286–287, 293–296, 301, 349

mail-order business (cont'd)
  resentment of, 319–321
  vs. retail stores, 317–318, 349
  returns in, 290–292
  shipping delays in, 290, 292
Maison Blanche, 87, 129
Mallet, Francois, 209
Mannix, Thomas, 273
Mansfield, Jacob, 232
Marcus, Betty Blum, 188, 372n
Marcus, Edward, 53, 187, 372n, 373n
Marcus, Herbert, xiv, 122, 156, 167–171, 172, 175, 177, 178, 180, 183, 188, 189, 190, 198
Marcus, Herbert, Jr., 187
Marcus, Jacob, xiii, 177, 360n, 380n
Marcus, Lawrence, 187
Marcus, Mary Cantrell (Billie), 187–188, 195
Marcus, Minnie Lichtenstein, 165, 168–169, 170, 187
Marcus, Stanley, 30, 53, 80, 94, 107, 147, 169, 174, 175–176, 178–200, 250, 333, 339, 372n, 373n
  art and book collections of, 180, 190–192, 198
  courageous public positions of, 193–194, 356
  early life of, 178–179
  employee selection of, 185–186
  public relations talent of, 180–185
  relationship with brothers of, 186–187
  reputation of, 195, 197–199
Marcus, Theo, 168, 170
Marcus family (the Marci), 164, 165, 167–200, 371n–373n
marriage:
  among merchant families, 18, 43–44, 68, 76–78, 82–83, 167, 187, 255
  to non-Jews, 61, 77, 143, 210–211, 229, 248–249, 261
  parental approval and, 248–249, 266–267
Marsh, Benjamin L., 10
Marshall, Louis, 300, 308
Marshall Field's, ix, 129, 162, 282, 283, 307, 349, 379n
Marx, Karl, 24, 221
Marx, Marcus, 311
Massell, Sam, Jr., 154
May Company, xi, 109, 110, 278, 348
May, David, x
Mayer, Louis B., 252
Mayo, William James, 335
Meadows, Algur, 193
Meier, Aaron, 263, 264, 269–270, 271, 275–278

Meier, Abe, 271
Meier, Fannie, 266, 268
Meier, Grace, 271
Meier, Jack, 276, 277–278, 377n
Meier, Jean, 267
Meier, Jeannette Hirsch, xvii, 264, 265–267, 270, 276
Meier, Julius, 270–271, 272–273, 275
Meier & Frank, 266, 269, 274, 275–276
Meiklejohn, Alexander, 164
Mellon, Ailsa, see Bruce, Ailsa Mellon
Mellon, Andrew, 94, 245, 367n
Mellon, Paul, 94, 108
Mellon, Richard, 94
Mellon, Richard King, 94, 107–108
Mellon, Thomas, 93–94
Mellon family, 93, 99, 103, 105, 107–108, 217
Memphis, 112–134, 369n–370n
    Civil War smuggling in, 116–117
    as river port, 112–113
    yellow fever in, 119–120
Mencken, H. L., 24, 104
Menuhin, Yehudi, 254
merchandising:
    boldness needed in, 122
    by creating demands, 286–287
    holidays and, 341–342
    to middle class, 346–347
    recordkeeping in, 20–21
    scientific, 6–8, 14–17, 20–21
    size displays and, 339
    see also advertising
Metropolitan Museum, 63, 67, 245, 356
Metropolitan Opera, xv, 76, 164, 188
Meyer, Julius, 210–211
Miller, Mrs. Michael, 260
Mitchell, Margaret, 140
Molyneaux, Edward, 250
Montgomery Ward, 197, 291, 296, 317, 318, 319, 349
Moody, Dwight, 170
Moran, George (Bugs), 311
Morgan, Anne, 54
Morgan, J. P., 190
Morgan, Junius Spencer, 10, 282
Morgan, Ruth, 80
Morgan family, 103, 151
Morgenthau, Henry, 51, 285, 364n
Moses, Raphael J., 143–144
Moses, Robert, 107
Mossiker, Frances, 165, 372n
Moynihan, Daniel P., 332
Mumford, Lewis, 91
Murchison, Clint, 192
music, 10, 164–165, 180, 188–189, 246, 254

names, changes of, xii, 27–29, 46, 60–61, 67–68, 83, 151, 217, 290, 332
Napoleon I, 27, 37, 238
Neely, Frank H., 141, 152, 154, 370n
    political influence of, 142–143
Neely, Rae Schlesinger, 143
Neiman, Abraham Lincoln (Al), 122, 156, 169–171, 172, 186
    salesmanship of, 169–170
    women and, 177–178
Neiman, Carrie Marcus, xii, xiv, xvi, 169, 170–171, 172, 175–176, 178, 180
Neiman-Marcus, 10, 16, 80, 127, 170–175, 181–186, 191–192, 194, 196–197, 199–200, 239, 251, 254, 346, 349, 354
    exclusivity reputation of, 181–183
    "Fortnights" of, 183–184
    sales technique at, 176–177
    specialty gift service of, 185
Nesbit, Evelyn, 101–102
Neustadter, David, 255
Neustadter, Dora Dannenberg, 255
Neustadter, Jacob H., 255
Neustadter, Josephine Dannenberg, 255
Newberry, J. J., 64
Newhall, C. Stevenson, 85
Newhouse, Samuel I., 83
newspapers, xiv, 26, 31, 86, 130–131, 181, 225, 274, 311
New York City, 36–68, 75–81, 363n–365n
Nickerson, Luthera M., 331
Nixon, Richard, 80, 192, 193, 252
Nunberg, Herman, 315–316
Nuñes, Samuel Ribeiro, 136
Nusbaum, Aaron, 286, 292, 313
    early business enterprises of, 283–284
    personality of, 288–290
    Sears interest of, 284, 288–289

Ochs, Adolph, 83, 117, 301
Ochs, Bertha, 117
Ogelthorpe, James, 135–136, 143
opera, xv, 45, 164–165, 181, 188, 254
Oppenheim Collins, 88
Oregon, 259–279, 377n–379n
Oriental art, 245–246
O'Sullivan, John L., 378n
Otis, Elisha Graves, 149–150
Otis, James, 22
Ottenheimer, Louis, 117–118, 119
outlaws, 221–222, 224, 311–313
Owens, Martha, 137

Pacific Union Club, 241, 257
Palestine, 45, 299–300, 333–334
Papert, Frederic, 161

Parkman, Francis, 262
Peacock, Alexander, 96
peddlers, peddling, 3–4, 18, 71, 123–124, 159, 201–205, 210–211, 260–262, 263, 349
  as adventurers, 202–203
  credit for, 37
  department stores vs., 349
  Jewish women as, 3, 158
  as traditional start for merchants, 37, 113–114, 237–238, 260, 264, 284
Penn, William, 90, 91
Penney, J. C., x, 197, 319, 347, 349
Perelman, S. J., 293
Pershing, John J., 54
Petroleum Club, 195
Pfeifer, Joseph, 14
Philadelphia, 69–75, 81–90, 365n–367n
Philadelphia Club, 70
philanthropy, 107–108, 152, 190, 297–301, 303–310, 326
  administration of, 309–310
Philomath Club, 255
Phoenix Country Club, 232
Piedmont Driving Club, 143, 153
Pittsburgh, 91–111, 367n–369n
  arts and culture in, 103–106
  economic growth in, 93–94
  pollution in, 106
  religious freedom in, 91–92
  scandals in, 101–102
  social reforms in, 106–108, 110–111
Pizitz, Louis, 136
Plough, Abe, 131
politics, 2–3, 25–26, 258
  advertising and, 293–294
  business interests served by, 128
  as duty, 234–235
  moral character in, 233–235, 356
  muckraking and, 22–24
  party membership and, 26, 53, 86, 228, 274–275
  profession, 356–357
  real estate and, 84–85, 128
Pool, Loretta, 119
premiums, merchandise, 295–296
Press, J., 153
price control, 193–194
price fixing, 195–196
price wars, 40–41, 53, 80
Printemps, 339
Puckett, B. Earl, 344
Pulitzer, Joseph, 83, 294

Quart, Thomas and Sarah Anne, 101

railroads, 47, 92, 157, 161–162, 205, 213
Randall, David A., 191
ready-made garments, 122, 140, 171–172
real estate, 78–79, 122–123, 346
  political influence and, 84–85, 128
Redondo, José Maria, 232
Regenstein, Julius, 137
Retail Research Association, 20–21
Rich, Bertha, 139
Rich, Daniel, 136
Rich, Emmanuel, 136, 139
Rich, M., & Bro. (Rich's), 135–143, 147–155
  community activities and, 139–140, 152, 154–155
  competitors of, 141–142
  credit policy of, 138–139, 152–153
  customer relations at, 137–138
  Federated Department Stores merged with, 154–155
Rich, Maud (Honey), 151
Rich, Michael Peter, 153, 154, 370n
Rich, Morris, 136–137, 151
Rich, Richard H. (Dick), 30, 151–154, 370n
  name change of, 152
  personality of, 153–154
Rich, Rosalind, 151
Rich, Virginia Lazarus, 153
Rich, Walter, 139, 142–143, 151, 370n
Rich, William, 136
Rich family, 54, 135–143, 151–155, 337, 370n–371n
Rivera, Diego, 105–106
Robinson, Boardman, 105
Rockefeller, Isabel, 151
Rockefeller, John D., 136, 310
Rockefeller, John D., Jr., 54, 64, 81, 302
Rockefeller, Mrs. John D., Jr., 54
Roebuck, Alvah Curtis, 282, 320
Roos, Achille, 242, 251
Roos, Adolphe, 242
Roos, Ernestine, 242, 251
Roos, George, 242–243
Roos, Leon, 242–243
Roos, Robert, 242–243
Roos Brothers, 242, 254
Roosevelt, Eleanor, 324
Roosevelt, Franklin D., 26, 53, 54, 63, 87, 186, 275, 340
Roosevelt, Sara Delano, 34
Roosevelt, Theodore, 47–48, 294
Roosevelt, Mrs. Theodore, 60
Rosenbaum's, 108
Rosenberg (tailor), 153
Rosenfield, John, 189, 358

Rosenheim, Herman, 151
Rosenheim, Rosalind Rich, 151
Rosenstein, Nettie, 184
Rosensweig, Harry, 232
Rosenthal, Andrew, 343
Rosenwald, Adele, see Levy, Adele
    Rosenwald
Rosenwald, Augusta Hammerslough, 284,
    327
Rosenwald, Augusta Nusbaum, 284, 286,
    288, 297, 300, 316, 325, 329–331, 334–
    335
Rosenwald, Edith, see Stern, Edith
    Rosenwald
Rosenwald, Julius, 79, 145, 284–292, 295,
    296–323, 327–330, 333, 334–335, 356
  American blacks aided by, 303–307, 320
  early life of, 284–286
  as father, 315–317, 325–326, 328–331
  honesty of, 287, 289, 302, 323
  mail-order business improved by, 290–
    292
  personality of, 289, 313–316, 335
  as philanthropist, 297–301, 303–310, 314
  Sears interest of, 284, 286, 288–291, 296–
    297, 302–303, 309, 322–323
  stock market collapse and, 322–323
  on success, 313–314
  white slavery investigation and, 312–313
Rosenwald, Lessing, 316–317, 318, 320,
    321–323, 331, 333, 335, 379n
Rosenwald, Marion, see Ascoli, Marion
    Rosenwald
Rosenwald, Mary, 334
Rosenwald, Morris, 285, 325
"Rosenwald, S., the C.O.D., one-price
    clothier," 285
Rosenwald, Samuel, 284–285
Rosenwald, William, 315, 316, 330–331,
    333, 379n
Rosenwald family, x, 36, 55, 82, 111, 284–
    335, 379n–380n
  generosity of, 297–308, 310, 313, 314,
    320–324, 326–327, 333–334
  as thrifty, 291, 324–326, 330, 331
Ross, Joseph, 186
Rothschild, Baron Alphonse de, 45
Rothschild, Carola Warburg, 44
Rothschild, Baron Edmond de, 45, 299
Rothschild, Baron Gustave de, 45
Rothschild, Walter, 44
Rothschild, Walter, Jr., 359n
Rouf, Maggie, 16
Ryan, Charlotte, 100
Ryan, Joseph, 100

Sacco, Nicola, 22, 33, 145
Sachs, Helen, 43
Sachs, Julius, 51
Sachs, Paul, 31
St. Augustine, xx
Sakowitz's, 198
Saks, Horace, 79
Saks & Company, 79
Saks Fifth Avenue, 16, 77, 80, 90, 181, 196,
    349, 352
Salomon, Haym, 70
saloons, 202, 206, 216, 220, 243–244
Sandburg, Carl, 336
Sanford, Stephen, 96
San Francisco, 237–258, 376n–377n
  earthquake reconstruction in, 254
  fashion in, 243
  French immigrants in, 239
  Gold Rush days of, 237–239
  hotel residences of, 251
  houses of, 255–256
  Jewish civic leadership in, 253–255
  as seller's market, 237–239
Sanger, Alex, 162, 165, 166, 167, 169, 173,
    175
Sanger, Claudia Meader, 248
Sanger, Cornelia, 166
Sanger, Dave, 161
Sanger, Eli, 164, 165, 166, 248–249
Sanger, Elias, 157–158
Sanger, Elihu, 167
Sanger, Evelyn, 166
Sanger, Isaac, 158–160
Sanger, Jake, 161
Sanger, Jessica, 166
Sanger, Lehman, 157–161, 372n
Sanger, Lois, 166–167
Sanger, Margaret, 164
Sanger, Morton, 179, 188, 372n
Sanger, Philip, 159–160, 162–163, 165–166,
    167, 168, 173
Sanger, Sophie, 161
Sanger Brothers, 162, 167, 169, 173, 174,
    196, 248–249, 346
Sanger family, 157–169
Sankey, Ira, 170
Sarnoff, David, 74
Sartre, Jean-Paul, 259
Saufley, Bill, 235
Scaife, Mrs. Alan M., 94
Schaffner, Joseph, 311
Scheible, Billie, 97–100
Schiff, Dorothy, 43
Schiff, Jacob H., 48, 300, 301, 310, 364n
Schiff, Mortimer, 51
Schlesinger, James, 332

Schlesinger, Rae, 143
Schlesinger, Sigmund, 263
Schlesinger & Mayer, 106, 282
Schloss, Ann Lazarus, 343, 380n
Schloss, Stuart, 343
Schumacher, John, 352
Schurz, Carl, 37, 47, 211
Schuster, Edward, 72
Schwab, Abraham, 123
Schwab, Sarah Ottenheimer, 123
Schwartz, Adolph, 14
Scott, Sir Walter, 70
Sears, Richard Warren, 284, 320, 335
    advertising talent of, 282, 286–288, 292–
        297
    creation of demands by, 286–287, 295
    early life of, 280, 281, 282
    ownership changes and, 284, 288–289
Sears, Roebuck, 21, 79, 141, 142, 145, 195,
        280, 286–287, 290–297, 301–303, 309,
        311–313, 317–319, 346, 347, 349, 351
    anti-Semitism at, 318–321, 379n
    catalogue of, 286, 293–296, 319
    operating capital needed for, 284
    postwar financial crisis of, 302–303
    retail stores of, 317–318
    superlative aspects of, 335
Selden (Straus), Percy, 60–61
Seligman, Arthur, 274
Seligman, Joseph, 57, 117, 207
selling:
    joys of, xix–xx, 175
    as seduction, 175–176
service:
    chain stores and, 349–350
    for customer complaints, 123–124, 137–
        138
    improved social conditions and, 355
    as personal treatment, 172, 175–177,
        182–183, 185, 199–200, 349
sex:
    in advertising, 293–294
    in brothels, 98–100, 270
    extra-marital, 95, 97–98, 102, 177–178,
        242, 269, 271
    "nice" women and, 98–99
    racism and, 144–145
Sharf, Renée, 334
Shaver, Dorothy, xvii
Shearer, Norma, 294
Shefferman, Nate, 196–197
Sherman, William T., 137, 210, 228
Shillito's, 338, 343
Shouse, Jouett, 29
Simon, Joseph, 91–92
Simon, Julius, 72

Sinclair, Upton, xvii–xviii, 75
Slaton, John, 145
Sloan, Alfred, P., 56, 292
Sloane, W. & J., 87
Smadbeck, Louis, 216
Smith, Alfred E., 53
Smith, Lillian, 307
Smith, Louise, 244
Snellenburg, Irene Horner, 82–83
Snellenburg, Joseph N., 82
Snellenburg, Morton E., 82
Snellenburg family, 72, 82
Snellenburg's, 88
Solomon, Charles, 214
Solomon, Ezekiel, 261
Solomon, Isidor Elkan, 213–214
Solomon, Morris, 212
Sondheimer, Joseph, 261
Sonnenberg, Ben, 180–181, 183, 343–344,
        363n, 380n
Sousa, John Philip, 150
Southwest, 201–236, 373n–375n
specialty shops, vs. department stores,
        349–350
Spencer, Herbert, 104, 298
Speyer, Albert, 204
Spiegelberg, Elias, 205, 209
Spiegelberg, Emanuel, 205, 207
Spiegelberg, Flora, 208–209
Spiegelberg, Lehman, 205, 210
Spiegelberg, Levi, 205, 208
Spiegelberg, Solomon Jacob, 205–206, 209
Spiegelberg, Willi, 205, 208–209, 236
Spiegelberg Brothers, 206
Spiegelberg family, 205–210, 211, 221, 223
Spreckels, Claus, 244
Standard Club, 143
Stanford, Leland, 238, 244
Stanford, Sally, 246–247
Stanton, Frank, 195
Starr, Belle, 224
Stearn's, 19
Steffens, Lincoln, 23–25, 26, 94
Stegner, Ann, xvii
Stein, Gertrude, 103, 192, 246
Stein, Nathan, 18
Steinhart family, 254
Stern, Alfred, 332
Stern, Audrey, 327
Stern, Edgar Bloom, 326, 328
Stern, Edith Rosenwald, 325–328, 330, 331,
        334, 379n
Stern, Julius David, 86
Stern, Malcolm H., 361n
Stern, Philip M., 328, 379n
Stern family, 254–255

Stevenson, Adlai, 53, 193
Stewart's, A. T., ix, 40, 74, 148
Stiles, Ezra, 1
Stotesbury, E. T., 85
Straus, Beatrice (Mrs. Levy), 326
Straus, Donald Blun, 60, 61–63, 363n
Straus, Edith Abraham, 43, 60
Straus, Ellen Sulzberger, 43
Straus, Emil, 45–46
Straus, Gladys Guggenheim, 43, 60, 68
Straus, Helen Sachs, 43
Straus, Herbert, 42, 50, 52, 53, 60, 63
Straus, Hermina, 37, 38, 42
Straus, Ida, 42, 49
Straus, Irma Nathan, 54, 64
Straus, Isidor, 37–42, 44, 46, 48–52, 59, 211
    advice of, 49–51
    as Confederate agent, 38–39, 363n
    death of, 49
    family life of, 41
Straus, Jack, 64–65, 141, 142, 363n
Straus, Jesse, 42, 57, 59–60, 64, 321
    as director of Macy's, 52–53
    early training of, 51–52
    political career of, 53–55
Straus, Lazarus, 37–39, 41, 45
Straus, Minnie, 42, 43
Straus, Nathan, 37, 40–42, 44–45, 49–50,
    59, 145, 310
Straus, Nathan, Jr., 43
Straus, Oscar, 37, 40, 41, 42, 45, 46–49,
    50, 55, 57, 60, 365n
Straus, Oskar (composer), 45
Straus, Percy Selden, 60–61
Straus, Percy Solomon (Selden), 42, 43, 50,
    51, 54, 60, 88
Straus, Ralph Isidor, 60, 67, 363n
Straus, Robert Kenneth, 28, 54, 60, 63, 363n
Straus, Roger Williams, 43, 60
Straus, Roger Williams, Jr., 68
Straus, Ronald Peter, 43, 68
Straus, Sara (Isidor's daughter), 42
Straus, Sara (Mrs. Lazarus Straus), 37–38
Straus, Therese Kuhn, 43, 61, 63–64
Straus, Vivian, 42, 43
Straus family, x, xii, xx, 36–68, 103, 299,
    363n–365n
    Abraham & Straus interests of, 39, 50
    art collections of, 62–63
    education in, 50–51
    European background of, 36–37, 45
    financial reputation of, 41
    luxury displays of, 63–65
    Macy's ownership by, 39–42
    obligations of children in, 61–62
    in South, 37–39

Strauss, Anna Lord, 68
Strauss, Jonas, 241
Strauss, Levi, 68, 237–239, 240, 255
Strauss, Levi, Company, 185, 194, 220, 255
Strauss, Lewis L., 68
Strauss, Louis, 240
Strauss, Robert, 319
Strawbridge & Clothier, 21, 72
Stuart, Gilbert, 2–3
Stuart, May, 245
Stutz, Geraldine, xvii
Stuyvesant, Peter, 205
Sullivan, Louis E., 106, 282
Sulzberger, Ellen, 43
Sulzberger, Germon, 326
Suslow, Robert J., 352
Sutter, John, 239, 240
Swanson, Gloria, 294

Taft, William Howard, 45, 109, 243, 304,
    337
Thalhimers, x, 125
Thaw, Harry Kendall, 101–102
Thaw, William, 93
Tiffany, Louis Comfort, 165
Tiffany & Co., 88
Tocqueville, Alexis de, 188
Truman, Harry S., 176, 258, 323
Tunney, Gene, 76
Tuskegee Institute, 305–306, 333
Twain, Mark, ix, 69, 345
Tweed, William (Boss), 42
Twentieth Century Fund, 35

Untermeyer, Samuel, 54

Valenstein, Lawrence, 161
Vanderbilt, William H., 190
Vanderbilt, Mrs. William K., 54
Vanzetti, Bartolomeo, 22, 33, 145
Vare, William S., 86
Veblen, Thorstein, xviii, 66
Verdier, Felix and Émil, 239

Wagner, Robert, 323
Wall, Tessie, 244
Wallace, Lew, 210
Walsh, Jack, 120
Wanamaker, John, 34, 73–74, 80, 296, 341
Wanamaker, Rodman, 43–44
Wanamaker family, 74
Wanamaker's, John, ix, 72, 73–74, 90, 379n
Warburg, Edward M. M., 32
Warburg, Felix, 55, 300
Warburg, James, 65
Warburg, Paul, 60, 65

Ward, Aaron Montgomery, 282
Ward, Montgomery, 197, 291, 296, 317, 318, 319, 349
Warner, Jack, 252
Washington, Booker T., 303, 304–305
Washington, George, 91, 92
Watson, Tom, 145, 370n
Waxman, Josephine Bennett, 101
Wayne, Joseph, Jr., 85
Webber, Oscar, 379n
Wechsler, Norman, 379n
Weil, Evelyn, 43
Weil, Julius E., 286
Weil, Minnie Straus, 42, 43
Weill, Alexandre, 240
Weill, Michel David, 242
Weill, Raphael, 239–242
Weizmann, Chaim, 258
Wemme, Henry, 272, 273
West:
    adventure-seeking in, 202–203, 262–263
    army posts and, 203, 211
    bandits in, 221–222
    exploitation of, 235
    freight problem in, 212–213, 221–224
    storekeepers' role in, 206, 227
    violence in, 219–221, 222
    wagon trains in, 212–213, 262
Westinghouse, George, 96, 101
Weston, Mrs. David, 342, 380n
Wharton School, xv, 7, 76, 130, 152
White, George, 97
White, R. H., 19, 88
White, Stanford, 101–102, 246
White, William Allen, 371n
Whitney, John Hay, 96
Wildenstein, Nathan, 245
Williams, G. Mennen, 233
Williams, Roger, 2, 230
Wilson, Woodrow, 275, 301
Winchell, Walter, 53
Winston, Harry, 175
Winston, Sid, 153
Wise, Stephen S., 55, 57, 310

Witte, Count Serquis de, 47
Wolf, Irwin Damasius, 108
Wolfe, Thomas, 144
women, xvi–xvii
    as board and committee members, 324
    as chief executives, xvii, 247
    extra-marital affairs and, 95, 97–98, 146–147, 242, 269, 271
    invisibility of, xvii, 129
    Jewish, sexuality of, 144, 370n
    Jewish discrimination against, 129
    merchandising to, 5, 10, 171, 182–183, 202, 294
    sexual freedom for, 242–243
    in South, 326
    strong-willed, 129–130, 161–162, 265–267
    Victorian sexuality and, 98–99, 163, 270, 294
    in work force, 137, 145–147, 311–313
Wood, Charles, 26
Wood, Robert Elkington, 316, 317–319, 320
Woodcock, Lindsay T., 138
Woodruff, Robert W., 141–142
Woolworth, Frank Winfield, 147, 320, 341
Wormser, Michael, 227, 375n
Wright, Frank Lloyd, 103, 105–106, 107–108

Yale University, 1, 31, 82, 94
Yellin, Samuel, 95
Yohamino, Julius Rosenwald, 329
Younkers, 147
Yulee, David Levy, 274

Zaharof, Basil, 54
Zeckendorf, A. & L., 223, 224
Zeckendorf, Aaron, 223–224
Zeckendorf, Louis, 223–224
Zeckendorf, William, 223–224
Zeckendorf family, 210, 223–224
Zellerbach, James David, 250–251
Ziegfeld, Florenz, 97
Zola, Émile, 148